lonely planet

Discover
Hawai'i, the
Big Island

Experience the best
of Hawai'i, the Big
Island

This edition written and researched by

Sara Benson
Luci Yamamoto

Contents

Kohala & Waimea
p93

Hamakua
p145 Coast

Mauna Kea &
Saddle Road

Hilo
p131
p165

p31 Kailua-Kona
& the Kona
Coast

p189

p205
Puna

Hawai'i Volcanoes
National Park

p231 Ka'u

This is Hawai'i, the Big Island

We doubt it's possible to get 'island fever' on Hawai'i. The aptly named Big Island is fantastically diverse, with miles of highways and – better yet – byways to explore, from age-old fishing villages to modern megaresorts, from snowy peaks to sandy beaches. Hawai'i is twice as big as the other Hawaiian islands combined, and its dramatic terrain will surprise you and take you to extremes.

Less than half a million years old, Hawai'i is a baby in geologic terms.

It's here you'll find the Hawaiian Islands' highest and largest volcanic mountains – and the world's most active volcano, spewing molten lava continually since 1983. Circumnavigate the Big Island and watch stark lava desert morph into rolling pastureland and misty valleys, weathered by rain, waves and time.

Ancient history looms large on Hawai'i, a place of powerful *mana* (spiritual essence).

The first Polynesians landed at Ka Lae, where the windswept coast remains pristine and undeveloped, and Kamehameha the Great was born in Kohala. Hula and *oli* (chant) are powerful forms of living history on the Big Island, which has birthed legendary hula and Hawaiian music masters, as well as the celebrated Merrie Monarch Festival.

Plantation days are long past, but not their colorful legacy.

Waves of immigrants who labored in the cane fields added their languages, foods and cultures to the mix. Today, there's no ethnic majority and common bonds are intangible: the pidgin vernacular, an easygoing manner and deep love of the *'aina* (land).

Hawai'i is untouristy.

Thanks to its sheer size, there's lots of legroom. While Kona caters to travelers en masse, most island towns are rural and made for residents instead. Even the capital seat, Hilo, is a former plantation town that's still slow-paced and populated by *kama'aina* (people born and raised in the Hawaiian Islands). Wherever you go, there's a sense of freedom and frontier. The Big Island is a guaranteed *big* experience.

> *Wherever you go, there's a sense of freedom and frontier*

Pololu Valley (p121)

PERSPECTIVES/GETTY IMAGES ©

4

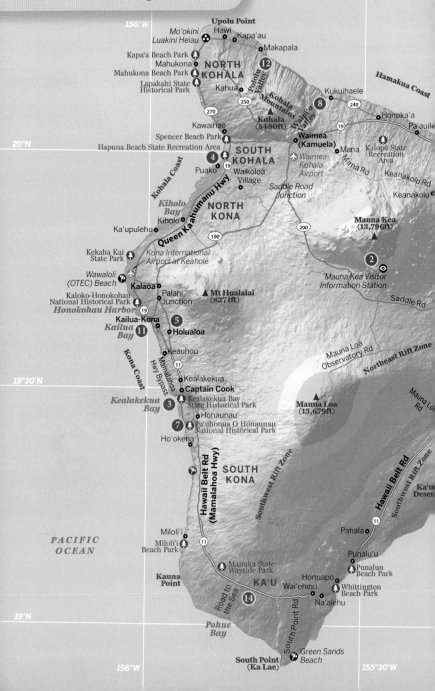

Hawai'i, the Big Island

Upolu Point

Mo'okini
Luakini Heiau — Hawi · Kapa'au
· Makapala

Kapa'a Beach Park
Mahukona
Mahukona Beach Park
Lapakahi State
Historical Park

**NORTH
KOHALA**

Kahua

Pololu
Valley

12

Kohala
Mountains

8

Kukuihaele

Hamakua Coast

270

250

Kohala
(5480ft)

Wai'pi'o
Valley

240

Kawaihae

Spencer Beach Park
Hapuna Beach State Recreation Area

4

**SOUTH
KOHALA**

19

Puako

Waikoloa
Village

Waimea
(Kamuela)

Mana

Waimea-
Kohala
Airport

Mana Rd

Kalopa State
Recreation
Area

Honoka'a

Pa'auil

19

Keanakolu Rd

Keanakolu

Kohala Coast

**Kiholo
Bay**

Kiholo

Ka'upulehu

**NORTH
KONA**

Saddle Road
Junction

200

**Mauna Kea
(13,796ft)**

2

Queen Ka'ahumanu Hwy

190

Kekaha Kai
State Park

**Kona International
Airport at Keahole**

Mauna Kea Visitor
Information Station

Saddle Rd

Wawaloli
(OTEC) Beach

Kalaoa

Palani
Junction

Kaloko-Honokohau
National Historical Park
Honokohau Harbor

19

▲ Mt Hualalai
(8271ft)

Kailua-Kona

5

**Kailua
Bay**

11

Holualoa

Mamalahoa Hwy Bypass

Keauhou

11

Mauna Loa
Observatory Rd

Northeast Rift Zone

Mauna Loa
Rd

19°30'N

Kealakekua
Captain Cook

Kealakekua Bay
State Historical Park

**Kealakekua
Bay**

3

Honaunau

7

Pu'uhonua O Honaunau
National Historical Park

Ho'okena

▲ **Mauna Loa
(13,679ft)**

Southwest Rift Zone

**SOUTH
KONA**

**Hawaii Belt Rd
(Mamalahoa Hwy)**

Hawaii Belt Rd

Southwest Rift Zone

**Ka'u
Deser**

**PACIFIC
OCEAN**

Miloli'i
Miloli'i
Beach Park

11

Pahala

11

Punalu'u

**Kauna
Point**

Manuka State
Wayside Park

KA'U

Honuapo

Wai'ohinu

Punaluu
Beach Park

Road to
the Sea

14

South Point Rd

Na'alehu

Whittington
Beach Park

19°N

**Pohue
Bay**

**South Point
(Ka Lae)**

Green Sands
Beach

156°W

155°30'W

155°W

N
0   40 km
0   20 miles

PACIFIC
OCEAN

ELEVATION

11,000ft
9000ft
7000ft
5000ft
4000ft
3000ft
2000ft
1000ft
0

20°N

Laupahoehoe
Point
Beach Park

19

Kolekole
Beach Park
Honomu
9
Akaka Falls
State Park

HILO

Papaikou

Hilo
Bay

Richardson
Ocean
Park

Leleiwi
Point

Wailuku River

Hilo
10 13
200

Hilo
International
Airport

19

Kea'au

Kaloli
Point

Stainback Hwy

130

Mountain
View

11

Cape
Kumukahi

Lava Tree
State
Monument

Kapoho

19°30'N

Glenwood

Pahoa

PUNA

Pohoiki Rd

Isaac Hale
Beach Park

14

Kamaili
Rd

MacKenzie State
Recreation Area

Kilauea
Caldera

Volcano

Hawai'i
Volcanoes
National Park

Pu'u O'o Vent

7

Kehena
Beach

1

137

Hilina Pali Rd

Chain of Craters Rd

6

Kaimu

19°N

155°W

14
Top Highlights

1. Hawai'i Volcanoes
   National Park
2. Mauna Kea Stargazing
3. Snorkeling in
   Kealakekua Bay
4. Hapuna Beach
5. Kona Coffee Farms
6. Chasing Lava
7. Pu'uhonua O Hōnaunau
   National Historical Park
8. Waipi'o Valley
9. Akaka Falls State Park
10. Merrie Monarch Festival
11. Manta Ray Night Dive
12. Hiking into Pololu Valley
13. Hilo
14. Caving in Puna & Ka'u

14 Hawai'i, the Big Island's Top Highlights

Hawai'i Volcanoes National Park

The eerie glow of a lava lake, secluded palm-fringed beaches, ancient petroglyphs pecked into hardened lava, and miles of hiking trails through smoking craters, rainforest and desert – there's always so much more to explore at Hawai'i's number-one attraction (p205). The park is also one of the island's top spots to experience traditional Hawaiian culture at hula dance performances, annual festivals, concerts and talks. After dark, warm up by the fireplace inside the landmark Volcano House lodge, perched right on the rim of Kilauea Caldera. Kilauea Iki crater (p211)

1

TODD GIPSTEIN/GETTY IMAGES ©

2

Mauna Kea Stargazing

It's breathless *and* breathtaking to be in the rarefied air of Mauna Kea (p138), Hawai'i's highest mountain and most sacred spot. Once the sun goes down, the stars come out – and so do the telescopes. Some of the world's clearest stargazing happens here. What you see through these telescopes, aided by enthusiastic amateur astronomers, you won't soon forget. For a trophy experience, show up here during a meteor shower. Above: Gemini Northern 8m Telescope, Mauna Kea

Snorkeling in Kealakekua Bay

It's all true – from teeming tropical fish to spinner dolphins lazily circling your kayak or catamaran. Tourist brochures hype this as the best snorkeling in the state, but in this case, you can believe it. New restrictions on kayaks can't tarnish the luster of this must-see spot (p71) – in fact, it's quite the opposite, as ecoconscious regulations are helping preserve the bay's underwater paradise. If kayaking doesn't float your boat, hike down instead to this historically significant spot, where Captain Cook perished.

The Best...
Scenic Drives

CHAIN OF CRATERS ROAD
National park highway links volcanic craters downhill to the sea. (p212)

KOHALA MOUNTAIN ROAD (HIGHWAY 250)
Emerald pastures with black lava and white-sand beaches on the horizon below. (p113)

PEPE'EKEO 4-MILE SCENIC DRIVE
Jungle ramble across rivers and moss-covered bridges. (p163)

MAUNA KEA SUMMIT ROAD
Hawaii's highest-elevation mountain drive – oh, the sunsets. (p135)

MAMALAHOA HIGHWAY (HIGHWAY 180)
Coffee and mac-nut farms with skyline views of Kona's coast. (p61)

11

The Best...
Hikes

KILAUEA IKI TRAIL
Hike across a moonscape in Hawai'i Volcanoes National Park. (p216)

POLOLU VALLEY TRAIL
Knees quake and spirits soar on this short, steep hike. (p121)

NAPAU CRATER TRAIL
Trek to the heart of an active volcanic eruption. (p217)

KIPUKA PUAULU
Native birdsong fills the sun-dappled forest on an easy nature walk. (p219)

MAUNA LOA OBSERVATORY TRAIL
Hard-core trek to a high-altitude summit – in just one day. (p142)

Hapuna Beach

4

Rock up to this half-mile-long powdery white-sand beach (p108), rent an umbrella and a bodyboard, and make one of Hawaii's most iconic beaches your personal playground. Surfboard, lounge chair or water wings – this beach has something for the whole family. While the basic A-frame camping cabins here are not for the finicky, the island's best beach is in your front yard – that's pretty hallucinatory. For more magic, detour just north to tranquil Mauna Kea Beach, sitting on crescent-shaped Kauna'oa Bay.

Kona Coffee Farms

5

Christian missionaries planted Kona's first coffee trees. What began as an ornamental floral fad became a thriving agro-industry, as coffee farms worked by immigrants spread across South Kona's rain-kissed 'coffee belt.' Today rural byways wind past small, family-owned coffee plantations (p61), many of which let you drop by for a quick tour and free tastings of 100% Kona brews. Every November the whole community celebrates with the prestigious Kona Coffee Cultural Festival.

Chasing Lava

Pele, Hawaiian goddess of fire and volcanoes, is notoriously fickle. But if you're lucky, you may get the chance to see live lava crawling over and under newly birthed land (p202). Lava usually flows inside or around Hawai'i Volcanoes National Park, sometimes plunging into the sea, sending a steam plume skyward as hot lava mixes with roiling surf. Feel the heat on a walking or boat tour out of Puna.

Right: Lava from Kilauea Volcano (p208)

Pu'uhonua O Hōnaunau National Historical Park

Ki'i (deity images) watch over ancient temples at this historical site (p77) – known as the Place of Refuge – an unforgettable introduction to traditional Hawaiian culture. There's no better place to gain an understanding of the kapu (taboo) system that once governed life across the Hawaiian Islands. At nearby snorkeling spot Two-Step, look for *honu* (green sea turtles).

Waipi'o Valley

You can linger at the scenic viewpoint overlooking this lush green valley (p152), but the waterfalls, wild horses and wilder black-sand beach beckon. Hike down, ride horseback or even take an old-fashioned mule-drawn wagon to get you there. Experts can kayak in – when conditions are right. The most spectacular panoramas are from the grueling Muliwai Trail – head up, up and up some more for the money shot.

The Best...
Beaches

HAPUNA BEACH
Often voted the island's all-round top beach. (p108)

KIHOLO BAY
Soft black sands, sea turtles and a swimmable lava tube. (p90)

MANINI'OWALI BEACH
Easy access to a powdery white-sand beauty. (p86)

MAKALAWENA BEACH
Save a half-day to explore this hard-to-reach, idyllic strand. (p86)

BEACH 69
Swim, snorkel or laze at a gay- and family-friendly hangout. (p107)

Akaka Falls State Park

Crashing through the rainforest choked with fragrant ginger and giant philodendrons, this 420ft-high waterfall is no less spectacular for its easy access. Drive up, stroll a half-mile through what feels like Hollywood's version of Hawaii and there you are. Like all waterfalls on Hawai'i's windward coast, the park's two falls (p161) are most impressive during seasonal rains when they spill violently over the verdant cliffs. Poke around the tiny sugar-plantation town of Honomu once you're done ogling the towering falls.

The Best... Local Food

DA POKE SHACK
Fresh off the fishing boat *poke* (cubed, marinated raw fish) and plate lunches. (p46)

TEX DRIVE-IN
King of sugary, hot and filled *malasadas* (Portuguese doughnuts). (p151)

SUPER J'S
All homemade, *'ono* (delicious) Hawaiian recipes. (p70)

CAFE 100
Where the *loco moco* (dish of rice, fried egg and hamburger patty topped with gravy) madness all began. (p182)

VILLAGE BURGER
Big Island ranchers, farmers and fishers stock this cowboy country grill. (p127)

10 Merrie Monarch Festival

What you saw at that resort luau? That's to hula what Velveeta is to cheese. If you really want to see how a hula *halau* (school) invokes the gods and legends through Hawaiian chants and dance, time your trip to attend this statewide hula competition (p177). Book early; people fly in from all over the globe for this one. Unless you're a serious hula aficionado, you're more likely to enjoy the pan-Pacific exhibition dances than the intense head-to-head competitions.

Manta Ray Night Dive

Diving at night is a thrill in itself, but once you turn on your light and attract a corps de ballet of Pacific manta rays, with wing spans of 10ft or more and tails like javelins, your life becomes segmented: before diving with mantas and after. Snorkeling with mantas can be even better because you're closer, but it's very popular, so don't be surprised if you get head-whacked by someone else's fins. Bring your own dive light and swim onto center stage with these graceful animals (p42).

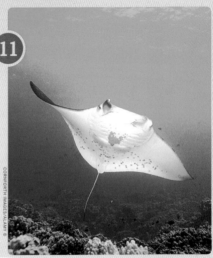

CORMORTH IMAGES/ALAMY ©

Hiking into Pololu Valley

Waipi'o Valley or Pololu Valley? It's a tough call as to which of Hawai'i's emerald valleys threaded with waterfalls and blessed with a black-sand beach is more beautiful. But little Pololu (p121) retains a tranquility lost to Waipi'o since the invention of the monster truck. It takes a 10-minute downhill hike to get here, and it's the only way in. Combine your visit with lunch and a stroll around diminutive Hawi, Kohala's alternative arts hub. This northern thumb of land is old Hawai'i at its most evocative.

Hilo

If one word describes Hilo (p168), that would be 'real.' This former sugar town had a life before tourism and remains refreshingly unpretentious, local and normal – if normalcy includes buoyant tropical greenery, drive-up beaches, unique museums, historic storefronts and sublime views of Mauna Kea and the Pacific. Here you'll rarely find tourist traps, but find yourself immersed in Hilo's diverse mix of residents, many whose ancestors arrived as plantation workers.
Left: Palace Theater (p185)

Caving in Puna & Ka'u

In Hawai'i, what you see on the surface is never the whole story. Beneath all the forest and volcanic flows lie elaborate systems of caves, caverns and lava tubes, multiplying by miles your exploration possibilities. The world's two longest lava tubes, Kazumura Cave (p192) and Kula Kai Caverns (p242), as well as a roadside lava tube that younger kids can walk through inside Hawai'i Volcanoes National Park, are among many options. Below: Kula Kai Caverns (p242)

The Best... For Kids

CATAMARAN CRUISE
Snorkel with tropical fish, spy wild dolphins and humpback whales. (p38)

ZIPLINING
Hands on the cable, your heart will be in your throat. (p159)

KIKAUA BEACH
A protected cove perfect for little ones learning to swim or snorkel. (p87)

DAHANA RANCH ROUGHRIDERS
Giddyap like a *paniolo* (Hawaiian cowboy). (p124)

KULA KAI CAVERNS
Marvel at geological wonders on an educational tour. (p242)

Hawai'i, the Big Island's Top Itineraries

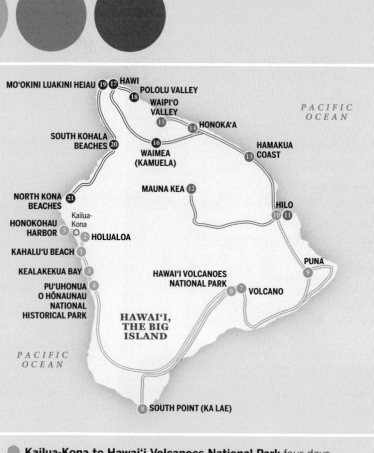

MO'OKINI LUAKINI HEIAU **19** **17** HAWI

POLOLU VALLEY **18**

WAIPI'O VALLEY **15**

HONOKA'A **14**

SOUTH KOHALA BEACHES **20**

WAIMEA (KAMUELA) **16**

HAMAKUA COAST **13**

PACIFIC OCEAN

MAUNA KEA **12**

NORTH KONA BEACHES **21**

Kailua-Kona

HILO **10** **11**

HONOKOHAU HARBOR **5**

KAHALU'U BEACH **1**

2 HOLUALOA

PUNA **9**

KEALAKEKUA BAY **3**

PU'UHONUA O HŌNAUNAU NATIONAL HISTORICAL PARK **4**

HAWAI'I VOLCANOES NATIONAL PARK

6 **7** VOLCANO

HAWAI'I, THE BIG ISLAND

PACIFIC OCEAN

8 SOUTH POINT (KA LAE)

- **Kailua-Kona to Hawai'i Volcanoes National Park** four days
- **Volcano to Hilo** six days
- **Hilo to Waipi'o Valley** eight days
- **Waimea to North Kona** 10 days

Kailua-Kona to Hawai'i Volcanoes National Park

4 DAYS

Kayaking on Kealakekua Bay

GREG ELMS/GETTY IMAGES ©

1 Kahalu'u Beach (p54)

Teeming with tropical fish and sea turtles, this roadside beach is great for snorkeling or a surfing or stand up paddling lesson.

2 Holualoa (p59)

In the afternoon, drive upcountry to Holualoa. Browse high-quality island art galleries, sample Kona coffee from small family farms, and catch a spectacular sunset.

3 Kealakekua Bay (p71)

For day two, make reservations in advance for a morning snorkeling cruise or to paddle a kayak to the underwater wonders by the Captain Cook Monument.

4 Pu'uhonua O Hōnaunau National Historical Park (p77)

On day three, take an easy coastal walk around South Kona's 'Place of Refuge,' where ancient Hawaiian history and spectacular natural scenery converge. Afterward, duck next door to Two-Step for gorgeous shoreline snorkeling.

5 Honokohau Harbor (p80)

Don't miss night diving (or snorkeling) with giant manta rays – book ahead for boat tours. Show up early for a sunset walk around the ancient fishponds of Kaloko-Honokohau National Historical Park.

6 Hawai'i Volcanoes National Park (p208)

Set out early on your fourth day for the 100-mile drive over to East Hawai'i to visit the world's most active volcano. Diverse hiking trails and (if you're lucky) glowing after-dark views of a roiling lava lake await.

➡ THIS LEG: 170 MILES

Volcano to Hilo

Rugged coastline of South Point (Ka Lae)

JULIE THURSTON/GETTY IMAGES ©

7 Volcano (p223)

On the morning of your fifth day, browse or buy original works – photos, ceramics, blown glass – and meet the artists who created them at eclectic galleries hidden in the rainforest that embraces rainy, romantic Volcano village.

8 South Point (Ka Lae) (p239)

Backtrack past Ka'u's coffee farms and the sea turtles at Punalu'u Beach to stand at the southernmost point in the USA. It's also the place where ancient Polynesians first rowed ashore on Hawai'i. After standing at wind-blown Ka Lae, get ready for a long hike (or hop in a 4WD 'taxi') to unusually colored Green Sands Beach.

9 Puna (p192)

Get lost on day six in Puna, a district as nonconformist as it is beguiling. Little-traveled rural byways let you explore this region's wonders including tide pools, a black-sand beach and lava tree molds, plus there's a chance to perhaps see red-hot lava flowing into the ocean. Book ahead for dramatic lava boat tours.

10 Hilo (p168)

Drive north to Hilo to bed down tonight. With its scenic bay and lush greenery, Hawai'i's capital is a charmer. Stroll the retro-flavored downtown, with its local cafes, sushi bars and shops, to the EHCC Hawai'i Museum of Contemporary Art and Palace Theater.

➡ THIS LEG: 200 MILES

Hilo to Waipi'o Valley

'Imiloa Astronomy Center of Hawai'i (p172), Hilo

ANN CECIL/GETTY IMAGES ©

⑪ Hilo (p168)

On the morning of day seven, step inside one of Hilo's fascinating museums to learn about the Big Islands' volcanic origins, modern astronomy or destructive tsunami. Grab lunch fixings from Hilo's farmers and fish markets, then picnic in Liliuokalani Park, a bayside gem with Japanese gardens, pagodas and bamboo groves.

⑫ Mauna Kea (p134)

Drive up Hawaii's highest peak in time for sunset – the island's top spot for it – and then stick around for free stargazing programs outside the visitor information station. Taking a summit tour maximizes the literally breath-taking experience.

⑬ Hamakua Coast (p148)

Begin day eight by meandering through storybook rainforest along the short Pepe'ekeo 4-Mile Scenic Drive, passing the Hawaii Tropical Botanical Garden. Continuing north, stop at Akaka Falls State Park.

⑭ Honoka'a (p148)

On your way to Waipi'o Valley, pause in laid-back Honoka'a. Amble around downtown's antiques and art shops, or reserve ahead for a tour of nearby boutique farms that grow vanilla, honey, tea and more. Don't forget to fuel up with *malasadas* (Portuguese doughnuts) from Tex Drive-In.

⑮ Waipi'o Valley (p152)

No matter how you experience this waterfall-strewn, sacred 'Valley of Kings' – with a guide, on horseback or on foot – it will be memorable. Go solo to kick back on the black-sand beach at your leisure.

⏩ **THIS LEG: 135 MILES**

Waimea to North Kona

Dahana Ranch, Waimea (Kamuela)

LONELY PLANET/GETTY IMAGES ©

16 Waimea (p122)

On day nine, giddyap on a morning trail ride (book ahead) across the heart of Hawai'i's *paniolo* (cowboy) country. Browse living-history exhibits at the town's heritage centers, then grab lunch.

17 Hawi (p113)

Follow scenic Kohala Mountain Rd (Hwy 250) through rolling green pasturelands to Hawi, a small, hang-loose town that's chock-full of art galleries and shops.

18 Pololu Valley (p121)

This valley offers eye candy from the road's-end lookout. A short, steep trail leads to the black-sand beach below.

19 Mo'okini Luakini Heiau (p115)

Unless you spent a lot of time swooning over Pololu Valley's rugged beauty, you'll also have time in the afternoon to visit this site, one of Hawaii's most sacred. It's nearby Kamehameha the Great's birthplace.

20 South Kohala Beaches (p97)

Don't miss sunset from one of South Kohala's drive-up beaches. Mauna Kea Beach is a favorite; Hapuna Beach is another all-around winner.

21 North Kona Beaches (p80)

Spend your last day adventuring to North Kona's wilder beaches – among the Big Island's very best. Dive into coconut-fringed Kiholo Bay, with its sea turtles and swimmable lava tube, or trek to Kekaha Kai (Kona Coast) State Park for powdery salt-and-pepper sands.

THIS LEG: 90 MILES

Get Inspired

📖 Books

o **Saturday Night at the Pahala Theatre** (1993) Lois-Ann Yamanaka's bracing stories written in Hawaiian pidgin reveal another side of 1970s Hilo.

o **Volcano: A Memoir of Hawai'i** (1996) Poet Garrett Hongo traces his family's roots back to the evocative rainforests and lava flows of East Hawai'i.

o **Big Island Journey** (2009) Sophia Schweitzer and Bennett Hymer share Hawai'i's rich history with 400-plus vintage photos.

🎬 Films

o **Keepers of the Flame** (1988) Eddie and Myrna Kamae (www. hawaiianlegacy.com) profile revered Hawaiian cultural practicioners Mary Kawena Pukui, Iolani Luahine and Edith Kanaka'ole.

o **Li'a: The Legacy of a Hawaiian Man** (1988) Another documentary by Eddie and Myrna Kamae celebrates prolific songwriter and musician Sam Li'a Kalainaina from remote Waipi'o Valley.

🎵 Music

o **Tell U What** (2012) Ukulele prodigy Brittni Paiva's latest collection shows off her range.

o **Kona** (2010) Master slack key guitarists Martin Pahinui, Daniel Akaka Jr and others highlight Hawaii's iconic instrument.

o **'Ohai 'Ula** (2010) Kainani Kahaunaele is a gifted *haku mele* (composer of Hawaiian songs).

🖱 Websites

o **Mountain Apple Company on YouTube** (www.youtube.com/user/ mountainapplecompany) Watch Israel 'Iz' Kamakawiwo'ole to better understand what it means to be Hawaiian.

o **Toward Living Pono on YouTube** (www. youtube.com/user/ towardlivingpono) Snippets on poi, aloha and the Hawaiian language from iconic Big Islanders.

o **KonaWeb** (www. konaweb.com) Despite the name, the whole island is covered, with handy links to cultural and performing-arts events,

farmers markets, unique local products and more.

o **Hawaiian Lava Daily** (http://hawaiianlavadaily. blogspot.com) Stunning photos and videos of Kilauea's red-hot lava action.

⏱ Short on time?

This list will give you instant insight into Hawai'i.

Read *Ancient Hawai'i* (1998) Artist and historian Herb Kawainui Kane depicts traditional Hawaiian ways in vivid detail.

Watch *The Punalu'u Experience* (2008) Danny Miller's documentary explains why Ka'u's pristine, black-sand beach is sacred.

Listen *Hawai'i Island...Is My Home* (2008) Slack key guitarist John Keawe's lilting instrumental and vocal tribute to the Big Island won a prestigious Na Hoku Hanohano award.

Log on GoHawaii.com (www.gohawaii.com/big-island) Official tourism website.

Hula performance with *ipu* (gourds)
WATERFALL WILLIAM/GETTY IMAGES ©

Hawai'i, the Big Island Month by Month

Top Events

⭐ **Merrie Monarch Festival** April

🏃 **Hawai'i Island Festival** September

🎽 **Ironman Triathlon World Championship** October

🍷 **Kona Coffee Cultural Festival** November

⭐ **Waimea Ukulele & Slack Key Guitar Institute** November

January

⭐ **Waimea Ocean Film Festival**

Watch eco documentaries, high-adrenaline sports footage and films about Hawaiian culture, with Q&A talks and outdoor activities over five days in Waimea and South Kohala in mid-January (www.waimea-oceanfilm.org).

March

🍷 **Kona Brewers Festival**

This beer fest (www.konabrewersfestival.com) on the second Saturday of March just keeps getting bigger. Sip dozens of handcrafted brews from across Hawaii, the western USA and elsewhere, all accompanied by live music and top island chef's food.

April

⭐ **Merrie Monarch Festival**

Hilo's premier event (p177) is a week-long celebration of Hawaiian arts and culture, starting on Easter Sunday. This Olympics of hula competitions draws top *halau* (schools) from all Hawaiian Islands, the US mainland and abroad. Plan ahead.

May

🏃 **Lei Day**

This statewide cultural festival kicks off on May 1 (Lei Day) at Kalakaua Park in downtown Hilo, with plenty of masterful lei on display, and continues with live music and hula at Hilo's beautiful Palace Theater.

(left) Dancers at the Merrie Monarch Festival
JOE CARINI/GETTY IMAGES ©

June

🏃 King Kamehameha Day

On June 11, a state holiday, join the crowds at King Kamehameha's birthplace in North Kohala for a flowery parade, arts-and-crafts fair, live music and food booths. More events take place on Mokuola (Coconut Island) in Hilo.

July

⭐ Fourth of July Rodeo

Held on the historic Parker Ranch, this annual event packs in *paniolo* (Hawaiian cowboys) and their fans for team roping, horse racing and other fun.

✳ Kilauea Cultural Festival

This day-long festival in early July draws crowds to Hawai'i Volcanoes National Park to celebrate Hawaiian culture: there are lei- and basket-making demonstrations, hula dancing and even nose-flute jams.

⭐ Big Island Hawaiian Music Festival

A must for Hawaiian music fans, this two-day concert in Hilo features virtuoso performances by ukulele strummers, steel and slack key guitarists and falsetto singers in mid-July.

August

🏃 Hawaiian International Billfish Tournament

Kailua-Kona is the epicenter of big-game fishing, and this is Hawaii's grand tournament in late July or early August. Watch the weighing of the catch at Kailua Pier.

Septem'

✳ Hawai'i Island

For '30 days of aloha' islandwide cultural celebration (w. hawaiiislandfestival.org) starts with a Hawaiian royal procession in South Kona and ends with a *paniolo* parade in Waimea. The Queen Lili'uokalani Canoe Races happen over Labor Day weekend.

October

🏃 Ironman Triathlon World Championship

This legendary triathlon is the ultimate endurance contest, combining a 2.4-mile ocean swim, 112-mile bike race and 26.2-mile marathon in Kailua-Kona on the second Saturday of October.

November

🍷 Kona Coffee Cultural Festival

Celebrate Kona's signature brew during the harvest season with 10 days of coffee tastings, farm tours, cultural events and a cupping competition in early November.

⭐ Moku O Keawe

In early November, this three-day dance festival brings together hula troupes from Hawaii, Japan and the US mainland for competitions, workshops and a crafts-and-clothing market, all in Waikoloa.

⭐ Waimea Ukulele & Slack Key Guitar Institute

In mid-November, aspiring musicians can study with Hawaii's foremost musicians at this three-day institute's workshops, whose legendary concerts and *kanikapila* (jam sessions) are open to the public.

Need to Know

Currency
US dollar ($)

Language
English, Hawaiian

Visas
Generally not required for Canadians or for citizens of Visa Waiver Program (VWP) countries for stays of 90 days or less with ESTA pre-approval.

Money
ATMs available in major towns. Credit cards widely accepted by most businesses (except some lodgings); often required for reservations. Traveler's checks (US dollars) occasionally used.

Cell Phones
Coverage spotty in remote areas. International travelers need GSM multiband phones; buy prepaid SIM cards locally.

Wi-Fi
Available at most accommodations; many hotels charge daily fees.

Internet Access
Cybercafes are scarce; access averages $6 to $12 per hour.

Tipping
Expected by bartenders, restaurant servers, taxi drivers etc. See p286.

When to Go

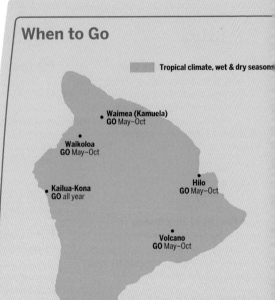

Tropical climate, wet & dry seasons

Waimea (Kamuela)
GO May–Oct

Waikoloa
GO May–Oct

Kailua-Kona
GO all year

Hilo
GO May–Oct

Volcano
GO May–Oct

High Season
(Dec–Apr & Jun–Aug)
- Accommodations prices up 50% to 100%
- Christmas to New Year and Easter most pricey, busiest
- Winter rainier (best for whale-watching and surfing)

Shoulder
(May & Sep)
- Crowds and prices drop slightly between schools' spring break and summer vacation
- Temperatures mild, mostly sunny days
- Hawai'i Island Festival in September

Low Season
(Oct–Nov)
- Airfares at lowest from US mainland and Canada
- More vacancies, accommodations rates lower
- Ironman World Championship (Oct), Kona Coffee Cultural Festival (Nov)

Advance Planning

- **Three months before** Decide which region's climate and attractions best match your interests. Search for internet deals on flights, cars and accommodations.

- **One month before** Reserve a spot on popular tours, such as nighttime snorkeling and diving with manta rays, lava-watching boats and Mauna Kea summit stargazing.

- **One week before** Confirm your travel bookings. Check weather forecasts to ensure you pack the right gear. Make spa and splurge-worthy restaurant reservations.

Daily Costs

Budget Less than $100
- Hostel dorm bed: $25–35
- Budget hotel or B&B room, shared bath: $55–80
- Local plate lunch: $5–10
- Bus fare (one way): $2

Midrange $100–250
- Room with private bath at midrange hotel or B&B: $100–200
- Rental car (excluding insurance and gas): per day/week from $35/150
- Dinner at casual sit-down restaurant: $20–40

Top End More than $250
- Luxury beach resort room: over $250
- Three-course meal and cocktail: $75–100
- Guided outdoor adventure tour: $80–200

Exchange Rates

Australia	A$1	$0.94
Canada	C$1	$0.92
Europe (euro)	€1	$1.38
Japan	¥100	$0.98
New Zealand	NZ$1	$0.87
UK	£1	$1.68

For current exchange rates see www.xe.com.

What to Bring

- **Driver's license** Needed to rent and drive a car.
- **Hands-free device** Talking or texting on a handheld cellphone while driving is illegal.
- **Hiking shoes** Broken in and sturdy enough for lava-rock terrain.
- **Long sleeves & pants** Breathable fabric to protect against sunburn and mosquito bites; lightweight waterproof jacket may be useful.
- **UV-protection sunglasses** For ocean glare and highway driving.
- **ID cards** Student, automobile association and AARP member cards for travel discounts.
- **Snorkeling gear** Bring your own if you'll snorkel often or are picky about fit and quality.

Arriving on Hawai'i, the Big Island

Kona International Airport at Keahole (KOA; p289)
Car Rental-car companies at airport.

Taxi & airport shuttle Around $25 to Kailua-Kona, $35 to Keauhou, plus tip.

Bus One to three daily buses (none Sunday; $2).

Hilo International Airport (ITO; p289)
Car Rental-car companies at airport.

Taxi Around $15 plus tip into town.

Getting Around

- **Car** Well-maintained highway circumnavigates island. Free parking widely available.
- **Bus** Hele-On Bus (fare $2) links major towns; limited runs, especially on weekends. Luggage, bicycle surcharge $1; no surfboards.
- **Bicycle** Decent roads for touring, but sun, wind and rain can be brutal.

Sleeping

- **Hotels & resorts** Prevalent on South Kohala and Kona coasts; top-end resorts offer the best beaches and splashy pools.
- **Condos** Mainly south of Kailua-Kona; ideal for independent travelers who prefer apartment-style amenities; discounted weekly rates.
- **B&Bs and inns** Generally reliable, with more space and amenities than comparably priced hotels; multinight stay often required.
- **Hostels** Simple private rooms and dormitory beds at rock-bottom prices.
- **Camping & cabins** Low-cost campsites and budget cabins at national, state and county parks; bring your own camping gear.

Be Forewarned

- **Vog** Volcanic smog can make sunny skies hazy. Short-term exposure not generally hazardous except for people with respiratory and heart conditions, pregnant women, young children and infants.
- **Coqui frogs** Nightly mating calls can disrupt sleep; inquire with accommodations if you're sensitive to noise.

Kailua-Kona & the Kona Coast

Since ancient Hawaiian times, the Kona Coast has been – and probably always will be – the Big Island's most popular playground. So alluring is this stretch of West Hawai'i's coast, it's not surprising that most travelers base themselves here. You can kayak and snorkel in aquamarine coves and lagoons one day, laze on a white- or black-sand strand the next, then cool off in the lush, green coffee belt on the slopes of Mt Hualalai. All the while, the natural beauty of Kailua Bay recalls its original role as an idyllic retreat for Hawaiian royalty. For visitors, the beach town of Kailua-Kona is a sunny delight and a hub for ocean sports. For locals who like to gripe, it's a sprawling suburb with nightmare rush-hour traffic, but others love the annual Ironman action and taking sunset cocktails by the surf. Stop by and see it all, then judge for yourself.

Kayaking, Kailua-Kona (p41)
ABRAHAM BOB/GETTY IMAGES ©

Kailua-Kona & the Kona Coast Itineraries

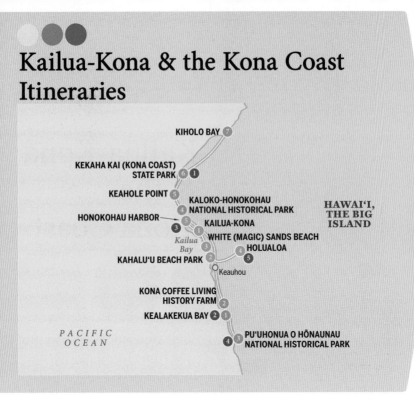

Two Days

1 Kailua-Kona (p34) Dive right into the bay at Kailua Pier with whatever floats your boat – stand up paddling (SUP), surfing or outrigger canoeing. Take a guided tour of historical Huliheʻe Palace, once a royal retreat, as you amble down oceanfront Aliʻi Dr. Grab sunset drinks at breezy Huggo's on the Rocks or the ocean-view lanai at Humpy's Big Island Alehouse.

2 Kahaluʻu Beach Park (p54) Roll out of bed early on day two, and check the weather first. Nice and calm? Head out for an early morning snorkel at this ever-popular beach, a quick drive or trolley ride south of Kailua-Kona. *Honu* (green sea turtles) and tropical fish abound in the bay's shallow waters.

3 White (Magic) Sands Beach (p34) If it's looking choppy out there in the ocean, don't despair. Join the locals bodyboarding instead at this crescent-shaped strand closer to downtown Kailua-Kona.

4 Holualoa (p59) In the afternoon, get out of town for a quick escape to this historic plantation community up in the hills. Do a slo-mo art-gallery crawl, followed by tastings and tours of Kona's famous coffee estates, only a short, scenic drive away.

5 Honokohau Harbor (p80) Book ahead for inspiring nighttime snorkeling cruises and scuba-diving tours that visit the hidden haunts of manta rays along the Kona Coast. Most boats leave from this sportfishing harbor, just north of Kailua-Kona.

 **THIS LEG: 30 MILES**

Four Days

1 Kealakekua Bay (p71) Begin your third day early, paddling a kayak across this crystalline bay and keeping an eye peeled for dolphins. The only way to enjoy some of Hawai'i's most phenomenal snorkeling at Ka'awaloa Cove is on a guided kayak tour or snorkel cruise, or by hiking.

2 Kona Coffee Living History Farm (p69) Travel back in time at this family-owned coffee farm that shows what life in South Kona was like for Japanese immigrant farmers in Hawai'i's prestatehood era.

3 Pu'uhonua O Hōnaunau National Historical Park (p77) Also known as the Place of Refuge, you can circumambulate ancient temples at this park deeply rooted in the Hawaiian religion and traditions. Have your snorkel gear handy for Two-Step.

4 Kaloko-Honokohau National Historical Park (p83) Start day four learning how ancient Hawaiians raised fish and crops on the inhospitable North Kona Coast. Fishponds and tide pools await at lava- and coral-strewn beaches.

5 Keahole Point (p85) Take in a lecture and tour of West Hawai'i's alternative-energy and sustainable-aquaculture projects; take the kids to Ocean Rider Seahorse Farm.

6 Kekaha Kai (Kona Coast) State Park (p86) These are the pristine, wild beaches you've been so eager to find – but you'll have to hike to reach the best of 'em. Then swim, snorkel and dream of sailing to Tahiti.

7 Kiholo Bay (p90) Hit this state-park reserve at the end of day four for wildlife spotting, a swimmable lava tube and one last brilliant sunset.

➡ THIS LEG: 75 MILES

Kailua-Kona & the Kona Coast Highlights

1 Best Beaches: Kekaha Kai (Kona Coast) State Park (p86) Hard to get to, easy to love: snorkeling; sea turtles; soft, white sand.

2 Best Snorkeling: Ka'awaloa Cove (p73) Hike, kayak or cruise into Kealakekua Bay to this legendary spot teeming with underwater life.

3 Best Diving: Garden Eel Cove (p81) Aka Manta Heaven. Enough said! Thrilling after-dark boat trips depart from nearby Kailua-Kona.

4 Best Hawaiian Cultural Experience: Pu'uhonua O Hōnaunau National Historical Park (p77) Explore an ancient Hawaiian place of refuge.

5 Best Small Town: Holualoa (p59) Traditional Hawaiian craft and art galleries tucked among family-owned coffee farms.

Snorkeling, Kona Coast
JAMES R.D. SCOTT/GETTY IMAGES ©

Discover Kailua-Kona & the Kona Coast

KAILUA-KONA

Kailua-Kona, aka 'Kailua,' 'Kailua Town' or just 'Town,' makes a convenient base for exploring the entire Kona Coast, with its wild beaches; snorkeling with sea turtles and manta rays; upcountry coffee farms; and ancient Hawaiian sites by the ocean. In town, sunset by the seawall with a cold brew and a fish taco may be just what you're looking for at the end of another glorious day in the tropical sun.

Even so, Kailua can be a love-it-and-leave-it kind of place. Along Ali'i Dr, the main oceanside drag, traffic crawls bumper-to-bumper past tacky souvenir shops, waterfront bars and seafood restaurants. Sidewalk 'tourist information' booths sell every kind of tour and activity you might imagine.

🏖 Beaches

Kailua-Kona might act like a beach town, but most of its in-town beaches don't rank among the Kona Coast's showstoppers.

White (Magic) Sands Beach Beach
(La'aloa Beach Park; Ali'i Dr; P) Over 3 miles south of Kailua-Kona toward Keauhou, this small but gorgeous roadside beach beckons with turquoise waters, tall palms and little shade. Its other nickname is 'Disappearing Sands,' because the sand can wash offshore literally overnight during high surf, exposing dangerous rocks and coral. As the surf settles, white sands magically return. It's a hot spot for body-boarding, or you can snorkel at the beach's southern end when waters are perfectly calm. Facilities include restrooms, outdoor showers, drinking water, picnic tables, a volleyball court and lifeguard tower.

Old Kona Airport State Recreation Area Beach
(www.hawaiistateparks.org; Kuakini Hwy; ⊙7am-8pm; P) The swimming is just so-so at this sandy but rock-strewn beach, just over a mile northwest of downtown Kailua-Kona. Come to picnic, explore tide pools and experience a laidback locals' beach. Just inside the south entrance gate is a pristine, sandy-bottomed pool for *na*

Kahalu'u Beach Park (p54)
ANN CECIL/GETTY IMAGES ©

34

keiki (kids). At low tide, tiny sea urchins, crabs and bits of coral resemble lava-rock aquariums. When the surf's up, local surfers catch an offshore break here. Facilities include restrooms, outdoor showers, covered picnic tables and drinking water.

There's also a popular running track here. Just further south, the county-run **Kailua Park Complex** has an outdoor swimming pool, kiddie playground, tennis courts and ball-sports fields.

Kamakahonu Beach   Beach

(🏖️) Kailua-Kona's only swimmable in-town beach is this teeny-tiny strand between Kailua Pier and Ahu'ena Heiau, where ocean waters are calm and usually safe for kids. Concession stands rent all kinds of beach gear here.

◎ Sights

Ali'i Dr bombards you with surf shops and ABC Stores, but amid the tourist kitsch are a handful of historic buildings and landmarks worth seeking out.

Hulihe'e Palace   Historic Building

(📞808-329-1877; www.huliheepalace.net; 75-5718 Ali'i Dr; adult/child $6/1; ⊙9am-4pm Mon-Sat) Imagine the life of Hawaiian royalty in this palace, a private oceanfront residence constructed in 1838 by Hawaii's second governor, John Adams Kuakini. It was originally built with lava rock, but in 1885 King Kalakaua plastered over it because he preferred a more polished style after his travels abroad. The two-story palace contains Western antiques collected on royal jaunts to Europe and ancient Hawaiian artifacts, most notably several of Kamehameha the Great's war spears.

Admission to the palace includes a 40-minute tour given by **Daughters of Hawai'i** (www.daughtersofhawaii.org) docents, who relate fascinating anecdotes about past royal occupants – including Princess Ruth Ke'elikolani, who typically slept outdoors in a *pili* (grass) hut.

Ahu'ena Heiau   Temple

(www.ahuena.com; 75-5660 Palani Road) FREE
After uniting the Hawaii's islands in 1810,

Kamehameha the Great established the kingdom's royal court in Lahaina on Maui, but he continued to return to the Big Island. After a couple of years, he restored this sacred site as his personal retreat and temple. Notice the towering carved *ki'i* (deity) image with a golden plover atop its helmet: these long-distance flying birds may have helped guide the first Polynesians to Hawaii.

When Kamehameha I died at Ahu'ena Heiau on May 8, 1819, his body was prepared for burial here. In keeping with ancient Hawaiian tradition, the king's bones were secreted elsewhere, hidden so securely no one has ever found them (though some theorists point to a cave near Kaloko Fishpond).

Step inside **King Kamehameha's Kona Beach Hotel** nearby to view historical paintings and a mural by legendary artist and Hawaiian historian Herb Kawainui Kane. Also on display are a rare feathered helmet and cloak once worn by *ali'i* (royalty), ancient Hawaiian war weapons and musical instruments, and a whale's-tooth pendant strung on a braided cord made of human hair.

Moku'aikaua Church   Church

(📞808-329-0655; www.mokuaikaua.org; 75-5713 Ali'i Dr; ⊙7:30am-5:30pm) FREE Completed in 1836, Moku'aikaua Church matches its island setting, with walls of lava rock hewn with stone adzes, smoothed with chunks of coral and held together by sand and coral-lime mortar. The interior posts and beams are constructed from ohia trees, while the pews and pulpit are made of koa, Hawaii's most prized native hardwood. The steeple tops out at 112ft, making this Kailua-Kona's tallest structure. The 11am Sunday worship service is usually followed by a short history lecture.

When the first Christian missionaries landed in Kailua Bay on April 4, 1820, their timing couldn't have been better. King Liholiho had abolished the traditional religion on that very spot just a few months before. He gave the missionaries this site, just a few minutes' walk from Ahu'ena Heiau, to establish Hawai'i's first Christian church.

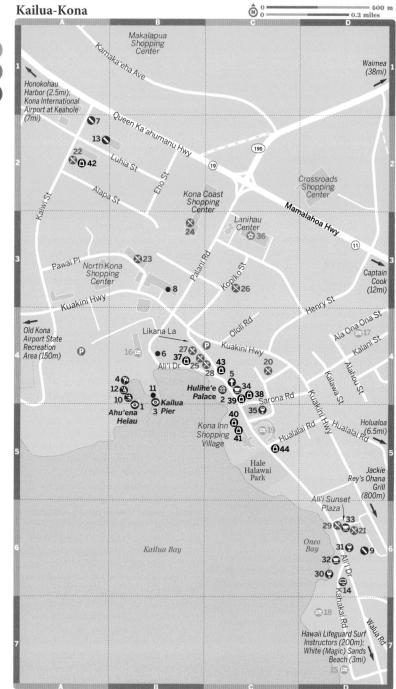

Makalapua
Shopping
Center

Kamaka'eha Ave

Waimea (38mi)

Honokohau
Harbor (2.5mi);
Kona International
Airport at Keahole
(7mi)

Queen Ka'ahumanu Hwy

7

13

22

42

Luhia St

Eho St

Kaiwi St

Alapa St

190

19

Crossroads
Shopping
Center

Mamalahoa Hwy

11

Kona Coast
Shopping
Center

24

Lanihau
Center

36

Captain
Cook
(12mi)

Pawai Pl

North Kona
Shopping
Center

23

Palani Rd

Kopiko St

26

Henry St

Ala Ona Ona St

17

Kuakini Hwy

8

Kalani St

Old Kona
Airport State
Recreation
Area (150m)

Likana La

Ololi Rd

Kuakini Hwy

Alahou St

P

16

6

27

37

25

28

P

20

Kalawa St

Kuakini Hwy

Hualalai Rd

4

12

10

1

11

Kailua
Pier

43

5

34

38

2 39

35

Sarona Rd

Holualoa
(6.5mi)

Ahu'ena
Heiau

Ali'i Dr

Hulihe'e
Palace

40

41

19

44

Kona Inn
Shopping
Village

Hale
Halawai
Park

Jackie
Rey's Ohana
Grill
(800m)

Ali'i Sunset
Plaza

29

33

21

Kailua Bay

Oneo
Bay

31

9

32

30

14

Ali'i Dr

18

15

Kahakai Rd

Wailua Rd

Hawaii Lifeguard Surf
Instructors (200m);
White (Magic) Sands
Beach (3mi)

Kailua-Kona

Kailua Pier　　　　　Landmark

Kailua Bay was once a major cattle-shipping area; animals were stampeded into the water and forced to swim to steamers waiting to transport them to Honolulu slaughterhouses. Now locals come to swim at lunchtime and canoe clubs launch their vessels here. The Hawaiian International Billfish Tournament (p43) kicks off here, continuing a sportfishing tradition begun in 1915 when the pier was built.

✪ Activities

Other activity outfitters and tour companies are based at Keauhou, about 5 miles south of Kailua-Kona.

SWIMMING

With rocky shores and rough waters, Kailua-Kona isn't ideal for swimming – for that head to North Kona Coast beaches. Still, Kahalu'u Beach Park (p54), 5 miles south in Keauhou, is a good bet when conditions are calm, as is Old Kona Airport State Recreation Area (p34), especially with kids in tow.

BODYBOARDING, SURFING & SUP

White (Magic) Sands Beach (p34) is a favorite spot for bodyboarding. Local experts board surf at Banyans, north of White Sands, and Pine Trees (p85), south of the airport near Wawaloli (OTEC) Beach. Newbies can surf at Lymans, south of Banyans.

Ever popular, stand up paddling (SUP) delivers a core workout in the company of dolphins, turtles and tropical fish. The best part is anyone can do it – even the less fit can groove to this easy, fun

37

The Best...
Kailua-Kona Sunset Views

1 Touching down at Kona International Airport (p52)

2 Kailua Pier (p37)

3 White (Magic) Sands Beach (p34)

4 Huggo's on the Rocks (p49)

5 Don's Mai Tai Bar (p50)

watersport. Give it a spin in Kailua Bay or Kahalu'u Bay, further south in Keauhou.

Hawaii Lifeguard Surf Instructors
Surfing, SUP

(HLSI; 808-324-0442; www.surflessonshawaii.com; 75-5909 Ali'i Dr; group/private lessons from $75/100) Skilled, professional HLSI instructors have a minimum of 15 years' surfing experience and are all certified lifeguards. Join a group surfing or SUP lesson, or book a private one-on-one session (which is the only way that kids aged three to 10 years are taught at this school).

Kona Boys Beach Shack
SUP

(808-329-2345; www.konaboys.com; Kamakahonu Beach; surfboard/SUP set rental from $25, SUP lesson/tour $75/150; 8am-5pm) Organizes SUP lessons for beginners as well as more ambitious coastal paddling tours, and rents SUP sets and surfboards right on the beach. Call in advance to arrange group or private surfing or SUP lessons.

Kona Surf Adventures
Surfing

(808-334-0033; www.konasurfadventures.com; 75-6129 Ali'i Dr, Ali'i Gardens Marketplace; surfing lesson $99-150) This surf school is run by California-born 'Kona Mike,' who comes with endorsements from novice students and veteran wave riders alike.

SNORKELING

For easy-access snorkeling, Kahalu'u Beach Park (p54), 5 miles south in Keauhou, is your closest and best option. To snorkel further afield, take a cruise from Honokohau Harbor or Keauhou Pier. Opt to depart in the morning, when conditions are calmer and clearer. Tour prices typically include snorkel gear, beverages and snacks; book ahead online for discounts.

Zodiac rafts are zippy and thrilling, capable of exploring sea caves, lava tubes and blowholes, but expect a bumpy ride and no shade or toilets. Catamarans are much larger, smoother and comfier but can't get as close into coves. Alternatively, many dive boats let snorkelers ride along at a cheaper rate.

Sea Paradise
Snorkeling

(800-322-5662, 808-322-2500; www.seaparadise.com; 78-6831 Ali'i Dr; snorkel cruise adult/child 5-12yr from $89/59) Highly recommended outfitter offers morning snorkel cruises to Kealakekua Bay and nighttime manta ray trips (free rebooking if you don't spot any the first time out) on a smaller 46ft-long catamaran with a friendly, professional crew.

Fair Wind
Snorkeling, Diving

(800-677-9461, 808-322-2788; www.fairwind.com; 78-7130 Kaleiopapa St; snorkel cruise adult/child 4-12yr from $75/45) The *Fair Wind II,* a two-story catamaran with two 15ft-long waterslides, sails to Kealakekua Bay every morning. Longer daytime cruises on the luxury hydrofoil catamaran *Hula Kai* explore less-trafficked waters ($149), while nighttime manta ray snorkel cruises are hugely popular ($99), so book ahead.

Captain Zodiac
Snorkeling, Whale-Watching

(808-329-3199; www.captainzodiac.com; Honokohau Harbor; snorkel cruise adult/child 4-12yr from $99/78) In business with a jaunty pirate theme since 1974, Captain Zodiac makes daily trips to Kealakekua Bay in 24ft-long rigid-hull inflatable rafts that each carry up to 16 passengers.

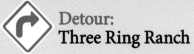

Detour:
Three Ring Ranch

Kona resident Dr Ann Goody communes with animals, fixes their broken bones and psyches, coaxes them back into their natural behavior and sets them free – or not: some rescued and exotic animals just can't cut it in the wild. That's when they become residents of her **Three Ring Ranch Exotic Animal Sanctuary** (☎808-331-8778; www.threeringranch.org; 75-809 Keaolani Dr, Kailua-Kona; suggested donation $35; ⏰tours 11am-1pm, by reservation only) 🌿, a short drive from downtown Kailua-Kona.

An internationally accredited animal sanctuary, Three Ring Ranch currently hosts South African–crowned cranes, David and Goliath (a pair of gigantic African spur-thigh tortoises) and endangered endemic species such as the Hawaiian owl and nene (Hawaiian goose). Rescued from the failed Moloka'i Ranch safari park, the zebra Zoe has amelanosis, meaning her stripes are the color of sand and her eyes the color of the ocean.

Dr Ann Goody – who has been struck by lightning, tossed by a tiger shark and survived breast cancer – is as good with people as she is with animals. This, along with the unflagging support of her husband and business partner Dr Norm Goody, has led to an enormously successful educational initiative. Tours are by reservation only (children must be at least six years old). No drop-in visitors allowed.

Kamanu Charters   Snorkeling
(☎800-348-3091, 808-329-2021; www.kamanu.com; Honokohau Harbor; adult/child under 13yr $95/50) Snorkel without crowds in the protected waters of Pawai Bay, just north of Old Kona Airport State Recreation Area. This 36ft catamaran maxes out at 24 people. Kamanu also offers a nighttime manta ray snorkel, but skip the dolphin swim – state law prohibits swimmers from getting closer then 150yd to these wild creatures to avoid disturbing them.

Snorkel Bob's   Snorkeling
(☎800-262-7725, 808-329-0770; www.snorkelbob.com; 75-5831 Kahakai Rd; ⏰8am-5pm) Rent snorkel masks (including corrective lenses for near-sighted folks), fins, reef walkers, wetsuits and flotation aids.

DIVING

The Kona Coast is known for calm, clear waters, unique lava formations and coral reefs. Near shore, divers can see steep drop-offs with lava tubes, caves and diverse marine life. Deeper waters contain dozens of popular boat-dive areas, including an airplane wreck off Keahole Point.

Most dive boats launch from Honokohau Harbor but have bricks-and-mortar offices in Kailua-Kona. Including all gear, the cost of a standard two-tank morning dive or one-tank night dive to see manta rays ranges from $110 to $150. Multiday PADI Open Water certification programs cost around $500 or more.

Jack's Diving Locker   Diving, Snorkeling
(☎800-345-4807, 808-329-7585; www.jacksdivinglocker.com; 75-5813 Ali'i Dr, Coconut Grove Marketplace, Bldg H; 👶) 🌿 For top-notch introductory dives and courses, plus extensive programs for kids, this ecoconscious dive outfitter has a 5000-sq-ft facility with a store, classrooms, tank room and Hawaii's only 12ft-deep indoor dive pool. Sign up for a boat or shore dive, as well as a night manta ray dive. Snorkelers are welcome on many dive-boat trips.

Sandwich Isle Divers   Diving
(☎888-743-3483, 808-329-9188; www.sandwichisledivers.com) This small charter dive-boat outfit run by a husband-and-wife team organizes personalized trips

(six-person maximum). These folks have decades of experience in Kona waters, and Captain Steve has a marine-biology degree.

Big Island Divers Diving, Snorkeling
(☎808-329-6068; www.bigislanddivers.com; 74-5467 Kaiwi St) Personable staff, an expansive shop and boat dives that are open to snorkelers all score big. This outfit specializes in night and manta ray dives. Black-water boat trips ($150 to $210) are for experienced – and, more importantly, fearless – divers only.

Kona Honu Divers Diving, Snorkeling
(☎888-333-4668, 808-324-4668; www.konahonudivers.com; 74-5583 Luhia St) Well-reviewed dive company schedules diverse boat trips, including manta ray night dives and Nitrox trips.

FISHING

Kailua-Kona is legendary for its big-game fishing, especially Pacific blue marlin (June to August are the best months), which can grow into 1-ton 'granders.' Sharing a charter boat starts at $95 per person for a four-hour trip or $250 all day. If you charter a whole boat, you can take up to six people for $450 to $600 for a half-day, or $750 or more for a full day. Ask whether the captain shares the catch.

Agencies book for so many boats that it's impossible to guarantee quality or consistency, but **Charter Desk** (☎888-566-2487, 808-326-1800; www.charterdesk.com; Honokohau Marina; ⊘6am-6pm) is reputable and can match you with 60 boats.

Captain Jeff's Charters Fishing
(☎808-895-1852; http://fishinkona.com) Captain Jeff is a straight shooter who offers tailored trips, insider advice and a share of the catch. Not for nothing, he has maintained the highest catch record in Kona for more than 15 years. Check his other website, **Kona Hawaii Fishing Report** (http://aloha-kona.com), for current sportfishing conditions.

Left: Surfing at Lymans Beach (p37) **Below:** Catamaran entering Keauhou Bay (p55)
(LEFT & BELOW) LONELY PLANET/GETTY IMAGES ©

Kayak Fishing
Hawai'i   Fishing, Kayaking

(📞808-936-4400; www.kayakfishing hawaii.com; guided tour $300) Imagine landing a 25lb ahi (yellowfin tuna) or *ono* (wahoo) fish from a kayak – not without a fight! This outfitter is based at Kawaihae Harbor, but travels island-wide.

OUTRIGGER CANOEING & KAYAKING

To see how outrigger canoeing pros do it, check out the January-to-May race schedule of the **Hawai'i Island Paddlesports Association** (www.hawaiipaddling.com). Over Labor Day weekend in late August and/ or early September, don't miss the **Queen Lili'uokalani Canoe Race** (www.kaiopua.org) from Kailua Bay south to Honaunau.

Kona Boys
Beach Shack   Canoeing, Kayaking

(📞808-329-2345; www.konaboys.com; Kamak ahonu Beach; tours $50-149; 🕐8am-5pm) Experience what the original Polynesian settlers must have felt with the water

rushing under their hull as they approached the volcanic shores of the Big Island. Paddle an outrigger canoe around Kamakahonu Bay or all the way from Keauhou to snorkel in Kealekekua Bay. Sea-kayaking tours often stop to snorkel too.

Kai 'Opua Canoe Club   Canoeing

(www.kaiopua.org; Kamakahonu Beach) 🏄 With this local club dedicated to traditional Hawaiian outrigger canoeing, visitors are welcome to join recreational paddling excursions leaving at 6am every morning except Sunday. There is no club office, so check the website for schedules and contact details. Trips launch next to Ahu'ena Heiau.

WHALE-WATCHING

Although snorkeling, diving and fishing tours often give you whale-watching opportunities during humpback season

41

Manta Ray Night Dives & Snorkeling

A night dive or snorkel cruise among Pacific manta rays is the aquatic thrill of a lifetime. Manta ray sightings are not guaranteed, no matter what boat operators promise, although some will let you repeat the cruise for free if none are sighted. If you're PADI-certified but rusty (or if it's your first night dive), a two-tank dive allows time to practice during the first afternoon dive.

Visit the **Manta Pacific Research Foundation** (www.mantapacific.org) website for responsible viewing guidelines for divers and snorkelers.

(December to April), you're more likely to see, and learn, more on specialized tours.

Dan McSweeney's Whale Watch
Whale-Watching

(☏ 888-942-5376, 808-322-0028; www.ilovewhales.com; Honokohau Harbor; 2½hr cruise adult/under 12yr $110/99) Captain McSweeney's winter excursions focus on humpback whale sightings, marine conservation and education. Several other species of whales and dolphins can be seen in Kona waters year-round. Hydrophones allow passengers to listen in on whale songs.

🏃 Tours

Body Glove Hawaii
Cruise

(☏ 808-326-7122, 800-551-8911; www.bodyglovehawaii.com; 75-5629 Kuakini Hwy; adult/child 6-17yr historical cruise incl dinner $115/83, incl lunch $88/68; ⏰ 1pm Wed, 4pm Tue, Thu-Fri & Sat; ♿) Popular historical cruises along the Kona Coast last three hours and feature a so-so buffet, live music and engaging historical narration. Staffed by a hospitable crew, the boat is wheelchair-accessible.

Kona Brewing Company
Tour

(☏ 808-334-2739; http://konabrewingco.com; 75-5629 Kuakini Hwy; ⏰ 30min tours 10:30am & 3pm) 🎫 FREE Since 1994, this ecoconscious company has anchored Hawai'i's microbrewery scene. The once-small, family-run operation is now one of the nation's fastest-growing microbreweries – from Maine to California, you can sip 'liquid Aloha.' Complimentary tours include tasting samples. No reservations accepted; sign up in person at the pub.

Hawaiian Walkways
Walking Tour

(☏ 800-457-7759; www.hawaiianwalkways.com; tour adult/child 8-12yr $119/99) Leads three-hour walking tours through the upland **Kona Cloud Forest Sanctuary**. Guides are knowledgeable about botany and geology, and the tour ends with a visit to Mountain Thunder Coffee Plantation (p61). Wear sturdy shoes.

Kailua Bay Charter Company
Cruise

(☏ 808-324-1749; www.konaglassbottomboat.com; Kailua-Kona Pier; 50min tour adult/child under 12yr $40/20; ⏰ usually 10:30am, 11:30am & 12:30pm daily; ♿) Gain a new perspective on Kailua-Kona's coastline, its underwater reef and sea life from a 36ft glass-bottomed boat with a cheery crew and onboard naturalist. Easy boarding available for passengers with mobility issues.

Atlantis Submarines
Boat Tour

(☏ 800-548-6262; www.atlantisadventures.com; 75-5669 Ali'i Dr; 45min tour adult/child under 13yr $109/45; ⏰ 10am; ♿) You read that right: a real-deal submarine descends up to 100ft into a coral-reef crevice and explores nearby shipwrecks. The battery-powered sub has 26 portholes and carries 48 passengers. Kids must be at least 36in tall.

✨ Festivals & Events

Kokua Kailua
Art, Food

(http://historickailuavillage.com) On the third Sunday of the month, local food vendors, artists and craftspeople set up booths along Ali'i Dr, which closes to vehicular traffic. The whole affair starts around 1pm and lasts until sunset, with free Hawaiian music and hula dancing at Hulihe'e Palace starting around 4pm.

Kona Brewers Festival   Beer, Food

(www.konabrewersfestival.com) On the second Saturday in March, Kona Brewing Company throws its annual beer bash, with proceeds benefiting local charities. Sample dozens of craft beers and island chefs' gourmet grinds. Buy tickets in advance online.

Hawaiian International Billfish Tournament   Fishing

(www.hibtfishing.com) Hawaii's most prestigious sportfishing contest encompasses five days of fishing followed by weigh-ins and festivities at Kailua Pier. The tournament starts in late July or early August.

Ironman Triathlon World Championship   Sports

(www.ironman.com) On the second Saturday in October, all traffic on Ali'i Dr halts for this human-powered endurance test that starts and finishes at Kailua Pier.

Kona Coffee Cultural Festival   Coffee

(www.konacoffeefest.com) For 10 days in early November during the harvest season, the community celebrates Kona coffee pioneers and their renowned beans. Dozens of events include a cupping competition, art shows, live music and hula performances, farm tours, coffee tastings, a recipe cook-off and a coffee cherry-picking contest.

Sleeping

The quality of hotels and condos along Ali'i Dr in walkable downtown Kailua-Kona is only fair to middling. Many condos and vacation rentals are either along or near Ali'i Dr heading toward Keauhou,

the beachy resort area just south of Kailua-Kona, or several miles upland on the cool slopes of Mt Hualalai.

Browse condo- and vacation-rental listings online at **Vacation Rentals by Owner** (VRBO; VRBO; www.vrbo.com), **Home Away** (http://www.homeaway.com/) and **Air B&B** (www.airbnb.com), or with local booking agencies **Affordable Paradise** (☏ 808-261-1693; www.affordable-paradise.com), **ATR Properties** (☏ 888-311-6020, 808-329-6020; www.konacondo.com), **Kona Hawaii Vacation Rentals** (☏ 800-244-4752, 808-329-3333 ; www.konahawaii.com), **Kona Rentals** (☏ 800-799-5662, 808-334-1199; www.konarentals.com), **Knutson & Associates** (☏ 800-800-6202, 808-329-6311; www.konahawaiirentals.com) and **SunQuest Vacations** (☏ 808-329-6438, from Canada 800-800-5662, from mainland USA 800-367-5168; www.sunquest-hawaii.com).

Wherever you stay, remember that oceanfront in Kona doesn't necessarily mean a sandy beach, as there's little sand along the rocky shoreline. Make reservations, especially during high season. Booking online in advance usually nets you the biggest savings.

Humpback whale, Kona Coast
STUART WESTMORLAND/GETTY IMAGES ©

The Best...
Kailua-Kona & the Kona Coast for Kids

1 Kahalu'u Beach Park (p54)

2 Ocean Rider Seahorse Farm (p85)

3 Scandinavian Shave Ice (p47)

4 Fair Wind snorkel cruise (p38) to Kealakekua Bay

5 Hawaii Lifeguard Surf Instructors (p38)

6 Three Ring Ranch Exotic Animal Sanctuary (p39)

Koa Wood Hale Inn/ Patey's Place
Hostel $

(✆808-329-9663; 75-184 Ala Ona Ona St; dm/r with shared bath from $25/55; ⊘reception 8am-noon & 5-10pm; @ 🛜) Kailua-Kona's only hostel is a backpacker crashpad, with basic fan-cooled dorms and private rooms, a common kitchen and the usual crowd of 20-somethings, misfits and the globally road-weary. It's on a residential street within walking distance of Ali'i Dr. No drugs, alcohol or shoes indoors.

Royal Sea-Cliff Resort
Condo $$

(✆info 866-733-0659, reservations 800-688-7444; www.outriggercondominiums.com; 75-6040 Ali'i Dr; studio/1br/2br apt from $145/175/230; P ❄ @ 🛜 🏊) This seven-floor timeshare complex feels almost like a hotel, giving you the best of both worlds. Immaculate units are generously sized and appointed with tropical furniture and lots of amenities – well-stocked kitchens, washer/dryers, two oceanfront pools, tennis courts and outdoor BBQ grills. Minimum two-night stay; mandatory cleaning fee ($40 to $60).

Kona Tiki Hotel
Hotel $$

(✆808-329-1425; www.konatikihotel.com; 75-5968 Ali'i Dr; r $85-159; P 🛜 🏊) You can afford oceanfront views at this retro three-story hotel, a quirky, well-kept 15-unit complex south of downtown Kailua-

Ironman Triathlon World Championship

JOHN P KELLY/GETTY IMAGES ©

Ironman Triathlon World Championship

When thousands of athletes and fans swoop into Kailua-Kona each October, locals gripe about traffic and crowds. But nobody can deny the thrilling spectacle of the Ironman Triathlon World Championship (p43). The granddaddy of triathlons is a brutal combination of a 2.4-mile ocean swim, 112-mile bike race and 26.2-mile run. And it has to be done in under 17 hours. Australian Craig Alexander set the current course record at eight hours, three minutes and 56 seconds in 2011.

Harsh conditions make the event the ultimate endurance test. Heat bouncing off the lava commonly exceeds 100°F (38°C), making dehydration and heat exhaustion major challenges. Many contenders arrive on the island weeks before to acclimatize. On race day, the world's toughest athletes are pushed to the max – in the past, they've included a 75-year-old nun, an Iraq war veteran amputee, and father–son Team Hoyt, with Rick pushing son Dick in a wheelchair (they're six-time finishers!).

Begun in 1978 by a US Navy man on a dare, the Ironman was labeled 'lunatic' by *Sports Illustrated*. Only 15 people competed the first year, and three didn't even cross the finish line. With that kind of crazy drama, the sports world was hooked. Today the event draws up to 2000 athletes from over 50 countries, everyone seeking the rights to 'Brag for the rest of your life!'.

Kona. Motel-style rooms are forgettably basic (no TVs, phones or air-con), but all have a fridge and enchanting lanai. Book well ahead, as the hotel regularly fills with nostalgic repeat guests. No credit cards.

Hale Kona Kai Condo $$
(☎800-421-3696, 808-329-6402; www.halekon akai-hkk.com; 75-5870 Kahakai Rd; 1br apt $150-215; P ❋ ☎ ☎) All condos overlook crashing surf at this well-managed, oceanfront complex off the busy commercial stretch of Ali'i Dr. The 22 one-bedroom units vary in style, but each has a separate living room, full kitchen and ocean-view lanai. Poolside wi-fi only. Minimum-night stay varies.

Casa de Emdeko Condo $$
(☎808-329-2160; www.casadeemdeko.org; 75-6082 Ali'i Dr; 1br apt from $100; P ❋ ☎ ☎) With Spanish-tile roofs, white stucco, immaculate gardens and two pools, this condo complex south of downtown Kailua-Kona is stylish and restful. Individually owned units are mostly up-to-date, peacefully quiet and reasonably priced.

Mango Sunset B&B B&B $$
(☎808-325-0909; www.mangosunset.com; 73-4261 Mamalahoa Hwy; r without/with private bath $100/120, all incl breakfast; P @ ☎) ❂ Hawaiiana-bedecked teak furnishings and bamboo accents spruce up the snug accomodations on this family-owned organic coffee farm. The best rooms offer sweeping ocean views from a shared lanai, and there's a common kitchenette. It's about a 15-minute drive from downtown Kailua-Kona, closer to the airport.

Kona Magic Sands Resort Condo $$
(☎800-244-4752, 808-329-3333; www.konaha waii.com/ms.htm; 77-6452 Ali'i Dr; studio apt $115-160; P ☎ ☎) Large studios all have oceanfront lanai, but the 2nd- and 3rd-floor units are best. The location south of downtown Kailua-Kona is perfect for beach-goers. An all-concrete building keeps out some noise and heat, but not all units have air-con.

Nancy's Hideaway B&B $$
(☎866-325-3132, 808-325-3132; www.nancy-shideaway.com; 73-1530 Uanani Pl; studio incl

breakfast $120-140, cottage incl breakfast $130-150; 🛜) At this peaceful retreat, 6 miles upslope from town, pick between a free-standing studio or a one-bedroom cottage, each contemporary in design with its own kitchenette. No young children allowed.

Uncle Billy's Kona Bay Hotel
Hotel **$$**

(📞808-329-1393, 800-367-5102; www.unclebilly. com; 75-5739 Ali'i Dr; r $99-135; 🅿🌸@🛜♨) In a pinch, head to this low-rent waterfront hotel. The good: it's right downtown with complimentary continental breakfast. The bad: street noise, frumpy interiors and kooky folks.

Kona Sugar Shack
Vacation Rental **$$$**

(📞877-324-6444, 808-895-2203; www.kona sugarshack.com; 77-6483 Ali'i Dr; ste $225-490; 🅿🌸🛜♨) 🍃 It hits the sweet spot for vacation rentals, right across the street from the beach. Friendly, artistic hosts have created a solar-powered oasis with funky, colorful and eclectic decor and relaxing, kid-friendly vibes. Extras include a shared outdoor kitchen, coin-op laundry, a miniscule pool and beach and baby gear to borrow. Rent the whole house for a family reunion. Expect a one-time cleaning fee ($125 to $275). Ouch.

King Kamehameha's Kona Beach Hotel
Hotel **$$$**

(📞808-329-2911, 800-367-2111; www. konabeachhotel.com; 75-5660 Palani Rd; r $150-305; 🅿🌸@🛜♨) A prime beach-front location and spiffy renovations are watchwords for the historic 'King Kam,' anchoring the north end of Ali'i Dr. Chic decor by the Courtyard Marriott chain, Herb Kawainui Kane's artwork and Hawaiian historical artifact exhibits in the lobby, a 24-hour fitness center and free wi-fi are all draws at this favorite with both vacationers and business types.

Royal Kona Resort
Resort **$$$**

(📞800-222-5642, 808-329-3111; www.royalkona. com; 75-5852 Ali'i Dr; r $140-300; 🅿🌸@♨) Spread over three ship-shaped towers, this breezy, 1970s Polynesian fantasy has a tropical theme that lets you know you're in Hawaii. Although all rooms are remodeled, those in the pricier Ali'i and Lagoon Towers are worth an upgrade. A protected, saltwater lagoon is perfect for kids. Check out the long menu of spa services at the **Lotus Center** (www.konaspa.com).

Honu Kai B&B
B&B **$$$**

(📞808-292-1775, 808-329-8676; www.honukai bnb.com; 74-1529 Hao Kuni St; d incl breakfast $220-255; 🅿@🛜) Amid tropical gardens, this plush, romantic four-room B&B is filled with rich fabrics, carved bedframes and Asian and Hawaiian decor. Guests share a hot tub, outdoor kitchen and rooftop lanai. Enclosed by rock walls, the private gated property is a 10-minute drive from downtown Kailua-Kona.

✖ Eating

You don't have to spend a lot to devour *'ono kine grinds* (good food), but you'll usually have to venture further afield than Ali'i Dr, where most waterfront restaurants are disappointing and overpriced.

Da Poke Shack
Seafood, Local **$**

(📞808-329-7653; http://dapokeshack.com; 76-6246 Ali'i Dr, Castle Kona Bali Kai; mains & meals $5-10; ⏱10am-6pm) What's *poke*? Hawaii-style raw cubes of fish mixed with soy sauce, sesame oil, some chiles, seaweed and...well, the sky's the limit. This is the spot to get it, because these awesome *brah* (brothers) offer a huge variety of fresh-off-da-boat, homemade *poke*, side salads and plate lunches. Eat at picnic tables in the parking lot or take it to the beach.

Basik Acai
Cafe **$**

(www.basikacai.com; 75-5831 Kahakai Rd; snacks & drinks $6-13; ⏱7am-4pm Mon-Fri, from 8am Sat & Sun; 🛜🍴) Healthy, wholesome acai bowls bursting with tropical fruity goodness, granola, nuts, shredded coconut and even cacao nibs, along with fresh juice smoothies, are made to order at this tiny upstairs kitchen that sources organic, local ingredients. It's expensive, but worth it.

Phuket Monkey
Thai **$**

(📞808-333-5395; www.phuketmonkey.com; 75-5660 Kopiko St, Kopiko Plaza; mains $7-13;

⏱10:30am-3:30pm & 5-9pm) Nearby Longs Drugs, this tiny strip-mall kitchen with a laughing monkey mascot dishes up real-deal authentic Thai food such as fiery lemongrass chicken, marinated beef salads and tangy pineapple curry. Order it 'super monkey' hot, if you dare.

Metal Mike's Twisted Pretzels
Fast Food $

(Likana Ln; snacks $3-5; ⏱usually 11:30am-10pm Mon-Thu, to midnight Fri & Sat, noon-10pm Sun; 🖊) Metal Mike, who seriously looks like he spent time as a roadie, runs this rock-and-roll pretzel stand on a narrow alley by a parking lot just above Ali'i Dr. Go ga-ga over a dozen kinds of pretzels and dipping sauces, from cheesy jalapeño to white chocolate mac-nut.

Kope Lani
Cafe

(www.kopelani.com; 75-5719 Ali'i Dr; snacks & drinks $3-7; ⏱7am-9pm) Ali'i Dr is chock-a-block with coffee shops vending 100% Kona brews from upcountry coffee plantations. This sweet spot stands out, not just for its ocean views and ice-blended espresso drinks, but also its two-dozen flavors of Big Island–made ice cream.

Island Naturals Market & Deli
Supermarket, Deli $

(www.islandnaturals.com; 74-5487 Kaiwi St; ⏱7:30am-8pm Mon-Sat, 9am-7pm Sun; 🖊) This health-conscious grocery store has a fantastic deli making sandwiches, wraps and salads to go, plus a hot-and-cold takeout bar. Some organic and gluten-free options too.

Scandinavian Shave Ice
Desserts $

(www.scandinavianshaveice.com; 75-5699 Ali'i Dr; snacks & drinks $3-8; ⏱11am-8pm Sun-Thu, to 9pm Fri & Sat; 🚹) Shave ice is piled up here in huge, psychedelic mounds that are as big as your head. Dither over a rainbow variety of flavored syrups, then borrow a board game to while away an hour.

KTA Super Store
Supermarket $

(www.ktasuperstores.com; 74-5594 Palani Rd, Kona Coast Shopping Center; ⏱5am-11pm) The Big Island's best grocery chain, with many Hawaii-made products, anything from La-vosh crackers to *liliko'i* (passion fruit) jam.

Kona Brewing Company
American $$

(📞808-334-2739; http://konabrewingco.com; 75-5629 Kuakini Hwy; mains $13-18; ⏱11am-9pm

Luau (Hawaiian feast), King Kamehameha's Kona Beach Hotel

Sun-Thu, to 10pm Fri & Sat; ⊕) ⬤ Expect a madhouse crowd at this sprawling, ecosustainable brewpub, with torch-lit outdoor seating and laidback waitstaff. Everyone's here for the handcrafted 'liquid aloha' made on-site (Pipeline Porter and Castaway IPA are our faves). Pizza toppings verge on gourmet, but crusts can be soggy; BBQ sandwiches and fish tacos are better. Enter the parking lot off Kaiwi St.

Island Lava Java   Cafe $$

(☎808-936-9766; www.islandlavajava.com; 75-5799 Ali'i Dr, Ali'i Sunset Plaza; breakfast & lunch mains $7-20; ⊙6:30am-9:30pm; 📶📷⊕) ⬤ A convivial gathering spot for Sunday brunch or a sunny breakfast (served til 11:30am) with ocean-view dining on the sidewalk patio. The menu aims for upscale diner but hits closer to greasy spoon. Not everyone minds – especially with huge portions, Big Island–raised meats and farm-fresh produce and 100% Kona coffee.

Big Island Grill   Local $$

(75-5702 Kuakini Hwy; mains $10-20; ⊙7am-9pm Mon-Sat, to noon Sun; ⊕) Big appetites are no match for the big portions served at this island-style diner. The island soul food is down-home country cooking, with loco moco (rice, fried egg and hamburger patty topped with gravy or other condiments), mahimahi fish-and-chips and slow-cooked kalua pork with cabbage always on the menu. Superfriendly service makes you feel like part of the 'ohana (extended family and friends).

Rapanui Island Cafe   Asian $$

(☎808-329-0511; 75-5695 Ali'i Dr, Kona Banyan Court; mains lunch $6-10, dinner $13-19; ⊙11am-2pm Tue-Fri, 5-9pm Mon-Sat) The New Zealand owners know Polynesian and Indonesian curries, which they prepare with tongue-tingling warmth. Various salads and satays, spiced pork and pawpaw chicken also make an appearance. Order the house coconut rice and wash it down with lemongrass-ginger tea.

Jackie Rey's Ohana Grill   Hawaii Regional Cuisine $$$

(☎808-327-0209; www.jackiereys.com; 75-5995 Kuakini Hwy; mains lunch $10-16, dinner $15-33; ⊙11am-9pm Mon-Fri, from 5pm Sat & Sun; ⊕) Jackie Rey's is a casual, family-owned grill with a delightfully retro-kitsch Hawaii vibe. Haute versions of local grinds (food) include guava-glazed ribs, wasabi-seared ahi and mochiko (rice-flour-battered) fish with Moloka'i purple sweet potatoes. Locals, tourists, kids, aunties – pretty much everyone loves it. Pop by between 3pm and 5pm on weekdays for half-price pupu (snack or appetizers), tropical cocktails and island microbrews. Reservations recommended for dinner.

Sushi Shiono   Japanese $$$

(☎808-326-1696; www.sushishiono.com; 75-5799 Ali'i Dr, Ali'i Sunset Plaza; a la carte dishes $4-17, lunch plates

Kona Brewing Company beers (p42)
NIELS VAN KAMPENHOUT/ALAMY©

$10-19, dinner combos $20-37; ⏱11:30am-2pm Mon-Sat, 5:30-9pm Sun-Thu, to 10pm Fri & Sat) Inside a minimall, wickedly fresh sushi and sashimi are complemented by a tempting sake list. The joint is owned by a Japanese expat, who employs an all-star, all-Japanese (and all-male) cast of sushi chefs behind the bar. Skip the surf-and-turf combo plates. Dinner reservations recommended.

🍷 Drinking

Kailua-Kona's bar scene is pretty touristy, but there are a handful of places for a cocktail or a beer. Always a good fallback, Kona Brewing Company (p47) usually has live Hawaiian music from 5pm to 8pm on Sundays.

Huggo's on the Rocks   Bar
(☎808-329-1493; http://huggos.com; 75-5828 Kahakai Rd; ⏱4-10pm Mon-Thu, to midnight Fri, 5pm-midnight Sat & 5-10pm Sun) Right on the water, with a thatched-roof bar and live music nightly, Huggo's is an ideal sunset spot. Whether it's worth staying longer depends on who's playing and who else shows up. In the mornings, it reverts to **Java on the Rock** (☎808-324-2411; www.javaontherock.com; 75-5828 Kahakai Rd; ⏱6-11am; 📶) serving coffee and espresso drinks (give the bland breakfasts a miss).

Humpy's Big Island Alehouse   Bar
(☎808-324-2337; www.humpyshawaii.com; 75-5815 Ali'i Dr, Coconut Grove Marketplace; ⏱11am-2am Mon-Fri, from 8am Sat & Sun) With its enviable location on the strip overlooking Kailua Bay, Alaskan Humpy's would probably survive in touristy Kailua-Kona even without having dozens of craft beers on tap. Perch on the upstairs balcony, with its sea breezes and views, while live bands rock out. The kitchen stays open till 10pm daily, with a limited bar menu available until midnight. Happy hour runs from 3pm to 6pm on weekdays.

Kanaka Kava   Cafe
(75-5803 Ali'i Dr, Coconut Grove Marketplace; ⏱bar 10am-11pm, kitchen till 9:30pm) This tiny, locals' grass-shack hangout is the place to try Hawaiian-style kava (the mildly

Local Knowledge

NAME: PAUL STREITER
OCCUPATION: CO-OWNER, JACKIE REY'S OHANA GRILL
RESIDENCE: KAILUA-KONA

1 WHERE DO YOU GO ON YOUR DAY OFF?
I like Magic Sands (p34) right in town. It's a local favorite for people-watching and bodysurfing. In the winter, it gets a little rough and loses some of its sand; it's better in summer. My favorite all-round beach is Hapuna (p108) – phenomenal.

2 WHAT DO YOU RECOMMEND FOR TRAVELERS WITH KIDS?
The Fair Wind (p38) snorkel cruise to Kealakekua Bay is great. The crew is fun and kids love jumping off the upper deck or riding the waterslide into the bay. They always have fun sea toys that make you feel safe while snorkeling.

3 LET'S TALK FISH. TELL US SOMETHING WE DON'T KNOW.
The Big Island has amazing fishing grounds right off the coast – it's the best of all the Hawaiian Islands for fresh fish. The KTA Super Store (p47) on Palani Rd has the best fish counter. Top quality, nothing is ever frozen – this is the real deal. Try the *poke* (cubed raw fish mixed with soy sauce, sesame oil, salt, chili pepper or other condiments). For sushi, I like Sushi Shiono (p48), owned by a Japanese businessman who wants guaranteed good sushi when he's on the island.

4 YOUR RESTAURANT IS ON THE OFFICIAL IRONMAN ROUTE. WHAT TIPS DO YOU HAVE FOR FANS?
Watch the swim portion from Kailua Pier. The finish line is also a blast. Cyclists can feel like an Ironman for a day by renting a top-end road bike and pedalling the official Kailua-Kona-to-Hawi route.

sedative juice of the *'awa* plant) or organic *noni* (Indian mulberry) juice, another herbal elixir. *Pupu* like squid luau and ahi *poke* are just an after-thought. Cash only.

Don's Mai Tai Bar
Bar

(☎808-930-3286; www.royalkona.com; 75-5852 Ali'i Dr, Royal Kona Resort; ⏰10am-10pm) For pure kitsch, nothing beats the lounge-lizard fantasy of Don's inside the Royal Kona Resort. Soak up the killer ocean views of the crashing surf – then lament the fact that the 10 different varieties of mai tai are all pretty lackluster (at least the little blue plastic monkey is yours to keep).

Real tiki fans roll in for **Don's Mai Tai Festival** (www.donsmaitaifest.com) in mid-August.

Sam's Hideaway
Bar

(75-5725 Ali'i Dr; ⏰9am-2am) Sam's is a dark, cozy (OK, some might say 'dank') nook of a dive bar. You'll rarely find tourists here, but there are always locals. On karaoke nights, don't act shocked when a 7ft Samoan guy tears up as he belts out 'The Snows of Mauna Kea.' The bar is hidden behind the shops fronting Ali'i Dr.

⭐ Entertainment

Kailua-Kona's two hokey, cruise-ship-friendly luau include a ceremony, a buffet dinner with Hawaiian specialties, an open bar and a Polynesian dinner show featuring a cast of flamboyant dancers and fire twirlers. Forego if any rain is forecast – an indoor luau ain't worth it.

KBXtreme
Bowling, Karaoke

(☎808-326-2695; www.kbxtreme.com; 75-5591 Palani Rd; ⏰9am-1am Sun-Thu, to 2am Fri & Sat; 👪) Make a rainy day or dull night fun for families with a bowling alley, arcade games, a sports bar and a karaoke lounge. 'Xtreme' blacklight bowling parties take over Friday and Saturday nights; weekday afternoon bowling is discounted.

Regal Makalapua Stadium 10
Cinema

(☎808-327-0444; 74-5469 Kamaka'eha Ave, Makalapua Shopping Center; adult/child $10.50/7) Catch first-run Hollywood movies on 10 screens. Matinee showings before 6pm are discounted.

Island Breeze Lu'au
Luau

(☎808-329-4969; www.islandbreezeluau.com; 75-5660 Palani Rd, Courtyard Marriott King Kamehameha's Kona Beach Hotel; adult/5-12yr $82/41; ⏰5pm Tue, Thu & Sun; 👪) Family-friendly luau benefits from a scenic oceanfront setting but crowds can reach up to 400.

Lava Legends & Legacies – Journeys of the South Pacific
Luau

(☎808-329-3111; www.royalkona.com; 75-5852 Ali'i Dr, Royal Kona Resort; adult/child 6-11yr $67/33; ⏰6pm Mon, Tue, Wed & Fri; 👪) Assuage your disappointment in the buffet by taking a photo with the lithesome dancers.

🔒 Shopping

Ali'i Dr is swamped with run-of-the-mill, dubious-quality Hawaiiana and souvenir shops. Beware of 'Made in China' fakes.

J Lambus Photography
Arts & Crafts

(☎808-989-9560; www.jlambus.com; 75-5744 Ali'i Dr, Kona Inn Shopping village; ⏰11am-8pm Tue-Sat, to 4pm Mon) Josh Lambus's celebrated underwater photography has been exhibited by the Smithsonian, and he has taken some of the first recorded snaps of several deep-sea species. Pop into his gallery, then check his blog for Big Island adventure stories.

Big Island Jewelers
Jewelry

(☎888-477-8571, 808-329-8571; http://bigislandjewelers.com; 75-5695A Ali'i Dr; ⏰9am-5:30pm Mon-Sat) Family owned for nearly four decades, with master jeweler Flint Carpenter at the helm, this storefront sells high-quality Hawaiiana bracelets, pendants, earrings and rings, including pieces made with Tahitian pearls. Custom orders welcome.

Honolua Surf Co
Clothing

(☎808-329-1001; www.honoluasurf.com; 75-5744 Ali'i Dr, Kona Inn Shopping Village; ⏰9am-9pm) This island-grown surfwear shop is split right down the middle between styles for *kane* (men) and *wahine* (women). Board shorts, bikinis, hoodies, T-shirts and beach cover-ups will last you as long as an endless summer.

Hula dance performance, King Kamehameha's Kona Beach Hotel (p46)

LONELY PLANET/GETTY IMAGES ©

Na Makana
Souvenirs

(☏808-938-8577; 75-5722 Likana Ln; ⊗9am-5pm) Poke around this hole-in-the-wall shop for authentic made-in-Hawaii gifts, souvenirs and collectibles, with such unusual finds as Japanese glass fishing floats. Variable opening hours epitomize 'Hawaiian time.'

Crazy Shirts
Clothing

(☏808-329-2176; www.crazyshirts.com; 75-5719 Ali'i Dr, Kona Marketplace; ⊗9am-9pm) Once maverick, now mainstream, Crazy Shirts are worn mainly by tourists these days. The best designs feature natural dyes like Kona coffee, hibiscus, *ti* (a native plant) leaves and volcanic ash.

Kona Bay Books
Books, Music

(☏808-326-7790; http://konabaybooks.com; 74-5487 Kaiwi St; ⊗10am-6pm) Hawai'i's biggest selection of used books, CDs and DVDs, including Hawaiiana titles.

Conscious Riddims Records
Music

(☏808-326-7685; www.consciousriddims.org; 75-5719 Ali'i Dr, Kona Marketplace; ⊗10am-7pm Mon-Fri, to 5pm Sun) Drop by for reggae and Jawaiian (Hawaii-style reggae) music and dope clothing.

Village Farmers Market
Souvenirs

(cnr Ali'i Dr & Hualalai Rd; ⊗8am-5pm Thu-Sun) Sells a lotta phony shell jewelry and pseudo-Hawaiian knickknacks, but also fresh produce and flower lei.

ⓘ Information

Media

Hawaii Tribune-Herald (www.hawaiitribune-herald.com) The Big Island's main daily newspaper.

West Hawaii Today (www.westhawaiitoday.com) Kona Coast's daily newspaper covers Kohala to Ka'u.

KAGB 99.1 FM (www.kaparadio.com) West Hawai'i home of Hawaiian and island music.

KKUA 90.7 FM (www.hawaiipublicradio.org) Hawaii Public Radio; classical music, talk and news.

KLUA 93.9 FM Native FM plays island tunes and reggae beats.

Medical Services

Kona Community Hospital (☏808-322-9311; www.kch.hhsc.org; 79-1019 Haukapila St; ⊗24hr)

51

West Hawai'i's most advanced (level-III) trauma center, about 10 miles south of Kailua-Kona.

Longs Drugs (📞808-329-1632; www.cvs.com; 75-5595 Palani Rd; ⏰store 7am-10pm daily, pharmacy 7am-8pm Mon-Fri, 8am-7pm Sat & 8am-6pm Sun) Centrally located drugstore and pharmacy.

Money

The following banks have 24-hour ATMs and islandwide branches:

Bank of Hawaii (📞808-326-3900; www.boh. com; 74-5457 Makala Blvd; ⏰8:30am-4pm Mon-Thu, to 6pm Fri, 9am-1pm Sat)

First Hawaiian Bank (📞808-329-2461; www. fhb.com; 74-5593 Palani Rd, Lanihau Center; ⏰8:30am-4pm Mon-Thu, to 6pm Fri, 9am-1pm Sat)

Websites

Big Island Visitors Bureau (www.gohawaii.com/big-island) Travel planning info and comprehensive listings for festivals and special events.

KonaWeb (www.konaweb.com) Homegrown website for locals and visitors, with an islandwide calendar of events.

ⓘ Getting There & Away

Air

Kona International Airport at Keahole (KOA; 📞808-327-9520; http://hawaii.gov/koa; 73-7200 Kupipi St) Mostly interisland and some US mainland and Canada flights arrive at Hawai'i's main airport, 7 miles northwest of Kailua-Kona.

Bus

Hele-On Bus (📞808-961-8744; www.heleonbus. org; 1-way fare $2, 10-ride ticket $15, monthly pass $60) Public buses run between Kailua-Kona and Captain Cook in South Kona (one to 1¾ hours) up to 10 times daily except Sunday; one or two also stop at the airport. Buses connect Kailua-Kona with Hilo (three hours) via Waimea (1¼ to 1¾ hours) three times daily except Sunday; one goes via South Kohala's resorts. Buses on the long-distance Pahala–South Kohala route (four hours) makes stops in Kailua-Kona, South Kona, Ka'u and sometimes at Kona's airport and in Keauhou; service is three times daily Monday through Saturday, once on Sunday.

All schedules and fares are subject to change; check the website. A $1 surcharge applies for luggage, backpacks or bicycles; no surfboards or bodyboards allowed on board. Children under 6 years old ride free.

Keauhou Trolley (📞808-329-1688; www. keauhouresort.com; 1 way $2; ⏰9am-9pm) Also called the 'Honu Express,' this tourist trolley makes five daily round-trips between Keauhou and Kailua-Kona. Stops include White (Magic) Sands Beach, Kona Brewing Company, Kailua Pier and various shopping centers and resort hotels. Check current schedules and fares online.

Car

The drive from Kailua-Kona to Hilo is 75 miles and takes at least 1¾ hours via Saddle Rd, 95 miles (two hours) via Waimea and 125 miles (three hours) via Ka'u and Volcano.

To avoid snarly commuter traffic on Hwy 11 leading into and away from Kailua-Kona, try the Mamalahoa Hwy Bypass Rd. It connects Ali'i Dr in Keauhou with Haleki'i St in Kealakekua, between the Mile 111 and the Mile 112 markers on Hwy 11.

ⓘ Getting Around

To/From the Airport

A car is almost necessary on Hawai'i, but if you're not renting one upon arrival at the airport, taxis are available curbside (book late-night pickups in advance). Taxi fares average $25 to Kailua-Kona or $35 to Keauhou, plus tip.

Speedi Shuttle (📞877-242-5777, 808-329-5433; www.speedishuttle.com; ⏰9am-last flight) Charges about the same as airport taxis, but may be economical for large groups. Book in advance.

Bicycle

Home of the Ironman Triathlon World Championship (p43), Kailua-Kona is a bike-friendly town.

Bike Works (📞808-326-2453; www.bikeworks kona.com; 74-5583 Luhia St, Hale Hana Center; bicycle rental per day $40-80; ⏰9am-6pm Mon-Sat, 10am-4pm Sun) Full-service bike shop rents high-quality mountain and road-touring bikes; rates include helmet, lock, pump and patch kit. Multiday and weekly discounts available. Second location in Waikoloa.

Hawaiian Pedals (📞808-329-2294; www. hawaiianpedals.com; 75-5744 Ali'i Dr, Kona Inn Shopping Village; bicycle rental per day $25-30;

9:30am-8pm) Rents well-used hybrid bikes for cruising around town; multiday and weekly discounts apply.

Bus

Both the public Hele-On Bus and privately operated Keauhou Trolley make stops within Kailua-Kona.

Car

Ali'i Dr in downtown Kailua-Kona is almost always congested. Free public parking is available in a lot between Likana Ln and Kuakini Hwy. Many shopping centers along Ali'i Dr have free parking lots for customers.

Moped & Motorcycle

Doesn't it look fun zipping down Ali'i Dr on a moped? And what a breeze to park!

Big Island Harley Davidson (☏888-904-3155, 808-217-8560; www.bigislandharley.com; 75-5633 Palani Rd; motorcycle rental per day/week $179/763; ⏱8:30am-6pm Mon-Fri, to 5pm Sat, 10am-4pm Sun) Well-maintained Harley motorcycles come with helmets and rain gear to borrow. Book ahead online.

Scooter Brothers (☏808-327-1080; www.scooterbrothers.com; 75-5829 Kahakai Rd; rental per 4hr/8hr/day moped $40/50/60, electric scooter $21/42/52; ⏱10am-6pm Mon-Sat, from 9am Wed, by reservation Sun) Get around town like a local, on a moped or electric scooter. The official riding area is from Hapuna Beach up north to Honaunau down south. Honda motorcycle rentals cost from $95 per 24 hours.

Taxi

Call ahead for pickups from the following taxi companies:

Aloha Taxi (☏808-329-7779; www.alohataxihi.com)

D&E Taxi (☏808-329-4279)

Laura's Taxi (☏808-326-5466; www.luanalimo.com)

AROUND KAILUA-KONA

Keauhou Resort Area

With its wide streets and manicured landscaping, Keauhou feels like a US mainland suburb: easy, pleasant and bland. Like most suburbs, there's no town center (unless you count the shopping mall).

View of Moku'aikaua Church and Hulihe'e Palace (p35), Kailua-Kona

PETER FRENCH/GETTY IMAGES ©

Rather, it's a collection of destinations: Keauhou Harbor for boat trips, beaches for snorkeling and surfing, condos and resort hotels for sleeping, and farmers markets for local flavor.

🏔 Beaches

Kahalu'u Beach Park   Beach

(🏖) Whether young or old, triathlete or couch potato, everyone appreciates the island's most thrilling, easy-to-access (and admittedly busy) snorkeling spot. Protected by an ancient breakwater (which, according to legend, was built by the *menehune*, or 'little people'), the bay is pleasantly calm and shallow. You'll spot tropical fish and *honu* (green sea turtles) without even trying. The lifeguard-staffed park has outdoor showers, restrooms, drinking water, snorkel and locker rentals and picnic tables.

Kahalu'u can be too popular for its own good, with snorkelers literally bumping into one another. The salt-and-pepper beach (composed of lava and coral sand) is often a mass of humanity, which you may find sociable or nauseating, depending. Come early; the parking lot may fill by 10am. Treading lightly is also important: follow coral-reef etiquette and stay back at least 50yd in the water (20ft on land) from all sea turtles.

When the surf's up (and it can rage here), expert surfers challenge the offshore waves and avoid strong rip currents on the bay's north side near the church. When conditions are mellow, beginners can learn to surf or stand up paddle here.

◎ Sights

Kahalu'u
Manowai   Archaeological Site

(www.keauhouresort.com/learn.html; 78-6740 Ali'i Dr) 🅿 FREE On the former grounds of the Outrigger Keauhou Beach Resort, just south of Kahalu'u Beach Park, three restored heiau (temples) and ancient Hawaiian petroglyphs are the centerpiece of a planned outdoor education and Hawaiian cultural center, sponsored by Kamehameha Schools and still under development in talks with the local community. For now, respectful visitors can explore the archaelogical sites during daylight hours. Check in at the security guardhouse and ask for a map.

At the north end of the complex is **Kapuanoni Heiau**, a restored fishing temple. Just south, **Hapaiali'i Heiau** was built 600 years ago and its construction aligns the temple with seasonal equinoxes and solstices. Both of these temples were painstakingly restored by Hawaiian cultural practioners, archaeologists and students in 2007. Furthest south is **Ke'eku Heiau**, also recently restored. Legends say that Ke'eku was a *luakini* (temple of

Green sea turtle, Kahalu'u Beach Park
DR PETER M FORSTER/GETTY IMAGES ©

human sacrifice). Most famously, a Maui chief who tried to invade the Big Island was sacrificed here, and the spirits of his grieving dogs are said to still guard the site. Along the shoreline look for teeming tide pools and *ki'i pohaku* (petroglyphs) visible among the rocks at low tide.

Keauhou Kahalu'u Heritage Center
Gallery

(www.keauhouresort.com; 78-6831 Ali'i Dr, Keauhou Shopping Center; ⊙10am-5pm) 🗗 FREE To learn about the restoration of Keauhou's *heiau* (temples), visit this unstaffed cultural center, where small exhibits and videos also describe *holua,* the ancient Hawaiian sport of lava-rock sledding, at nearby He'eia Bay. The center is on the KTA Super Store side of the mall, hidden behind the post office near the public restrooms.

Keauhou Bay
Harbor

Many tour cruises launch from the small pier at this protected bay. While not worth going very far out of your way for, the small beach, picnic tables and sand volleyball courts bring out locals. Facilities include restrooms and outdoor showers.

Against the hillside, a **plaque** marks the site where Kamehameha III was born in 1814. The prince is said to have been stillborn and brought back to life by a visiting kahuna (healer) who dunked him in a healing freshwater spring here.

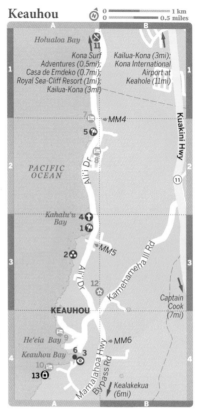

Keauhou

KAILUA-KONA & THE KONA COAST KEAUHOU RESORT AREA

Keauhou

Right: Sunset over Kahalu'u Bay **Below:** St Peter's Church

(RIGHT) ALVIS UPITIS/GETTY IMAGES ©; (BELOW) BOB POOL/GETTY IMAGES ©

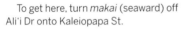

To get here, turn *makai* (seaward) off Ali'i Dr onto Kaleiopapa St.

St Peter's Church   Church

The much-photographed 'Little Blue Church' practically sits in Kahalu'u Bay. Made of clapboard and a corrugated-tin roof in the 1880s, it was moved here from White (Magic) Sands Beach in 1912. The church is on the *makai* side of Ali'i Dr, north of the Mile 5 marker.

Incidetally, an ancient Hawaiian temple, Ku'emanu Heiau, once stood here. Hawaiian *ali'i* (royalty), who surfed at the northern end of Kahalu'u Bay, prayed at the temple before hitting the waves.

Original Hawaiian Chocolate Factory   Farm

(☏ 888-447-2626, 808-322-2626; www.ohcf.us; 78-6772 Makenawai St; tour adult/child under 12yr $15/free; ⏰ usually 9am Wed & Fri, by reservation only; 👪) A must for chocolate fans, these one-hour farm tours detail how the *only* Hawaiian chocolate is grown, harvested, processed and packaged, followed by chocolate sampling and sales. Book tours by phone or email at least a week ahead. The factory is inland from Hwy 11 and King Kamehameha III Rd.

🏃 Activities

Some snorkel cruises and fishing trips booked out of Kailua-Kona depart from Keauhou Pier.

Kona Eco Adventures   Ziplining

(☏ 808-324-4111; www.konazip.com; 78-8631 Ali'i Dr, Keahou Shopping Center, Suite 148; 3hr tour per person $149; ⏰ hourly departures 8am-3pm, by reservation only) Hop aboard a shuttle to the upland slopes of Mt Hualalai, where two suspension bridges add to the thrill of eight short ziplines through ohia forest. Tours include snacks and drinks; participants must wear closed-toed shoes and weigh between 80lb and 250lb. The outfitter's storefront is not far from KTA Super Store.

🛏 Sleeping

Cheaper rates may be available by booking ahead online.

Outrigger Kanaloa at Kona
Condo $$$

(☎800-688-7444, 808-322-9625; www.outriggerkanaloaatkonacondo.com; 78-261 Manukai St; 1br/2br apt from $229/275; P✳@🛰🏊) Tropical townhouse-style condos feel exclusive, sitting behind a private gate on an oceanfront lava ledge. Incredibly spacious, immaculate and fully equipped units gather in small clusters. One-bedroom condos easily fit a family of four. With three pools, night-lit tennis courts and an adjacent golf course, you can practically stay put. Multiple-night minimum stay (cleaning fee from $50).

Sheraton Kona Resort & Spa at Keauhou Bay
Resort $$$

(☎866-716-8109, 808-930-4900; www.sheratonkona.com; 78-128 'Ehukai St; r/ste from $215/379; P✳@🛰🏊) Keauhou's only bona fide resort, the family-friendly Sheraton has a sleek modern design with hip boutique-hotel appeal. Despite having over 500 rooms, an oceanfront bar and restaurant with fire pits and live music (usually 6pm to 9pm nightly), and a massive pool with a spiral waterslide, unfortunately there's no beach. Manta rays gather off the rocky shoreline at night.

A mandatory resort fee (over $30 per night) covers self-parking, wi-fi, unlimited Keauhou Trolley rides, a morning yoga class and Hawaiian cultural activities.

🍴 Eating

Drop by Keahou's twice-weekly farmers markets for tasty, cheap *grinds*.

KTA Super Store
Supermarket $

(78-6831 Ali'i Dr, Keauhou Shopping Center; ⏱7am-10pm) Locally owned supermarket chain stocks groceries, beach snacks and drinks, with a full-service deli and bakery.

57

Peaberry & Galette
Cafe $$

(📞808-322-6020; www.peaberryandgalette.com; 78-6831 Ali'i Dr, Keauhou Shopping Center; mains $7-14; ⏱7am-7pm Mon-Thu, to 8pm Fri & Sat, 8am-6pm Sun) With 100% Kona estate-grown coffee, Illy espresso and Euro-bistro style, this cafe dishes up sweet and savory French crepes, plus satisfying salads, sandwiches, quiches and *liliko'i* (passion fruit)-lemon bars for dessert.

Kenichi Pacific
Japanese, Fusion $$$

(📞808-322-6400; www.kenichihawaii.com; 78-6831 Ali'i Dr, Keauhou Shopping Center; a la carte dishes $3-18, mains $23-38; ⏱5-9pm Sun-Thu, to 9:30pm Fri & Sat) Ignore the mall setting. Just savor the beautifully presented Pacific Rim fusion cuisine including tender miso black cod, Hawaiian *ono* (white-fleshed wahoo) topped with a cloud of *ponzu* (Japanese citrus sauce) and macadamia-nut-encrusted lamb. Sushi and sashimi cuts are fresh and generous. Happy hour (4:30pm to 6:30pm daily) brings half-price sushi rolls and drinks to the bar.

Sam Choy's Kai Lanai
Hawaii Regional Cuisine $$$

(📞808-333-3434; www.samchoy.com; 78-6831 Ali'i Dr, Keauhou Shopping Center; mains lunch $10-14, dinner $17-36; ⏱11am-9pm Mon-Thu, to 9:30pm Fri, 7am-9:30pm Sat, 7am-9pm Sun; 🅿🚸) Sam Choy is one of the pioneers of Hawaii Regional Cuisine, an island-grown version of Pacific Rim fusion. At this casual eatery with dynamite sunset panoramas, the dinner menu is stuffed with haute fusion gastronomy like lamb chops broiled with soy, ginger and local bird-peppers, although execution falls short of the chef's sterling reputation. During happy hour (3pm to 5pm daily), nosh on *pupu* on the breezy ocean-view lanai.

⭐ Entertainment

Haleo Luau
Luau

(📞866-482-9775; www.haleoluau.com; 78-128 'Ehukai St, Sheraton Keauhou Bay Resort; adult/child 6-12yr $82/52; ⏱usually 4:30pm Mon, also 4:30pm Fri late May-early Aug) The Sheraton's touristy luau weaves together Hawaiian themes and tales of ancient kings and battles, along with fiery dances from across Polynesia. The buffet is about as generic as you'd expect, but there's an open bar.

Regal Keauhou Stadium 7
Cinema

(📞808-324-0172; 78-6831 Ali'i Dr, Keauhou Shopping Center) Hollywood flicks fill seven screens. Matinee showings before 6pm are discounted.

Keauhou Shopping Center
Music, Dance

(www.keauhouvillageshops.com; 78-6831 Ali'i Dr) **FREE** This shopping mall has hula shows from 6pm to 7pm most Friday nights. It also usually runs free Hawaiian craft workshops from 10am to noon every Thursday. Check the website for more cultural activities and special events.

🔒 Shopping

Ho'oulu Community Farmers Market
Market

(www.hooulufarmersmkt.com; 78-128 Ehukai St, Sheraton Keauhou Bay Resort; ⏱usually 9am-2pm Wed & Sat) Unlike the touristy Kailua-Kona farmers market selling knickknacks from who-knows-where, this twice-weekly event focuses on small-scale farm and fishing bounty, including genuine Kona coffee and flower lei. Live music, island artists and takeout food vendors make this a must-do lunchtime stop.

Keauhou Farmers Market
Market

(www.keauhoufarmersmarket.com; 78-6831 Ali'i Dr, Keauhou Shopping Center; ⏱8am-noon Sat; 🚸) 🍃 At this parking-lot farmers market with live Hawaiian music and a neighborly spirit, everything is Big Island–grown including seasonal fruits and veggies, organic coffee, homemade preserves and fresh flowers.

Kona Stories
Books

(📞808-324-0350; www.konastories.com; 78-6831 Ali'i Dr, Keauhou Shopping Center; ⏱10am-6pm Mon-Fri, to 5pm Sat, 11am-5pm Sun) Independent bookstore with a strong Hawaiiana section hosts community events for kids and adults. It's near KTA Super Store.

ℹ️ Information

Bank of Hawaii (www.boh.com; 78-6831 Ali'i Dr, Keauhou Shopping Center, Suite 131; ⏰9am-6pm Mon-Fri, to 2pm Sat & Sun) ATM available inside KTA Super Store.

Keauhou Urgent Care Center (📞808-322-2544; www.konaurgentcare.com; 78-6831 Ali'i Dr, Suite 418, Keauhou Shopping Center; ⏰9am-7pm) Walk-in clinic for nonemergency medical matters.

Longs Drugs (www.cvs.com; 78-6831 Ali'i Dr, Keauhou Shopping Center; ⏰store 7am-10pm, pharmacy 8am-8pm Mon-Fri, 9am-7pm Sat, to 6pm Sun) Convenient drugstore and pharmacy.

ℹ️ Getting There & Around

Nicknamed the 'Honu Express,' Keauhou Trolley (p52) makes five daily round trips between Keauhou and Kailua-Kona, stopping at White (Magic) Sands Beach, Kailua Pier, various shopping centers, resort hotels and elsewhere. Check current schedules and fares online.

Holualoa

POP 8540

It's well worth going out of your way to visit Holualoa, a bohemian coffee-farming village perched on the lush slopes of Mt Hualalai. Ramshackle retro buildings, a tight-knit community and a slower pace of life preserve old Hawaii right alongside contemporary art galleries. At 1400ft elevation, the climate is cooler and wetter, and the coastal views are magnificent.

◎ Sights & Activities

Donkey Mill Art Center Arts Center (📞808-322-3362; www.donkeymillartcenter.org; 78-6670 Mamalahoa Hwy; ⏰10am-4pm Tue-Sat Aug-May, 9am-3pm Mon-Fri Jun & Jul; 👫) FREE The Holualoa Foundation for Arts & Culture established this community art center in 2002. There are free exhibits, arts-and-crafts workshops, literary readings, performance art and film nights. If you're wondering about the name, the building was once a coffee mill with a donkey painted on its roof. It's 3 miles south of the village center.

Malama I'ka Ola Holistic Health Center Health & Fitness
(📞808-324-6644; www.malamatherapy.com; 76-5914 Mamalahoa Hwy) Inside a 19th-century doctor's office, this alternative-minded oasis offers yoga and Pilates classes, and massage, acupuncture, Chinese herbal medicine and organic skin treatments.

⭐ Festivals & Events

Coffee & Art Stroll Art, Food (www.konacoffeefest.com) During early November's Kona Coffee Cultural Festival (p43), Holualoa hosts an incredibly popular, day-long block party.

Sushi platter, Kenichi Pacific
LONELY PLANET/GETTY IMAGES ©

Music & Light Festival   Art, Music

(www.holualoahawaii.com) A small-town Christmas celebration with live music and a tree-lighting ceremony in mid-December.

🛏 Sleeping

Lilikoi Inn   B&B $$

(📞808-333-5539; www.lilikoiinn.com; 75-5339 Mamalahoa Hwy; r incl breakfast $125-165; 📶) All four rooms have an airy, modern art-gallery-in-the-tropics kind of vibe, blending cool monochromes with tasteful Hawaiiana. Each has a private entrance and access to a hot tub, guest laundry, kitchen and pick-your-own avocado and fruit trees. Enjoy the chef's restaurant-worthy breakfasts on a garden lanai. It's 3 miles north of Holualoa village.

Haleakala B&B   B&B

(📞808-322-6053; www.haleakalabedbreakfast.com; 78-6612a Mamalahoa Hwy; d $130-150; 📶) Setting this breezy, welcoming B&B apart are the breathtaking views – over coffee farms and mac-nut orchards all the way to the startling blue Pacific – from your private lanai or the shared hot tub.

For *ipo* (sweethearts), the Kokua Nest is a private cottage suite with an outdoor garden shower. Rates include a local cafe breakfast voucher.

Holualoa Inn   B&B $$$

(📞800-392-1812, 808-324-1121; www.holualoainn.com; 76-5932 Mamalahoa Hwy; r/ste/cottage incl breakfast from $345/385/550; 📶📷) From gleaming eucalyptus floors to river-rock showers, serene beauty shines in every soul-soothing detail here. Common rooms are graced with Polynesian and Asian art and exquisite carved furniture that segue seamlessly into outdoor gardens and a pool, while the rooftop gazebo surveys the ocean. It's a peaceful, intimate retreat you'll long remember. No TVs, phones or children under 13 years old.

🍴 Eating

Holuakoa Gardens & Café   Local, Organic $$

(📞808-322-2233; www.holuakoacafe.com; 76-5900 Mamalahoa Hwy; mains brunch $12-20, dinner $17-32; ⏰cafe 6:30am-3pm Mon-Fri, from 8am Sat & Sun, restaurant 10am-2:30pm Mon-Fri,

Decorated *ipu* (gourds), Ipu Hale Gallery

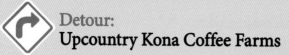

Detour:
Upcountry Kona Coffee Farms

Kona coffee has had gourmet cachet for decades, and today many coffee farms have opened roadside visitor centers and gift shops, where they give free samples and quickie tours. The best time to visit is during the harvest season, running from August through February, when 'Kona snow' (white blossoms) and 'cherries' (mature berry fruit) cluster on the coffee trees.

Mountain Thunder Coffee Plantation (☎ 888-414-5662, 808-325-2136; www.mountainthunder.com; 73-1944 Hao St, Kailua-Kona; 20min tour free, 3hr VIP tour adult/child under 6yr $135/free; ⊙tours hourly 10am-4pm, VIP tours 10am Mon-Fri by reservation only) 🌿 is an award-winning farm lies upland in lush Kaloko Mauka, a 20-minute drive from downtown Kailua-Kona or Holualoa village. VIP tours (call 808-345-6600 at least one day in advance) give you a more in-depth look at Kona coffee, and let you roast a half-pound of beans to take home.

With jaw-dropping ocean views on a breezy lanai, an epicurean tasting room and eco-conscious farm, **Hula Daddy Kona Coffee** (☎ 808-327-9744; www.huladaddy.com; 74-4944 Mamalahoa Hwy, Holualoa; ⊙10am-4pm Mon–Sat) 🌿 is the place to learn about cupping. Ask about unusual coffee-production techniques used to create its signature Kona Oli and Kona Sweet beans. It's less than 5 miles north of Holualoa.

Holualoa Kona Coffee Company (☎ 800-334-0348, 808-322-9937; www.konalea.com; 77-6261 Mamalahoa Hwy, Holualoa; ⊙8am-4pm Mon-Fri) at Kona Le'a Plantation does not use pesticides or herbicides on its small organic-certified farm, less than 2 miles south of Holualoa. As you drive up, watch for the free-ranging geese who do double duty as lawn mowers and fertilizers!

Kona Blue Sky Coffee (☎ 877-322-1700; www.konablueskycoffee.com; 76-973 Hualalai Rd, Kailua-Kona; ⊙visitor center & gift shop 8:30am-4pm Mon-Sat, tours 9am-3:30pm Mon-Sat) 🌿 is a convenient choice if your time is limited. This tiny coffee estate in Holualoa village offers a free walking tour that passes traditional open-air drying racks and includes an educational video.

from 9am Sat & Sun, also 5:30-8:30pm Mon-Sat; 🖥) 🌿 The storefront cafe serves 100% Kona coffee, baked goods and sandwiches. Out back an organic, slow-food restaurant serves a sophisticated yet casual bistro-style menu that make the most of fresh, Big Island grown produce. Book ahead for dinner.

As one of Hawai'i's most dedicated establishments to supporting local farmers, it's no surprise there's a seasonal **Saturday farmers market** (⊙9am-noon Sat Apr-Oct) here.

🔒 Shopping

Holualoa is a tiny village but don't underestimate the quality of its artists.

Along the Mamalahoa Hwy (Hwy 180) you'll find internationally known, highly commissioned artists creating art beyond the stereotypical tropical motifs. Most galleries and shops are closed on Sunday and Monday.

Ipu Hale Gallery   Arts & Crafts
(☎ 808-322-9069; www.holualoahawaii.com/member_sites/ipu_hale.html; 76-5893 Mamalahoa Hwy; ⊙10am-4pm Tue-Sat) 🌿 Magnificent *ipu* (gourds) are decoratively carved with Hawaiian imagery and dyed using an ancient method unique to Ni'ihau island, knowledge of which had been lost for over a century until a scholar rediscovered it in 1980.

Island Insights

Hawaiians wove the dried *lau* (leaves) of the hala (pandanus) tree into floor mats, hats, baskets, fans and other household items. Strong and flexible, *lauhala* is surprisingly hardy and long-lasting. Today, most *lauhala* is actually mass-produced in the Philippines and sold cheaply to unwitting tourists. But Holualoa's **Kimura Lauhala Shop** (808-324-0053; www.holualoahawaii.com/member_sites/kimura.html; cnr Hualalai Rd & Hwy 180; 9am-5pm Mon-Fri, to 4pm Sat) , run by the Kimura family's fourth generation, sells high-quality, genuine Hawaiian *lauhala* handmade by local weavers, from traditional hats to signature lined tote bags.

Holualoa Ukulele Gallery   Music
(808-324-4100; www.konaweb.com/uke gallery/index.html; 76-5942 Mamalahoa Hwy; 11am-4:30pm Tue-Sat, other times by appt) Inside a historic post office, owner Sam Rosen displays beautifully handcrafted ukulele made by himself and other island luthiers. He's happy to talk and show you his workshop. If you've got 10 days, he'll even teach you how to build your own uke.

Studio 7 Fine Arts   Arts & Crafts
(808-324-1335; http://studio7hawaii.com; 76-5920 Mamalahoa Hwy; 11am-5pm Tue-Sat) A serene, museum-like gallery featuring prominent artist-owner Hiroki Morinoue's watercolor, oil, woodblock and sculpture pieces, and his accomplished wife Setsuko's pottery.

Dovetail Gallery & Design   Arts & Crafts
(808-322-4046; www.dovetailgallery.net; 76-5942 Mamalahoa Hwy; 10am-4pm Tue-Sat) Showcases elegant contemporary work by Big Island sculptors, painters, photographers and furniture designers.

ℹ Getting There & Away

Holualoa village straggles along Hwy 180 (Mamalahoa Hwy), north of the Hualalai Rd intersection. Parking in the free village lot or along the highway's shoulder is easy most of the time, except during special events.

SOUTH KONA COAST

The dozen or so miles heading south from Kailua-Kona to Kealakekua Bay are among Hawai'i's most action-packed, historically speaking. It's here that ancient Hawaiian *ali'i* (royalty) secretly buried the bones of their ancestors, kapu (taboo) breakers braved shark-infested waters to reach the *pu'uhonua* (place of refuge), and British explorer Captain Cook and his rabble-rousing crew fatally first stepped ashore in Hawaii.

But you'd never know all that today, simply judging by the sleepy, small, yesteryear towns lined up along the Mamalahoa Hwy (Hwy 11). Upcountry lies Kona's coffee belt, where the slow pace of agricultural life continues on family-owned coffee farms and mac-nut plantations. Hidden down below, the coast may be short on sandy beaches, but it's long on snorkeling, diving and kayaking spots.

Most people drive to and around South Kona, but the public Hele-On Bus (p52) runs between Kailua-Kona and Captain Cook and buses on the long-distance Pahala–South Kohala route also make stops in Kailua-Kona and South Kona.

Honalo

At a bend in the road where Hwys 11 and 180 intersect, little time-warped Honalo is your first sign that more than miles separate you from touristy Kailua-Kona.

◎ Sights & Activities

Daifukuji Soto Mission   Temple
(808-322-3524; www.daifukuji.org; 79-7241 Mamalahoa Hwy; usually 8am-4pm Mon-Sat) On the *mauka* (inland) side of Mamalahoa Hwy, this Buddhist temple founded in

1914 inhabits a quirky red-and-white Hawaiian farmhouse. Inside are two altars, large drums and spiritual sculptures. Anyone is welcome to join the Zen meditation and tai chi sessions, Buddhist services and festival days.

Aloha Kayak Co Kayaking, SUP
(☎877-322-1444, 808-322-2868; www.alohakayak.com; 79-7248 Mamalahoa Hwy; 24hr kayak rental s/d/tr $35/60/85, tours $75-99; ☺usually 7:30am-5pm) This Hawaiian-owned outfit knows local waters, offers half-day (noon to 5pm) kayak rentals and stand up paddling (SUP) gear rental. Kayak-snorkel tours go to Kealakekua Bay and other spots along the coast, seeking out sea caves and manta rays at night.

 Eating

Teshima's Restaurant Japanese, Local $$
(☎808-322-9140; www.teshimarestaurant.com; 79-7251 Mamalahoa Hwy; dinner mains $13-23; ☺6:30am-1:45pm & 5-9pm; ♦) For a real window into local life, grab a table at this family-run restaurant, which has been dishing up Japanese comfort food since the 1950s. It's more about the vintage atmosphere than the country-style cooking, which has as many misses as hits. That said, the sashimi is always superfresh and the tempura lightly crisp and golden.

Kainaliu

Packed with antiques shops, art galleries and eclectic boutiques, Kainaliu is a lunch-and-linger town – handy if you get caught in the infamous 'Kainaliu crawl' traffic jam along the two-lane Mamalahoa Hwy.

 Eating

Rebel Kitchen Sandwiches $$
(☎808-322-0616; http://rebelkitchen.com; 79-7399 Mamalahoa Hwy; mains $9-16; ☺11am-5:30pm Mon-Fri; ♪) Expect playful anarchy here, from the young counter staff to punk and reggae sounds streaming out

of the kitchen. You know what else comes out of the kitchen? Amazing sandwiches. We'll fight you for the blackened *ono* with spicy Cajun mayo or Southern-style BBQ pulled pork.

Annie's Island Fresh Burgers Burgers $$
(www.anniesislandfreshburgers; 79-7460 Mamalahoa Hwy, Mango Court; burgers $9-14; ☺11am-8pm; ♪♦) ✐ Annie's is where grass-fed Big Island beef and *panko* (Japanese-style breadcrumbs)–crusted fish with locally grown veggie sides (try

Kona Coast

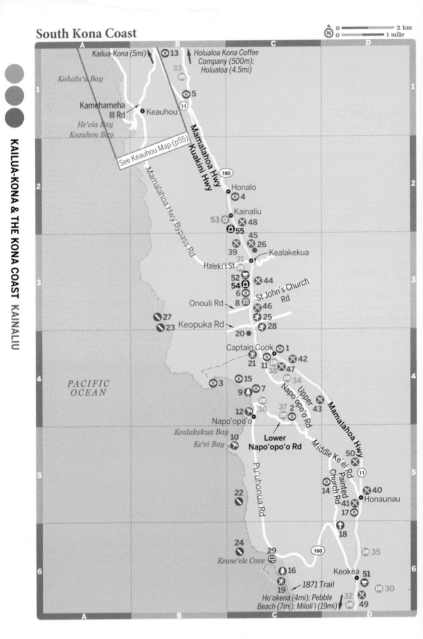

South Kona Coast

0 ──── 2 km
0 ──── 1 mile

Kailua-Kona (5mi)

Holualoa Kona Coffee Company (500m); Holualoa (4.5mi)

Kahalu'u Bay

Kamehameha III Rd

Keauhou

He'eia Bay
Keauhou Bay

See Keauhou Map (p55)

Mamalahoa Hwy
Kuakini Hwy

Mamalahoa Hwy Bypass Rd

Honalo

Kainaliu

Kealakekua

Haleki'i St

St John's Church Rd

Onouli Rd

Keopuka Rd

Captain Cook

PACIFIC OCEAN

Napo'opo'o

Kealakekua Bay
Ke'ei Bay

Lower Napo'opo'o Rd

Upper Napo'opo'o Rd

Middle Ke'ei Rd
Painted Church Rd

Mamalahoa Hwy

Honaunau

Pu'uhonua Rd

Keone'ele Cove

1871 Trail

Ho'okena (4mi); Pebble Beach (7mi); Miloli'i (19mi)

Keokea

the purple potato salad) satisfy hungry road-trippers. Vegetarian? No worries – dig into a portobello mushroom 'burger' stuffed with Parmesan cheese and bulgur wheat.

⭐ Entertainment

Aloha Theatre   Theater, Cinema
(☎808-322-9924; www.apachawaii.org; 79-7384 Mamalahoa Hwy; tickets $10-25; ☺box office

South Kona Coast

10am-4pm Mon-Fri) Repertory plays, indie films and live-music shows are on the program at this historic theater.

🔒 Shopping

Kiernan Music
Music

(☎808-323-4939; www.kiernanmusic.com; 79-7401 Mamalahoa Hwy; ◷10am-6pm Tue-Fri, to 5pm Sat) Friendly owner Brian Kiernan has a talent for restoring vintage ukuleles and guitars, and he's a wonderful resource whether you're a curious beginner or a serious musician looking to buy a custom-made uke or archtop guitar.

Lavender Moon Gallery
Arts & Crafts

(☎808-324-7708; www.lavendermoongallery. com; 79-7404 Mamalahoa Hwy; ◷11am-6pm Tue-Fri, to 5pm Sat) High-quality original paintings, prints, jewelry, pottery and handmade bags by Big Island artists fill the colorful storefront windows.

Kimura Store
Arts & Crafts

(79-7408 Mamalahoa Hwy; ⊙9am-5pm Mon-Sat) Long-standing family shop rolls out yards of colorfully patterned Hawaiian and Japanese fabrics.

Kealakekua

A sacred place whose name means 'pathway of the gods,' Hawaiian heiau (temples) and the secret burial caves of ali'i (chiefs) sat high upon these cliffs centuries ago. Today, this workaday town spread out along the busy Mamalahoa Hwy is South Kona's commercial center.

◉ Sights

HN Greenwell Store Museum
Museum

(☎808-323-3222; www.konahistorical.org; 81-6551 Mamalahoa Hwy; adult/child 5-12yr $7/3; ⊙10am-2pm Mon & Thu) Housed in one of Kona's oldest buildings, this museum is a taste of old Hawai'i. Built in 1875 and meticulously restored, here educational docents in period dress bring Kona's multicultural and agricultural history to life as they wield dry goods and talk story. You'll usually smell sweet bread baking in the traditional Portuguese bread oven outside after 11am on Thursdays.

The museum is between the Mile 111 and the 112 markers on Hwy 11.

Greenwell Farms
Farm

(☎808-323-2295, 888-592-5662; www.greenwellfarms.com; 81-6581 Mamalahoa Hwy; ⊙8am-5pm, tours 8:30am-4:30pm) **FREE** Run by the Greenwell family and their descendants since 1850, this is one of Kona's oldest and best-known coffee plantations, roasting coffee cherries from over 300 local growers. Take a free tour (offered continuously throughout the day) and sample coffee and fruit at a shady picnic table. You can also purchase Kona Red, a juice made from coffee cherries.

The farm is between the Mile 111 and the Mile 112 markers on Hwy 11.

🏃 Activities

Adventures in Paradise
Water Sports

(☎info 808-323-3005, reservations 800-979-3370; www.bigislandkayak.com; 81-6367 Mamalahoa Hwy, Kealakekua; surfboard/SUP rental per day $25/35, kayak-snorkel tour $80; ⊙usually 8am-5pm) At this professional water-sports outfitter, guides look after beginners well and lead kayak-snorkeling trips to Kealakekua Bay. Rental gear includes surfboards, bodyboards, wetsuits, stand up paddling (SUP) sets and prescription snorkel masks.

Kona Boys
Water Sports

(☎808-328-1234; www.konaboys.com; 79-7539 Mamalahoa Hwy; s/d/tr kayak rental per day $47/67/87, tours $99-250; ⊙7am-5pm) This laid-back pro water-sports outfitter is South Kona's largest. Kayaking, snorkeling and outrigger-canoe sailing trips visit Kealakekua Bay, or learn surfing and SUP from these brahs. Snorkel gear, SUP, surfboard and kayak rentals available. Call ahead for tour and gear-rental reservations.

Mamalahoa Hot Tubs & Massage
Spa

(☎808-323-2288; www.mamalahoa-hottubs.com; 81-1016 St John's Church Rd; hot tub per hour for 2 people $40-50; ⊙noon-9pm Wed-Sat, by appointment only) Soak away your blisters or blues in a lush garden mini-oasis. The two teak-wood tubs, sheltered by thatched roofs that allow for stargazing, are open-sided yet private. Many types of massage, from Swedish to traditional Hawaiian lomilomi and hot stone, are available. Reservations required; ask about discount packages.

Kings' Trail Rides
Horseback Riding

(☎808-345-0661, 808-323-2388; www.konacowboy.com; 81-6420 Mamalahoa Hwy; 2hr ride incl lunch $135; ⊙by reservation only) This family-run outfitter leads horseback trips across ranch lands on the slopes of Mauna Loa. Ask if trail rides along the coast near Kealakekua Bay have resumed.

🛏 Sleeping

Areca Palms Estate B&B   B&B $$
(📞808-323-2276; www.konabedandbreakfast.com; 81-1031 Keopuka Mauka Rd; d incl breakfast $120-145; @ 🛜) Country comfort and aloha spirit seamlessly combine in this spotless, wooden home. Airy rooms are meticulously outfitted, with lots of pillows and lush robes, and your hosts share their local knowledge freely. Kick back in the family room or watch a sunset from the hot tub. You'll eat like royalty with fresh breakfasts daily. Guests can borrow beach and snorkel gear.

Banana Patch   Vacation Rental $$
(📞800-988-2246, 808-322-8888; www.bananabanana.com; Mamao St; studio $115, 1br/2br cottage $125/150; @) Let it all hang out in one of these comfortable, clothing-optional cottages secluded amid tropical foliage. Clean and tasteful, these rustic retreats are terrific for DIY naturists, who share the full kitchen and a hot tub.

✕ Eating & Drinking

Dave's Hawaiian Ice Cream   Ice Cream $
(www.daveshawaiianicecream.com; 81-6592 Mamalahoa Hwy; snacks $3-6; 🕐11:30am-9pm) Made on O'ahu, Dave's creamy concoctions are bursting with island flavors: *poha* (cape gooseberry), guava, *liliko'i*, coconut, *ube* (purple yam), chocolate-mac-nut, Kona coffee and more. Get a scoop inside a cup of rainbow shave ice.

Ke'ei Café   Fusion $$$
(📞808-322-9992; www.keeicafe.net; 79-7511 Mamalahoa Hwy; mains $15-29; 🕐5-9pm Tue-Sat; 🚶) At this long-standing outpost of haute island-fusion cooking, cracking peanut-miso papaya salad sets the stage for fresh catch of the day in fiery Thai curry sauce, tamed by sweet *liliko'i* cheesecake or mango cobbler for dessert. Some nights, the staff and kitchen are simply off their game, however. Reservations recommended; request a lanai table. No credit cards.

Kona coffee plant

Mi's Italian Bistro   Italian $$$

(📞808-323-3880; www.misitalianbistro.com; 81-6372 Mamalahoa Hwy; mains $14-35; ⌚4:30-8:30pm; 🚗) This intimate eatery with class run by husband-and-wife team chef Morgan Starr and Ingrid Chan features homemade pasta, cioppino (seafood stew), meaty mains with organic Big Island–grown vegetables and housemade tiramisu soaked in Kona coffee for dessert. Reservations advised.

Orchid Isle Café   Cafe

(www.orchidislecoffee.com; 81-6637 Mamalahoa Hwy; ⌚6:30am-2pm; 📶) Hang out on the ocean-view lanai, surf the internet and refuel with Kona coffee and quiche at this cozy coffeehouse.

🛍 Shopping

Discovery Antiques   Antiques

(81-6593 Mamalahoa Hwy; ⌚10am-5pm Mon-Sat, 11am-4pm Sun) Tin toys and aloha shirts, bric-a-brac and vintage Hawaiiana – who knows what you'll find at this secondhand antiques and curiosities shop. Bonus: it sells scoops of Tropical Dreams ice cream, made in Hilo.

South Kona Green Market   Market

(www.skgm.org; ⌚9am-2pm Sun) Currently setting up at the Amy BH Greenwell Ethnobotanical Garden, this small farmers market with live music vends organic island-grown produce, artisanal foodstuffs and funky crafts.

ℹ Information

First Hawaiian Bank (📞808-322-3484; www.fhb.com; 81-6626 Mamalahoa Hwy; ⌚8:30am-4pm Mon-Thu, to 6pm Fri)

Kona Community Hospital (📞808-322-9311; www.kch.hhsc.org; 79-1019 Haukapila St) Level-III trauma center with a 24-hour emergency room.

ℹ Getting There & Away

The long-awaited Mamalahoa Hwy Bypass Rd between Keauhou and Kealakekua allows drivers to avoid the worst of commuter traffic into and out of Kailua-Kona. The road connects Haleki'i St in Kealakekua (*makai* off Hwy 11 between the Mile 111 and the Mile 112 markers) to Ali'i Dr in Keauhou.

Captain Cook Monument (p72), Kealakekua Bay

Captain Cook

As the Mamalahoa Hwy winds south and the tropical greenery thickens, Captain Cook is a small town boasting big ocean views. Named after the ill-fated circumnavigator who died at Kealakekua Bay below, the town is peppered with B&Bs, roadside coffee-tasting rooms and kayaking outfitters.

◉ Sights

Kona Coffee Living History Farm
Historic Site

(☎808-323-2006; www.konahistorical.org; 82-6199 Mamalahoa Hwy; 1hr tour adult/child 5-12yr $15/5; ⏰10am-2pm Mon-Thu, hourly tours until 1pm) 🌿 Many coffee-farm tours are perfunctory 15-minute affairs. This tour run by the Kona Historical Society, an affiliate of the Smithsonian Institute, is different and deep. More than just an exploration of how coffee is grown and harvested, it's an evocative look at rural Japanese immigrant life in South Kona. Restored to Hawai'i's pre-statehood era, this 5.5-acre working coffee farm once belonged to the Uchida family, who lived here until 1994.

Several of the docents grew up on area coffee farms, so they speak from experience as they show you around the orchards, processing mill, drying roofs and main house. On easy walking tours, you'll learn how to pick coffee cherries and prepare a traditional *bentō* (Japanese boxed lunch).

The farm is between the Mile 110 and the Mile 111 markers on Hwy 11.

Amy BH Greenwell Ethnobotanical Garden
Gardens

(☎808-323-3318; www.bishopmuseum.org/greenwell; 82-6160 Mamalahoa Hwy; adult/child under 12yr $7/free; ⏰9am-4pm Tue-Sun, guided tours 1pm Tue-Sat) 🌿 Without pottery or metals, ancient Hawaiians fashioned most of what they needed from plants. This ethnobotanical garden preserves Hawai'i's endemic species dating from before Western contact and Polynesian-introduced plants in an *ahupua'a* (land division). Walk yourself along landscaped

The Best...
Kona Coast Outdoor Activities

1 Night dive or snorkel with manta rays near Kailua-Kona (p39)

2 Kayaking and snorkeling Kealakekua Bay (p66)

3 Hiking in Kaloko-Honokohau National Historical Park (p83)

4 Snorkeling at Two-Step (p77)

5 Off-roading or hiking to remote beaches in Kekaha Kai (Kona Coast) State Park (p86)

6 Lava-tube swimming at Kiholo State Park Reserve (p90)

paths or take a guided tour to go more in-depth. Bring insect repellent.

The garden is between the Mile 110 and the Mile 111 markers on Hwy 11.

Big Island Bees
Farm

(☎808-328-7318; www.bigislandbees.com; 82-5780 Napo'opo'o Rd; ⏰10am-4pm) At this roadside gift shop and tiny historical museum, genial staff will let you in on all the secrets of beekeeping, then give you a peek inside a living apiary and teach you how their award-winning, single-varietal and certified organic honey gets made. Taste a free sample of ohia lehua blossom honey spiced with cinnamon or the macnut blossom honey, and you'll be hooked.

🛏 Sleeping

Manago Hotel
Hotel $

(☎808-323-2642; www.managohotel.com; 82-6151 Mamalahoa Hwy; s/d $56/59, with shared bath from $33/36; 🖥) This no-frills, historical hotel has been hosting travelers and islanders since 1917. Run by the family's third generation, the Manago has clean, spare, motel-style rooms without air-con; the best have private bathrooms and ocean-view lanai on the 3rd floor. Book far ahead, especially for the Japanese-style tatami room with futons and a *furo* (Japanese bathtub).

A koi pond and garden add to the breezy tropical atmosphere. This local landmark is between the Mile 110 and the Mile 111 markers on Hwy 11.

Pineapple Park
Hostel $

(☎877-800-3800, 808-323-2224; www.pineapple-park.com; 81-6363 Mamalahoa Hwy; dm $30, r shared/private bath $69/85; ⊙office 8am-8pm; @☎) South Kona's only hostel is your basic backpacker crashpad, run by a friendly if iron-willed proprietress. A sociable vibe makes up for cramped dorms (No 10 is best) and more comfortable (but still overpriced) private rooms. Look for colorful kayaks out front, between the Mile 110 and the Mile 111 markers on Hwy 11.

Ka'awaloa Plantation & Guesthouse
B&B $$

(☎808-323-2686; www.kaawaloaplantation.com; 82-5990 Upper Napo'opo'o Rd; r $125-150, cottage $159, ste $199, incl breakfast; @☎) Some places embody Hawaii's beauty effortlessly – like this guesthouse with wrap-around lanai, unparalleled coastal views and gracious hosts who show genuine aloha. Exquisitely decorated rooms (not all have private baths) with fine linens and cottages set amid organic coffee and macadamia-nut orchards are ideal for romance; so is soaking in the outdoor hot tub watching the sunset.

Luana Inn
B&B $$

(☎808-328-2612; www.luanainn.com; 82-5856 Lower Napo'opo'o Rd; d incl breakfast $170-210; ✳@☎✲) Welcome to spotless Luana Inn, where each spacious, uncluttered and tastefully understated room has its own private entrance and kitchenette. Two rooms open right onto the pool and hot tub with jaw-dropping bay views, while two spacious suites share a sunny cottage. Over a lavish breakfast, pick your hosts' brains for Hawai'i travel tips – they've been around.

✗ Eating

Super J's
Hawaiian, Local $

(☎808-328-9566; 83-5409 Mamalahoa Hwy; plates $8-12; ⊙10am-6:30pm Mon-Sat) The full title of this place is 'Ka'aloa's Super J's Hawaiian Food,' but everyone calls it Super J's. They also call it freakin' delicious. The *laulau* (pork, chicken or fish wrapped inside taro or *ti* leaves) is steamed until it's so tender it melts under your fork, the *lomilomi* salmon is perfectly salty – you'll even want second helpings of *poi* (mashed taro).

Site of Captain Cook's first landing in Hawai'i, Kealakekua Bay
SHELDON LEVIS/GETTY IMAGES ©

Best of all is the setting: you're basically eating in a welcoming Hawaiian family's kitchen. It's on the *makai* side of Hwy 11, between the Mile 106 and the Mile 107 markers.

Mahina Cafe
Cafe $

(☎808-323-3200; 82-6123 Mamalahoa Hwy; breakfast & lunch mains $6-12; ⏱7am-3pm daily, 5-8:30pm Fri-Mon) Just south of the Manago Hotel, this simple diner run by two sisters serves made-from-scratch comfort food like pancakes slathered in *haupia* (coconut cream), *loco moco* bowls and mixed-plate lunches. Grab fresh, hot *malasadas* (Portuguese doughnuts) from the drive-through window.

Patz Pies
Pizzeria $

(☎808-323-8100; 82-6127 Mamalahoa Hwy; slices/pies from $3/17; ⏱10am-9pm) Thin crust, zesty sauce: claims to dishing authentic NYC pizza are only slightly exaggerated at this native NYer's kitchen, just south of the Manago Hotel.

ChoiceMart
Supermarket $

(82-6066 Mamalahoa Hwy; ⏱5am-10pm) South Kona's largest grocery store lets you stock up on beach picnic supplies.

Coffee Shack
Cafe $$

(☎808-328-9555; www.coffeeshack.com; 83-5799 Mamalahoa Hwy; meals $10-15; ⏱7:30am-3pm) Perched precariously next to the highway, this longtime favorite banks on its vertigiounous views of Kealakekua Bay from the back deck – truly, you may never have another cup of 100% Kona coffee with a more inspiring vista. Sandwiches, salads and breakfasts can feed two easily, but taste so-so. Homemade desserts are killer: *liliko'i* cheesecake and Kona lime, coconut-cream or mac-nut pie.

Look for the historic building on the *makai* side of Hwy 11, between the Mile 108 and the Mile 109 markers.

Manago Restaurant
Japanese, Local $$

(www.managohotel.com; 82-6155 Mamalahoa Hwy; mains breakfast $4-6, lunch & dinner $6-14; ⏱7-9am, 11am-2pm & 5-7:30pm Tue-Sun; 👪)

Don't be put off by the bingo-hall ambience at this historic travelers' stopover, where locals devour the pork chops topped with gravy and onions, or try the fried whole '*opelu* (mackerel scad) or fresh catch in butter sauce. Each dinner plate is accompanied by Japanese pickles, miso soup and big bowls of rice. Simple diner-style breakfasts may be South Kona's cheapest.

🔒 Shopping

Reading Garden
Books

(☎808-323-9540; http://thereadinggarden. blogspot.com; 82-6125 Mamalahoa Hwy; ⏱9am-6pm Mon-Sat, from 11am Sun) Teetering stacks of used volumes spread about in an ordered chaos, wrapping over walls and up staircases and even extending outdoors. Inside you may find proprietor Marcus Medler, whose hobby is restoring rare and vintage books.

Kealakekua Bay

Kealakekua Bay blends supreme natural beauty with ancient sacred sites possessing powerful mana (spiritual essence). Besides being of religious importance to Hawaiians, this also marks the spot where Captain Cook, and by extension the entire outside world, first set foot on Hawai'i, irrevocably altering the fate of the entire archipelago and the indigenous people.

This wide, calm bay, sheltered by a low lava point to the north, tall *pali* (cliffs) in the center and miles of green mountain slopes to the south, is both a **state historical park** (www.hawaiistateparks.org; ⏱sunrise-sunset) FREE and a marine-life conservation district. Off the Mamalahoa Hwy (Hwy 11), narrow Napo'opo'o Rd twists downhill for 4.5 miles to the bay, leaving behind rainy uplands and arriving at the often sunny coast. The road ends by the Napo'opo'o Wharf parking lot. Public restrooms are near the heiau (turn right).

ride the long reef break here. Bayside, there's a small canoe and kayak launch and a few fishing shacks, but no public facilities. Be respectful of local residents – you're essentially walking in their front yards.

To get here, take the ragged 4WD road leading *makai* off Pu'uhonua Rd, about 0.3 miles south of Manini Beach Rd (if you hit Ke'ei Transfer Station, you've gone too far). Paved Pu'uhonua Rd continues another few miles south to Place of Refuge.

🏔 Beaches

Manini Beach
Beach

On its southern side, Kealakekua Bay is rocky and exposed to regular northwest swells, so swimming and snorkeling conditions are poor. That said, Manini Beach makes a scenic, shady picnic spot. If you do want to take a dip, despite the scattered, sharp coral and *a'a* (rough, jagged lava) along the shoreline, the best ocean access is to your right upon arriving at the beach.

From Napo'opo'o Rd, turn left onto Pu'uhonua Rd, then right onto Manini Rd. There's limited roadside parking.

Ke'ei Beach
Beach

South of Kealakekua Bay, Ke'ei Beach is an attractive cove that's mostly too rough and rocky for swimming, except for a narrow sandy stretch at its northern end. When conditions are right, local surfers

👁 Sights

Captain Cook Monument
Historic Site

From Napo'opo'o Wharf, this tall white obelisk is visible a mile away at Ka'awaloa Cove. It marks the spot where Captain Cook was killed in an armed confrontation with Hawaiians in 1779. In 1877, as an act of diplomacy, the Kingdom of Hawai'i deeded the land that the monument

stands on to Britain. Behind lie the ruins of the ancient village of Ka'awaloa.

Hiki'au Heiau
Temple

Veer right at the base of Napo'opo'o Rd to reach this large platform temple. In front of the heiau, a stone beach makes a moody perch from which to observe the stunning scenery, but the surf is too rough to swim. Climbing on the ruins is kapu (forbidden).

Pali Kapu o Keoua
Historic Site

Above Kealakekua Bay, the 'sacred cliffs of Keoua' were named for a chief and rival of Kamehameha I. Several high, inaccesible caves in these cliffs served as burial places for Hawaiian royalty, and it's speculated that some of Captain Cook's bones ended up here as well.

😀 Activities

SNORKELING

At Kealakekua Bay's northern end, protected **Ka'awaloa Cove** ranks among Hawai'i's premier snorkeling spots. Protected from ocean swells, its aquamarine waters are especially clear. Tropical fish and coral are brilliantly abundant, and those with iron stomachs can swim out 100ft from shore to hang over the blue abyss of an underwater cliff.

If you're lucky, *honu* (green sea turtles) and spinner dolphins might join you, but remember not to approach these wild animals. By law, you must remain at least 50yd away from turtles, dolphins, whales and seals in the water. All Hawaiian sea turtles are endangered, so give 'em a break and never touch or try to ride them.

At the time of research, you could only visit Ka'awaloa Cove on a snorkel cruise leaving from Kailua-Kona or Keahou, on a guided kayaking tour by a South Kona outfitter or by hiking the Captain Cook Monument Trail.

KAYAKING

Controversy over overcrowding and environmental impact on the bay has resulted in new legal regulations for

73

kayakers. Special recreational permits for transiting the bay, but not for landing at Ka'awaloa Cove or launching from Napo'opo'o Wharf, are currently available to individual kayakers in advance from the **Division of State Parks** (☎808-951-9540; www.hawaiistateparks.org; 75 Aupuni St, Hilo; ☺8:30am-3:30pm Mon-Fri).

Otherwise, your only other option (for now) is a guided kayaking tour by a state-permitted outfitter; check the website www.hawaiistateparks.org for a current list. Most tours launch from Napo'opo'o Wharf, paddling 30 to 45 minutes across the bay to Ka'awaloa Cove. Prevailing winds are from the northwest, so returning is usually faster and easier.

At the time of research, the only outfitters permitted to lead guided kayaking tours of Kealakekua Bay were Kona Boys (p66) in Captain Cook, Aloha Kayak Co (p63) in Honalo and Adventures in Paradise (p66) in Kealakekua.

DIVING

There are many good dive sites clustered around Kealakekua Bay, including **Ka'awaloa Cove**, with its exceptionally diverse coral and fish. Other sites further north include **Hammerhead**, a deep dive with pelagic action; **Coral Dome**, a big, teeming cave with a giant skylight; and **Driftwood**, featuring lava tubes and white-tip reef sharks.

In the aptly named **Long Lava Tube**, an intermediate site just north of Kealakekua Bay, lava 'skylights' shoot light through the ceiling of the 70ft-long tube, and you may see crustaceans, morays – even Spanish dancers. Outside are countless lava formations sheltering conger eels, triton's trumpet shells and squirrelfish.

HIKING

Captain Cook Monument Trail
Hiking

While not a particularly interesting hike, the steep Captain Cook Monument Trail down to Ka'awaloa Cove gives a different perspective than paddling over in a kayak. Go early to avoid the heat, bring snorkel gear and pack plenty of water and insect repellent. The one-way hike down takes about an hour, losing 1300ft of elevation in less than 2 miles.

To get to the trailhead, turn *makai* off the Mamalahoa Hwy onto Napo'opo'o Rd; within the first 10th of a mile, park along the narrow road shoulder, wherever it's safe and legally signposted to do so. To find the trailhead, count five telephone poles from the start of the road – it's *makai* across from three tall palm trees.

The trail can be hot and buggy, with inspiring lookouts on the way down. The route is fairly easy to follow; when in doubt, stay to the left. Plan on twice as long for the uphill return, when you should stay alert for the trail's right-hand turn back up onto the lava ledge, or you'll end up on a 4WD road heading north along the coast – for miles.

🛏 Sleeping

Kealakekua Bay Bed & Breakfast
B&B $$

(☎808-328-8150, 800-328-8150; www.keala.com; 82-6002 Lower Napo'opo'o Rd; r/ste $165/240, 2br cottage $360; 🛜) 🅿 Gourmet breakfasts served in a Mediterranean-style villa are reason enough to stay here. Local goat cheese, macadamia-nut pancakes, fresh fruit plucked from the garden – you can't go wrong. That goes for the property itself too: three bright, sun-kissed rooms filled with tropical accents, and the six-person Ohana Kai Guest House, a hill-perched cottage with postcard views of Kealakekua Bay.

Honaunau

Growing by leaps and bounds amid thick coffee and macadamia-nut groves, Honaunau invites exploring without any must-do stops. Of course, nearby Place of Refuge (Pu'uhonua O Hōnaunau National Historical Park) is the star attraction, but meander down Painted Church Rd, stopping at fruit stands, honey farms and coffee shacks with sea views for less-trafficked diversions.

Sights & Activities

St Benedict's Painted Church
Church

(📞 808-328-2227; www.thepaintedchurch.org; 84-5140 Painted Church Rd; 🕐 services 7am Tue & Thu-Fri, 4pm Sat, 7:15am Sun) **FREE** A pulpit with a view, gravestones cradled by tropical blooms and a little chapel with floor-to-ceiling 'outsider art' make this church a picturesque side trip. A self-taught artist and Catholic priest, John Velghe, came to Hawai'i from Belgium in 1899 and he modeled the vaulted nave on a Gothic cathedral in Burgos, Spain. His trompe l'oeil artwork is delightful, in a naive art kind of way. Come early or late, when the light is softer and birds sing out.

Paleaku Gardens Peace Sanctuary
Gardens

(📞 808-328-8084; www.paleaku.com; 83-5401 Painted Church Rd; adult/child 6-12yr $10/3; 🕐 9am-4pm Tue-Sat) Seven acres of shrines and meditation nooks await at this tranquil garden sanctuary tucked along Painted Church Rd. The innovative 'galaxy garden' is a mini Milky Way rendered in plants. A self-guided tour is a peaceful introduction to this unique, peaceful place. Check online for schedules of drop-in yoga classes and special events.

Society for Kona's Education & Art
Arts Center

(SKEA; 📞 808-328-9392; www.skea.org; 84-5191 Mamalahoa Hwy) 🌀 SKEA is a hotbed of activity, with pilates, Polynesian dance, tai chi and Japanese ink painting classes, art shows and poetry read-

ings; check the online calendar. Around back at the **Kona Potter's Guild**, you can watch potters at work and buy their handmade creations.

The center is between the Mile 105 and the Mile 106 on Hwy 11.

Sleeping

Aloha Guest House
B&B $$

(📞 800-897-3188, 808-328-8955; www.alohaguesthouse.com; 84-4780 Mamalahoa Hwy; r incl breakfast $125-230; @ 🛜) If you're coming all the way to Hawai'i, you should have the finest digs. Heady views from the shared lanai, guest living room and, for the lucky ones, your own king-sized bed will make you swoon, guaranteed. Ocean vistas are complemented by luxurious amenities such as organic bath products and full breakfasts with local fruit and estate-grown coffee.

Access is via a unpaved one-lane farm road that's very steep and bumpy.

St Benedict's Painted Church
JOHN ELK/GETTY IMAGES ©

Hale Hoʻola B&B
B&B **$$**

(☏877-628-9117, 808-328-9117; www.hale
-hoola.com; 85-4577 Mamalahoa Hwy; r incl
breakfast $125-165; @ 🛜) This remark-
ably hospitable roadside B&B provides
a homey, relaxed stay with three small
but comfortable rooms downstairs in
the main house. Despite comfy beds and
private lanai with ocean views, the
unfortunately thin-walled rooms are
jammed together – they're not recom-
mended for honeymooners or antisocial
types. Robust breakfasts somewhat
compensate.

Kane Plantation
B&B **$$$**

(☏808-328-2416; http://kaneplantationhawaii.
com; 84-1120 Telephone Exchange Rd; d incl
breakfast $155-255; 🛜) You'll be in excellent
hands at this upscale historic home,
where renowned Hawaiian artist Herb
Kane once lived. Perched on a lush *mauka*
hillside, the B&B shares the grounds with
an avocado farm. Upstairs the most spacious Kanaloa Suite boasts a king-sized
canopy bed and views of Kealakekua Bay
from a private lanai. Breakfasts are gourmet, and the hosts are charming.

✗ Eating & Drinking

South Kona Fruit Stand
Market, Cafe **$**

(☏808-328-8547; www.southkonafruitstand.com;
84-4770 Mamalahoa Hwy; items $3-10; ⊙9am-
6pm Mon-Sat, 10am-4pm Sun) Baskets overflow
with everything from tart apple bananas to
filling breadfruit, creamy *abiu* (sapote) and
purple jaboticaba berries. Slurp a smoothie
on the outdoor patio with gorgeous coastal
views. Look for the pineapple flags on the
mauka side of Hwy 11, between the Mile
103 and the Mile 104 markers.

Bong Brothers & Sistahs
Health Food, Deli **$**

(www.bongbrothers.com; 84-5227 Mamalahoa
Hwy; items $3-8; ⊙9am-6pm Mon-Fri, noon-6pm
Sun; 🖉) 🌱 Food is politics at this small
organic health-food store, vegetarian
take-out deli and coffee shop inside a
historic 1929 building.

Big Jake's Island B-B-Q
BBQ **$$**

(☏808-328-1227; 83-5308 Mamalahoa Hwy;
most mains $7-12; ⊙11am-6pm Sun-Thu, to 7pm
Fri & Sat) Barbecued ribs, pork and chicken
are slowly cooked up in the barrel smoker

Puʻuhonua O Hōnaunau National Historical Park

IMAGES ETC LTD/GETTY IMAGES ©

parked by the Mile 106 marker on Hwy 11. Chow down at picnic tables out back, or for DIY surf-and-turf, pick up some *poke* from the seafood shop next door.

Kona Coffeehouse & Cafe   Cafe

(84-4830 Mamalahoa Hwy; ⏱7am-4pm Tue-Sat, 8:30am-2pm Sun) On the *mauka* side of Hwy 11, at the turnoff to Place of Refuge, this coffee shop is serious about 100% Kona brews, espresso and more. Gooey mac-nut caramel pies and *liliko'i* bars are homemade.

Pu'uhonua O Hōnaunau National Historical Park

Standing at the edge of thorny coastal plains and lava desert, this **national park** (☎808-328-2326, 808-328-2288; www.nps.gov/puho; off Hwy 160, Honaunau; 7-day entry per car $5; ⏱park 7am-sunset, visitor center 8:30am-4:30pm) 🖝 fronting Honaunau Bay is one of the state's most evocative experiences of ancient Hawai'i. You'll almost always hear this park referred to as 'Place of Refuge,' because the name, meaning 'a place of refuge at Honaunau,' is such a tongue-twister.

Early morning or late afternoon is an optimal time to visit to avoid the midday heat and crowds. On the weekend closest to July 1, show up for the park's annual **cultural festival**, an extravaganza of traditional food, hula dancing, Hawaiian crafts and cultural demonstrations.

◎ Sights

A half-mile walking tour easily encompasses the park's major sights. The sandy trail begins below the visitor center, where you can pick up self-guiding tour brochures and beach wheelchairs to borrow. Sights nearest the water require traversing rough lava, which makes them wheelchair-inaccessible.

The park comprises two sections: the royal grounds and the *pu'uhonua* (place of refuge). You enter via the royal grounds – a little village, really – where *ali'i* (chiefs) and their warriors lived. Leading up to the heiau is the **Great Wall** separating the royal grounds from the *pu'uhonua*. Built around 1550, this stone wall is more than 1000ft long and 10ft high.

The authentically reconstructed temple on the cove's point, **Hale o Keawe Heiau**, was first built around 1700. In ancient times, it contained the sacred bones of chiefs whose mana (spiritual essence) bestowed sanctity on those who entered the grounds. Surrounding the temple, ohia trees carved into *ki'i* (deity images) up to 15ft high stand guard.

Honu (green sea turtles) nibble and rest around small, sandy **Keone'ele Cove**, which was once the royal canoe landing. Also nearby are a royal fishpond, lava-tree molds, hand-carved koa canoes with coconut-fiber lashings and an open-sided, thatch-roofed *hale* (hut) where the park's cultural demonstrator talks story and carries on traditional crafts.

After wandering the self-guided trail, you might like to try some wildlife watching: humpback whales swim offshore in winter, along with sea turtles and dolphins year-round, and even hoary bats can be seen (after sunset is best).

🤸 Activities

Two-Step   Snorkeling, Diving

Immediately north of Pu'uhonua O Hōnaunau National Historical Park, concealed within a (usually) placid bay, are ridiculously beautiful, vibrant coral gardens where reef and marine life seem locked in a permanent race to outstrip each other with the most eye-catching color palette. From above the water, your only indication of the action is the presence of boats leading snorkeling, diving, kayaking and SUP tours, plus the crowds gathering at the titular two steps.

There's no beach here – snorkelers use a stepped lava ledge beside the boat ramp to access about 10ft of water, which quickly drops to about 25ft. Look for, but by no means touch, the predatory, razor-sharp 'crown of thorns' starfish feasting on live coral polyps. Scuba divers can investigate a ledge a little way out that drops off about 100ft.

Island Insights

In ancient Hawai'i the kapu (taboo) system regulated every waking moment. A *maka'ainana* (commoner) could not look at *ali'i* (chiefs) or walk in their footsteps. Women couldn't cook for men, nor eat with them. Fishing, hunting and gathering timber was restricted to certain seasons. And on and on.

Violators of kapu were hunted down and killed. After all, according to the Hawaiian belief system, breaking kapu infuriated the gods. And gods wrought volcanic eruptions, tidal waves, famine and earthquakes, which could be devastating to the entire community.

There was one loophole, however. Commoners who broke kapu could stave off death if they reached the sacred ground of a *pu'uhonua* (place of refuge). A *pu'uhonua* also gave sanctuary to defeated warriors and wartime noncombatants (men who were too old, too young or unable to fight).

To reach the *pu'uhonua* was no small feat. Since royals and their warriors lived on the grounds surrounding the refuge, kapu breakers had to swim through violent, open ocean, braving currents and sharks, to safety. Once inside the sanctuary, priests performed ceremonies of absolution to placate the gods. Kapu breakers could then return home to start afresh.

The *pu'uhonua* at Honaunau was used for several centuries until 1819, when Hawai'i's old religious ways were abandoned after King Kamehameha II and regent Queen Ka'ahumanu ate together in public, overthrowing the ancient kapu system forever.

The best time to go is during a rising tide, when there are more fish. Year-round, freshwater springs can create blurry patches in the water, however. High winter surf means rough waters.

A privately operated parking lot here costs $3, or try to squeeze in along the road's shoulder.

1871 Trail
Hiking

A 2-mile round-trip oceanfront hike leads to the abandoned village of Ki'ilae, where there's very little left to see. The visitor center stocks trail guides describing ancient Hawaiian archaeological sites along the way; among other things, you pass a collapsed lava tube and a tremendous, if overgrown, *holua* (lava-sledding course) that *ali'i* raced sleds down. Watch out for feral goats (but they're usually benign).

Ho'okena & Around

Most tourists zip right by the turnoff for Ho'okena, between the Mile 101 and the Mile 102 markers on Hwy 11. But meander just a couple of miles downhill to this fishing community and you'll be surprised by a gorgeous bayfront beach that locals love and, more importantly, are willing to share.

Ho'okena was once a bustling Hawaiian village. Novelist Robert Louis Stevenson wrote about his 1889 visit in *Travels in Hawaii*. In the 1890s, Chinese immigrants moved into Ho'okena, a tavern and a hotel opened, and the town got rougher and rowdier. In those days, Big Island cattle were shipped from the Ho'okena landing, but when the circle-island road was built, Honolulu-bound steamers stopped coming and most people moved away.

🏖️ Beaches

Ho'okena Beach Park
Beach

This modest, charcoal-colored beach is backed by a steep green hillside. When calm, the bay's waters are good for swimming, kayaking and snorkeling (although the bottom drops off quickly). Coral abounds, as do strong currents further out. When the winter surf is up, local kids hit the waves with bodyboards. You might spot dolphins and humpback whales offshore between December and April. Facilities include restrooms, outdoor showers, drinking water, campsites, a picnic pavilion and a concession stand.

Camping is right on the sand at the base of the cliffs. Ongoing security issues have been addressed by implementing a guard patrol and through the activism of the **Friends of Ho'okena Beach Park** (📞808-328-7321; http://hookena.org); you can obtain required camping permits and rent camping gear online or in person. Camping permits can also be obtained in advance from the county.

Pebble Beach
Beach

Not quite pebbles, the smoky stones of this nonsandy beach at the bottom of the Kona Paradise subdivision range from gumdrop to palm-sized. It's a popular kayak put-in and offers a good dose of peace and quiet. Lounge for a bit, paddle a while or just watch the sun go down. If you enter the water, watch out for potentially fatal 'sneaker' waves.

The beach is a mile down very steep, winding Kaohe Rd, accessed between the Mile 96 and the Mile 97 markers on Hwy 11. Signs say 'private road' and 'keep out,' although the subdivision is ungated. Always ask permission from locals before entering.

Miloli'i

Miloli'i is a fishing village fighting to maintain its traditional ways while an upscale subdivision rises from the lava landscape around it. Miloli'i means 'fine twist,' and historically the village was known for skilled sennit twisters, who used coconut-husk fibers to make fine cord and highly valued fishnets. Villagers still live close

Hawaiian spinner dolphin, Ho'okena

to the sea, and many continue to make a living from it.

Privacy is paramount in these parts and curious tourists are tolerated – barely. The turn-off to Miloli'i is just south of the Mile 89 marker on Hwy 11; the village is 5 miles down a steep, winding, single-lane road that cuts across a 1926 lava flow.

🏖 Beaches

Miloli'i Beach Park   Beach
This locals-only county beach park is pocked with tide pools. Visitors are generally unwelcome and facilities are limited to restrooms and picnic tables. Camping along the rocky shore is allowed (but not recommended due to security problems) with an advance county permit.

Honomalino Beach   Beach
Instead of feeling like the unwanted guest you are at Miloli'i Beach Park, instead head to Honomalino Bay, less than a mile's walk south. With sand the color of all Big Island beaches crushed into one – green, gold, tawny and black – this beach has gentle swimming (for kids too) and reef snorkeling. Look for the marked public path beginning just beyond Miloli'i's public basketball courts by the yellow church and up the rocks.

When in doubt, keep to the right fork along the trail. Respect all private property and kapu (no trespassing) signs.

NORTH KONA COAST

If you imagine the Big Island is all jungle rainforest and white-sand beaches, the severity of the North Kona Coast will come as a shock. Infinite fields of black, broken lava-rock desert blanket this forbidding-looking shoreline. Yet always, at the edge of the horizon, the bright, sparkling blue waters of the Pacific beckon.

Turn off the Queen Ka'ahumanu Hwy (Hwy 19) and make your way across the eerie lava fields to snorkel with sea turtles, bask on almost deserted black-sand beaches and catch an iconic Kona sunset. On clear days, gaze *mauka* at panoramas of Mauna Kea and Mauna Loa volcanoes, both often snow-dusted in winter, and in the foreground between the two, Mt Hualalai.

Honokohau Harbor

Almost all of Kona's catch comes in at this harbor, about 2 miles north of downtown Kailua-Kona, including granders (fish weighing over 1000lb). Most fishing charters, dive boats and snorkeling and whale-watching cruises booked out of Kailua-Kona depart here.

Sunset, Honomalino Beach
ALVIS UPITIS/GETTY IMAGES ©

To reach the harbor, turn *makai* on Kealakehe Pkwy, just north of the Mile 98 marker on Hwy 19. The harbor provides public access to Honokohau Beach (p84) inside Kaloko-Honokohau National Historical Park.

🏃 Activities

DIVING & SURFING

From Honokohau Harbor south to Kailua Bay is a marine-life conservation district, accessible only by boat. This stretch of coast is littered with dive sites, including **Turtle Pinnacle**, a premier turtle-spotting site straight out from the harbor. Northbound toward the airport is **Garden Eel Cove**, aka 'Manta Heaven.'

Another good diving spot is off **Kaiwi Point**, south of Honokohau Harbor, where sea turtles, large fish and huge eagle rays swim around some respectable drop-offs. Nearby is **Suck 'Em Up**, a couple of lava tubes you can swim into, letting the swell pull you through.

Ocean Eco Tours   Diving, Surfing
(☎808-324-7873; www.oceanecotours.com; 74-425 Kealakehe Pkwy, Honokohau Harbor; snorkel/dive boat trips from $99/119, group/private surfing lesson $95/150) For surfing lessons, this is the only operator permitted to surf within the boundaries of Kaloko-Honokohau National Historical Park. It also guides snorkeling and scuba trips along the coast, including night dives with manta rays. Stop by the small shop at the harbor to rent surfboards, bodyboards and snorkel or scuba gear.

FISHING

Scads of fishing charters leave from Honokohau Harbor. If you're just after the money shot, you can watch the boats as they pull up and weigh their haul at around 11:30am and 3:30pm. Entering the harbor area, take the first right, park near the gas station and walk toward the dock behind Bite Me Fish Market Bar & Grill.

KAYAKING

Plenty Pupule   Kayaking
(☎808-880-1400; www.plentypupule.com; 73-4976 Kamanu St, Kaloko Industrial Park; kayak rental per day s/d $25/38, tours $80-250; ⏱10am-5:30pm Tue-Sat) One of the island's top outfitters for adventure kayaking, these folks can recommend the best put-ins and snorkel spots, customize tours, teach you to kayak surf or take you kayak sailing, the latter particularly memorable during winter whale-watching season.

👉 Tours

Hawaii Forest & Trail   Van Tours
(☎800-464-1993, 808-331-8505; www.hawaii-forest.com; 74-5035B Queen Ka'ahumanu Hwy; tours adult/child from $159/139) ✈ This multiaward-winning outfitter caters to active travelers who want to delve into the Big Island's greenest depths. From the always popular Mauna Kea summit and stargazing van tours to exclusive guided bird-watching hikes in Hakalau Forest National Wildlife Refuge, you won't regret an adventure with these expert naturalists and ecosustainability stewards.

🍴 Eating & Drinking

**Bite Me Fish Market
Bar & Grill**   Seafood $$
(☎808-327-3474; www.bitemefishmarket.com; 74-425 Kealakehe Pkwy, Honokohau Harbor; mains $8-23; ⏱6am-9pm; 🛜♿) Steps from the harbor boat ramp, stop into this bamboo-fenced place for a bottle of Longboard Lager and to spin yarns after a day of fishing. At dockside picnic tables, chow down on just alright fish sandwiches, tacos, ceviche, *poke* and seafood and *pupu* platters. Service from the tattted-out servers can be lackadaisical.

**Kona Coffee & Tea
Company**   Cafe
(www.konacoffeeandtea.com; 74-5035 Queen Ka'ahumanu Hwy; ⏱7am-5:30pm Mon-Fri, 8am-5pm Sat, 10am-3pm Sun; 🛜) Life is too short for bad coffee: head here for award-winning 100% Kona grown on sustainable

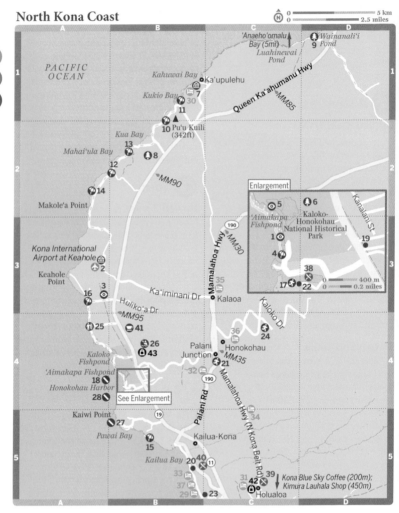

farms. Freshly roasted beans and toothsome mac-nut pies mitigate the location behind a gas station.

Kona Mountain Coffee · Cafe

(☎808-329-5005; www.konamountaincoffee.com; 73-4038 Hukiloa Dr; ☺8am-6pm Mon-Fri, to 5pm Sat & Sun) Just over 2 miles north of the harbor turnoff along Hwy 19, this farm-grown coffee roaster's retail shop and coffee bar also stocks baked goodies and snacks. It's a quick stop on the way to the airport.

🔒 Shopping

Kailua Candy Company · Food

(☎808-329-2522, 800-622-2462; http://kailua-candy.com; 73-5612 Kauhola St, Kaloko Industrial Park; ☺9am-5pm Mon-Sat) A detour to this chocolate factory shop is mandatory for every sweet tooth. Savor free samples of Mauna Kea 'snowballs' (white chocolate with shredded coconut), Kona coffee swirls, Hawaiian 'turtles' and tropically flavored truffles. To get here, turn *mauka*

North Kona Coast

onto Hina Lani St off Hwy 19, then right on Kamanu St.

Kaloko-Honokohau National Historical Park

Just north of Honokohau Harbor, this 1160-acre **national park** (☎808-326-9057; www.nps.gov/kaho; ⊗visitor center 8:30am-4pm, park 24hr) FREE may be the Kona Coast's most underappreciated ancient Hawaiian site. Hidden among lava fields lies evidence of the innovations that allowed Hawaiians to thrive in this hostile landscape: fish traps, lava planters used to grow taro and other staples, plus the

ahupua'a (land division) between Kaloko and Honokohau that gives the park its name. There are also heiau, burial caves and petroglyphs.

Despite the seemingly endless expanse of lava rock and unbearable midday heat, this is a good place to explore. Go in the early morning, late afternoon or when skies are overcast. *Kokua* (please) remember not to climb on, move, alter or deface any rock structures. Take special care not to disturb the endangered *honu* (green sea turtles), who haul out here to rest, feed and bask in the sun – it's illegal to approach them closer than 20ft away on land, or 50yd in the water.

The park's main entrance is off Hwy 19 between the Mile 96 and the Mile 97 markers, where there's a parking lot and a small, but informative ranger-staffed visitor center.

◉ Sights

Honokohau Beach   Beach
At this beautiful hook-shaped beach with a mix of black lava, white coral and wave-tossed shells, the water is usually too cloudy for snorkeling, but just standing on shore you'll see *honu* (green sea turtles). You may spot more *honu* munching on *limu* (seaweed) around the ancient **'Ai'opio fishtrap**, bordered by a Hawaiian **heiau** at the beach's southern end. Inland are **anchialine ponds** – pools of brackish water that make unique habitats for marine and plant life.

To get here, turn right into the first parking lot at Honokohau Harbor (look for the small public coastal access sign). Near the end of the road is the signposted trailhead; a five-minute walk on a well-beaten path leads to the beach. You could also take the more scenic, if longer route by hiking to the beach along the 0.75-mile **Ala Hele Iki Trail** from the visitor center.

Kaloko Fishpond   Historic Site
At the park's northern end, Kaloko Fishpond is one of the most interesting sites because its massive rock retaining wall is being completely rebuilt, so it can once again be fished in the traditional way. Some speculate that the bones of Kamehameha the Great were secretly buried in a cave nearby.

From the park's visitor center, drive north on Hwy 19 until you reach a separate gated entrance at Ala Kaloko Rd. Alternatively, it's about a 1-mile hike north from the visitor center along the coastal **Ala Kahakai National Historic Trail**, a restored ancient Hawaiian footpath.

'Aimakapa Fishpond   Historic Site
In the park's southern section, 'Aimakapa is the largest fishpond on the Kona Coast. It's home to *ae'o* (Hawaiian black-necked stilt) and *'alae kea* (Hawaiian coot), both of which are endangered native waterbirds. Neaby look for the ancient remains of a *holua* (lava-sledding course).

Heiau, Kaloko-Honokohau National Historical Park

Keahole Point

Funny place, Keahole Point. Just offshore, the seafloor drops abruptly, providing a continuous supply of both cold water from 2000ft depths and warm surface water. These are ideal conditions for ocean thermal-energy conversion (OTEC), deep sea water extraction and aquaculture. All of this is happening here, plus there's a beach and one of the island's best surf breaks.

🏖 Beaches

Wawaloli (OTEC) Beach   Beach
(Makiko Bay Dr; ⏰6am-8pm) At the *makai* end of the access road to the Natural Energy Laboratory of Hawaii (Nelha), this quiet locals' beach is perfectly positioned for sunsets – never mind the jets flying overhead. Swimming isn't good here, except at high tide when the oodles of protected **tide pools** along the lava-rock coastline overflow. Bring a picnic and the kids. Facilities include restrooms and outdoor showers.

◎ Sights

Hawaii Ocean Science & Technology Park   Building
(HOST Park; 📞808-327-9585; http://nelha. hawaii.gov; 73-4660 Queen Ka'ahumanu Hwy; lecture & tour adult/student & senior/child under 9yr from $8/5/free) 🌿 That funny-looking building with the gigantic solar panels is the **Natural Energy Laboratory of Hawaii (Nelha)**. This 'zero-net energy facility' was voted one of the USA's 10 greenest buildings in 2007. Learn about OTEC and research into alternative and renewable-energy technologies at Nelha's public presentations, which are followed by an abalone farm tour and tasting on Monday, Wednesday and Thursday or a solar-energy plant tour on Tuesday. Friday's 'Grand Tour' (reservations required) visits OTEC Tower and kampachi and abalone farms.

About 40 businesses call Nelha's HOST Park home, including **Kampachi Farms** (www.kampachifarm.com) 🌿, the aquaculture gurus responsible for yellowfin tuna seen on haute island restaurant menus; **Kona Deep** (www.gotdeep.com), 100% Hawaii deep-sea water that's desalinated and bottled here, then sold as a tonic internationally; and **Ocean Rider Seahorse Farm** (📞808-329-6840; www.seahorse.com; 73-4388 Ilikai Pl; tours adult/child 4-9yr $36/26; ⏰gift shop 9:30am-3:30pm, tours noon & 2pm Mon-Fri, also 10am Mon-Fri late Dec-Apr & Jun-late Aug; 🚹), the only one of its kind in the country.

The turnoff is just over a mile south of Kona International Airport, between th Mile 94 and the Mile 95 markers on Hwy 19.

Astronaut Ellison S Onizuka Space Center   Museum
(📞808-329-3441; http://hawaii.gov/koa/; Kona International Airport; adult/child under 12yr $3/1; ⏰8:30am-4:30pm; 🚹) This little museum pays tribute to the Big Island native who perished in the 1986 *Challenger* space-shuttle disaster. Sitting between the aiport's departure and arrival buildings, you'll find kid-friendly exhibits and educational videos about space and astronauts. Items on display include a moon rock, a NASA space suit and scale models of spacecraft.

🏃 Activities

Pine Trees   Surfing
Pine Trees is one of West Hawai'i's best surfing breaks. The break stretches along a pretty beach that is rocky enough to make swimming difficult. The final bay gets the most consistent yet more forgiving waves. An incoming midtide is favorable, but as the swell picks up in winter these breaks often close out.

Get friendly with local regulars if you want in on the action – this hot spot draws crowds, especially on weekends. Where the access road to Nelha veers to the right, look left for a rutted dirt road leading about 2 miles further south. You'll need a high-clearance 4WD to make it, or you can walk, but it's hot. The access road gates are locked between 8pm and 6am.

Kekaha Kai (Kona Coast) State Park

Most only accessible by 4WD or on foot, the gorgeous beaches of this **state park** (www.hawaiistateparks.org; ⊙9am-7pm) FREE are all the more memorable for being tucked away on the far side of a vast desert of unforgiving black lava. Several beaches have remote coves where sea turtles gather and calm pools for swimming. The majority of the 1600-acre park is wonderfully undeveloped and brutally hot; bring water, food, sunscreen, a hat and sturdy hiking shoes or a 4WD vehicle.

Hard-core hikers can tackle a section of the coastal **Ala Kahakai National Historic Trail** from Kua Bay north via Kikaua Beach to Kukio Beach (2 miles each way), or south via Makalawena Beach to Mahai'ula Beach (4.5 miles each way). But beware that temperatures by midmorning can be broiling, and the trail has painful stretches of nothing but *a'a* lava.

🏖 Beaches

Manini'owali Beach (Kua Bay)   Beach

(www.hawaiistateparks.org; ⊙9am-7pm)
At this crescent-shaped beach with powdery white sand and little shade, sparkling turquoise waters are first-rate for swimming and bodyboarding (the latter especially in winter), and there's even decent snorkeling when waters are calm. Manini'owali draws major crowds, especially on weekends. To get here, turn onto the (unsigned) paved access road between the Mile 88 and the Mile 89 markers on Hwy 19, opposite West Hawaii Veterans Cemetery.

Mahai'ula Beach   Beach

Kekaha Kai (Kona Coast) State Park's largest beach has salt-and-pepper sand, rocky tide pools, shaded picnic tables and pit toilets. Swimming usually isn't good here, but during big winter swells, surfing happens. Walk a few minutes north along the coast to find a second, less rocky beach with soft tawny sands (nicknamed **Magoon's**), perfect for sunbathing and swimming. Access to Mahai'ula is via a chunky lava road between the Mile 90 and the Mile 91 markers on Hwy 19.

Although 4WD is recommended, many locals drive down the unpaved beach access road in a standard passenger car. Alternatively, you could traverse the 1.5 miles on foot from Hwy 19. Park at an improvised lot just inland from the highway and start walking or thumb it – drivers may take pity on your sun-beaten head and give you a lift.

Makalawena Beach   Beach

If what you're after is an almost deserted, postcard-perfect scoop of

Manini'owali Beach (Kua Bay)
TOM BENEDICT/GETTY IMAGES ©

soft, white-sand beach cupping brilliant blue-green waters (are you sold yet?), head to 'Maks.' Although popular, this string of idyllic coves absorbs crowds so well, you'll still feel like you've found paradise. The northernmost cove is sandier and gentler, while the southernmost cove is (illegally) a naked sunbathing spot. Swimming is splendid, but beware of rough surf and rocks in the water. Bodyboarding and snorkeling are more possibilities.

Practice aloha during your visit by packing out all trash and respecting the privacy of others. For locals, this is an unofficial camping and fishing getaway, and the growing popularity of these beaches among outsiders is contentious for some. Always give endangered sea turtles a wide berth – it's illegal to approach them closer than 20ft away on land, or 50yd in the water.

Getting to Makalawena requires extra effort. Take the unpaved Kekaha Kai (Kona Coast) State Park access road (4WD recommended, although many locals drive it in a standard passenger car), off Hwy 19 between the Mile 90 and the Mile 91 markers. Less than 1.5 miles later, at the road junction before the parking lot for Mahai'ula Beach, turn right. Park on the road shoulder near the cables restricting vehicle access to a service road, then walk north for 30 minutes across the lava flow and sand dunes to the beach, either following the service road or a rougher footpath over crunchy *a'a* lava.

Makole'a Beach   Beach
Amazingly, this secluded black-sand beach belongs to Kekaha Kai (Kona Coast) State Park. Although there's no shade and it's too rocky for swimming, its natural beauty rewards those who make the effort to visit. To reach this small, dark treasure on foot, head south along Mahai'ula Beach and either follow the road or the coastline while making toward a lone tree.

With a 4WD, turn left at the road junction by Mahai'ula Beach, drive south for about 1000yd until you reach a path marked by white coral, then get out and hoof it as the lava becomes too rough.

Ka'upulehu

Once a thriving fishing village among many dotting this length of coast, Ka'upulehu was wiped out by the 1946 tsunami and abandoned until the Kona Village Resort opened here in 1965. The resort closed indefinitely in 2011 after more tsunami damage caused by a massive earthquake in Japan. The luxurious Four Seasons Resort Hualalai remains open, however, as do some fine public beaches that you can visit for free.

🏖 Beaches

Kikaua Beach   Beach
(🚹) Obviously artificial (a thin layer of sand laid over concrete is hard on the feet), Kikaua Beach has some things going for it. There's lots of shade, and a completely protected cove is perfect for teaching *keiki* (children) to swim and even snorkel. Around the kiawe-covered point are gaggles of sea turtles. Facilities include restrooms, outdoor showers and drinking water.

Public beach access is through a private country club and residential development. It's limited to 28 cars per day, so it never feels that crowded. To get here, turn *makai* onto Kuki'o Nui Rd

Right: Manini'owali Beach (Kua Bay) **Below:** Four Seasons Resort Hualalai golf course

(RIGHT) TOM BENEDICT/GETTY IMAGES ©; (BELOW) PETER FRENCH/GETTY IMAGES ©

near the Mile 87 marker on Hwy 19. Drive to the security guardhouse and request a parking pass and directions to the beach.

Kukio Beach
Beach

From Kikaua Beach you could walk north to the scalloped, palm-fringed coves of Kukio Bay, officially part of the Four Seasons Resort Hualalai. There the sand is soft, the swimming is good (even for kids) and there's a paved trail leading north along the rocky coastline to another beach. Facilities include restrooms, outdoor showers and drinking water.

To drive here, turn onto Ka'upulehu Rd (unsigned) between the Mile 86 and the Mile 87 markers on Hwy 19. Drive straight ahead to the Four Seasons security guardhouse and request a beach parking pass. The 50-car beach parking lot almost never fills up.

◉ Sights

Ka'upulehu Cultural Center
Gallery

(☑ 808-325-8520; 72-100 Ka'upulehu Dr, Four Seasons Resort Hualalai; ⊗ 8:30am-4pm Mon-Fri) **FREE** Inside the Four Season's Hawaiian cultural center, small but museum-quality displays are organized around a collection of 11 original paintings by Herb Kawainui Kane. Each painting is accompanied by a hands-on exhibit about traditional Hawaiian culture: shake an 'uli'uli (feathered hula rattle), test the heft of a kapa (bark-cloth) beater or examine stone adze heads. On-site Hawaiian cultural practitioners actively link the present with the past by teaching classes (usually reserved for resort guests only) and giving impromptu Hawaiian arts-and-crafts demonstrations.

At the Four Seasons security guardhouse, tell them you're visiting the cultural center. Drive all the way downhill

to the resort's self-parking lot, from where it's a short walk to the center.

🛏 Sleeping

**Four Seasons Resort
Hualalai**   Resort **$$$**
(📞800-819-5053, 808-325-8000; www.foursea
sons.com/hualalai; 72-100 Ka'upulehu Dr; r/ste
from $675/1475; ❄ @ 🛜 ⛱) The island's
only five-diamond resort earns its ac-
colades with top-flight service and lavish
attention to details like fresh orchids in
every room, embracing lush gardens and
an oceanview infinity pool. Some poolside
rooms have rejuvenating lava-rock garden
outdoor showers. The golf course and spa
are both outstanding, or snorkel with 75
species of tropical fish in the King's Pond.

🍴 Eating & Drinking

**'Ulu Ocean Grill +
Sushi Lounge**   Hawaii Regional **$$$**
(📞808-325-8000; www.uluoceangrill.com;
72-100 Ka'upulehu Dr, Four Seasons Resort

Hualalai; mains $24-45, tasting menu from
$65; 🕐restaurant 5:30-9pm, sushi lounge
5:30-10pm) *'Ulu* means 'breadfruit,' and
this sustainably minded restaurant is all
about locally sourced produce, seafood
and meat – in fact, 75% of its dishes are
made with Hawai'i-grown ingredients.
The menu mixes tastes from *makai* to
mauka: currried Kona mussels, kiawe-
smoked potatoes and wild boar glazed
with *liliko'i* (passion fruit). Too bad the
food doesn't live up to the hype – or the
sky-high prices.

The atmosphere is casually elegant,
with glass-ball partitions and island
artwork. Soak up sunset views from
the 10-seat bar inside the sushi lounge.
Dinner reservations are recommended
for the restaurant.

Beach Tree   Californian **$$$**
(📞808-325-8000; www.fourseasons.com/
hualalai; 72-100 Ka'upulehu Dr, Four Seasons
Resort Hualalai; mains lunch $14-22, dinner $16-
39; 🕐11:30am-8:30pm; 👶) You can't beat
catching sunset from a cabana-style sofa

while imbibing pricey tropical cocktails and noshing on *pupu*. A Cal-Italian menu of pastas, salads, sandwiches, burgers and pizzas is nothing to write home about, but the open-air oceanfront setting definitely has that barefoot romantic wow-factor. Live Hawaiian music plays until 8pm daily, and sometimes a solo hula dancer performs too.

Kiholo Bay

If you're looking for a beach with a little something for everyone, head to 2-mile-wide **Kiholo State Park Reserve** (www.hawaiistateparks.org; ⏱7am-7pm Apr-1st Mon in Sep, to 6pm 1st Tue in Sep-Mar). Incredibly, this oasis in the lava is not thronged by visitors, despite its gorgeous beaches, good chances for wildlife viewing and swimming through a lava tube.

At the south end of the main beach, take the lava-rock path toward the coconut grove in the distance, where there's a series of secluded, soft black-sand beaches. The lower the tide, the bigger the beaches, and when waters are calm, you can swim. Look for whales breaching offshore in winter. The coconut grove rings **Luahinewai**, a large, cold, spring-fed pond on private property (no trespassing).

Back at the main beach, you can explore on foot far to the north, especially when the tide's out. Seaweed-covered tide pools abound with *honu* (green sea turtles). Remember to keep back at least 20ft on land and 50yd in the water to avoid disturbing these endangered creatures – it's the law.

Once the gravel footpath heading north ends, look inland for **Keanalele (Queen's Bath)**, a lava tube filled with crystalline freshwater that beckons to strong, adventurous swimmers. Lots of folks stop here to wash off salt water, but because there's a living ecosystem inside the lava tube, don't enter it if you're wearing any sunscreen.

You can keep trekking north along the bay past an abandoned mansion and an authentic **Balinese house** (keep a respectful distance from both, as they're on private property). Past the remains of a gigantic ancient **fishpond** built during the reign of Kamehameha I, you'll come

Kiholo Bay

PHILIP ROSENBERG/GETTY IMAGES ©

Avoiding Car Break-ins at Beaches & Trailheads

For many, the Big Island's remote beaches and hikes are the main event – but they also make your rental car a prime target for thieves. Follow local advice: leave nothing of value in your car (yes, this includes the trunk). It's smart to get all your gear packed up before arriving at your destination.

Another local tip is to leave your doors unlocked so would-be ne'er-do-wells know there's nothing of value in the car. In this way, you can avoid a smashed window – which, as the confetti of broken glass in beach and trailhead parking areas proves, occurs fairly frequently.

Check your rental-car insurance policy before considering doing the same, however. This strategy can backfire, as it leaves your car wide open to stinky feral animals who may hop inside and make a huge mess that's impossible to clean up.

to **Wainanali'i Pond**, a lagoon where *honu* congregate.

To get to Kiholo Bay, turn *makai* onto the unmarked dirt road off Hwy 19 between the Mile 82 and the Mile 83 markers, just south of the scenic viewpoint. Drive downhill for less than a mile, taking the left-hand fork and parking by the abandoned roundhouse. You can also hike in about a mile from a small, rocky parking lot on the *makai* side of Hwy 19, just north of the Mile 81 marker.

Kiholo is a popular weekend **camping** spot for locals (get an advance state-park permit), but there's no potable water.

Kohala & Waimea

Kohala is a study in contrasts.
South Kohala is the archetypal sun-and-sea resort mecca. Since the 1960s, swanky resorts and golf courses have transformed this stretch into the Gold Coast. From Waikoloa to Kawaihae, Hawaiian history is preserved in ancient trails, heiau (temples), fishponds and petroglyphs – although all you'll see from the highway is stark lava desert. In counterpoint to the south's desert climate and man-made attractions, North Kohala is lushly otherworldly, with magnificent pastureland, quaint plantation towns and Pololu Valley's cascading cliffs. It proudly remains rural with nary a high-rise in sight. Waimea, a ranch town in between, is a central stop for cross-island travelers.

Pololu Valley (p121)

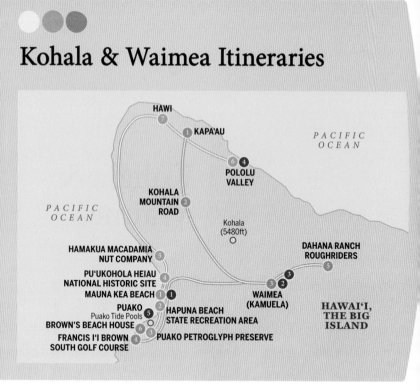

Two Days

① **Mauna Kea Beach** (p108) Start your first day at this picture-perfect beach accessed through the Mauna Kea Beach Hotel, which reserves 40 parking spots for nonguests.

② **Hapuna Beach State Recreation Area** (p108) As an alternative, try this awesome, easy-access public beach. Escape into shade for lunch at Monstera an *izakaya* spot (Japanese pub serving tapas-style food) at the Shops at Mauna Lani.

③ **Puako Petroglyph Preserve** (p104) A mini hike leads you to a fascinating tableau of petroglyphs. Explore sea life or watch the sunset from the Puako Tide Pools.

④ **Pu'ukohola Heiau National Historic Site** (p110) On day two, head to North Kohala, a world away with its lush forestland and village charm. Along the way, stop at this historic heiau, built by Kamehameha the

Great during his fight for supremacy over the Hawaiian Kingdom.

⑤ **Hamakua Macadamia Nut Company** (p110) Who doesn't like macadamia nuts? Stop here for a free tour and ample samples.

⑥ **Pololu Valley** (p121) At the highway's end awaits Pololu Valley. The view from the lookout will only whet your appetite for deeper exploration into this mysterious valley. Hike down the short but steep and slippery trail to the beach.

⑦ **Hawi** (p113) End your day at this tiny town with outstanding art galleries.

● THIS LEG: 32 MILES

Four Days

1 **Kapa'au** (p116) Follow the two-day plan, then join a morning zipline tour with Kohala Zipline or Big Island Eco Adventures. You'll be ferreted away into thick forest for aerial thrills and otherwise-inaccessible sightseeing.

2 **Kohala Mountain Road** (p113) This bucolic, two-lane highway has such stunning views of the vast island, it's almost a traffic hazard.

3 **Waimea (Kamuela)** Take a lunch break at Merriman's, one of the pioneering restaurants focusing on fresh local ingredients. Don't miss Isaacs Art Center, an impressive collection of fine art by late and living masters. Check the schedule for Kahilu Theatre, which hosts big-name performers.

4 **Francis I'i Brown South Golf Course** (p104) The next day, head to this golf course at the Mauna Lani Bay Hotel & Bungalows. The juxtapositions of rugged lava rock and immaculate greens, massive mountains and the great Pacific, make Big Island courses distinctive.

5 **Dahana Ranch Roughriders** (p124) Nongolfers can go horseback riding instead. At this ranch, even beginners learn to ride free on the range, not fixed 'nose to tail.'

6 **Brown's Beach House** (p106) End your visit with a culinary extravaganza at this oceanfront icon, specializing in Hawaii Regional Cuisine (an island-grown version of Pacific Rim fusion) and stunning sunsets.

THIS LEG: 35 MILES

Kohala & Waimea Highlights

1 **Best Beach: Mauna Kea Beach** (p108) Find powdery white sand and glassy water at this picture-perfect spot.

2 **Best Art Venue: Isaacs Art Center** (p123) Size isn't everything, as this impressive fine-art collection proves.

3 **Best Drink: Big Island Brewhaus & Taqueria** (p127) Prepare to be impressed by the lineup at this award-winning microbrewery.

4 **Best Views: Pololu Valley** (p121) The lookout is the first of countless spectacular views along the valley trail.

5 **Best Ocean Adventure: Kohala Kayak** (p108) Can't decide between paddling and snorkeling? Do both in the pristine waters of Puako.

Black-sand beach in Pololu Valley (p121)
TAN YILMAZ/GETTY IMAGES ©

Discover Kohala & Waimea

SOUTH KOHALA

The Queen Ka'ahumanu Hwy (Hwy 19) cuts through stark fields of lava. But a series of sumptuous resorts have created tropical oases along the water's edge, some containing the island's best beaches, some building their own. Meet the Gold Coast.

The waters off the Kohala Coast are pristine and teeming with marine life – and they're relatively uncrowded. The reef here drops off more gradually than along the Kona Coast, so you see sharks, dolphins, turtles and manta rays, but not large schools of tuna and other deepwater fish. Kohala is the oldest area of the Big Island: see lush coral growth and lots of lava tubes, arches and pinnacles.

A car is essential to get around South Kohala. While **Hele-On Bus** (☎808-961-8744; www.heleonbus.org) routes stop at the major hotels, they're geared for commuting hotel staff and run very early in the morning!

Waikoloa Resort Area

POP 6362

Among South Kohala's resort areas, the **Waikoloa Beach Resort** (www.waikolo beachresort.com) is the most affordable and bustling. Its two mega hotels and golf courses aren't as prestigious as those further up the coast, but it does offer two shopping malls and the lion's share of events. Note that the Waikoloa Beach Resort is not Waikoloa Village, a residential community further inland. To get to the resort area, turn *makai* (seaward) just south of the Mile 76 marker on Hwy 19. To get to the village for general services, such as a post office, turn *mauka* (mountainward) onto Waikoloa Rd north of the Mile 75 marker.

Beaches

'Anaeho'omalu Beach Park Beach
(Waikoloa Beach Dr; ⏱6am-8pm) 'A Bay' boasts easy access, salt-and-pepper sand and calm waters; it's the only place suited to windsurfing on Hawai'i. Classically beautiful, it's backed by hundreds of palm trees and makes for fantastic sunset viewing.

Golf course at the Waikoloa Beach Resort
GREG VAUGHN/GETTY IMAGES ©

Drinking water, showers and restrooms are available.

The Waikoloa Beach Marriott fronts the beach's north end, but **ancient fishponds** add a buffer zone between the two. In that area, there's decent snorkeling directly in front of the sluice gate, where you'll find coral formations, a variety of fish and possibly sea turtles.

'Anaeho'omalu was once the site of royal fishponds, and archaeologists have found evidence of human habitation here dating back more than 1000 years. A short footpath with interpretive plaques starts near the showers.

To get here, turn left off Waikoloa Beach Dr opposite the Kings' Shops.

Sights

Waikoloa Petroglyph Preserve
Historic Site

(Waikoloa Beach Dr; ⊙dawn-dusk, 1hr tour 9:30am) FREE This collection of petro-glyphs carved in lava rock is so easy-access that it merits a stop, although the Puako Petroglyph Preserve (p104) further north is more spectacular and not neighboring a shopping mall. Dating back to the 16th century, they're rather vague.

To get here, park at the Kings' Shops mall and walk for five minutes on the signposted path. Free guided tours of the petroglyphs are offered from 9:30am to 10:30am most Thursdays and Fridays, starting at the mall.

Activities

Ocean Sports
Water Sports

(📞888-724-5924, 886-6666; www.hawaiiocean sports.com; 69-275 Waikoloa Beach Dr) Ocean Sports monopolizes the ocean-activity market in South Kohala. Fortunately the company is well run, if slightly steep in its pricing. Cruises include whale-watching ($119) and snorkeling tours ($147) aboard a 49-passenger catamaran. Departures from 'Anaeho'omalu Bay and Kawaihae Harbor.

At Anaeho'omalu Beach Park and the Hilton Waikoloa Village, this outfit also rents beach equipment.

The Best...
South Kohala Beaches

1 Mauna Kea Beach (p108)

2 Beach State Recreation Area (p108)

3 'Anaeho'omalu Beach Park (p96)

4 Beach 69 (p107)

Waikoloa Beach & Kings' Courses
Golf

(📞886-7888; www.waikoloabeachgolf.com; 69-275 Waikoloa Beach Dr, Waikoloa Beach Marriott; green fees guest/nonguest $135/165) The Waikoloa Beach Marriott boasts two top golf courses: the coastal **Beach course** is known for its par-five 12th hole; the **Kings' course** is more challenging and offers Scottish-style links. Tee off later and pay less (11:30am/1pm/2pm $115/105/85). Carts are mandatory.

Star Gaze Hawaii
Stargazing

(📞323-3481; http://stargazehawaii.biz; adult/child 5-11yr $30/15) Take advantage of Kohala's consistently clear night skies with professional astronomers and equipment. Locations include **Fairmont Orchid** (1 North Kaniku Dr; ⊙7:30-8:30pm Fri), **Hapuna Beach Prince Hotel** (62-100 Kauna'oa Dr; ⊙8-9pm Sun & Wed) FREE and **Hilton Waikoloa Village** (425 Waikoloa Beach Dr; ⊙8-9pm Tue & Thu). Reservations are required.

Dolphin Quest
Wildlife

(📞800-248-3316, 886-2875; www.dolphinquest. com; 425 Waikoloa Beach Dr, Hilton Waikoloa Village; per person from $210, family encounter $1400; ⊙9am-4pm) Minds differ on the ethics of captive dolphins. Judging by the popularity of this program, however, many have no qualms about paying big bucks for an encounter with this adored sea creature.

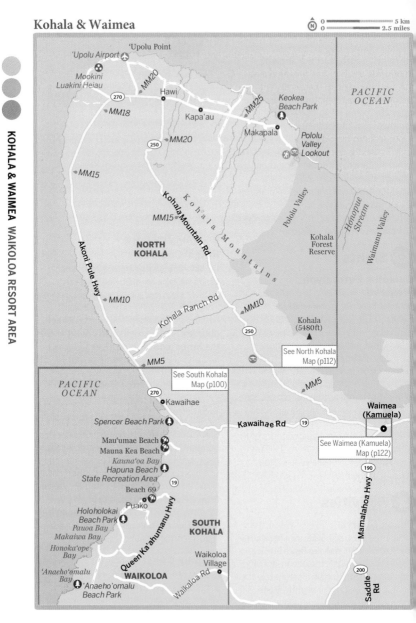

Hilton Waikoloa Village Pools
Swimming

(☎ 800-221-2424, 886-1234; www.hilton waikoloavillage.com; 425 Waikoloa Beach Dr; nonguest pool pass up to 4 people $90; 👪) Chances are, the pools at this over-the-

top resort will thrill your kids. Besides two serpentine pools with multiple waterslides and waterfalls, there's a man-made beach. If your group numbers four, the fee *might* be worth a splash.

Ancient Hawaiian Art

Ancient Hawaiians carved *ki'i pohaku* (stone images), called **petroglyphs**, into *pahoehoe* (smooth lava). These mysterious carvings are most common on the Big Island, perhaps because it is the youngest island, with the most extensive fields of *pahoehoe*. The sketchy images include human figures, animals and canoes and other important objects. They're typically found along major trails or on the boundaries of *ahupua'a* (land divisions).

Touching the petroglyphs will damage them, so never step on or make rubbings of them. Photography is best done in the early morning or late afternoon.

⭐ Festivals & Events

A Taste of the Hawaiian Range
Food

(www.tasteofthehawaiianrange.com; Hilton Waikoloa Village; admission advance/door $40/60) Celebrated Big Island chefs work magic with local range-fed meats and local produce in late September or early October.

Moku O Keawe
Hula

(www.mokif.com; Waikoloa Resort Area; admission per night $15-25) This early November hula competition includes *kahiko* (ancient), *'auana* (modern) and *kupuna* (elder) categories. A decent alternate to the sell-out Merrie Monarch Festival in Hilo around Easter.

🛏 Sleeping

Waikoloa Beach Marriott
Hotel $$$

(☎888-924-5656, 886-6789; www.waikoloa beachmarriott.com; 69-275 Waikoloa Beach Dr; r $200-450; ⓟ❄@🛜🏊) This airy, 555-room hotel fronts 'Anaeho'omalu Bay and thus boasts an awesome beach setting, plus three oceanfront pools. Renovated in late 2013, rooms feature quality beds (down comforters and high-count linens), tastefully muted decor and standard amenities, from cable TV to refrigerator.

Internet access is wi-fi in public areas and wired in rooms. Book ahead and online for deep discounts. There's a resort fee of $25 per day.

Hilton Waikoloa Village
Resort $$$

(☎886-1234, 800-221-2424; www.hilton waikoloavillage.com; 425 Waikoloa Beach Dr; r from $225; ⓟ❄@🛜🏊) You'll either love or hate the showy, theme-park features of this 62-acre, 1240-room megahotel. There's no natural beach, so its highlights are manmade. Rooms are comfy enough but they're standard business class and neither luxury nor oceanfront. Due to sheer property size, getting around can be a hike and service somewhat impersonal.

The hotel is showing its age, but its larger-than-life decor could be a diversion for kids, with its monorail and boats navigating between three towers. Visitors must shell out $15/21 per day for self/valet parking. and $25 per day for resort fees.

🍴 Eating

Increase your dining options at Kings' Shops and Queens' MarketPlace, both located near the resort areas, and at Waikoloa Highlands Shopping Center, across the highway in Waikoloa Village. On Wednesdays, another option is the **Waikoloa Kings' Shops Farmers Market** (Kings' Shops; 🕗8:30am-3pm Wed), which sells locally grown and produced edibles.

Island Gourmet Markets
Market $

(Queens' MarketPlace; ☎886-3577) Spectacularly maintained and stocked, this is a one-stop shop for takeout food, freshly

99

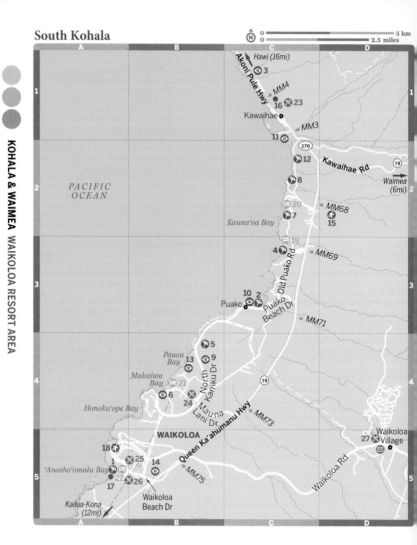

made sushi, basic and specialty groceries, magazines, gifts and more. There's a small patio for diners. A great option for healthy eats.

Inside the market, a little sushi bar called **Sushi Shiono** (☎886-3588; www. sushishiono.com; Queens' MarketPlace; ⊙7am-11pm) prepares rolls and *nigiri* (oblong-shaped sushi) by request, as well as packs to go.

Waikoloa Village Market   Supermarket $

(☎883-1088; 68-3916 Paniolo Ave, Waikoloa Highlands Shopping Center; ⊙6am-9pm) Located *mauka* of the highway in Waikoloa Village, this branch of the excellent KTA Super Stores is a full-service grocery store with deli, bakery and ATM.

Pueo's Osteria   Italian $$

(☎339-7566; http://pueososteria.com; 68-1845 Waikoloa Rd, Waikoloa Highlands Shopping Center; pizzas $14-18, mains $17-29; ⊙5pm-midnight

South Kohala

Mon-Sat, 8:30am-1:30pm & 5-9pm Sun) Run by a former top resort chef, this hidden gem will satisfy your cravings for gourmet-rustic Italian fare: pizzas, pastas and classics, including a yummy gorgonzola gnocchi. Everything is homemade and it's obvious. The Sunday brunch menu, from lemon-ricotta pancakes to a cherrywood bacon BLT, surpasses the standard buffet line.

Located in the Waikoloa Highlands Shopping Center, inland of the highway.

Sansei Seafood Restaurant & Sushi Bar
Japanese $$$

(☏886-6286; www.sanseihawaii.com; Queens' MarketPlace; mains $25-45, rolls $5-20; ⏲5:30-10pm, to 1am Fri & Sat) Local celebrity chef DK Kodama is known for innovative, fusion Japanese cuisine, such as his signature flash-fried ahi roll, and an extensive wine list. This newest branch might be a letdown to fans, with inconsistent service and less impressive execution. But it's worth a try, especially with the fantastic

50% early-bird discount. Free karaoke on Friday and Saturday after 10pm.

Roy's Waikoloa Bar & Grill
Hawaii Regional Cuisine **$$$**

(☎886-4321; www.roysrestaurant.com; Kings' Shops; mains $30-35; ⏰5:30-9:30pm) Always ridiculously bustling and noisy, Roy's will either delight or disappoint. We suggest that you focus on the food and not the atmosphere or sketchy service. The main courses, such as rack of lamb in a *liliko'i* (passion fruit) cabernet sauce or blackened ahi with pickled ginger, are less than cutting-edge today, but they generally don't disappoint.

Merriman's Market Cafe
Mediterranean **$$$**

(☎886-1700; www.merrimanshawaii.com; Kings' Shops; mains $20-30; ⏰11:30am-9:30pm) Foodies from sophisticated cities might find the Mediterranean-inspired fare unremarkable, but the kitchen does feature organic, island-grown produce and fresh local fish. Lunch is better value, with salads, sandwiches, pizzas and pastas under $20. Compared with the Waimea flagship, this alfresco cafe is more casual, affordable and touristy.

⭐ Entertainment

For nightlife, check **Waikoloa Nights** (www.waikoloanights.com) for special events, from rock concerts to hula shows. Free early-evening concerts featuring slack key guitar, ukulele and hula can be had at the Kings' Shops and Queens' MarketPlace shopping malls.

Waikoloa Beach Marriott Sunset Luau
Luau

(☎886-6789; www.waikoloabeachmarriott.com; 69-275 Waikoloa Beach Dr; adult/child 6-12yr $97/43; ⏰5pm Wed & Sat) This oceanfront luau features a Hawaiian-style dinner buffet, open bar and various Polynesian perfomances, including the Samoan fire dance.

Left: 'Anaeho'omalu Beach Park (p96); Below: Hilton Waikoloa Village (p99)
(LEFT) DANITA DELIMONT/GETTY IMAGES ©; (BELOW) WATERFALL WILLIAM/GETTY IMAGES ©

Legends of the Pacific
Luau

(☎ 886-1234; www.hiltonwaikoloavillage.com/dining/luau.cfm; Hilton Waikoloa Village; adult/child 5-12yr/senior & teen 13-18yr $109/54/99; ⏱ 5:30pm Tue, Fri & Sun) The 'Legends of the Pacific' luau show features various South Pacific dances and includes a dinner buffet and one cocktail.

Mauna Lani Resort Area

Constructed in 1983 by a Japanese company, the Mauna Lani Resort Area resembles its neighbors, with high-end hotels, condos and golf courses. But it deserves special attention for its significant historical sites and for the Mauna Lani Bay Hotel & Bungalows' open attitude toward nonguests who come to explore its fishponds and trails.

Beaches

The best beaches for swimming or snorkeling are small and located around the two large hotels.

The beach fronting the Mauna Lani Bay Hotel & Bungalows is protected and relatively calm, but the water is shallow. Just 10 minutes south of the hotel by foot, In **Makaiwa Bay**, there's a small, calm lagoon fronting the Mauna Lani Beach Club condo. To get here, park at the hotel and walk south along the path past the fishponds.

One mile south of the hotel, there's a small salt-and-pepper beach at **Honoka'ope Bay**. When seas are calm, swimming and snorkeling are fine but not fantastic. The resort development fronting the beach reserves 20 daily parking spaces for nonresidents. To get here, drive toward the golf courses, turn left at Honoka'ope Pl and check in at the entry gate.

Located at the Fairmont Orchid, **Pauoa Bay** is an excellent, little-known snorkeling spot, which unfortunately is accessible only to hotel guests.

Holoholokai Beach Park   Beach

(⊙6:30am-6:30pm) Forget about sand and swimming here. Instead enjoy picnicking and strolling at this pleasantly uncrowded beach, blanketed by chunks of white coral and black lava. Facilities include restrooms, showers, drinking water, picnic tables and grills.

To get here, take Mauna Lani Dr and veer right at the circle; turn right on the marked road immediately before the Fairmont Orchid. The trail to the Puako petroglyphs starts here.

◎ Sights

Puako Petroglyph
Preserve   Historic Site

With more than 3000 petroglyphs, this preserve is among the largest collections of ancient lava carvings in Hawaii. The simple pictures might not make sense to you, but viewed altogether, they are fascinating and worth a visit.

The three-quarter-mile walk from Holoholokai Beach Park to the preserve adds to the experience: take the well-marked trail at the parking lot. The walk is easy but rocky; wear sturdy footwear and expect blazing sun.

Kalahuipua'a Historic
Trail   Historic Site

(68-1400 Mauna Lani Dr, Mauna Lani Bay Hotel & Bungalows; P) ✎ FREE The first segment of this easy trail meanders through a 16th-century Hawaiian settlement, passing **lava tubes** once used as cave shelters and a few other archaeological and geological sites marked by interpretive plaques.

The trail then skirts ancient **fishponds** lined with coconut palms and continues out to the beach, where there's a thatched shelter with an outrigger canoe and a **historic cottage**. Continue southwest past the cottage to loop

around the fishponds and back to the start (about 1.5 miles, round-trip).

Located on Mauna Lani Bay Hotel & Bungalows grounds, this trail starts at a marked parking lot opposite the hotel convenience store.

Kalahuipua'a
Fishponds   Historic Site

✎ These ancient fishponds are among the island's few remaining working fishponds and, as in ancient times, they're stocked with *awa* (Hawaiian milk fish). Water circulates from the ocean through traditional *makaha* (sluice gates), which allow small fish to enter, but keep mature, fattened catch from escaping.

To access the fishponds directly (without taking the trail), exit the lobby of Mauna Lani Bay Hotel & Bungalows and go south toward the beach.

◉ Activities

Mauna Lani Sea
Adventures   Water Sports

(☎885-7883; http://maunalaniseaadventures.com; 68-1400 Mauna Lani Dr, Mauna Lani Bay Hotel & Bungalows; snorkeling tour adult/child 3-12yr $99/45, whale-watching cruise $85/45) For snorkeling, whale-watching and diving tours, this outfit offers almost daily tours at decent prices. While Kailua-Kona is the Big Island's hub for snorkeling and scuba diving, the waters off Mauna Lani are excellent and much less crowded. You can also try stand up padding (SUP; rental and instruction $30/50 per 30/60 minutes).

Francis I'i Brown North &
South Golf Courses   Golf

(☎885-6655; 68-1400 Mauna Lani Dr, Mauna Lani Bay Hotel & Bungalows; green fees guest/nonguest $165/215) Mauna Lani boasts two world-class golf courses. The **South course** is more scenic and popular, with its signature 15th hole featuring a tee shot over crashing surf. The **North course** is more challenging and interesting, however, with a par-three 17th hole within an amphitheater of black lava rock.

🛏 Sleeping

Mauna Lani Bay Hotel
& Bungalows   Resort $$$

(📞808-885-6622, 800-367-2323; www.mau
nalani.com; 68-1400 Mauna Lani Dr; r from $400;
P❄️📶♿) 🌿 The 342-room Mauna Lani
has a loyal clientele for unfussy vibe and
commitment to Hawaiian cultural stewardship. The grounds feature well-tended
tropical gardens, hundreds of towering
coconut palms and precious historic
sites. Geared more for couples than kids,
this is a solid upscale, if shy of luxurious,
hotel.

Rates include basic services (eg
parking, phone, internet access). Eco
policies include use of solar power,
drought-resistant grass and recycled
water for irrigation. The **Mauna Lani
Spa** (📞881-7922; www.maunalani.com;
68-1400 Mauna Lani Dr, Mauna Lani Bay
Hotel & Bungalows; massages & facials from
$159; ⏰treatments 10am-4pm) boasts
lush landscaping and a lava-rock
sauna; treatments are pricey, perhaps
overpriced, but a memorable splurge.

Fairmont Orchid   Hotel $$$

(📞866-54004474, 885-2000; www.fairmont.
com/orchid-hawaii; 1 North Kaniku Dr; r $360-
700; P❄️@📶♿) Elegant and almost
formal (for Hawai'i), the Orchid never lets
you forget that you're at an exclusive,
luxury hotel. The architecture feels rather
continental, but the meticulously maintained grounds are buoyantly tropical.
The 540 rooms are clean, modern and
comfortable.

Amenities, such as in-room internet
access ($14.50 per day), are rather
pricey. Spa fans can experience outdoor
treatments at **Spa Without Walls** (📞887-
7540; www.fairmont.com/orchid; 1 North Kaniku
Dr, Fairmont Orchid; massages & facials from
$169; ⏰7am-6pm), hidden amid orchids,
palms and waterfalls.

1 WHAT ARE HAWAI'I'S MOST HISTORICALLY SIGNIFICANT SITES?

Accessible heiau, such as Pu'ukohola Heiau
(p110), Mo'okini Luakini Heiau (p115), and
Pu'uhonua O Hōnaunau (p77), are foremost. I'd
also recommend visiting Hulihe'e Palace (p35) in
Kailua-Kona and Hawai'i Volcanoes National Park
(p208). Waipi'o Valley (p152) is also impressive,
not only for preservation of *kalo* (taro) culture
but because it was once the seat of this island's
government.

2 WHAT'S A HAWAIIAN TRADITION THAT CONTINUES TODAY?

Hawaiians always shared their bounty. No one
went hungry. It was not quite barter, but more
like mutual gift giving. If you grew taro in Waipi'o
Valley and I had well-stocked fishponds, we would
exchange and thus enjoy both. Likewise, today
we never arrive for family visits empty-handed.
I might go to Honolulu taking dried *'opelu* [pan-
sized mackerel scad] and poi, and return with dim
sum from Chinatown.

3 WHAT DOES ALOHA REALLY MEAN?

The word 'aloha' is a sacred Hawaiian word:
'Alo' means being in the presence of another
(or of the Supreme Creator, God). *'Ha'* refers to
one's breath, life force or spirit. In the traditional
greeting between Hawaiians, two people would
come into each other's *alo,* touch nose to
nose, which is known as *honi ihu,* breathing
and sharing each other's *ha.* It was a spiritual
exchange.

4 HOW IS ALOHA USED TODAY?

The word 'aloha' is used lightly today,
to say hello and goodbye; but the profound
meaning of aloha is to share spirit with one
another.

Island Insights

In ancient Hawaii, the fish raised in fishponds were reserved for the *ali'i* (chiefs and royalty). Commoners who stole fish for their own consumption could be punished by death. When a chief wanted fish, the pond caretaker would simply net the biggest as they gathered for feeding. Sometimes, trained runners would transport fresh fish to distant royal tables. According to legend, they were wrapped in wet *limu* (seaweed) and arrived still wriggling, proof of freshness.

Eating

Foodland Farms Supermarket **$**
(☏887-6101; 68-1330 Mauna Lani Dr, Shops at Mauna Lani; ☉6am-11pm) Full-service gourmet supermarket with an impressive deli selection.

Monstera Japanese **$$**
(☏887-2711; www.monterasushi.com; 68-1330 Mauna Lani Dr; plates $16-30, sushi rolls $10-20; ☉5:30-10pm) Chef Norio Yamamoto left his namesake restaurant at the Fairmont Orchid to launch his own *izakaya* (Japanese pub) venue. It's a looser, cooler place, where the menu ranges from classic *nigiri* sushi and tuna *tataki* (tuna seared and seasoned with ginger) to sizzling plates of kimchi stir-fried pork loin and teriyaki chicken.

Brown's Beach House Hawaii Regional Cuisine **$$$**
(☏887-7368; 1 North Kaniku Dr, Fairmont Orchid; mains $40-60; ☉5:30-8:30pm Thu-Mon, til 9pm Tue & Wed) 🍽 Brown's remains a standout for those willing to pay. Expect gracious service and the finest local ingredients: the 'Sustainable Seafood Trio' features *shutome* (swordfish), mahimahi and *ono* (wahoo) from Kona waters, short ribs are braised with Kona coffee and the creamy risotto includes five types of Hamakua mushrooms.

Puako Petroglyph Preserve (p104)

LASZLO PODOR PHOTOGRAPHY/GETTY IMAGES

Canoe-House Hawaii Regional **$$$**
(☎881-7911; 68-1400 Mauna Lani Dr, Mauna Lani Bay Hotel & Bungalows; mains $35-44; ⏱6-9pm) 🍴 The Mauna Lani's flagship restaurant showcases local ingredients creatively, but simply. Those seeking a huge punch might find the dishes lackluster. A decadent option is the 'Captain's Table' (two to eight diners), a five-course meal specially designed in collaboration with the chef (per person $100). No complaints about the setting and service.

🍷 Drinking & Entertainment

Luana Lounge Bar
(☎885-2000; 1 North Kaniku Dr, Fairmont Orchid; ⏱4-11pm) A nice spot to unwind at sunset, with specialty drinks and tapas (small plates). The fish or burger sliders (three per order for under $20) make for a light, relatively affordable meal.

Gathering of the Kings Luau
(☎326-4969; http://www.gatheringoftheking-ings.com; Fairmont Orchid; adult/child 6-12yr $99/65; ⏱Sat from 4.30pm) This luau spins a thread of storytelling to highlight slightly modernized versions of Polynesian and Hawaiian dance and music. It's notable for its above-average Polynesian dinner buffet and an open bar.

Puako

POP 772

Puako, a longtime beach community, is essentially a mile-long row of homes. The single road through 'town' is marked with numerous 'shoreline access' points. To get here, turn *makai* down Puako Beach Dr between Mile 70 and Mile 71 markers. You'll pass the **Hokuloa United Church** on your right. This cute little seaside church was originally built in 1860.

Vacation rentals abound here. Check www.2papayas.com and www.hawaiianbeachrentals.com for listings.

The Best...
Kohala & Waimea for Kids

1 Horseback riding in Waimea or in North Kohala (p117)

2 Paddling with Kohala Kayak (p108)

3 Splashing around at Spencer Beach Park (p110)

4 Ziplining in Kapa'au (p116)

5 Exploring the Puako Tide Pools (p107)

6 Cooling off with shave ice at Anuenue (p111)

🏖 Beaches

Beach 69 Beach
(⏱7am-8pm; 👪) This lovely crescent of white sand is a local favorite but remains somewhat off the tourist radar. Both family-friendly and gay-friendly, the calm, protected waters are ideal for morning snorkeling. Around the boundary, shady trees provide welcome relief. Restrooms and showers are available; no lifeguards.

From Puako Beach Dr, take the first right turn onto Old Puako Rd. Find telephone pole No 71 (originally numbered No 69) to the left and park. Follow the 'road' to its end, and then tramp along the footpath that runs parallel to a wooden fence.

Puako Tide Pools Landmark
Puako is known for giant tide pools, some deep enough to shelter live coral and other marine life.There's no sandy beach, but a narrow strip of pulverized coral and lava covers the shore. It's ideal for beach walks and you might even see *honu* (sea turtles) sunning on the rocks.

To get to the pools, park along the road near one of six signposted 'beach access' paths.

🏃 Activities

For diving tours, book with Kawaihae-based Kohala Divers (p111).

Kohala Kayak   Kayaking
(☎882-4678; www.kohalakayak.org; 3hr tour $70; ⊙depart 9am) Paddle and snorkel in Puako's pristine, less-traveled waters with knowledgeable, customer-service-oriented guides. Water depth is about 20ft; swim through underwater arches 10ft below. All levels are welcome; pedal kayaks are available for more stability.

Hapuna Beach State Recreation Area

Hapuna Beach is world famous for its magnificent half-mile sweep of white powder sand and fabulously clear waters. In summer, waves are calm and allow good swimming, snorkeling and diving, although the fish population has woefully declined since the 1980s. When the surf's up in winter, bodyboarding is awesome, thanks to reliable swells from the northwest. In general, Hapuna waters are too choppy for tots or nonswimmers. Waves over 3ft should be left for experts; drownings are not uncommon here.

The restrooms and picnic area at this **state recreation area** (www.hawaiistateparks.org/parks/hawaii; ⊙gate 7am-8pm; P) can be crowded and, at worst, grungy. Lifeguards are on duty. For nonresidents, parking costs $5 per vehicle.

To get here, take Hapuna Beach Rd just south of the Mile 69 marker. Arrive early to snag a parking space and a good spot. Bring industrial-strength sunscreen because there's virtually no shade.

Stay overnight in one of six state-owned **A-frame cabins** (per night residents/nonresidents $30/50) near the beach, an awesome location for sunset watching. While rather makeshift for the price, each

sleeps four people on wooden platforms (bring your own bedding). Restrooms, showers and a cooking pavilion are available.

Mauna Kea Resort Area

The pioneering Mauna Kea development began in the early 1960s when the late Laurance Rockefeller obtained a 99-year lease on the land around Kauna'oa Bay from Richard Smart, owner of Parker Ranch. The Mauna Kea Beach Hotel was the first luxury hotel on the Neighbor Islands. 'Every great beach deserves a great hotel,' Rockefeller apparently said. Not everyone would agree, but he got his way here.

🏖 Beaches

Mauna Kea Beach   Beach
Crescent-shaped Kauna'oa Bay (nicknamed 'Mauna Kea Beach' after Rockefeller built his landmark hotel on it) is blanketed in powdery white sand, while the clear waters are calm and shallow (generally less than 10ft). Snorkeling is best at the north end along the rocky ledge. This wonderfully uncrowded beach is open to the public through 40 parking spaces set aside daily for nonguests. Arrive by 9am and stop at the entry gate for a parking pass and directions.

Mau'umae Beach   Beach
Lovely white sand, shady trees and glassy waters – this intimate beach can feel like your own. The downside: no restrooms. Plan accordingly and tread lightly on this locals' beach.

To get here, go toward Mauna Kea Beach Hotel, turn right on Kamahoi and cross two wooden bridges. Look for telephone pole No 22 on the left and park next to the other cars. Walk down the trail to the Ala Kahakai sign and turn left toward the beach. You can also walk here from Spencer Beach Park to the north.

Detour:
Ala Kahakai Trail from Kawaihae to Puako

For diehard sun worshippers, access South Kohala's signature beaches via a 6-mile stretch of the 175-mile **Ala Kahakai National Historic Trail** (www.nps.gov/alka/index.htm). You'll also cover pristine shoreline and natural anchialine ponds (pools of brackish water that provided drinking water to the ancients). You can start at any point along the way.

From the north, start at the southern end of Spencer Beach Park, where you'll pass thick kiawe groves until you reach Mau'umae Beach and eventually the Mauna Kea Resort Area, including the renowned golf course. After you navigate the Hapuna Beach, the trail continues down to Beach 69. The whole hike, especially the last leg, is scorching. Of course, you can turn back at any point.

Activities

Mauna Kea & Hapuna Golf Courses
Golf

(☎Hapuna Beach Prince Hotel 880-3000, Mauna Kea Beach Hotel 882-5400; www.princeresorts hawaii.com; Mauna Kea Beach Hotel, Hapuna Beach Prince Hotel; green fees Mauna Kea Golf Course guest/nonguest $230/255, Hapuna Golf Course $125) Designed by Robert Trent Jones, Sr, the **Mauna Kea course** is a 72-par championship course that consistently ranks among the top courses in the USA. The **Hapuna course** has a 700ft elevation gain and was designed by Arnold Palmer and Ed Seay.

Sleeping

Room rates vary significantly by season.

Hapuna Beach Prince Hotel
Hotel $$$

(☎880-1111, 888-977-4623; www.princeresorts hawaii.com; 62-100 Kauna'oa Dr; r $200-500; ❄🛜🏊) The Mauna Kea Beach Hotel's 'sister' hotel offers good value and a primo beach setting. The architectural design is rather heavy-handed and rooms could use a facelift, but they're clean and come with large bathrooms. This hotel shares amenities with Mauna Kea Beach, and buses transport guests between the two.

Mauna Kea Beach Hotel
Hotel $$$

(☎866-977-4589, 882-7222; www.maunakea beachhotel.com; 62-100 Mauna Kea Beach Dr; r $325-760; P❄🛜🏊) This grand hotel on the Gold Coast is understated, quietly confident of its reputation. At first glance it might not wow you, but there is history here, among loyal returning guests and longtime staff. Rooms are regularly renovated and nicely maintained. The hotel's crowning jewel, however, is simply its location on Kauna'oa Bay, arguably the island's best beach.

Entertainment

Mauna Kea Hawaiian Luau
Luau

(☎882-5707; www.princeresortshawaii.com; 62-100 Mauna Kea Beach Dr; adult/child 5-12yr $96/48; ⏱6pm Tue & Fri) This outdoor luau show features standard entertainment (thrilling fire dance, group hula) and gorgeous beach setting. Buffet is generous and above average.

Kawaihae & Around

Kawaihae is a drab port town, where fuel tanks and cargo containers give off an industrial vibe. There's noteworthy dining, a family beach and historic heiau (temple) toward the south. For an insider's view of Kawaihae, see the **Pacific Worlds Kawaihae** (www.pacificworlds.com/kawaihae) site.

🏖 Beaches

Spencer Beach Park
Beach

(🚻) Shallow, sandy and gentle, this beach lacks the dramatic sweep of Mauna Kea or Hapuna, but it's ideal for kids and popular with local families. Come to swim rather than to snorkel; the waters are slightly silty due to Kawaihae Harbor to the north.

Located off the Akoni Pule Hwy just north of the Mile 2 marker, the park has a lifeguard, picnic tables, barbecue grills, restrooms, showers, drinking water and campsites (permit required). The campsites are exposed and crowded together, but it's the best camping beach north of Kona.

👁 Sights

Pu'ukohola Heiau National Historic Site
Historic Site

(📞 882-7218; www.nps.gov/puhe; 62-3601 Kawaihae Rd; ⏰ 7:45am-4:45pm) 🍃 FREE
By 1790 Kamehameha the Great had conquered Maui, Lana'i and Moloka'i. But power over his home island of Hawai'i was a challenge. When told by a prophet that he'd rule all of the Hawaiian Islands if he built a heiau dedicated to his war god Kuka'ilimoku atop Pu'ukohola (Whale Hill) in Kawaihae, Kamehameha built this massive structure.

He and his men formed a human chain 20 miles long, transporting rocks hand to hand from Pololu Valley in North Kohala. After finishing the heiau by summer 1791, Kamehameha held a dedication ceremony and invited his cousin and rival Keoua, chief of Ka'u. When Keoua came ashore, he was killed and taken to the *luakini* heiau (temple of human sacrifice) as the first offering to the gods. With Keoua's death, Kamehameha took sole control of the Big Island and by 1810 ruled all Hawaiian Islands.

Back then Pu'ukohola Heiau was adorned with wooden *ki'i* (statues) and thatched structures, including an oracle tower, an altar, a drum house and shelter for the high priest. After Kamehameha's death in 1819, his powerful widow Ka'ahumanu and son Liholiho, who abolished the kapu (taboo) system, destroyed the deity images and the heiau was abandoned.

Today, only the basic rock foundation remains, but it's still a massive 224ft by 100ft, with 16ft- to 20ft-walls. To get here, turn *makai* off the Akoni Pule Hwy halfway between the Mile 2 and 3 markers.

Hamakua Macadamia Nut Company
Factory

(📞 888-643-6688, 882-1690; www.hawnnut.com; 61-3251 Maluokalani St; ⏰ 8am-5pm) 🍃 FREE
It's a tourist stop, but a darned good one, featuring a spanking-clean factory, gift shop and generous free samples.

Pu'ukohola Heiau National Historic Site
CASEY MAHANEY/GETTY IMAGES ©

Sacred Sites

Ancient Hawaiians built a variety of heiau (temples) for different gods and different purposes: healing the sick, sharing the harvest, changing the weather, offering human sacrifice and succeeding in warfare.

While some were modest thatched structures, others were enormous stone edifices, which today exist in eroded ruins that only hint at their original grandeur. After Kamehameha II (Liholiho) abolished the kapu (taboo) system in 1819, many were destroyed or abandoned. But on the Big Island, two of the largest and best-preserved heiau remain: Pu'ukohola Heiau (p110) and Mo'okini Luakini Heiau (p115).

Luakini heiau, for human sacrifice, were always dedicated to Ku, the war god. Only Ku deserved the greatest gift, a human life, and only the highest chiefs could order it. An enemy slain in battle was an acceptable sacrifice. But the victim had to be a healthy man, never a woman, a child or an aged or deformed man.

An eco-conscious company, it generates 75% of its energy needs from solar power and 10% from ground macnut shells. The Hamakua-grown nuts are excellent in quality and reasonably priced. To get here, turn *mauka* just north of the Mile 4 marker.

Activities

Kohala Divers Water Sports
(📞882-7774; www.kohaladivers.com; 61-3665 Akoni Pule Hwy, Kawaihae Shopping Center; 1-/2-/3-tank dive $100/139/239; ⏰8am-6pm) This longtime outfit leads excellent diving trips throughout Kohala waters, plus snorkeling and seasonal whale-watching. One memorable trip visits a *honu* (sea turtle) 'cleaning' station where the turtles allow fish to pick parasites off their bodies.

Sleeping & Eating

In this rural residential area, the only lodging options are B&Bs and vacation rentals.

Hale Ho'onanea B&B $$
(📞877-882-1653, 882-1653; www.houseofrelaxation.com; Ala Kahua Dr; ste $130; 📶) About 5 miles north of Kawaihae, find a terrific-value B&B suite atop peaceful grassy knolls 900ft above sea level. The Bamboo

Suite includes kitchenette, private lanai, satellite TV, wi-fi, high ceiling, hardwood floor and stunning 180-degree horizon view.

Anuenue Ice Cream $
(📞882-1109; Akoni Pule Hwy, Kawaihae Shopping Center; cones from $2.50, fast food $3.50) Since 1998, Tim Termeer has delighted all comers with snowy shave ice and premium ice cream. Among his 35 flavors are ginger lemongrass, citrus mint and lavender lemonade. He also offers hot dogs, veg burgers and chili bowls.

Kohala Burger & Taco Burgers, Mexican $
(📞880-1923; www.kohalaburgerandtaco.com; Akoni Pule Hwy, Kawaihae Shopping Center; mains under $10; ⏰11am-7pm Mon-Fri, to 4pm Sat & Sun) When only a real burger will do, come here for local grass-fed quarter-pounders with specialty toppings. But the real standouts are the fish tacos, quesadillas and dreamy shakes and malts.

Cafe Pesto International $$
(📞882-1071; www.cafepesto.com; Akoni Pule Hwy, Kawaihae Shopping Center; lunch $11-14, pizza $9-20, dinner mains $17-33; ⏰11am-9pm Sun-Thu, to 10pm Fri & Sat) This well-loved favorite, serving eclectic, innovative cuisine you might

KOHALA & WAIMEA NORTH KOHALA

call Mediterranean with an Asian twang or Italian with an island twist. Choose from curries and Greek salads, seafood risotto and smoked salmon alfredo, piping-hot calzones and thin-crust gourmet pizzas.

Blue Dragon Musiquarium   Hawaii Regional **$$$**

(☏808-882-7771; www.bluedragonhawaii.com; 61-3616 Kawaihae Rd; mains $18-36; ⏱5-10pm Wed-Thu & Sun, to 11pm Fri & Sat) This roofless restaurant under towering palms features great live music five nights a week, starting at 6pm. The cuisine is hard to pin down, from stir-fries to curries to rib-eye steaks, but generally good. It's a convivial, family-oriented place for dinner; later, the potent specialty cocktails might tempt you to the dance floor.

NORTH KOHALA

Rural North Kohala is a charming mix of farmers and artists, of Native Hawaiians and haole (Caucasian) transplants, of rustic storefronts and dream homes. It makes for a fantastic day trip (or serene retreat), but because it's off the main highway, it remains a hidden gem.

Geologically the oldest part of the Big Island, North Kohala is the birthplace of King Kamehameha I and is rich in ancient history. In modern times, this region was sugar country until the Kohala Sugar Company closed in 1975. Today, Hawi and Kapa'au contain just enough art galleries, boutiques and distinctive eateries to succeed as tourist attractions.

North Kohala

At the road's end, time and the elements have carved the lush landscape into dramatic contours, culminating in Pololu Valley, the jewel of North Kohala.

This region has virtually no bus service, so driving is your only option.

Hawi & Around

POP 1081

Hawi (hah-*vee*) can fit all of its businesses within two blocks, but it looms large in picturesque charm, notable restaurants and shopping treasures. Mainland transplants are bringing big money to little Hawi and leading its transformation from boondocks to tourist destination. But it still offers only basic services, such as a post office, grocery store and gas station. Thank goodness, say the residents.

There are two ways to get here: the coastal **Akoni Pule Hwy** (Hwy 270) and the mountainous **Kohala Mountain Road** (Hwy 250). The latter is arguably the Big Island's best scenic drive, affording stupendous views of the coastline and three majestic volcanic mountains: Mauna Kea, Mauna Loa and Hualalai.

To experience both routes, go north to Hawi on the Akoni Pule Hwy, which navigates a region largely undeveloped and with spectacular views of the Pacific (and Maui in the distance). Just south of the Mile 14 marker, **Lapakahi State Historical Park** (☎882-6207; ⊙8am-4pm, closed state holidays) 🅿 **FREE** re-creates an ancient fishing village along an unshaded, 1-mile loop trail. Nothing is elaborately presented, so you need a wild imagination to appreciate the modest remains.

Further along, **Mahukona Beach Park** and **Kapa'a Beach Park** are fine for picnicking and sunset watching, but too rocky and rough for swimming.

On your return, go south on Kohala Mountain Rd, which gives more opportunity to witness the spectacular panorama. This road is called Hawi Rd close to town.

🛌 Sleeping

Kohala Village Inn
Inn **$**

(☎889-0404; www.kohalavillageinn.com; 55-514 Hawi Rd; r $75-85, ste $130; 🛜) For budget travelers or those seeking digs in the heart of Hawi, this inn offers terrific value. In a plantation-era, motel-style building, no-frills rooms are clean and cozy, with wood-plank floors, pleasant lighting and cable TV.

Walls are rather thin and there's no view, but it's a fine place to rest your head.

Hawi Plantation House B&B
B&B $$

(☎(888) 465-8565; www.hawiplantationhouse bandb.com; r $169-249; 🛜) In a magnificently restored plantation house, choose from six lovely bedrooms of various sizes and sleeping configurations. All are smartly appointed and share a kitchen, a laundry room, a swimming pool, a gym and a tennis court.

Kohala Lodge
Vacation Rental $$$

(☎884-5105; www.vacationhi.com; 56-867 Kamalei St; $225-300; 🛜) Tucked away in a treeline with sweeping views, this reproduction 19th-century *paniolo* (Hawaiian cowboy) ranchhouse (formerly known as Cabin in the Treeline) is unique in every way. The owner has showered attention to every architectural detail, from the lava rock fireplace to the period plumbing to retro-style appliances (that are actually high tech).

The house is located about 2 miles from Hawi, off Kohala Mountain Rd. Rates vary depending on season and number of guests. Book well in advance.

Puakea Ranch
Vacation Rental $$$

(☎315-0805; www.puakearanch.com; 56-2864 Akoni Pule Hwy; cottages $289-799; 🛜♨) Dreaming of a secluded country estate? Live the dream in one of four meticulously restored cottages. Ranging from two to six bedrooms, each cottage enjoys its own bucolic grounds and includes kitchen, laundry facilities, and detached bathhouse with Japanese-style *furo* hot tub.

Striking just the right balance of luxury and authenticity, Puakea Ranch offers a unique alternative to the Gold Coast resorts. Located off a gated dirt road 3 miles from Hawi center.

Hawaii Island Retreat
Inn $$$

(☎889-6336; www.hawaiiislandretreat.com; At Ahu Pohaku Ho'omaluhia; r $425-500; 🛜♨) 🌿 Modern-day seekers with money are the target audience for this high-end, off-the-grid, organic retreat center on 50 gorgeous acres. Here, leaving urban life behind doesn't mean giving up creature comforts, from spa services to an infinity pool. In addition to nine spacious rooms in the cliffside villa, there are seven yurts (per night $195).

Sushi Rock restaurant

Detour:
Mo'okini Luakini Heiau

Remote and strangely moving, **Mo'okini Luakini Heiau** (📞373-8000; 🕐9am-8pm, closed Wed) 🎫**FREE**, near 'Upolu Point, is among the oldest (c AD 480) and most historically significant Hawaiian sites. Measuring about 250ft by 125ft, with walls 6ft high, the massive stone ruins sit solitary and brooding on a windswept grassy plain.

According to legend, the heiau was built from 'sunrise to first light' by up to 18,000 'little people' passing stones in complete silence from Pololu Valley – 14 miles away – under the supervision of Kuamo'o Mo'okini.

Five hundred years later Pa'ao, a priest from Samoa, raised the walls to 30ft and rebuilt the altar as his *ho'okupu* (offering) to the gods. He initiated human sacrifice, making this the first *luakini* heiau (human sacrifice temple).

In 1963 the National Park Service designated Mo'okini Heiau as Hawaii's first registered National Historic Landmark. Fifteen years later, it was deeded to the state. In 1978, the *kahuna nui* (high priestess) Leimomi Mo'okini Lum, the seventh high priestess of the Mo'okini bloodline, lifted the kapu (taboo) that restricted access to the temple.

To get here, take Old Coast Guard Rd, between the Mile 18 and 19 markers for just over a mile. Turn right onto a red-cinder road, blocked by a locked cattle gate. Call ahead for the gate to be unlocked (this is state land); otherwise park here (without blocking the gate) and walk 15 minutes to the heiau. There's an alternate route if you have 4WD: drive toward 'Upolu Airport, then turn south onto the gutted coastal road, which is impassable after rains.

🍴 Eating

Takata Store   Supermarket $
(📞889-5413; Akoni Pule Hwy; 🕐8am-7pm Mon-Sat, to 1pm Sun) For groceries, try this well-stocked, family-run market between Hawi and Kapa'au.

Kohala Coffee Mill   Cafe $
(📞889-5577; 55-3412 Akoni Pule Hwy; drinks $2-4, sandwiches $6-10; 🕐6am-6pm Mon-Fri, 7am-6pm Sat & Sun) A comfy place to hang out and treat yourself to muffins, fresh-brewed Kona coffee and heavenly Tropical Dreams ice cream. For breakfast, the souffléd eggs with cheese, onion, tomato, pesto and/or bacon is a winner.

Sushi Rock   Sushi $$$
(📞889-5900; www.sushirockrestaurant.net; 55-3435 Akoni Pule Hwy; sushi rolls $7-19, mains $18-32; 🕐noon-3pm & 5:30-8pm Sun-Tue & Thu, to 9pm Fri & Sat) This ever-popular sushi bar is famous for its fusion tropical sushi rolls, which might include papaya, mac nuts, Fuji apple or goat cheese. The menu also includes vegetarian/vegan rolls, creative salads and sandwiches, plus a wild selections of cocktails. Staff go out of their way to serve. Arrive early.

Bamboo   Hawaii Regional Cuisine $$$
(📞889-5555; Akoni Pule Hwy, Kohala Trade Center; lunch $11-16, dinner $25-35; 🕐11:30am-2:30pm Tue-Sun, 6-8pm Tue-Sat; 🍴) Like a once-cool, now-retro aunt, this local icon is lovable and impossible to ignore. It's a winning combination, but don't expect innovation or mind-blowing dining. That said, the food is fine and the inviting interior – suspended Balinese umbrellas, twinkling Christmas lights and warm wood walls – is cheerful and pure Hawi.

Don't miss checking out the gallery upstairs.

🔒 Shopping

Living Arts Gallery   Arts & Crafts
(www.livingartsgallery.net; 55-3435 Akoni Pule Hwy; ⏱10:30am-5pm, to 8pm Fri) To appreciated the Big Island's extraordinary amount of artistic talent, come to this artists co-op. Members staff the gallery, giving you firsthand contact with some of the 65 artists represented here.

L Zeidman Gallery   Arts & Crafts
(Hwy 270; ⏱10am-5pm) The exquisitely crafted, museum-quality wood bowls made by the owner are mesmerizing en masse. Take one home for $150 to $2500.

Hawi Gallery   Music
(☎206-235-1648; www.hawigallery.com; 55-3406 Akoni Pule Hwy; ⏱10am-5pm Mon-Sat, 11am-3pm Sun) The ukulele as a work of art? Definitely, as this fascinating collection proves. In addition to gorgeous classics, check out the Cuban model made from a cigar box and the curvaceous Polk-a-lay-lee, a rare

1960s promotional item from a Chicago furniture store.

Elements   Jewelry, Accessories
(www.elementsjewelryandcrafts.com; 55-3413 Akoni Pule Hwy; ⏱10am-6pm) This jewelry and gift shop carries an eclectic collection of locally made finery.

Kapa'au
POP 1734

Kapa'au is another former sugar town refashioned into an attractive tourist destination. Although more scattered than Hawi, Kapa'au has a few good eateries and serves as a meeting point for several outdoor adventure tours.

🏖 Beaches

Keokea Beach Park   Beach
(off Akoni Pule Hwy; ⏱gate 7am-11pm) While it has no beach to speak of, this park about 3.5 miles from Kapa'au has the best picnic spot around: an elevated pavilion with smashing views of a rocky bay and the motley crew of local surfers brave enough to test its dangerous shore breaks and strong currents.

Besides picnic tables, there are BBQ grills, showers, drinking water and portable toilets. The marked turnoff is about 1.5 miles before the Pololu Valley Lookout.

⊙ Sights

Kamehameha the Great Statue   Monument

The statue on the front lawn of the North Kohala Civic Center has a famous twin in Honolulu, standing across from Iolani Palace. The Kapa'au one was the original, constructed

Kamehameha the Great statue
CHEL BEESON/GETTY IMAGES ©

Ranch Life

Windswept pastureland. Grazing cattle. Cloud-dappled skies. North Kohala makes city slickers yearn to be a *paniolo* (cowboy), at least for a day. These working ranches give you that chance. Also see Hawaii Paso Finos (p118) in Kapa'au.

For horseback riding, **Paniolo Riding Adventures** (☎889-5354; www.panioloadventures.com; Kohala Mountain Rd; rides $69-159) offers a variety of rides (short, long, picnic and sunset) across 17-sq-mile Ponoholo Ranch and accommodates all levels. Horses are matched to a rider's level. This is the best choice for experienced riders. Boots, hats, chaps and jackets are provided.

Na'alapa Stables (☎889-0022; www.naalapastables.com; Kahua Ranch Rd; rides $65-85) offers rides across the pastures of 13-sq-mile Kahua Ranch, with nice views of the coast from its 3200ft elevation. Group rides are adjusted to the level of the least-experienced rider, so most rides are nose-to-tail.

If a down-home country barbecue is more your style, join the Richards family of **Kahua Ranch** (☎882-7954; www.exploretheranch.com; Kahua Ranch Rd; with transportation $119, without $95, child 6-11yr half price, under 5yr free; ☺6-9pm Wed summer, 5:30-8:30pm Wed winter; 👫) for a hearty buffet dinner (including beer) followed by country music, line dancing, a campfire and Piggly Wiggly, the performing pig. The sprawling pastureland is perfect for sunset watching and stargazing by telescope.

---

in 1880 in Florence, Italy, by American sculptor Thomas Gould. When the ship delivering it sank off the Falkland Islands, a duplicate statue was cast from the original mold and erected in downtown Honolulu in 1883. Later the sunken statue was recovered and sent here, to Kamehameha's childhood home.

Kamehameha Rock   Landmark

According to legend, Kamehameha carried this rock uphill from the beach to demonstrate his prodigious strength. Much later, when a road crew attempted to move it elsewhere, the rock stubbornly fell off the wagon – a sign that it wanted to stay put. Not wanting to upset Kamehameha's mana (spiritual essence), the workers left it alone. Don't blink or you'll miss it, on the inland roadside about 2 miles east of Kapa'au, on a curve just past a small bridge.

🎯 Activities

Kohala Zipline   Ziplining

(☎331-3620; www.kohalazipline.com; 54-3676 Akoni Pule Highway; adult/child 8-12 $159/$139) Once you're up in the trees, you stay up for the whole canopy tour, which includes nine easy zips, five elevated suspension bridges between platforms, and two rappels. There are no superlong zips, but also no walking between elements. The course is built to blend with nature and cause no harm to trees.

Max eight per group; mandatory weight range 70lb to 270lb (kids must be at least eight years). A dozen three-hour tours go out daily.

Big Island Eco
Adventures   Ziplining

(☎889-5111; www.thebigislandzipline.com; 53-496 'Iole Rd; $169) The forest wilderness near Pololu Valley is a perfect setting for zipping, which you do eight times on this excellent tour, which also includes one

117

Below: Lei drape the Kamehameha the Great statue to commemorate the North Kohala Kamehameha Day Celebration; **Right:** Kahua Ranch (p117)

(BELOW) DANITA DELIMONT/GETTY IMAGES ©; (RIGHT) PETER FRENCH/GETTY IMAGES ©

suspension bridge beside a 60ft waterfall. The three-hour tour departs at least four times daily. Max 10 per group; mandatory weight range 90lb to 250lb.

Meet a half-mile up 'Iole Rd and then ride a 6WD military vehicle to the course.

Hawaii Paso Finos
Horseback Riding

(instructional tours $85-130) Paso Finos are the smoothest-riding horses in the world. Experience their bounceless gait and engaging demeanor in private or small-group activities. Learn horsemanship, riding, therapeutic communication and even yoga on horseback. A unique option for experienced equestrians.

Kohala Ditch Adventures
Kayaking

(☎ 888-288-7288, 889-6000; www.kohaladitch adventures.com; 53-324 Lighthouse Rd, btwn Mile 24 & 25; adult/child 5-11yr $139/75; ⊙ 7-11am & 12:15-4pm Mon-Sat) After an off-road

excursion by Pingauer, a six-wheel Austrian military vehicle, you embark on a leisurely 2.5-mile kayaking trip through historic plantation irrigation ditches or flumes, including 10 tunnels. Guides are well-versed in island history. A unique culture journey, not a fast-paced action adventure.

Kamehameha Park & Golf Learning Center
Swimming, Golf

(☎ golf center 345-4393, gym 889-6505, pool 889-6933; 54-540 Kapa'au Rd; ⊙ pool 10-11:45am, 1-4:45pm, golf 8am-7pm, gym noon-8pm Mon-Thu, 7:45am-4:30pm Fri, 10am-4pm Sat) This county park includes a huge pool (call for schedule updates), tennis courts, gym with basketball courts and weight room, and playground. In back there's a privately run six-hole golf learning center where you can rent equipment and play all day for $10.

KOHALA & WAIMEA KAPA'AU

🎇 Festivals & Events

Kohala Country Fair
Fair

(www.kohalacountryfair.com; Akoni Pule Hwy opposite 'Iole Rd) **FREE** This old-fashioned fair, held in the first week in October, brings together a smorgasbord of local artists and food, plus events including a Spam-carving contest, frog catching, equestrian demonstrations, tug of war and who knows what else.

North Kohala Kamehameha Day Celebration
Historic Celebration

(www.kamehamehadaycelebration.org) **FREE** On June 11 join islanders in honoring Kame-hameha the Great in his birthplace. The spectacular parade of floral-bedecked horseback riders and floats culminates in an all-day gathering with music, crafts, hula and food.

🛏️ Sleeping

Kohala Club Hotel
Inn $

(☎889-6793; www.kohalaclubhotel.com; 54-3793 Akoni Pule Hwy; r/cottage $56/90) Less than half a mile from Kapa'au, this laid-back inn offers clean rooms with private bathrooms for an unbelievable price. The main house contains four small, no-frills rooms with either a queen bed or two twins. The two-bedroom cottage is perfect for families.

Kohala Country Adventures Guest House
Inn $$

(☎866-892-2484, 889-5663; www.kcadventures.com; off Akoni Pule Hwy; r $85-175; 🛜) For country livin', try this relaxed, lived-in house on 10 acres of ungroomed tropical gardens, with fruit trees, livestock and coastal views. The Sundeck Suite is comfy for families, with kitchenette, three beds and an open loft layout. Host Bobi Moreno puts everyone at ease.

Island Insights

South of Mo'okini Heiau is the apparent **site of Kamehameha's birth**, marked by stone-walled foundations. According to legend, when Kamehameha was born on a stormy winter night in 1758, his mother received a kahuna's prophecy that her son would be a powerful ruler and conquer all the islands. Upon hearing this, the high chief of Hawai'i ordered all male newborns killed. Thus, after Kamehameha was taken to the Mo'okini Heiau for his birth rituals, he was spirited away into hiding.

To get here, turn *makai* (seaward) on the dirt road about a quarter-mile south of Mo'okini Heiau.

🍴 Eating

Nambu Courtyard   Cafe $
(📞889-5546; 54-3885 Akoni Pule Hwy; mains $9-12; ⏰6:30am-2:30pm Mon-Fri, 7am-noon Sun) Pleasantly low-key, this owner-run cafe serves freshly made salads and sandwiches, espresso drinks and an unbelievable blueberry bread pudding. With lots of seating, indoor and outdoor, it manages to be both airy and cozy.

Gill's Lanai   Cafe $
(📞315-1542; 54-3866 Akoni Pule Hwy; mains $6-9; ⏰11am-5pm) With its umbrella-shaded patio and tiny kitchen, this avocado-colored road-side cafe offers a beach vibe and yummy fish tacos. Other favorites include bowls of ahi *poke* (cubed, marinated raw fish) and veg quesadillas. Service can be slow.

Minnie's   Diner $
(📞889-5288; 54-3854 Akoni Pule Hwy; meals $7-9; ⏰11am-8pm Mon-Thu, 11am-3pm & 6-8:30pm Fri, 11am-3pm Sat) This local-favorite family restaurant serves up generous burgers, sandwiches and plate lunches including mahimahi, Korean chicken and the house specialty, roast pork.

Sushi to Go   Sushi $
(📞756-0132; 54-3877 Akoni Pule Hwy; rolls $6-10) Nothing fancy, just decent takeout sushi.

🔒 Shopping

Dunn Gallery   Arts & Crafts
(📞884-5808; dunngallerywoodart.com; 54-3862 Akoni Pule Hwy; ⏰10am-5pm Tue-Sat) Of the many wood art shops on the island, this one stands alone. The distinctive works here, gathered from 30 Big Island artists, represent a museum-quality collection. Contemporary, traditional, and functional pieces range from $20 to five figures.

Ackerman Galleries   Arts & Crafts
(📞889-5138; www.ackermangalleries.com; 55-3897 Akani Pule Hwy; ⏰10am-6pm) The Ackerman family has managed to combine art and commerce for 30 years. They have two galleries: the Gift Gallery has an excellent array of wooden bowls, glasswork and jewelry. Across the street, the Fine Art Gallery displays Gary Ackerman's impressionistic paintings of Hawaii and France (open from October to March and by request).

Rankin Gallery & Studio   Arts & Crafts
(📞889-6849; www.patricklouisrankin.net; 53-4380 Akoni Pule Hwy; ⏰11am-5pm Tue-Sat & noon-4pm Sun-Mon) Located midway between Pololu Valley and Kapa'au, this gallery is noted for its landscapes of Hawaii and the American West (and for the conviviality of Patrick Rankin, a local character happy to show you around his studio).

Also check out the adjacent Tong Wo Society building, a nicely restored temple that was once an opium den.

Pololu Valley

Marked by a row of mystical cliffs, this ancient valley is utterly memorable. It was once abundant with wetland taro, when Pololu Stream carried water from the deep, wet interior to the valley floor. When the Kohala Ditch was built in 1906, however, it diverted the water for sugar production. The valley's last residents left in the 1940s, and the area is now forest reserve.

The Akoni Pule Hwy ends at the Pololu Valley Lookout, the endpoint for those who do not hike down the trail.

🏃 Activities

Pololu Valley Lookout & Trail
Hiking

From the lookout, you can admire the spectacular coastline toward the east, but you must hike down to see Pololu Valley. The steep, rocky trail is doable for most, thanks to switchbacks and its 0.75-mile distance. Avoid trekking down after rainfall, since the mud-slicked rocks will be precarious. Makeshift walking sticks are often left at the trailhead. Parking is tight; there are no facilities.

At the mouth of the valley lies a rugged black-sand beach. The surf is rough, with rip currents year-round. Swimming is out of the question, even if you see local surfers testing the waves.

Hawaii Forest & Trail
Hiking, Swimming

(☏ 331-8505, 800-464-1993; www.hawaii-forest.com; adult/child under 12

The Best...
Fine Art in Kohala & Waimea

1 Isaacs Art Center (p123)

2 Gallery of Great Things (p129)

3 Living Arts Gallery (p116)

4 Dunn Gallery (p120)

$159/139) The Kohala Waterfalls Adventure includes a leisurely 1.5-mile loop trail to waterfalls (swimming included). Transportation from the Waikoloa Resort Area is included.

Parker Ranch (p127)
PETER FRENCH/GETTY IMAGES ©

Waimea (Kamuela)

Waimea (Kamuela)

◎ Sights
| 1 Isaacs Art Center | B2 |
| 2 WM Keck Observatory Office | C2 |

✦ Activities, Courses & Tours
| 3 Mountain Road Cycles | D1 |

🛏 Sleeping
| 4 Kamuela Inn | A2 |

✕ Eating
5 Aka Sushi Bar	C2
6 Big Island Brewhaus & Taqueria	D2
7 Hawaiian Style Cafe	A2
8 Healthways II	C3
9 KTA Super Store	C2
10 Lilikoi Cafe	C3

Merriman's	(see 11)
11 Pau	A2
12 Village Burger	C3
13 Waimea Coffee & Co	B2
14 Waimea Town Farmers Market	B2

◎ Entertainment
| 15 Kahilu Theatre | C3 |

🛍 Shopping
Gallery of Great Things	(see 13)
16 Parker Ranch Center	C3
17 Parker Square	B2
Reyn's	(see 8)
18 Waimea Center	C2
Waimea General Store	(see 13)

WAIMEA (KAMUELA)

POP 9212

The misty rolling pastureland surrounding Waimea is perhaps Hawai'i's most unexpected face. This is *paniolo* (cowboy) country, and nearly all of it, including Waimea itself, is controlled by Parker Ranch, the fifth-largest cow-calf ranch in the USA.

From the highway, all you see are suburban strip malls, but closer inspection finds an extraordinary art scene, wide-ranging dining options, a shopper's paradise and rich cowboy heritage. Then there's the variety of transplants, including organic farmers, astronomers, artists and retirees.

Geographically, the town is split into a 'dry side' (west) and a 'wet side' (east), with the town center at the intersection of Kawaihae Rd (Hwy 19) and Mamalahoa Hwy (Hwy 190) roughly marking the transition.

For visitors, Waimea makes a good base to explore Kohala, Mauna Kea and the Hamakua Coast. The 2670ft elevation and evening fog can spell relief, but be prepared for chilly nights.

From Hilo, Hwy 19 is commonly called the Mamalahoa Hwy or Hawai'i Belt Rd, but west of Hwy 190 it becomes Kawaihae Rd, while Hwy 190 continues as the Mamalahoa Hwy.

◎ Sights

Isaacs Art Center
Art Gallery

(☏885-5884; www.isaacsartcenter.hpa.edu; 61-1268 Kawaihae Rd; ☉10am-5pm Tue-Sat) FREE Set in a meticulously relocated 1915 schoolhouse, this series of bright, charming galleries displays a diverse collection of local and international fine art. The permanent collection features mostly renowned late masters, while the pieces for sale are by living artists. As you enter, take note of Herb Kawainui Kane's classic *The Arrival of Captain Cook at Kealakekua*

Bay in January 1779. Works include paintings, pottery, furniture, jewelry and Hawaiian arts.

For deep pockets seeking the ultimate gift, this gallery is not to be missed. All proceeds go to the Hawai'i Preparatory Academy Scholarship Fund.

Rare Hawaiian Honey Company
Farm Store

(☏775-1000, 888-663-6639; www.rareha-waiianhoney.com; 66-1250 Lalamilo Farm Rd; ☉9am-4pm Mon-Fri) ✎ Sample unusual honey (imagine a pearlescent butter) at this welcoming sales/tasting room. The 'Rare Hawaiian Organic Kiawe Honey' (8oz jar $17 to 18) comes from a forest of kiawe trees in Puako. The thriving family-run business is the brainchild of former lawyer Richard Spiegel, who in the mid-1970s began collaborating with bees and the sweet nectar of kiawe flowers.

Anna Ranch Heritage Center
Historic Site

(☏885-4426; www.annaranch.org; 65-1480 Kawaihae Rd; ☉10am-3pm Tue-Fri) The life and times of Hawaii's 'first lady of ranching,' Anna Leialoha Lindsey Perry-Fiske, are celebrated at this 14-room historic ranch

Black-sand beach in Pololu Valley (p121)

Island Insights

Waimea is also known as **Kamuela**, which is the Hawaiian spelling of Samuel, apparently for Samuel Parker of Parker Ranch. Maps generally list both names; the post office and phone book use Kamuela to distinguish this Waimea from those on O'ahu and on Kaua'i.

house, which contains impressive koa furniture, Anna's bountiful wardrobe and other memorabilia. Tours (10am and 1pm, $10) must be booked in advance. Located 1 mile west of town center.

Paniolo Heritage Center   Museum
(✆854-1541; www.paniolopreservation.org; Pukalani Rd; ⊙9am-4pm Wed) FREE The Paniolo Preservation Society is developing this museum at Pukalani Stables, where Parker Ranch once bred horses. It's a work in progress, currently housing a photo exhibit and a saddle-making operation. The real reward is the personal touch: staffers are happy to talk story about *paniolo* history.

Open on Wednesdays along with the Waimea Midweek Market (p127).

**WM Keck Observatory
Office**   Visitor Center
(✆885-7887; www.keckobservatory.org; 65-1120 Mamalahoa Hwy; ⊙10am-2pm Tue-Fri) The lobby of this working office is open to the public. See models of the twin 33ft Keck telescopes, fascinating photos and a telescope trained on Mauna Kea. Informative volunteers prep you for a trip to the Mauna Kea summit.

Church Row   Churches
FREE Home to Christians, Buddhists and Mormons, Church Row is a living history of religious life on the island. There are several noteworthy, if humble, structures along this curved street, including the much-photographed, all-Hawaiian **Ke**

Ola Mau Loa Church. Look for the green steeple.

Next door is **Imiola Congregational Church**, Waimea's first Christian church, which originated as a grass hut in 1830 and was built entirely of koa in 1857. Here lies the grave of missionary Lorenzo Lyons, who arrived in 1832 and spent 54 years in Waimea. He wrote many hymns in Hawaiian, including the classic 'Hawai'i Aloha.'

🏃 Activities

**Dahana Ranch
Roughriders**   Horseback Riding
(✆888-399-0057, 885-0057; www.dahanaranch.com; 90min ride adult/child $80/70; ⊙rides 9am, 11am, 1pm & 3pm) Ride American quarter horses bred, raised and trained by third- and fourth-generation *paniolo*. On offer are open-range rides for kids as young as three, but also advanced rides for those who can canter. The ranch, owned and operated by a Native Hawaiian family, is 7.5 miles east of Waimea, off Mamalahoa Hwy. Reservations required.

Mountain Road Cycles   Cycling
(✆885-7943; www.mountainroadcycles.com; 64-1066 Mamalahoa Hwy; bikes per day $30-45; ⊙9:30am-5:30pm Mon-Fri, 10am-3pm Sat) In addition to renting bicycles, this full-service bike shop arranges mountain-biking and road tours starting at $50. It prefers small groups and serious riders.

🎆 Festivals & Events

Waimea Ocean Film Festival   Film
(✆854-6095; www.waimeaoceanfilm.org) In early January, films, speakers, receptions and art exhibits showcase the beauty, power and mystery of the ocean. It's held in multiple venues in Waimea, Kohala and Kona.

**Waimea Cherry Blossom
Heritage Festival**   Japanese Culture
(✆961-8706; waimeacherryblossom@gmail.com; Parker Ranch Center & Church Row Park) FREE Dark pink blossoms are greeted with *taiko* drumming, *mochi* (sticky rice

cake) pounding and other Japanese cultural events on the first Saturday in February.

Fourth of July Rodeo   Rodeo
(☏885-2303; 67-1435 Mamalahoa Hwy, Parker Ranch Rodeo Arena; admission $6) Celebrating over 45 years of ranching, this event includes cattle roping, bull riding and other hoopla.

Waimea Paniolo Parade & Ho'olaule'a   Parade
(☏885-3110; www.waimeatown.org) This mid-September parade of authentic *paniolo*, island princesses and beautiful steeds begins at historic Church Row Park and makes its way through town, followed by a lively fair in Waimea Park. In conjunction with statewide Aloha Festivals.

Round-Up Rodeo   Rodeo
(☏885-5669; www.parkerranch.com; 67-1435 Mamalahoa Hwy, Parker Ranch Rodeo Arena; admission $5) This whip-cracking event is held on the first Monday in September after Labor Day weekend.

Waimea Ukulele & Slack Key Guitar Institute Concert   Music
(☏885-6017; www.kahilutheatre.org; admission $20-64) This annual concert in mid-November is a dream opportunity to see Hawaii's musical greats. Past headliners include Ledward Ka'apana and Cyril Pahinui.

Christmas Twilight Parade   Christmas
In early December, the town gets into the Kalikimaka (Christmas) spirit with a block party.

🛏 Sleeping

Kamuela Inn   Inn $
(☏800-555-8968, 885-4243; www.thekamuelainn.com; 1600 Kawaihae Rd; r incl continental breakfast $69-94, ste $109-119; 🛜) Resembling a typical motor inn, this local institution is an awesome value. Nothing's fancy, but rooms are clean and comfy, with a range of bed configurations and kitchen amenities. Rooms in the renovated Mauna Kea Wing are worth the extra cost, with open-beam ceilings and spiffier decor. The

Anna Ranch Heritage Center (p123)

spacious Executive Suite ($189) with full kitchen is ideal for families.

Waimea Garden Cottages
Vacation Rental $$

(☏ 885-8550; www.waimeagardens.com; studio $155, cottages $170-185, incl breakfast; 🛜) On a well-tended property, find three spruce, well-equipped, country cottages around the owners' home. The largest, Kohala Cottage, has a full kitchen, enormous bath and adjacent walled garden. The cozy Waimea Cottage offers a fireplace, kitchenette and private patio. There's also a spacious studio near a seasonal stream.

Located a quick 2 miles west of town, near the intersection of Kawaihae Rd and Hwy 250. Three-day minimum stay.

Aaah, the Views B&B
B&B $$

(☏ 885-3455; www.aaahtheviews.com; 66-1773 Alaneo St; r incl breakfast $189; 🛜) Run by a welcoming family, this B&B takes advantage of a uniquely designed house with lots of windows, peaceful mountain views and charming ladder-accessible lofts. The two-bedroom Treetop Suite is an especially sweet deal, with four beds and a private deck.

Enjoy generous breakfasts in your room or on a pleasant shared lanai. Located 3 miles west of town.

Jacaranda Inn
Inn $$

(☏ 885-8813; www.jacarandainn.com; 65-1444 Kawaihae Rd; r/ste/cottage from $129/179/250; 🛜) Built in 1897, the Jacaranda has seen better days. While each of the eight rooms are indulgent, antique-filled visions (think four-poster beds, opulent tiled baths, carved furniture and oriental rugs), the property feels somewhat forlorn. Consider it a backup.

✕ Eating

Waimea has a remarkable surplus of eateries to fit various tastes and budgets. The two malls, Waimea Center and Parker Ranch Center, offer numerous inexpensive restaurants, although some are only fast-food joints. You can also stock up on groceries at **KTA Super Store** (☏ 885-8866; 65-1158 Mamalahoa Hwy, Waimea Center; ⏰ 6am-11pm), a large supermarket and deli with a pharmacy, and at **Healthways II** (☏ 885-6775; 67-1185 Mamalahoa Hwy, Parker Ranch Center; ⏰ 9am-7pm Mon-Sat, to 5pm Sun), a natural food store and deli.

Waimea Town Farmers Market
Market $

(⏰ 8am-1pm Sat) 🍴 With a circle of vendors around a grassy field, this farmers market has a friendly, cohesive vibe. Find artisan edibles, including handcrafted pasta and sausages, Thai plates and bread freshly baked in a mobile oven. While the specialty items such as tea, jam and honey are delightful, the selection of basic produce

Horseback riding, Dahana Ranch

Of Cattle & Cowboys

Parker Ranch (www.parkerranch.com) was once the nation's largest privately owned ranch, peaking at 391 sq miles. Recently, however, the ranch has had to sell off parcels, including 37.5 sq miles to the US military in 2006. Today it's the fifth-largest cow-calf ranch in the USA, with at least 12,000 mother cows on 203 sq miles, and producing 12 million pounds of beef annually.

Big Island ranching goes back to 1793, when British Captain George Vancouver gifted King Kamehameha with a herd of long-horned cattle. Protected by the king's kapu (taboo), the herd proliferated and by 1815 was a menace.

Massachusetts mariner John Palmer Parker, who arrived here in 1809 at age 19, was deft with a rifle and hired to control the cattle problem. After successfully cutting the herd down to size, he received not only top-quality cows, but also the hand of one of Kamehameha's granddaughters and a prime piece of land. Parker Ranch was born in 1847.

is surprisingly limited. Located in front of Parker School in town.

Waimea Homestead Farmers Market
Market $

(⏲7am-noon Sat) This market, spread out on a grassy field, has a scruffy, local feel. It offers fruits and vegetables, eggs, preserves, flowers, meats, cheeses, tea, coffee, massages and scrumptious breakfasts. Located in front of the Hawaiian Home Lands office, near Mile 55 marker on Hwy 19.

Waimea MidWeek Market
Market $

(Pukalani Stables; ⏲9am-4pm Wed) This midweek market offers goodies including local organic produce, honey, handmade soaps, hot plate lunches and live *paniolo* music. Before browsing, visit the Paniolo Heritage Center, also at the stables.

Village Burger
Burgers $

(☎885-7319; www.villageburgerwaimea.com; 67-1185 Mamalahoa Hwy, Parker Ranch Center; burgers $8-12; ⏲10:30am-4pm Mon-Sat, to 6pm Sun) Burger connoisseurs, prepare to be impressed. Big Island beef, veal and lamb burgers are juicy and tender, while vegetarian options (Waipi'o Valley taro or Hamakua mushroom) are equally scrumptious. All major ingredients pass muster with locavores. Freshly cut fries and aptly named 'Epic Shakes' top it off. Seating is very limited, but there's ample space in the adjacent food court.

Big Island Brewhaus & Taqueria
Mexican $

(☎887-1717; www.bigislandbrewhaus.com; 64-1066 Mamalahoa Hwy; mains $7.50-16; ⏲11am-8:30pm Mon-Sat, noon-8:30pm Sun) The former Tako Taco has upped its game as a quality brewpub. Owner Thomas Kerns has created over a dozen memorable beers, including White Mountain Porter, rich with coffee and coconut, and Golden Sabbath Belgian Ale, which has a tremendous aroma. The setting is casual verging on sloppy. Go for the beer.

Lilikoi Cafe
Cafe $

(☎887-1400; 67-1185 Mamalahoa Hwy, Parker Ranch Center; meals $9-12; ⏲7:30am-4pm Mon-Sat) 🌿 This cheery cafe serves healthy, innovative food such as a breakfast burrito with eggs, tofu and sweet red pepper, and hearty vegetable lasagne. Drink the fresh carrot, apple, beet and ginger 'House Cocktail' ($5.50) and conquer the world. Hidden in the back of the shopping center.

The Best...
Live Performances in Kohala & Waimea

Waimea Coffee & Co   Cafe **$**
(☎885-8915; www.waimeacoffeecompany.com; Kawaihe Rd, Parker Sq; sandwiches $8-10; ⏰6:30am-5:30pm Mon-Sat, 8am-2pm Sun; 📶) If you can snag a patio table, this is a lively hangout for espresso drinks and light fare. Service can be hit or miss, however.

Hawaiian Style Cafe   Diner **$**
(☎885-4295; 64-1290 Kawaihae Rd, Hayashi Bldg; dishes $7.50-10; ⏰7am-1:30pm Mon-Sat, to noon Sun) Big eaters will meet their match at this local favorite greasy spoon, especially popular for breakfast. Expect enormous Man v Food portions of *loco moco* (rice, fried egg and hamburger patty topped with gravy or other condiments), pancakes, fried rice, burgers and more. Not the place for health nuts and dieters.

Aka Sushi Bar   Sushi **$$**
(☎887-2320; 65-1158 Mamalahoa Hwy, Waimea Shopping Center; sushi $5-10, bowls $12-16; ⏰10:30am-2:15pm & 5-8:30pm Tue-Sat) Ignore the strip-mall setting: this is a gem for reasonably priced or takeout sushi. *Nigiri* (oblong-shaped sushi) and rolls have a high fish-to-rice ratio, and everything is fresh. Be sure to try the succulent *hamachi kama* (grilled yellowtail collar).

Pau   Sandwiches, Pizzeria **$$**
(☎885-6325; www.paupizza.com; 65-1227 Opelo Rd, Opelo Plaza; pizza $17-28; ⏰11am-8pm) This

Wok-charred ahi at Merriman's

casual eatery serves reliably creative, tasty and healthful salads, sandwiches, pastas and over a dozen crisp, thin-crust pizzas.

Fish & the Hog Market Cafe
BBQ $$

(☎ 885-6268; www.hulisues.com; 64-957 Mamalahoa Hwy; sandwiches $10-13, barbecue $15-24; ⏰ 11:30am-8:30pm Mon-Sat) Formerly known as Huli Sue's, this sit-down restaurant serves ribs, pulled pork, beef brisket and other kiawe-smoked meats with their signature BBQ sauces. Fish dishes, from gumbo to tacos, are well done. Save room for the famous banana cream pie.

Merriman's
Hawaii Regional $$$

(☎ 885-6822; www.merrimanshawaii.com; 65-1227 Opelo Rd, Opelo Plaza; lunch $11-15, dinner $30-50; ⏰ 11:30am-1:30pm Mon-Fri, 5:30-8pm daily) Chef-owner Peter Merriman's Waimea namesake has long wowed diners with creative use of organic, island-grown ingredients. Today there are four sister restaurants and his original flagship might be slipping. But it's still the best fine-dining spot in town. The mahimahi marinated in *ponzu* (Japanese citrus sauce), wok-charred ahi and crispy molten chocolate 'purse' are classics. Lunch offers good value.

⭐ Entertainment

Kahilu Theatre
Theater

(☎ 885-6017, box office 885-6868; www.kahilutheatre.org; 67-1185 Mamalahoa Hwy, Parker Ranch Center; admission $20-54; ⏰ box office 9am-3pm Mon-Fri, show times vary) A hotspot for music and dance, this theater offers a variety of top performances – for example Hawaii icon The Brothers Cazimero, the latest Van Cliburn winner and the annual Waimea Ukulele & Slack Key Guitar Institute Concert. Check the website for upcoming shows.

🔒 Shopping

Three shopping malls line Hwy 19 through town: **Parker Ranch Center** (67-1185 Mamalahoa Hwy), where the stop signs say 'Whoa,' **Waimea Center** (65-1158 Mamalahoa Hwy)

and **Parker Square** (65-1279 Kawaihae Rd). The first two have groceries and basics, plus restaurants and fast food; Parker Square aims for discriminating, upscale gift buyers.

Gallery of Great Things
Arts & Crafts

(☎ 885-7706; www.galleryofgreatthingshawaii.com; 65-1279 Kawaihae Rd, Parker Sq; ⏰ 9am-5.30pm Mon-Sat, 10am-4pm Sun) This unpretentious gallery is crammed with antiques, high-quality art and collectibles from Hawaii, Polynesia and Asia. Among the Hawaiian crafts for sale is *kapa,* bark cloth painstakingly handmade by traditional methods. Best, there's something for every budget.

Waimea General Store
Gifts, Homewares

(www.waimeageneralstore.com; 65-1279 Kawaihae Rd, Parker Sq) Shoppers, browsers and homemakers will enjoy the eclectic mix here, from Le Creuset and Japanese tableware to fancy toiletries and vintage hula-girl cards.

Reyn's
Clothing

(www.reyns.com; Parker Ranch Center; ⏰ 9:30am-5:30pm Mon-Sat, to 4pm Sun) If you want to dress like a local, shop at Reyn's. Its classic, understated aloha shirts (which use Hawaiian fabrics in reverse) never go out of style.

ℹ Information

North Hawaii Community Hospital (☎ 885-4444; 67-1125 Mamalahoa Hwy) Emergency services available 24 hours.

Post Office (☎ 800-275-8777; 67-1197 Mamalahoa Hwy; ⏰ 8am-4:30pm Mon-Fri, 9am-noon Sat) Address all Waimea mail to Kamuela.

ℹ Getting There & Around

Kailua-Kona is 37 miles away along Hwy 190; Hilo is 51 miles away on Hwy 19.

On Monday to Saturday the Hele-On Bus (p96) goes from Waimea (Parker Ranch Center) to Kailua-Kona on its 16 Kailua-Kona route (65 minutes) and to Hilo on its 7 Downtown Hilo route (80 minutes).

Mauna Kea & Saddle Road

Caution: you're entering hallowed ground. According to the Hawaiian creation myth, this sacrosanct peak is home to the gods, the place between heaven and earth where *na kanaka maoli* (Native Hawaiians) were created. With its summit soaring 13,796ft above sea level, Mauna Kea – more precisely, its true summit, Pu'u Wekiu – is also Hawaii's highest peak, and the tallest volcano anywhere in the world's oceans.

Sacred status and chart-topping elevation aren't the only reasons to head up Mauna Kea. Travelers from the world over make their way to this literally breath-taking mountain for stellar stargazing and high-altitude hiking. Astronomers, too, covet the summit: with its unmatched collection of high-tech astronomical observatories, it's one of the best places on earth to observe the night sky.

Even just the trip getting here – along rolling Saddle Rd, then up Mauna Kea's skyscraping summit road – is adventure.

Mauna Kea summit at sunset
ROSENBERG PHILIP/GETTY IMAGES ©

Mauna Kea & Saddle Road Itineraries

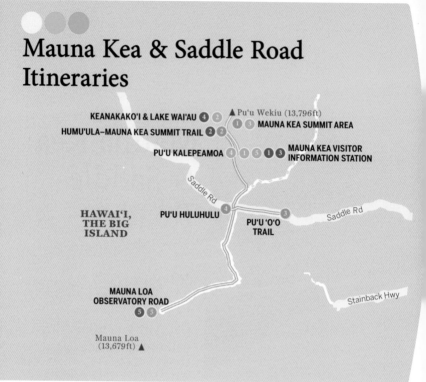

Pu'u Wekiu (13,796ft)

KEANAKAKO'I & LAKE WAI'AU ❹ ②

HUMU'ULA–MAUNA KEA SUMMIT TRAIL ② ②

MAUNA KEA SUMMIT AREA ❶ ③

PU'U KALEPEAMOA ❹ ❶ ❺ ❶ ❸

MAUNA KEA VISITOR INFORMATION STATION

Saddle Rd

HAWAI'I, THE BIG ISLAND

PU'U HULUHULU ❹

PU'U 'O'O TRAIL ❸

Saddle Rd

MAUNA LOA OBSERVATORY ROAD ❺ ❺

Stainback Hwy

Mauna Loa (13,679ft) ▲

One Day

❶ Mauna Kea Visitor Information Station (MKVIS) (p135) You'll probably be feeling the altitude by the time you reach this way station at 9200ft. Spend some time acclimatizing and picking the rangers' brains for fascinating facts about the mountain, modern astronomy and Hawaiian cultural traditions.

❷ Keanakako'i & Lake Wai'au (p135) With a low-gear 4WD vehicle, if the weather is cooperating, keep driving up the mountain on its summit road. Stop partway up to hike to a shrinking prehistoric lake and an ancient Hawaiian adze quarry inside the Mauna Kea Ice Age Natural Area Reserve.

❸ Mauna Kea's Summit Area (p135) You've made it! Drive the summit loop road around the 'golf ball' observatories perched high on the mountaintop. If it's a weekday, step inside the visitor gallery at the WM Keck Observatory.

❹ Pu'u Kalepeamoa (p135) Drive slowly down from the summit back to the MKVIS. Across the road, take a 15-minute, mostly uphill hike to this top spot for sunset views. Have a flashlight handy for the after-dark return trip.

❺ Stargazing (p138) Want your mind blown? Get some hot chocolate, bust out the warm jacket and mittens, and peer through powerful telescopes at distant corners of the universe during the MKVIS's free public stargazing programs held nightly, weather permitting.

➡ **THIS LEG: 16 MILES**

Two Days

1 **Sunrise on Mauna Kea** (p135)
Although light on traffic, dark and windy
Saddle Rd makes a fairly challenging
predawn drive – make sure the coffee is
flowing as you catch the sun coming up over
the clouds.

2 **Humu'ula–Mauna Kea Summit Trail**
(p138) Fit and prepared hikers will want
to hit this challenging trail by 6am, adding
Hawaii's tallest mountain to their list of
achievements. You'll be hiking at the knife's
edge of the volcano and the sky. A short spur
at the very top leads to Mauna Kea's true
summit, Pu'u Wekiu.

3 **Pu'u 'O'o Trail** (p143) For a day hike
that's not as heart-stoppingly strenuous,
head east on Saddle Rd for this lovely loop.
You'll cross forest, meadows and old lava
flows in profound solitude, and you may spy
colorful Hawaiian honeycreepers, such as
the *'apapane* and *'i'iwi*.

4 **Pu'u Huluhulu Trail** (p143) Start this
short leg-stretcher just before sunset. After
a short walk up 'Shaggy Hill,' the entire
Saddle Rd region will be laid out before you
on clear evenings: Mauna Kea, Mauna Loa
and Hualalai. The contrast between the lava
flows and green shrubbery of the *kipuka*
(oasis) is wild.

5 **Mauna Loa Observatory Rd** (p142)
Here's yet another sunset option. Reaching
the Mauna Loa Observatory (weather
forecast: *cold*) at 11,150ft is a bit of a tricky
drive, but you may be rewarded by seeing
the mystical 'Mauna Kea shadow' over Hilo
as you watch the sun go down. Inspired by
the views? Come back tomorrow to tackle
the hard-core Mauna Loa Observatory Trail.

 THIS LEG: 42 MILES

Mauna Kea & Saddle Road Highlights

1 **Best View: Mauna Kea stargazing** (p138)
Spy on our universe from Hawai'i's most
sacred mountain.

2 **Best Hike: Humu'ula–Mauna Kea
Summit Trail** (p138) Traipse among giant
volcanic cinder cones above the clouds.

3 **Best Place to Learn: Mauna Kea Visitor
Information Station (MKVIS)** (p135) Free
stargazing programs, escorted summit tours
and more fun for science geeks.

4 **Best Ancient Hawaiian Site: Lake
Wai'au** (p135) Hawai'i's spiritual umbilical
cord connects heaven and earth.

5 **Best Adventure: Mauna Loa
Observatory Trail** (p142) Climb this
massive mountain – in just one day.

WM Keck Observatory (p137)
MAGRATH PHOTOGRAPHY/NIELSEN/GETTY IMAGES ©

Discover Mauna Kea & Saddle Road

MAUNA KEA

Mauna Kea (White Mountain) is called Mauna O Wakea (Mountain of Wakea) by Hawaiian cultural practitioners. While all of the Big Island is considered the first-born child of Wakea (sky father) and Papahanaumoku (earth mother), the deity progenitors of the Hawaiian race, Mauna Kea is the sacred *piko* (navel) connecting the land to the heavens.

For the scientific world, it all began in 1968 when the University of Hawai'i (UH) began observing the universe from atop the mountain. Smart folks: the summit is so high, dry, dark and pollution-free that it allows investigation of the furthest reaches of the observable universe. Today, astronomers from 11 countries staff 13 observatories on Mauna Kea's summit – the largest conglomeration of high-powered telescopes anywhere in the world. They huddle in a small area of the Mauna Kea Science Reserve, a chunk of land leased by UH that encompasses almost everything above 12,000ft.

Many Hawaiians are opposed to the summit 'golf balls' – the white observatories. While not antiscience, they believe unchecked growth on the mountain threatens the *wahi pana* (sacred places) there, including heiau (temples) and burial sites. In a dramatic episode in 2006, an *ahu lele* (spiritual altar) built for ceremonies on the mountain was desecrated. Toxic mercury spills from some observatories have occurred, and damage to the mountain's fragile ecosystem is another arrow in the activists' antidevelopment quiver.

Nevertheless in 2011, plans were approved to build the Thirty Meter Telescope (TMT) here. While TMT will be the world's most advanced and powerful telescope, its structural footprint will be larger than all the observatories currently on the summit, with all the possible disruptions of natural and cultural resources that implies.

Saddle Road

◎ Sights

Mauna Kea Visitor Information Station
Visitor Center

(MKVIS; ☎808-961-2180; www.ifa.hawaii.edu/info/vis; ◎9am-10pm) **FREE** Modestly sized, MKVIS packs a punch with astronomy and space-exploration videos, virtual observatory tours and exhibits on the mountain's history, ecology and geology. Budding astronomers of all ages geek out in the gift shop, where knowledgeable staff will help you pass the time acclimatizing to the 9200ft altitude.

Free public stargazing programs (p138) happen from 6pm until 10pm nightly, weather permitting. If you have a low-gear 4WD vehicle, escorted summit tours (p140) usually leave at 1pm on Saturdays and Sundays.

Inside the **gift shop** you can buy hot chocolate, coffee, packets of instant noodles and freeze-dried astronaut food to munch on; hoodies, hats and gloves to stay warm; and books about science and Hawaiian culture. Check the website for upcoming special events, such as lectures about science and Hawaiian culture, typically held on Saturday nights.

Across from MKVIS, a 15-minute uphill hike crests **Pu'u Kalepeamoa** (9394ft), a cinder cone offering glorious sunset views. Directly off the MKVIS parking lot is a small enclosed area where rare and endangered **silversword plants** grow.

As you drive 6 miles and 2500ft uphill from Saddle Rd to the MKVIS, you'll break through the cloud cover. The road is paved and normally accessible by 2WD vehicles as far as MKVIS.

Keanakako'i & Lake Wai'au
Archaeological Site, Lake

Just after the Mile 6 marker en route to Mauna Kea's summit area from MKVIS, pull into a paved parking area. Below is the trailhead to **Lake Wai'au**, the third-highest lake in the USA (it's disappearing fast), and **Keanakako'i**, a protected ancient Hawaiian adze quarry. It'll take an hour or so to hike to both the lake and the quarry, depending on your level of fitness and acclimatization.

A sacred place to Hawaiians, Lake Wai'au is the *piko* (navel, or umbilical cord) connecting heaven and earth. To ensure a baby has the strength of the mountain, real umbilical stumps were traditionally placed in the lake. Clay formed long ago by volcanic ash holds the water, fed by melting snow, permafrost and minimal annual rainfall. Since 2010, the lake has dramatically shrunk to 2% of its former size, and is now less than 1ft deep, but scientists don't know exactly why.

During Mauna Kea's ice age, molten lava erupted under its glacier, creating an extremely hard basalt, which ancient Hawaiians chipped into tools and weapons at Keanakako'i quarry. Some of these tools were used on Hawai'i to peck massive fields of symbolic drawings into hardened lava, including the Pu'u Loa petroglyphs in Hawai'i Volcanoes National Park. Entering the quarry is discouraged, as it's a fragile archaeological site of importance to Hawaiians, but the views from the trail are still worth seeing.

Mauna Kea's Summit Area
Landmark

At the top of Mauna Kea, massive round observatories rise up white and silver from stark terrain. It's a striking juxtaposition – you may feel like you've discovered a futuristic human colony on an alien planet. Staffed by scientists from around the world, these observatories compose the greatest collection of optical, infrared and millimeter/submillimeter telescopes on earth. At almost 14,000ft, the summit is above 40% of the earth's atmosphere and 90% of its water vapor, resulting in many cloudless nights.

It's a veritable UN on the mountaintop, with a bevy of countries administering different telescopes – Taiwan and the USA collaborate on the **Submillimeter Array**; the UK and Canada run the **James Clerk Maxwell Telescope (JCMT)**; and six nations share the **Gemini Northern 8m Telescope**. The **University of Hawai'i 0.9m Telescope** is now used mostly for training undergraduates. Most of these observatories are closed to the public,

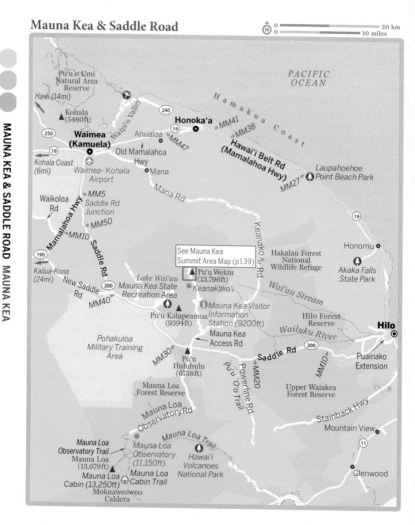

and none allow public viewing through their telescopes.

Sunsets are phenomenal from around the summit. All of Hawai'i lies below as the sun sinks into an ocean of clouds – while the telescopes silently unshutter and turn their unblinking eyes to the heavens. Look east to see 'the shadow' – the gigantic silhouette of Mauna Kea looming over Hilo. Moonrises can be equally as impressive: the high altitude may make the moon appear squashed and misshapen, or sometimes resemble a brushfire.

Be sure to bring long pants, a thick coat (or lots of layers), a warm hat and gloves. It gets cold up here. If you have a 4WD, you may drive to the summit in the daytime, but you must descend 30 minutes after sunset. It takes about half an hour to drive the 8-mile summit road, the first 4.5 miles of which are slippery gravel. Just before the pavement picks up again, the area on the east side of the road is dubbed **Moon Valley**, where Apollo astronauts rehearsed with their lunar rover before their journey to the real moonscape.

WM Keck Observatory Observatory
(808-935-6268; www.keck .org; visitors gallery 10am-4pm Mon-Fri) FREE Near Mauna Kea's summit, the WM Keck Observatory has a visitors gallery with scientific displays, public restrooms and partial views inside the Keck I dome. Currently the world's largest and most powerful optical and infrared telescopes are housed here, a joint project of the California Institute of Technology (CalTech), the University of California and NASA. The two interchangeable telescopes can function as one – like a pair of binoculars searching the sky – allowing them to study incredibly distant galaxies.

In 1992, **Keck I** made a breakthrough in telescope design using a unique honeycomb feature made up of 36 hexagonal mirror segments that function as a single piece of glass. A replica of the first telescope, **Keck II**, went online in 1996. In 2013, scientists using Keck I discovered the most distant galaxy ever observed, a mere 13.1 billion light-years away.

Subaru Telescope Observatory
(www.naoj.org; tours usually 10:30am, 11:30am & 1:30pm Tue-Thu) FREE Inaugurated in 1999 after almost a decade of construction, its $300 million price tag makes Japan's Subaru Telescope the most expensive observatory constructed to date. Its 22-ton mirror, reaching 27ft in diameter, is one of the largest optical mirrors in existence. Incidentally, Subaru is the Japanese word for the Pleiades constellation.

Observatory tours, which don't include looking through the telescope, are given in Japanese or English, but not both – so sign up early for your preferred language. Reserve tours online at least one week in advance. Children under 16 years old are not allowed on tours. No public restrooms.

Pu'u Wekiu Mountain
The short trail up this cinder cone to Mauna Kea's true summit (13,796ft) begins opposite the UH 2.2m Telescope. The hike is harder than it looks, and it's not necessary to go just to watch the sunset. Hawaiian cultural practitioners counsel against hiking due to the area's environmental fragility and cultural significance. At the true summit is a US Geological Survey (USGS) marker and an *ahu* (altar). Given the biting winds, high altitude and extreme cold, most people don't linger.

Island Insights

First snow is falling on Mauna Kea and, near the visitor information station, ranger James Keali'i Pihana – 'Kimo' as he's known – is blocking the frozen road in his pickup truck and explaining what Mauna Kea means to Hawaiians.

'To us, Mauna Kea is "the heavens." It is the place between heaven and earth... Mauna Kea is the center of our "Biblestory."

'Mauna Kea is the home of the snow goddess, Poliahu. Ceremonies are still conducted: equinox, solstices, first light. Lake Wai'au is sacred water. Umbilical cords were put in the lake for the protection of children.'

Kimo and others walked up the mountain in 1998 to voice their deep concern over the observatories. Sacred places and burial sites had been built on and disturbed, and new observatories were going up without consulting Hawaiians.

Consequently, a rally was held. Kimo says, 'Our people were ready to shut the road down.' It was a pivotal moment, and the politicians and astronomers responded. A Hawaiian advisory council was created, Kimo conducted cleansing rituals, and then he applied for a job. His most important task is communicating with Hawaiian leaders about what's happening on their sacred mountain.

The Best...

Mauna Kea Webcams

1 CFH Telescope Timelapse Webcam

2 Joint Astronomy Centre Webcam

3 MKVIS Live Allsky Cam

4 NASA Infrared Telescope Facility Cameras

5 Subaru Telescope Webcams

🐾 Activities

STARGAZING

Although the high-tech telescopes inside Mauna Kea's summit observatories are closed to the public, the MKVIS (p135) hosts free nightly stargazing programs, weather permitting (no reservations necessary). Specialists focus high-powered scopes on the night skies, and travelers in wheelchairs have the use of adaptive scope attachments.

During big meteor showers like the Leonides in mid-November, MKVIS often hosts all-night star parties. Lunar eclipses and the monthly full moon are also popular with stargazers. Call ahead for special events and current viewing conditions.

HIKING

For sunset views without going to the summit, take the 15-minute, steep hike up **Pu'u Kalepeamoa**, starting across the road from MKVIS (p135). Heading toward Mauna Kea's summit area, you can hike to Keanakako'i & Lake Wai'au (p135).

Humu'ula–Mauna Kea Summit Trail   Hiking

This daunting, all-day hike starts at 9200ft, then climbs almost 4600ft over the next 6 miles to Mauna Kea's summit. Expect thin air, steep grades and biting weather on this utterly exposed trail, where it often feels like you're going to step off the mountain into the sky. Plan on eight hours for the round-trip hike and bring a gallon of water per person – dehydration is a real danger at these altitudes. Don't hike in inclement weather.

Start by 6am to give yourself the maximum hours of daylight. Before hiking, register at the MKVIS (p135), where you can grab a hiking map and consult with rangers about current weather and trail conditions. (If it's closed, fill out a self-registration form and place it in the drop box.) Remember to take your time acclimatizing, with frequent rest and water breaks.

Park at MKVIS and walk up the summit road to where the pavement ends. Turn left onto a dirt side road and follow the brown-and-yellow Na Ala Hele signs for the Humu'ula Trail. The trail begins climbing doggedly upward, gradually getting slightly less steep after the first mile while it weaves among cinder cones. It's marked with poles and reflectors, as well as rock cairns. Avoid false spurs leading back to the summit road, which reappears after about an hour.

Most of the hike passes through the **Mauna Kea Ice Age Natural Area Reserve**. After about three hours you'll enter a broad valley, followed by a sharp, short ascent on crumbly soil over a rise to Keanakako'i (p135), an ancient adze quarry, with large piles of bluish-black basalt chips. Do not disturb anything in this protected area. Another mile-long ascent brings you to a four-way junction, where a 10-minute detour to the left reaches Lake Wai'au (p135). Back at the four-way junction, make your way north for the final upward push to the summit.

Suddenly the observatories pop into view and straight ahead is **Millimeter Valley**, nicknamed for the cluster of submillimeter observatories. The trail

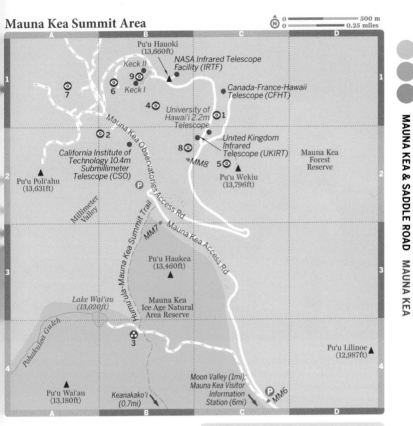

ends here at the road's Mile 7 marker, just below the hairpin turn; turn back here and you can descend the way you came on the trail or walk along the road instead. The latter is 2 miles longer, but faster and easier, and you're more likely (though not guaranteed) to get a lift down by hitchhiking.

If you really need to place a boot toe on Pu'u Wekiu (p137), Mauna Kea's true summit, follow the summit loop road up to the right (not the spur road into Millimeter Valley) for just over a mile. Past Mile 8 marker, where the road forks, veer right and look for a 'trail' opposite the **University of Hawai'i 2.2m Telescope**. This short spur trail-of-use descends steeply east, crosses a saddle and then scrambles up to the summit.

Mauna Kea Summit Area

SKIING & SNOWBOARDING

In January or February, enough snow may fall on Mauna Kea's heights to allow for winter sports. The so-called 'slopes' are crowded with locals using skis, snowboards, surfboards, bodyboards, inner tubes – whatever!

What concerns activists and conservationists is increased mountaintop usage during snowfall, combined with the degradation caused by monster trucks used to access the 'slopes,' thereby eroding natural habitat and culturally significant sites.

For those chasing this trophy experience, know that skiing Mauna Kea is entirely DIY. There are no groomed trails, no lifts, no patrols; exposed rocks and ice sheets are constant dangers.

Tours

MKVIS Escorted Summit Tour
Guided Tour

(📞808-935-6268; www.ifa.hawaii.edu/info/vis; 🕐usually 1pm Sat & Sun) **FREE** You must provide your own low-gear 4WD vehicle to take advantage of these free guided summit tours (no reservations accepted). You'll spend the first hour acclimatizing and watching astronomy videos. After the orientation, you'll caravan up to the summit, where a docent talks about the telescopes, their history and what they're typically looking at. Tours visit at least one of the summit observatories, ending around 4:30pm. Most people stay for the sunset, then drive back down on their own.

Tours don't run when bad weather closes the road, so call ahead to check weather and road conditions. Children must be at least 16 years old.

Hawaii Forest & Trail
Van Tour

(📞800-464-1993, 808-331-8505; www.hawaii-forest.com; tour $199; 🕐tours nightly, weather permitting) 🍃 This top-notch, ecotour outfitter hosts a sunset and stargazing tour, with parkas, gloves and a picnic dinner at a private location. Knowledgeable guides take you to the summit, then conduct a tour of the heavens with an 11in Celestron telescope outside MKVIS. Pick-ups from near Kailua-Kona, Waiakoloa and the Hwys 190 and 200 junction. Participants must be at least 16 years old. Book early.

Left: Observatories on Mauna Kea's Summit Area (p135); **Below:** Hikers at the Mauna Kea summit

(LEFT) MICHELE FALZONE/GETTY IMAGES ©; (BELOW) GREG ELMS/GETTY IMAGES ©

Mauna Kea Summit Adventures
Van Tour

(☏ 888-322-2366, 808-322-2366; www. maunakea.com; tour $204) The granddaddy of Mauna Kea tours has been taking folks to the summit for over 20 years. This outfit has vans with extra-tall windows and spacious seating. A hot dinner outside MKVIS, cold-weather parkas to borrow and stargazing through a 11in Celestron telescope are included. Pick-ups from Kailua-Kona, Waikoloa and the Hwys 190/200 junction. Children must be at least 13 years old.

Arnott's Mauna Kea Adventures
Van Tour

(☏ 808-339-0921; www.arnottslodge.com; 98 Apanane Rd, Hilo; tours $130-180; ⊗ Mon, Wed & Fri-Sun) Arnott's Lodge tours are for budget travelers, not serious stargazers. They're cheaper, leave from Hilo (or you can drive your own car and meet them on Saddle Rd) and the astronomy is bare-bones, with guides relying on laser pointers. BYO food and warm clothes.

Sleeping

The closest accommodations besides camping are in Waimea and Hilo.

Mauna Kea State Recreation Area
Cabin $

(www.hawaiistateparks.org; Saddle Rd; cabin $80) At the Mile 35 marker is this public recreation area, with five bare-bones cabins (currently available on weekends only, but double-check this). Used mainly by local hunters, each cabin has six bunk beds, a basic kitchen and a toilet, but no water. Bring your own bedding and towels. Military maneuvers at nearby Pohakuloa Training Area can be very noisy.

❶ Information

There are no restaurants, gas stations or emergency services anywhere on Mauna Kea or along Saddle Rd. Come prepared with a full tank of gas, warm clothing, sunglasses, sunscreen, snacks and plenty of water.

Dangers & Annoyances

Even at the MKVIS (9200ft), some visitors experience shortness of breath and mild 'altitude sickness' (acute mountain sickness, or AMS). At the 13,796ft summit, atmospheric pressure is less than 60% of sea level, and AMS is common. The risk increases with faster ascents and greater exertion; being physically fit offers no protection. All travelers to the summit should stop first at MKVIS for at least 30 minutes to acclimatize.

Symptoms of AMS include nausea, headaches, drowsiness, impaired reason, loss of balance, breathlessness and dehydration. AMS can lead to life-threatening pulmonary or cerebral edema. If you feel ill, descend immediately. Children under 16 years, pregnant women and those with high blood pressure or circulatory conditions should not go to the summit. Do not scuba dive for 24 hours before or after visiting Mauna Kea.

Be prepared for rapidly changing (and possibly severe) weather conditions, with daytime temperatures anywhere from 50°F (10°C) to below freezing and possible high winds. In winter, several feet of snow can fall, with road closures on the morning following a storm. Check weather and road conditions with the **Mauna Kea Weather Center** (📞808-935-6268; http://mkwc.ifa. hawaii.edu/) before heading up. Even when the fog's as thick as pea soup on Saddle Rd, it's crystal clear at the mountaintop 325 days a year.

🛈 Getting There & Around

Coming from Kona or Waimea, Saddle Rd (Hwy 200) starts just south of the Mile 6 marker on Hwy 190. From Hilo, drive *mauka* (inland) on Kaumana Dr (Hwy 200) or Puainako Extension (Hwy 2000), both of which become Saddle Rd. Start with a full tank of gas – Saddle Rd has no gas stations.

To get to MKVIS and the summit beyond, turn onto Mauna Kea Access Rd, near the Mile 28 marker on Saddle Rd. It takes about an hour to get to MKVIS from Hilo, Waimea or Waikoloa, or around 90 minutes from Kailua-Kona. MKVIS is 6 miles uphill from Saddle Rd; the summit is another 8 miles beyond the information station. Call 📞(808) 935-6268 for current road conditions.

Driving to the summit requires a low-gear 4WD vehicle – there have been many accidents to underscore this point. Over half of the summit road is gravel, sometimes at a 15% grade. The upper road can be covered with ice, and loose cinders are always challenging. Drive in low gear and be particularly careful on the way down *not* to ride your vehicle's brakes, which can overheat and

fail. Driving when the sun is low – in the hour after sunrise or before sunset – can create hazardous, blinding conditions. Plan to drive up to the summit during the daytime: the use of vehicle headlights is discouraged between sunset and sunrise, as they interfere with astronomical observations.

SADDLE ROAD

Off Saddle Rd you'll discover a few exceptional wilderness hikes, as well as one high-altitude scenic drive.

◉ Sights & Activities

Mauna Loa Observatory Road   Scenic Drive

Mauna Loa is somewhat of an enigma for visitors – it looms large all around, but how do you actually get on 'Long Mountain'? The answer is simple: drive up Mauna Loa Observatory Rd. This unsigned road starts near the Mile 28 marker on Saddle Rd, almost opposite Mauna Kea Access Rd and next to Pu'u Huluhulu. Delivering kicking views, the single-lane, 17.5-mile asphalt road ends at a parking area just below the **Mauna Loa Observatory** (11,150ft).

When weather conditions are just right, you can glimpse the 'Mauna Kea shadow' at sunset from here – a curious atmospheric phenomenon whereby Mauna Kea casts a blue-purple shadow behind itself over Hilo. The narrow road is passable in a standard car, but it's in varying condition and bedeviled by blind curves. Allow almost an hour. The road sometimes is closed in winter.

Mauna Loa Observatory Trail   Hiking

The easiest way to summit Mauna Loa (Long Mountain) is via this trail. Drive up to Mauna Loa Observatory at 11,150ft, then pick up the 6.4-mile trail for the remaining 2500ft to the top. It's a steep, exhausting, all-day adventure, but an exceptional one that allows experienced hikers to conquer a 13,000ft mountain in one day.

Start before 8am. You want to be off the mountain, or at least descending, by the time afternoon clouds roll in. Starting from the road's end near the observatory, the trail is marked by *ahu* (cairns) that disappear in fog, rain and snow; if that happens, rangers advise seeking shelter and waiting until visibility improves. The faster and/or higher you hike the more likely your risk of altitude sickness.

The trail starts by crisscrossing a series of *'a'a* (rough) and *pahoehoe* (smooth) lava flows. After 3.8 miles and 2000ft in elevation gain, you'll arrive at majestic **Moku'aweoweo Caldera**. From the trail junction, it's just over 2.6 miles northwest to Mauna Loa's **summit** (13,679ft) or 2.1 miles southwest to Mauna Loa Cabin (13,250ft). It should take about half as long to descend. All told, plan on a 10-hour day. Bring plenty of extra water, food and a flashlight.

Day hikers do not need a permit, but if you want to overnight at Mauna Loa Cabin near the summit, register the day before at Hawai'i Volcanoes National Park's Backcountry Office (p216), where rangers can tell you about current trail conditions and water-catchment levels at the cabin. An alternative backpacking route to the summit, the multiday Mauna Loa Trail (p219), starts inside the national park.

Pu'u Huluhulu Trail   Hiking

The easy 0.6-mile trail up the cinder cone **Pu'u Huluhulu**, 'Shaggy Hill' (6758ft), makes a piquant appetizer before going up Mauna Kea. Inside a *kipuka* (volcanic oasis), the 20-minute hike climbs through native forest to the hilltop, from where there are panoramic views of Mauna Kea, Mauna Loa and Hualalai on clear days. The trailhead parking area is almost opposite the turnoff to Mauna Kea, near the Mile 28 marker on Saddle Rd. Don't confuse this hike with the Pu'u Huluhulu Trail (p217) in Hawai'i Volcanoes National Park.

Pu'u 'O'o Trail   Hiking

For a peaceful yet substantial ramble, take the Pu'u 'O'o Trail, a 7.5-mile loop traversing meadows, old lava flows and pretty *kipuka* forests filled koa and ohia trees and the songs of Hawaiian honeycreepers and other native birds. The signed trailhead parking area is almost exactly halfway between the Mile 22 and 23 markers on Saddle Rd. The trail is marked by *ahu*; it's easy to follow in good

weather, less so in rain or fog. If in doubt, simply retrace your steps the way you came. Eventually, the trail connects with Powerline Rd (marked with a sign), a 4WD road that can be used as a return route, although this road dumps you out about a mile away from the trailhead parking area.

Hamakua Coast

Stretching from Waipi'o Valley to Hilo, the Hamakua Coast is wildly fertile and ruggedly beautiful. Here you'll find rocky shores and pounding surf, tropical rainforests and thunderous waterfalls. The color green takes on new meaning, especially in Waipi'o Valley, where farmers still grow taro, a native staple. Farther inland, farmers grow vanilla, tea, mushrooms and other innovative crops, modernizing and diversifying island agriculture. While drivers now speed along the highway, trains chugged along the coast during 'old plantation days,' when towering bridges spanned the gulches and sugarcane was king. Go slow here, taking back roads and stepping back in time.

Akaka Falls State Park (p161)
PETER FRENCH/GETTY IMAGES ©

Hamakua Coast Itineraries

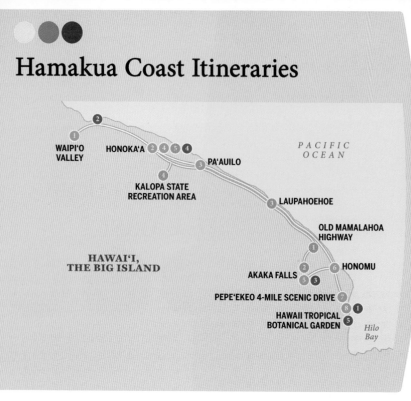

Two Days

1 Waipi'o Valley (p152) Start day one with the main event: hiking down into the valley. The view from the lookout is rewarding enough, but walk the 25% grade road to the bottom and write home about it!

2 Honoka'a (p148) Stop at this leisurely plantation/cowboy town and fuel up on *malasadas* (Portuguese doughnuts) at Tex Drive-In.

3 Hawaiian Vanilla Company (p148) Next is a trip to upcountry Pa'auilo, the island's bountiful breadbasket. Experience vanilla like you never have before at the Vanilla Experience Luncheon.

4 Café il Mondo (p151) End the day by returning to Honoka'a for freshly baked calzones and pizzas: you might even be serenaded by a guitar-strumming Brazilian.

5 Akaka Falls State Park (p161) The next day, head southeast to view the falls in flattering morning light; afternoon viewing guarantees gloomy backlit photos.

6 Hilo Sharks Coffee (p162) Stop in Honomu for locally grown coffee and chocolate, an unbeatable combination. Don't miss Mr Ed's Bakery for homemade preserves in 100 flavors.

7 Pepe'ekeo 4-Mile Scenic Drive (p163) Take this scenic drive and stop at What's Shakin' for a fresh fruit smoothie.

8 Hawaii Tropical Botanical Garden (p162) Leave lots of time to stroll amid wildly lush flora: gorgeous rain or shine.

↪ **THIS LEG: 40 MILES**

Three Days

1 **Old Mamalahoa Hwy** (p151) If you have three days, start by following the two-day itinerary. On day three, detour to the old highway. Sometimes narrow and winding, it forces you to slow down, look around and truly appreciate the *'aina* (land).

2 **Ziplines** (p159) Get a bird's-eye view of the island's emerald expanse of forestland, plus waterfalls. Choose from two zip parks near Umauma Falls and one near Akaka Falls.

3 **Laupahoehoe** (p158) If zipping isn't your thing, take an agri-gourmet tour at Hamakua Mushrooms. Stop at the Laupahoehoe Train Museum and also the tsunami memorial at Laupahoehoe Point.

4 **Kalopa State Recreation Area** (p157) In the afternoon, luxuriate in your own private expanse of green. Hike the trails through native forest, play Frisbee on the lawn and breathe that fresh air.

5 **Honoka'a** (p148) Stay in town for the evening, catching a movie or show at the picturesque Honoka'a People's Theatre, built in 1930 and once the liveliest spot in town.

➡ **THIS LEG: 50 MILES**

Hamakua Coast Highlights

1 **Best Garden: Hawaii Tropical Botanical Garden** (p162) Take a leisurely stroll through a rainforest jungle that meets the sea.

2 **Best Room with a View: Waipio Rim B&B** (p156) Behold Waipi'o Valley's green amphitheater from your bedroom!

3 **Best Waterfall: Akaka Falls** (p161) Walking to the lookout, past giant bamboo, ginger, ferns and orchids, is half the fun.

4 **Best Local Color: Honoka'a Trading Company** (p151) Browse through a mishmash of antiques and talk story with local characters.

5 **Best History Lesson: Hawaii Plantation Museum** (p163) See fascinating artifacts from plantation days, when Hawaii's multiethnic culture was born.

Laupahoehoe Train Museum (p159)
ANN CECIL/GETTY IMAGES ©

Discover
Hamakua Coast

Honoka'a & Around

POP HONOKA'A TOWN 2258

Who would guess that Honoka'a was once the third-largest town across Hawaii, after Honolulu and Hilo? It was the hub for the powerful cattle and sugar industries, but was forced to reinvent itself when those industries crashed. By the time Honoka'a Sugar Company processed its last harvest in 1993, the town had dwindled in size and struggled to find new economic niches.

Eventually, entrepreneurial farmers diversified their crops and found success with niche edibles, such as mushrooms, tomatoes and lettuces, sold at farmers markets and prized by gourmet chefs.

You can catch Hele-On Bus (p96) to Honoka'a from Hilo or from Kailua-Kona, but service is infrequent. In and around town, you'll definitely need a car.

◎ Sights

The following farms are located in pastoral **Pa'auilo** and **Ahualoa**, on the *mauka* (inland) side of the highway. All are small, family-run working farms, so you must book ahead for tours.

Hawaiian Vanilla Company   Farm

(☏776-1771; www.hawaiianvanilla.com; Pa'auilo; tasting $25, afternoon tea $29, lunch per adult/child under 12yr $39/19; ⊙tasting 10:30am Mon-Fri, afternoon tea 3pm Sat, lunch 12:30pm Mon-Fri) The first commercial vanilla operation in the USA, this family-run farm is a model for successful agritourism. All of the edible tours are decently priced and worth your time. If time is short, stop by the **gift shop** (⊙10am-5pm) for vanilla-infused coffee, tea, bath and body products, and of course prime beans and extracts.

Mauna Kea Tea   Farm

(☏775-1171; www.maunakeatea.com; 46-3870 Old Mamalahoa Hwy, Ahualoa; 60-90min tours per 2/3/4 or more people $30/25/20) ✎ If you're into tea, organic farming and philosophical inquiry, arrange a tour at this small-scale, family-run plantation. Its green and oolong teas are intended to represent the inherent 'flavor' of the land, not artificial fertilizers.

Taro farms in Waipi'o Valley (p152)
GREG VAUGHN/GETTY IMAGES ©

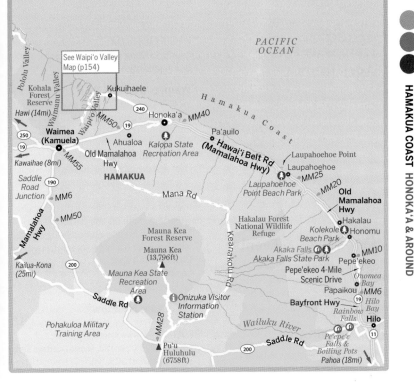

You can also meet the farmers at the Waimea Homestead Farmers Market (p127) on Saturday mornings.

Long Ears Coffee
Farm

(📞775-0385; www.longearscoffee.com; tours $35) 🍃 Try unique three-year 'aged' Hamakua coffee at this family farm. Wendell and Irmanetta Branco process their own and other Hamakua farms' beans, creating a sustainable agricultural economy for farmers here. On tour, you'll see the entire process: growing trees, harvesting cherry, pulping, drying, husking and roasting. Directions to the farm are given upon booking a tour.

Motta Ceramics
Studio

(📞775-0856; http://gordonmotta.com; 46-4030 Pu'aono Rd) FREE After four decades as a potter, Gordon Motta knows a few things about throwing clay on the wheel. He also offers a free tour of his ceramics studio, stocked with high-quality porcelain stoneware at all stages of production, including finished gift items. Call for reservations.

NHERC Heritage Center
Museum

(📞775-8890; http://hilo.hawaii.edu/academics/nherc/heritagecenter.php; 45-539 Plumeria St; ⏰9am-4pm Mon-Fri, to 1pm Sat) FREE Honoka'a will make a lot more sense if you visit here. Sponsored by the Northern Hawai'i Education and Research Center, it's mainly a large photo collection documenting the plantation era and its demise, but each picture speaks a thousand words.

From the main intersection downtown, follow Plumeria St uphill, turning right on Lehua St.

The Best... Hamakua Farm Agri-Tours

1 Hawaiian Vanilla Company (p148)

2 Hamakua Mushrooms (p159)

3 Mauna Kea Tea (p148)

4 Onomea Tea Company (p163)

5 Long Ears Coffee (p149)

Festivals & Events

Honoka'a Western Week   Rodeo
(Mamane St) FREE In late May, sleepy Mamane St saddles up with a block party, parade, foot-stomping music and a rodeo.

Sleeping

Your best options lie just outside Honoka'a town, in misty upcountry Ahualoa and Pa'auilo pastureland. If money's not an issue, consider Kukui-haele and its incomparable views of Waipi'o Valley.

Keolamauloa   Vacation Rental $$
(776-1294; www.keolamauloa.com; 43-1962 Pa'auilo Mauka Rd, Pa'auilo; house per 2/3/4 people $100/125/150; 🛜) This well-tended family homestead in Pa'auilo offers a

Island Insights

The only Native Hawaiian governor in the history of the USA, John D Waihee III (served 1986–94), hails from Honoka'a.

modern homestay. The comfy two-bedroom house includes full kitchen, laundry facilities and access to the grounds: koa and fruit trees, vegetable gardens, pond and livestock. Guests are encouraged to participate in farm life. Discounts for long stays; surcharge for under four nights; plus there's a cleaning fee.

Waipi'o Wayside B&B   B&B $$
(800-833-8849, 775-0275; www.waipioway side.com; Hwy 240; r incl breakfast $110-180; 🛜) Loaded with character, this attractively furnished 1932 plantation house is a classic B&B, complete with welcoming host and sociable homemade breakfast. The five rooms differ markedly, but each enjoys designer touches, such as iron-bed frames, a wooden Chinese barber chair, shower skylight and hardwood floors.

Common areas include a living room with books and a large-screen TV (with DVDs), plus a spacious, secluded lanai. Located about 2 miles north of Honoka'a on Hwy 240.

Mountain Meadow Ranch   Vacation Rental $$
(775-9376; www.mountainmeadowranch. com; 46-3895 Kapuna Rd, Ahualoa; cottage $150, ste incl breakfast $115; 🛜) This equestrian ranch on 7 acres offers a peaceful two-bedroom cottage that sleeps four and includes full kitchen, wood stove and washer/dryer. The B&B suite, attached to the main house, is ideal for two and, though lacking a kitchen, has a microwave, small fridge, and soothing dry sauna.

Waianuhea B&B   B&B $$$
(775-1118, 888-775-2577; www.waianuhea. com; 45-3503 Kahana Dr, Ahualoa; r $225-350, ste $400, incl breakfast; 🛜) This striking inn combines eco thinking (solar power) with fine art and design (Tiffany lamps, Philippe Starck chairs, bright skylights and gleaming hardwood floors). Here, you get excellent hotel professionalism in rural solitude, but the vibe is strangely detached. Gourmet dinners (per person $58 to $68) are served on-site with 48 hours' notice.

🍴 Eating

Much of Honoka'a is closed on Sundays and possibly Mondays, too.

Tex Drive-In Bakery, Local $
(📞808-775-0598; www.texdriveinhawaii.com; Hwy 19; mains $5-10; ⏱6:30am-8pm) A *malasada* is just a doughnut, but Tex is famous for serving them hot and fresh. They come plain (96¢) or filled (add 35¢). Tex also serves decent plate lunches and *loco mocos* (rice, fried egg and hamburger patty topped with gravy or other condiments), with fish options and seasonal taro burgers.

Simply Natural Cafe $
(📞775-0119; 45-3625 Mamane St, Honoka'a; dishes $5-12; ⏱9am-3pm Mon-Sat, 11am-3pm Sun; 📶) A cozy go-to spot for wholesome eats, from taro pancakes to an open-faced spicy tuna melt. Kiddie menu and biodegradable takeout containers add to the appeal.

Honoka'a People's Theatre Cafe Cafe $
(📞775-9963; www.honokaapeople.com; 45-3574 Mamane St, Honoka'a; espresso drinks $2.50-4.50, sandwiches $5.50-8; ⏱7am-7:30pm Tue-Sun) In the theatre lobby, this friendly cafe serves espresso drinks, sandwiches and other light meals. A cozy hangout with counter or table seating.

Honoka'a Farmers Market Market $
(Mamane St, Honoka'a; ⏱7:30am-noon Sat) A small gathering, with fresh produce, directly from the farmers. Located in front of Honoka'a Trading Company.

Café il Mondo Italian $$
(📞775-7711; www.cafeilmondo.com; 45-3626a Mamane St, Honoka'a; pizzas $12-24; ⏱11am-8pm Mon-Sat) Honoka'a's gathering place specializes in pizzas, pastas and enormous calzones packed to bursting point. Sit at the convivial central table and mingle with locals. Bring your own wine and don't hesitate to share it.

Ahualoa Pastoral

For a peaceful meander, turn off Hwy 19 onto the Old Mamalahoa Hwy, just west of the Mile 52 marker. (Coming from Hilo, turn left at the Mile 43 marker opposite Tex Drive-In and then take the next immediate right.) This 10-mile detour winds through hill country, with small roadside ranches, old wooden fences and grazing horses. Take it slow, snap some pictures and get a taste of old-time Waimea. It's even more picturesque by bike.

⭐ Entertainment

Honoka'a People's Theatre Theater
(📞775-0000; www.honokaapeople.com; 45-3574 Mamane St, Honoka'a; movie tickets adult/child/senior $6/3/4; ⏱showings 5pm & 7pm Tue-Sun) In a historic building dating from 1930, this theater shows movies and hosts special events.

🔒 Shopping

Honoka'a Trading Company Antiques
(Mamane St, Honoka'a; ⏱10:30am-5pm) If a couple of Honoka'a aunties emptied their attics, basements and garages, it would look like this hangar-sized store. Weave through a worthy collection of vintage aloha wear, antiques, used books (great Hawaiiana selection), rattan and koa furniture, and real Hawaiian artifacts. Then talk story with the owner, quite a character herself.

Big Island Grown Gifts
(📞775-9777; bigislandgrown@hotmail.com; 45-3626 Mamane St, Honoka'a; ⏱9am-5pm Mon-Sat) Support local! This store carries an assortment of Big Island items, including bamboo T-shirts, koa jewelry, coffee and tea and natural soap (made by unforgettably named island brand Filthy Farmgirl).

Taro Patch Gifts
(Mamane St, Honoka'a; ⏱9am-5pm) With a
little of everything, this welcoming shop
is a one-stop for souvenirs, from colorful
ceramic dishes and breezy island apparel
to Waipi'o Valley mouse pads and organic
soaps. The shopkeeper's organic macadamia nuts, roasted in shell, are awesome.

Waipi'o Valley

At the end of the road on Hwy 240, you'll
be blown away by the sight of Waipi'o
Valley, the largest of seven spectacular
amphitheater valleys descending from
the Kohala Mountains. The valley goes
back 6 miles, an emerald patchwork of
forest and taro, where waterfalls plunge
earthward from 2000ft vertical *pali*
(cliffs). A river runs through it all, into a
black-sand beach. Few sites rival sacred
Waipi'o for dramatic beauty.

For 'stop and click' tourists, the scenic
lookout is the final destination. To enter
the valley, check out our two hiking
options and talk to the ranger at the
information booth (⏱8am-dusk).

HISTORY

Known as the Valley of the Kings, Waipi'o
was the island's ancient breadbasket and
also the political and religious center,
home to the highest *ali'i* (ruling chiefs). According to oral histories, several thousand
people lived here before Westerners arrived, and the remains of heiau (temples)
can be seen today. In 1823 William Ellis, the
first missionary to descend into Waipi'o,
estimated the population to be around
1300. In the 1880s Chinese immigrants
began to settle in the valley's green folds,
adding rice to the native taro cultivation.

In 1946 Hawai'i's most devastating
tsunami struck the valley, traveling over a
mile inland. Interestingly, no one perished
despite the massive flooding. Once the
waters receded, however, most people
resettled 'topside' in Kukuihaele. The
valley floor has been sparsely populated
ever since, attracting only a few dozen
nature lovers, recluses, pot farmers,

Left: Cliffs of Waipi'o Valley; **Below:** Waipi'o Wayside B&B (p150), Honoka'a
(LEFT) TAN YILMAZ/GETTY IMAGES ©; (BELOW) LONELY PLANET/GETTY IMAGES ©

hippies and *kama'aina* (people born and raised in Hawaii; literally, 'child of the land') seeking to reclaim their history.

Taro cultivation and poi production are building blocks of Hawaiian identity, and both valley residents and Native Hawaiians across the island fiercely guard Waipi'o Valley. It is strongly advised that you stick to established trails and avoid trespassing on private property if you enter the valley.

◉ Sights & Activities

In addition to hiking, experienced sea kayakers can arrange custom tours with Plenty Pupule (p81) in Kona. Waipi'o Beach isn't swimmable, however, due to rip currents and treacherous undertow.

Hiking Etiquette in Waipi'o Valley

The first rule of backpacking etiquette is to leave no trace. This is critical in pristine, sacred places such as Waipi'o Valley. Inexcusably, some stick their garbage into crevices in the lava-rock walls surrounding the campsites. This attracts roaches and other pests. Some even abandon unneeded gear in the valley: tents, mattress pads, beach chairs, reef shoes, rope, canned goods, you name it. Carry out what you carry in.

Waipi'o Valley

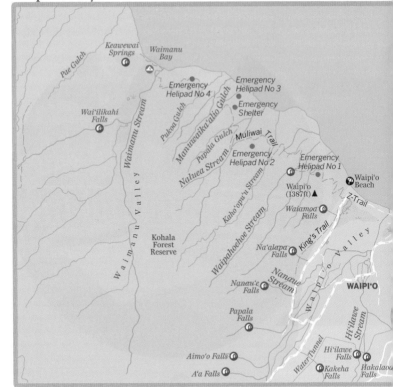

Waipi'o Valley Lookout   Lookout

Located at the end of Hwy 240, this lookout provides a jaw-dropping view across
the valley. One of Hawaii's iconic images.

Waipi'o Valley Hike   Hiking

To reach the valley floor, you must walk or
drive the incredibly steep road from the
lookout. The road leads to Waipi'o Beach,
and to explore further, the adventurous
can follow the King's Trail to Nanau'e Falls.

Don't underestimate the steep road.
If by car, you must have 4WD and use
your gears for braking. Do not attempt it
otherwise, as the road has a 25% grade
and ends in a rutted mess that's even
worse when wet. The trip takes about 15
minutes one way. If you hike down (allow
for 30 minutes down, 45 minutes up),
wear fitted shoes, as the decline will jam

your toes. There's no shade or potable
water.

Once on the valley floor, follow the road
to **Waipi'o Beach**, passing the twisted
remains of vehicles here to stay. There
are bathrooms near the beginning of
the black-sand beach. Don't even think
of swimming here, even if you see local
surfers paddling out. Midway down
you'll have to cross **Waipi'o Stream**,
which flows into the sea; best to do so by
wading in the ocean, where there are no
rocks. If there has been rain, you can see
Kaluahine Falls cascading down the cliffs
from whence you came. High surf makes
getting to the falls more challenging than
it looks. Ahead you'll see the Muliwai Trail
zig-zagging up the cliffs on the other
side of the valley, on its way to distant
Waimanu.

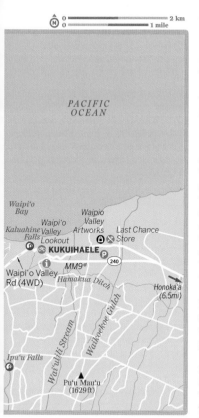

fruit), monkeypods, papaya, elephant ear, avocado, and lots more. You might see friendly wild horses, descendents of domesticated animals left behind after the tsunami.

After a mile or so you'll reach a wire fence (passable on this public trail) and shortly thereafter **Nanau'e Falls**.

Muliwai Trail
Hiking

For expert trekkers only, this 8-mile backcountry trail goes from Waipi'o Valley to Waimanu Valley, traversing steep, slippery and potentially treacherous ground. It takes 6½ to eight hours one way and requires crossing 13 gulches – brutal to ascend and descend, but lovely nonetheless, with little waterfalls and icy cold pools for swimming. Plan on camping in Waimanu Valley for at least one night. Don't attempt this hike during or after rains.

For detailed hiking information, contact **Na Ala Hele** (☏974-4382; http://hawaiitrails. ehawaii.gov) Trail and Access Specialist Clement Change in Hilo. Following is a general description of the hike.

To get to the Muliwai trailhead, you must first hike down into Waipi'o Valley. For overnight parking, your best bet is Waipi'o Valley Artworks (per day $15), a few miles from the Waipi'o Valley Lookout. Hike down into Waipi'o Valley and cross Waipi'o Stream, heading west.

The Muliwai Trail begins at the base of the cliffs on the west side of Waipi'o Valley. It starts by ascending over 1200ft in a mile of killer switchbacks. The hike out to Waimanu Valley is harder than the hike back, and the final 1200ft descent is extremely tricky. The trail is poorly

Once you cross to the base of the cliffs, you will see a trail that heads inland, next to a gate. The trail soon forks, with the Muliwai Trail heading upwards, and the **King's Trail** further inland, along a fence. As it parallels the valley walls the King's Trail passes through a natural botanical garden featuring coffee, *liliko'i* (passion

Island Insights

Kukuihaele means 'light that comes and goes' in Hawaiian, referring to the *huaka'ipo* (night marchers) – torch-bearing ghosts of Hawaiian warriors who pass through Kukuihaele to Waipi'o. As the legend goes, if you look at the night marchers or get in their way, you die. Survival is possible only if one of your ancestors is a marcher – or if you lie face down on the ground.

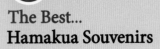

The Best...
Hamakua Souvenirs

maintained and extremely hazardous and partly washed out, with sheer drop-offs into the ocean and no handholds. If the descent is questionable, head back to a previous trail shelter for the night. Throughout, expect mud, mosquitoes, sun exposure and breathtaking views.

GUIDED HIKES & RIDES

Less-experienced hikers should consider exploring Waipi'o backcountry with guides.

Hawaiian Walkways   Hiking
(📞808-457-7759; www.hawaiianwalkways.com; guided hikes adult/child $119/99; ⏰tours 9:30am) Go to waterfalls and swimming holes via a private trail.

Walking Waipi'o   Hiking
(📞345-9505; www.walkingwaipio.com; adult/child 7-12yr $120/75; ⏰tours 8am Mon-Fri) An uncommon five-hour hiking trip on the valley floor, including swimming, led by a valley resident.

**Waipi'o Ridge
Stables**   Horseback Riding
(📞877-757-1414, 775-1007; www.waipioridgestables.com; rides $85-165; ⏰tours 8:45am) Tour the valley rim to the top of Hi'ilawe Falls (2½ hours) or combine with a forest trail ride (five hours), ending with a picnic and waterfall swim. Caters for all abilities.

Na'alapa Stables   Horseback Riding
(📞775-0419; www.naalapastables.com; rides $85; ⏰tours 9am & 12:30pm Mon-Sat) Visit the valley on a 2½-hour horseback ride; children eight and over are welcome. Caters for all abilities.

**Waipi'o Valley Wagon
Tours**   Wagon Ride
(📞775-9518; www.waipiovalleywagontours.com; adult/child $60/30; ⏰tours 10:30am, 12:30pm & 2:30pm Mon-Sat) This 1½-hour jaunt in a mule-drawn wagon carts visitors around the valley floor.

🛏 Sleeping

Backcountry camping in Waimanu Valley requires a state permit from the **Division of Forestry & Wildlife** (📞974-4221; http://camping.ehawaii.gov; 19 E Kawili St, Hilo, HI 96720; fee per night nonresident/resident $18/12; ⏰8am-4:30pm Mon-Fri) for a maximum of six nights. There are nine campsites (No 2, No 6 and No 9 are recommended) and facilities include fire pits and composting outhouses. For water, there's a spring about 10 minutes behind campsite No 9; all water must be treated.

Except for the yurt, there are no accommodations on the Waipi'o Valley floor. But there are excellent options in Kukuihaele, the residential community on the rim of the valley, including cliffside properties with spectacular views.

**Waipi'o Valley
Yurt**   Vacation Rental $
(📞345-9505; www.walkingwaipio.com; Waipi'o Valley; yurt per night/week $75/450) This off-the-grid, 14ft yurt by Waipi'o Stream is a unique opportunity to stay in the valley. It includes a kitchen with propane fridge and gas stove, plus a hot shower. The bed sleeps two but the kitchen/living area can accommodate more.

Waipio Rim B&B   B&B $$$
(📞775-1727; www.waipiorim.com; studio $200) Get away from it all at this handsome studio, gloriously perched on a cliff near the lookout. From the private deck, all-around windows keep the fabulous view in sight. Microwave, refrigerator, fifth night free.

Cliff House

Hawaii   Vacation Rental $$$

(☎ 800-492-4746, 775-0005; www.cliffhouse
hawaii.com; Waipi'o Rd; 2br house $199, each
additional person $35; @) Set on sprawling
acres of pastureland, this house assures
privacy and space. It's well equipped with
two bedrooms, full kitchen, living and
dining rooms, wrap-around lanai, satellite
TV, washer/dryer and even a telescope
for whale-watching. The same parcel
contains the less dramatic but still beauti-
fully situated **Hawaii Oceanview House**
(☎ 775-9098; www.hawaiioceanviewhouse.com;
2-br house $165, each additional person $35).
Minimum two-night stay.

🔒 Shopping

Waipi'o Valley
Artworks   Arts & Crafts

(☎ 800-492-4746, 775-7157, 775-0958; www.
waipiovalleyartworks.com; ⏰ 8am-5pm) This
inviting little shop wears many hats: stop
for ice cream, sandwiches and snacks;
browse the koa wood furniture, bowls
and other crafts. It's also the best place
to park your car overnight, if camping in
Waimanu Valley (per day $15).

Kalopa State Recreation Area

Don't miss this idyllic 100-
acre **state park** (www.
hawaiistateparks.org/parks/
hawaii/index.cfm?park_id=45;
⏰ daylight hrs) FREE,
with camping (first left
as you enter), cabins
(second left) and vari-
ous gentle trails. Set in
a quiet, native forest at
2000ft, it's fantasti-
cally lush and a great
place for beginner or
family camping. Group
cabins (eight people
max) have bunk beds,
linens and blankets, plus

hot showers and a fully equipped kitchen.
Permits (residents/nonresident $60/90) are
required.

The park comprises two overall trail
systems (see the large map near the
cabins). The first trail system starts where
the road by the cabins ends. The easy
0.75mi **Nature Trail** passes through old
ohia forest, where some trees measure
over 3ft in diameter. The path can be
overgrown so watch for the established
trail. Skip the **Dryland Forest Trail**, which
only goes 100 yards, and the **Arboretum
Trail**, which is so overgrown that you
might get lost. A small **Polynesian
Garden** contains a dozen of the original
25 canoe plants, introduced to Hawaii by
the original Polynesian voyagers for food,
medicine and clothing.

The second, more-interesting, trail
system leads into the adjoining forest
reserve with old-growth forest and
tremendous tree ferns. It starts along
Robusta Lane, on the left between the
caretaker's house and the campground,
and goes about 600yd to the edge of
Kalopa Gulch, through a thick eucalyptus

Muliwai Trail (p155)
JAMES OSMOND/ALAMY©

The Best... Hamakua Coast for Kids

1 See Waipi'o Valley by horseback (p156)

2 Eat Tex Drive-In (p151) *malasadas* (doughnuts) with abandon

3 Stay on a family farm at Keolamauloa (p150)

4 Go ziplining

5 Go retro at the Back to the 50s Highway Fountain Diner (p160)

forest. The trail continues along the gulch rim for another mile, while several side trails branch off and loop back into the recreation area via the **Perimeter Trail**. Signage is confusing so you should sketch the map near the cabins for reference along the way. You can go over 4 miles on these scenic but spottily maintained trails.

To get here, turn *mauka* off the Hawai'i Belt Rd near the Mile 42 marker, at Kalopa Dr. Follow park signs for 3 miles.

Laupahoehoe

Laupahoehoe had its heyday when sugar was king, but it remains a solid village community with a pleasant beach park and a handful of attractions.

On April 1, 1946, tragedy hit the small plantation town when a tsunami 30ft-high wiped out the schoolhouse on the point, killing 20 children and four adults. After the tsunami the whole town moved uphill.

In February, the **Laupahoehoe Music Festival** (Laupahoehoe Point Beach Park; admission $10; ⏲9am-5pm) comes to the beach park to raise scholarship money for local students. There's good eating, quality hula and tunes by favorite local musicians.

Laupahoehoe peninsula

PETER FRENCH/ALAMY

Hamakua Ziplines

Ziplines are being strung all over Hamakua's rainforests and waterfalls. Which course is best for you?

Skyline EcoAdventures Akaka Falls (☎888-878-8400; www.zipline.com; 28-1710 Honomu Rd; $170; ☉tours 10am-3pm) Skyline has the single best zip and it's a jaw dropper. The seven zips on this course get progressively longer and higher until you whoosh directly over a 250ft waterfall on a 3350ft ride! Weight 80lb to 260lb, ages 10 and up.

Umauma Falls & Zipline Experience (☎930-9477; http://umaumaexperience.com; 31-313 Old Mamalahoa Hwy; $189; ☉tours 8am-3pm) The most consistently thrilling. None of its nine zips has the grandeur of Skyline's magnificent climax, but there are no bunny-slope lines and you'll see 18 waterfalls. Weight 35lb to 275lb, ages four and up.

Zip Isle Zipline Adventures (☎888-947-4753, 963-5427; www.zipisle.com; $147; ☉tours between 9am-3:30pm) A good choice for kids and anxious first-timers. There are seven gentle zips, including a dual line, and a 150ft suspension bridge. Located at World Botanical Gardens, which you can enter for free. Weight 70lb to 270lb.

For other ziplines, see Kapaʻau in North Kohala (p116).

🏖 Beaches

Laupahoehoe Point Beach Park
Beach

Only real crazy *buggahs* would swim at windy, rugged Laupahoehoe, where the fierce surf sometimes crashes over the rocks and onto the parking lot. But it's strikingly pretty, with a scenic breakwater and fingers of lava rock jutting out of the waves. It's popular with local families for picnics and camping (full facilities available).

Stop here to view the memorial for the 24 students and teachers who died in the 1946 tsunami. The school stood around the colossal banyan tree toward your right as you approach the park.

⊙ Sights

The 1.5-mile **scenic drive** to the point winds through a dense tropical jungle and longstanding plantation houses.

Hamakua Mushrooms
Farm

(☎962-0305; www.hamakuamushrooms.com; 36-221 Manowaiopae Homestead Rd; 70min tours per adult/child 3-11yr/senior $20/10/ 17.50; ☉Tours 9:30am, 11am & 1:30pm Tue, Wed & Fri, 1:30pm Mon & Thu) A hugely successful boutique crop, Hamakua Mushrooms is favored by top chefs statewide. Its specialty mushrooms are cultivated in bottles and are immediately recognizable, especially the hefty Aliʻi Oyster. The husband-and-wife owners give informative guided tours with a personal touch, including sautéed samples. Their passion for mushrooms is contagious.

Laupahoehoe Train Museum
Museum

(☎962-6300; www.thetrainmuseum.com; 36-2377 Mamalahoa Hwy; adult/senior/student $6/5/3; ☉9am-4:30pm Tue-Fri, 10am-2pm Sat & Sun; P) This unassuming little museum is brimming with fascinating artifacts and photographs of the plantation railroad era, all contained in an old station agent's house. Don't miss the video of the long-gone coastal train, which showcases the amazing bridges that once curved along (and across) Hamakua gulches, until demolished by tsunami. Located between the Mile 25 and 26 markers.

The Best...
Hamakua Green Oases

1 Waipi'o Valley (p152)

2 Hawaii Tropical Botanical Garden (p162)

3 Pepe'ekeo 4-Mile Scenic Drive (p163)

4 Akaka Falls State Park (p161)

5 Kalopa State Recreation Area (p157)

6 Scenic drive to Laupahoehoe Point Beach Park (p159)

🛏 Sleeping & Eating

Old Jodo Temple B&B $$
(📞962-6967; www.vrbo.com/236574; r per night/week $150/950; 📶) This historic Buddhist temple (c 1899) is a gem hidden in the tropical valley near Laupahoehoe Point. Nicely restored by the owner-hosts, it's simple, retro and downright charming. Downstairs, the B&B area has two large bedrooms (sleeps up to seven), spacious living and dining rooms, airy porches and full kitchen.

For an additional charge, you could rent the entire house, which includes a large yoga space (formerly the temple), bedroom and bathroom upstairs. Washer and dryer available. Directions to the B&B are given upon booking.

Back to the 50s Highway Fountain Diner Diner $
(📞962-0808; 35-2704 Mamalahoa Hwy; burgers $4-7, plates $8-10; ⏰8am-7pm Wed & Thu, to 8pm Fri & Sat, to 3pm Sun) Nostalgia reigns in this wonderful homage to Elvis, Marilyn and the boppin' '50s. Built in a historic plantation house, the old-fashioned counter and booths set the mood for burgers (made with local beef) and shakes. The menu has island favorites including fried *ono* (wahoo) filets with mashed potatoes, chili bowls, and pancake and egg breakfasts.

Hakalau & Around

It's a stretch to call Hakalau a 'town,' but it's home to an active residential community of old-timers and newcomers. There are no restaurants here, but stock up on homemade taro chips and other snacks at **Aaron's Blue Kalo** (📞963-6929; 29-2110 Hwy 19; chips per bag $5-10; ⏰9:30am-2pm Mon, Wed & Fri).

🏖 Beaches

Kolekole Beach Park Park
Beneath a highway bridge, this park sits alongside Kolekole Stream. It's not a must-see, but there are pretty little waterfalls and full facilities. Daredevil locals surf and bodyboard at the river-mouth, but don't try it; it's rocky and currents are dangerous. Camping is allowed with a county permit, but the narrow area can get crowded and boisterous with picnicking local families.

To get here, turn inland off Hawai'i Belt Rd at the southern end of Kolekole Bridge, about 1300yd south of the Mile 15 marker.

◉ Sights

World Botanical Gardens Gardens
(📞963-5427; www.wbgi.com; MM16, Hwy 19; adult/child 5-12yr/teen 13-17yr $13/3/6; ⏰9am-5:30pm) Under development since 1995, this garden remains a work in progress. It is an admirable effort but plays second fiddle to the Hawaii Tropical Botanical Garden closer to Hilo. To get here from Hwy 19, turn *mauka* (inland) near mile marker 16, at the posted sign.

Sleeping

Akiko's Buddhist Bed & Breakfast
B&B, Vacation Rental $

(963-6422; www.akikosbnb.com; s/d incl breakfast from $65/75, studio cottage $65-85, 3br house from $150;) Immersed in tropical foliage, this peaceful retreat offers a variety of accommodations. The B&B rooms, with shared bath, are simple and clean, while two off-the-grid studio cottages allow a rare indoor-outdoor experience. For those seeking more space and privacy, the well-kept Hale Aloha house, with full kitchen, three bedrooms and two baths, is a fantastic value.

Most compelling might be owner Akiko Masuda, who invites guests to join morning meditation and coordinates a popular New Year's Eve *mochi* (Japanese rice cake) pounding festival. To get here, turn inland toward Wailea-Hakalau between the Mile 15 and 16 markers.

Honomu

Honomu is a quaint old sugar town that might be forgotten today if it weren't for its proximity to Akaka Falls. Life here remains rural and slow paced, now with retro wooden buildings sprouting shops and eateries.

Sights

Akaka Falls State Park
Park

(www.hawaiistateparks.org; Akaka Falls Rd; entry per car/pedestrian $5/1) A worthwhile excursion, this park is visually outstanding and easily accessible. A half-mile paved path loops through enchanting rainforest, stopping at two lookouts. Your first stop, 100ft **Kahuna Falls**, is just a teaser for the truly grand **Akaka Falls**, which plunges 420ft into a deep green pool. Lush foliage includes banyan and monkeypod trees, seasonally blooming heliconia and giant bamboo groves.

To get here, turn onto Hwy 220 between the Mile 13 and 14 markers and then drive 4 miles inland. Cash or credit cards accepted.

Local Knowledge

NAME: AKIKO MASUDA

OCCUPATION: B&B OWNER SINCE 1991, COMMUNITY ORGANIZER, ARTIST, CHILDREN'S BOOK AUTHOR

RESIDENCE: HAKALAU

1 HOW CAN VISITORS HAVE A DEEPER CULTURAL EXPERIENCE HERE?

If you want to delve deeper on your trip, be willing to stay in one place, so staff or neighbors recognize you. Greet them every morning. The key is to develop trust with local people, and that takes time and lots of friendliness.

2 ANY ADVICE FOR VISITORS ON TRIP ITINERARIES?

Stay for a minimum of five days (or ideally two weeks). You can circle the island in a weekend and 'see a lot' but it's the people who make Hawai'i a very special place. Meeting people will change your life. Seeing the island... you might get a few nice pics.

3 ARE THERE RULES ON INTERACTING WITH LOCALS?

Locals are low-key, but appreciate a thoughtful gesture. One of my guests accepted free paddle boarding lessons from a local guy. I told [my guest], 'Don't take that at face value. Figure out a reasonable hourly rate. Then put cash in an envelope with a nice thank-you note.'

4 WHAT ARE SOME OTHER CULTURAL EVENTS WORTH SEEING?

The Merrie Monarch Festival (p177) showcases many cultures: hula is Hawaiian, but dancers have diverse ethnic backgrounds and *halau* (schools) come from Japan and the mainland. I'd also suggest the Waimea Cherry Blossom Heritage Festival (p124) and the King Kamehameha Day (p119) parade in North Kohala.

🛏 Sleeping

Palms Cliff House Inn
B&B $$$

(☏963-6076; www.palmscliffhouse.com; r incl breakfast $299-449; ❄ 🛜) As elegant as a fine hotel, this well-run inn is also warm and welcoming. The eight ocean-view rooms are spacious, with upscale furnishings, and guests rave about the full hot breakfasts. Rates are steep, but discounts are often offered.

🍴 Eating

Hilo Sharks Coffee
Cafe $

(☏963-6706; www.hilosharkscoffee.com; sandwiches $6-7; ⏰8am-6pm Mon-Sat, to 4pm Sun; 🛜) This is *the* place to hang out in Honomu: great locally grown coffee, outdoor seating, wi-fi, creative sandwiches, refreshing smoothies, homemade chocolate and attractive prices.

Woodshop Gallery & Cafe
Cafe $

(☏963-6363; www.woodshopgallery.com; Hwy 220; lunch dishes $6-9; ⏰11am-5:30pm) From burgers and lemonade to homemade ice cream and espresso, it's all good and served with aloha. Following lunch, browse or splurge on the extraordinary collection of handcrafted bowls, photos and blown glass.

Mr Ed's Bakery
Bakery $

(☏963-5000; www.mredsbakery.com; Hwy 220; ⏰6am-6pm Mon-Sat, 9am-4pm Sun) Check out the staggering selection of homemade preserves featuring local fruit (jar $7.50). Pastries are hit or miss; some are cloyingly sweet, but the Portuguese sweet bread is a winner.

Onomea Bay & Around

Pepe'ekeo, Onomea and Papaikou are three plantation villages admired for their gorgeous landscapes and views.

◎ Sights & Activities

Hawaii Tropical Botanical Garden
Gardens

(☏964-5233; www.hawaiigarden.com; 27-717 Old Mamalahoa Hwy, Papaikou; adult/child $15/5; ⏰9am-4pm) This is an absolutely fabulous botanical garden, beautifully situated by the ocean and superbly managed. A paved trail meanders through 2000 species of tropical plants set amid streams and waterfalls. Give yourself at least an hour for the walk, which ends at Onomea Bay.

The garden is located halfway along the Pepe'ekeo 4-Mile Scenic Drive. Park and buy your ticket at the yellow building on the *mauka* side of the road. A guided tour ($5) is offered on Saturday at noon.

Hawaii Tropical Botanical Garden
TOM BENEDICT/GETTY IMAGES ©

Hawaii Plantation Museum
Museum

(☏443-7679; http://memoriesofhawaiibigisland. com; 27-246 Old Mamalahoa Hwy; adult/child/ senior $8/3/6; ☺10am-3pm Tue-Sat) Don't miss this well-done museum highlighting Hawai'i's sugar industry, which spanned the mid-1880s to 1996. Museum curator Wayne Subica has single-handedly amassed this collection, which includes plantation tools, memorabilia from 'Mom & Pop' shops, vintage photos and retro signage.

To get here from Hilo, turn left just past the Mile 6 marker on the main highway; from Kona, turn right just past the Mile 8 marker.

Pepe'ekeo 4-Mile Scenic Drive
Drive

The gorgeous rainforest jungle along this stretch of the Old Mamalahoa Hwy proves that those annoying showers are worth it. Cruising the narrow road, you cross a series of one-lane bridges spanning little streams and waterfalls, under a tangle of trees.

You can begin the drive from either end, but approaching from the south (Hilo side) involves an easy right turn between the Mile 7 and Mile 8 markers on the main highway.

Onomea Tea Company
Farm

(☏964-3283; www.onomeatea.com; 27-604 Alakahi Pl; tasting $25) This 9-acre tea plantation offers tea tastings and tours. It's a small-scale operation, allowing for friendly chatting about tea and its cultivation. Website reservations are required.

Onomea Bay Hike
Hiking

For a quick, scenic hike to the bay, take the Na Ala Hele trailhead on the *makai* (seaward) side of the road, along the Pepe'ekeo 4-Mile Scenic Drive. From Hilo, turn onto the scenic drive and go about 1.75 miles; look for a small sign marking the trailhead. Parking is tricky, but there's a small pullover spot just north of the sign.

After a 10-minute hike down a slippery jungle path, you'll come to a finger of lava jutting into the sea. A spur to the right leads to a couple of small waterfalls and a cove. Continuing straight brings you to the diminutive bluffs overlooking the batik blues of Onomea Bay. Hawaiian monk seals have been sighted here.

🍴 Eating

What's Shakin'
Health Food $

(☏964-3080; smoothies $6; ☺10am-5pm) 🌿 Your fondest memory of the Pepe'ekeo 4-Mile Scenic Drive might be this fantastic roadside eatery. Just over a mile from the north end, look for the cheerful yellow cottage, which pumps out fantastic homemade food and killer smoothies (all fruit, no filler).

Hilo

Hilo should have an inferiority complex. It gets less than half of Kailua-Kona's tourists. But the townsfolk know better. Sure, it's rainy. But 130in of annual rainfall guarantees a leafy landscape, where waterfalls gush and every homeowner has a green thumb. Sure, it seems ordinary and familiar (despite its tropical splendor). But Hilo has enough critical mass to be a real community. This ain't no tourist town! Locals will outnumber you wherever you go. Since the 1990s, moneyed outsiders have been noticing this most livable place, boosting real-estate values and somewhat changing its boondocks reputation. But Hilo remains staunch to its plantation-era roots and unpretentious vibe.

Mission House (p169)
JOHN ELK/GETTY IMAGES ©

Hilo Itineraries

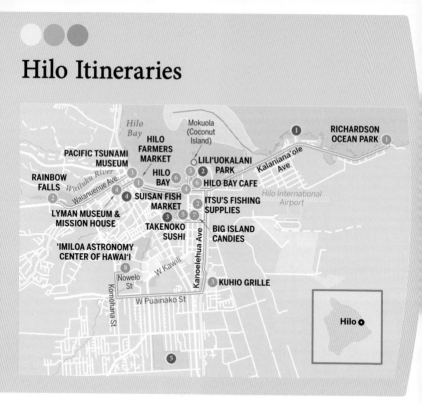

One Day

1 **Hilo Farmers Market** (p181) Time your trip for Wednesday or Saturday, when the market is in full swing. Go early to avoid traffic jams and bring cash for sweet bananas, juicy star fruit and fresh coconut.

2 **Rainbow Falls** (p173) If you're a waterfall aficionado, go in the morning for an optimal photo op.

3 **Pacific Tsunami Museum** (p172) It's impossible to understand Hilo's true grit without learning about its two catastrophic 20th-century tsunami. While downtown, stroll through old Hilo town, notable for its retro architecture, indie shops and scenic bay setting. Don't miss the stunning nature photography at Extreme Exposure Fine Art Gallery.

4 **Suisan Fish Market** (p181) Stop by for an assortment of takeout ahi *poke* (marinated raw fish) and succulent dried marlin.

5 **Lili'uokalani Park** (p169) Spend a leisurely afternoon picnicking or crossing the quaint bridges and stepping stones, all with a panoramic view of Hilo Bay. Walk across the paved footbridge to Mokuola (Coconut Island), another family favorite.

6 **Hilo Bay Cafe** (p183) To savor Hawaii Regional Cuisine, Hilo style, try this foodie favorite for dinner.

 THIS LEG: 6 MILES

Three Days

1 **Richardson Ocean Park** (p169) After following the one-day itinerary, next morning, wake early for a beach day. With sunning, swimming and snorkeling options here, there's something for everyone.

2 **Itsu's Fishing Supplies** (p184) Cool off with a rainbow ice shave from one of Hilo's iconic mom-and-pop shops.

3 **Kuhio Grille** (p183) Sate your appetite (and your curiosity about Hawaiian food) at this restaurant, known for its '1lb *laulau*' (pork or chicken and salted butterfish, wrapped in taro and *ti* leaves and steamed), *kalua* pork and poi.

4 **Lyman Museum & Mission House** (p169) History buffs can see a variety of collections, from geology to ancient Hawaiian artifacts to plantation life. Don't miss the guided tour of the Mission House.

5 **Takenoko Sushi** (p184) Reservations are imperative at this superlative eight-seat sushi bar.

6 **Hilo Bay** (p168) On your third day, take the opportunity to revisit your favorite beach or park. If you've been itching to try stand up paddle (SUP) surfing – rent a board and launch into the calm waters of the bay.

7 **Big Island Candies** (p184) Looking for gifts? The signature chocolate-dipped macadamia shortbread cookies are sure to delight.

8 **'Imiloa Astronomy Center of Hawai'i** (p172) Spend a few hours here, especially if you're heading to the Mauna Kea summit. Catch an awesome planetarium show.

THIS LEG: 15 MILES

Hilo Highlights

1 **Best Children's Beach: Onekahakaha Beach Park** (p168) Splash in kid-deep waters with lots of newfound playmates.

2 **Best Picnic Spot: Lili'uokalani Park** (p169) Find a patch of lawn amid serene ponds, towering trees and Japanese bridges.

3 **Best Local Food: Cafe 100** (p182) For local-style comfort food, join the lineup of locals at this iconic drive-in.

4 **Best Block Party: Black & White Night** (p177) On the first Friday in November, downtown Hilo comes alive. Monthly 'First Friday' street fairs keep the party going year round.

5 **Best Bargain Activity: Hilo Municipal Golf Course** (p174) Who cares if there are no seaside holes or resort glamour? This well-kept course is a fantastic value.

Lili'uokalani Park (p169)
LONELY PLANET/GETTY IMAGES ©

Discover Hilo

HISTORY

Since its first Polynesian settlers farmed and fished along the Wailuku River, Hilo has been a lively port town. In the 20th century, it was the trading hub for sugarcane grown in Puna and Hamakua, connecting in both directions with a sprawling railroad, the Hawaii Consolidated Railway.

Back then, townsfolk set up homes and shops along the bay. But after being slammed by two disastrous tsunami in 1946 and 1960, no one wanted to live downtown anymore. Today, you'll find parks, beaches and open space along Kamehameha Ave.

When the sugar industry folded in the 1980s and '90s, Hilo focused its economy on diversified agriculture, the university, retail and, of course, tourism. While downtown Hilo is still the charming heart of town, the go-to retail destinations are the big chain stores (Walmart, Target, Home Depot, etc) south of the airport.

🐦 Beaches

Except for Honoli'i Beach Park, Hilo's beaches are located in the Keaukaha neighborhood. Here, they're listed as you'd reach them driving out of central Hilo. On weekends, expect jammed parking lots and steady traffic along Kalaniana'ole Ave.

All beach parks listed below have restrooms, showers and picnic areas.

Reeds Bay Beach Park   Beach

At the end of Banyan Dr, this calm little cove is ideal for kids or stand up paddleboard (SUP) beginners. While centrally located, within sight of buildings and passing cars, it's a picturesque spot. Warning: a behemoth cruise ship might be docked in the distance.

Onekahakaha Beach Park   Beach

Popular with local families, this beach has a broad, shallow, sandy-bottomed pool, protected by a boulder breakwater. The water is only 1ft to 2ft deep in spots, creating the perfect 'baby beach.' An unprotected cove north of the protected pool is deeper but can be hazardous due to pokey *wana* (sea

Richardson Ocean Park
LONELY PLANET/GETTY IMAGES ©

urchins) and rough surf. Lifeguards on weekends and holidays.

James Kealoha Beach Park   Beach
(Carlsmith Beach Park) Best for older kids and snorkelers, this county beach is nick-named 'Four Miles' (the distance between the park and the downtown post office). For swimming and snorkeling, head to the eastern side, which has a deep, protected basin with generally calm, clear water and pockets of white sand. The park's western side is open ocean and much rougher. Locals surf here in winter or net fish. No lifeguards.

Wai'olena and Wai'uli Beach Parks   Beach
(Leleiwi Beach) Rocky and ruggedly pretty, these side-by-side beaches (commonly known by their former name, **Leleiwi Beach**) are Hilo's best shore-dive site. You might see turtles, interesting coral growth and a variety of butterfly fish. The water is freezing until you go past the reef, and the entrance is tricky (ask for advice at Nautilus Dive Center). Lifeguards on weekends and holidays.

Richardson Ocean Park   Beach
Near the end of Kalaniana'ole Ave, this pocket of black sand is Hilo's best all-round beach. During calm surf, the pro-tected waters are popular for swimming and snorkeling, with frequent sightings of friendly sea turtles (keep your distance, at least 50yd in the water). High surf at-tracts local bodyboarders. Shaded by lots of coconut trees, the beach also makes a sweet picnic spot. Daily lifeguards.

Honoli'i Beach Park   Beach
Less than 2 miles north of downtown Hilo, this protected cove is Hilo's best **surfing** and **bodyboarding** spot. When surf's up, it's jammed with locals and not a place for novices. Don't expect a sandy beach or ideal swimming conditions. It's all about the waves. Daily lifeguards.

From Hilo, take the Bayfront Hwy north; after the Mile 4 marker, turn right onto Nahala St and then left onto Kahoa St. Park on the roadside and walk down to the park.

◉ Sights

Most sights are found in downtown Hilo, where historic early-20th-century buildings overlook the coast, which locals call 'bayfront.' Farther east sits Hilo's landmark dock, Suisan Fish Market, and the Keaukaha beaches.

Lili'uokalani Park   Park
Savor Hilo's simple pleasures with a picnic lunch in **Japanese gardens** over-looking the bay. Named for Hawaii's last queen (r 1891–93), the 30-acre county park has manicured lawns, shallow ponds, bamboo groves, arched bridges, pagodas and a teahouse. At sunrise or sunset, join the locals and jog or stroll the perimeter, or simply admire the Mauna Kea view.

While here, cross the paved footbridge to **Mokuola (Coconut Island)**, a tiny island always lively with families, picnicking and swimming. Also adjacent to the park is **Banyan Drive**, Hilo's mini 'hotel row,' best known for the giant banyan trees lining the road. Royalty and celebrities planted the trees in the 1930s, and, if you look closely, you'll find plaques beneath the trees identifying Babe Ruth, Amelia Earhart and Cecil B DeMille.

Lyman Museum & Mission House   Museum
(☎808-935-5021; www.lymanmuseum.org; 276 Haili St; adult/child $10/3; ☉10am-4:30pm Mon-Sat) Compact yet comprehensive, this gem of a museum encompasses the tremendous variety of Hawaii's natural and cultural history. The adjacent Mis-sion House, built by the Reverend David Lyman and his wife, Sarah, in 1839, adds a human element to the hinstorical facts. Well-trained docents give half-hour tours of the house at 11am and 2pm.

Downstairs in the museum, geologic exhibits include fascinating examples of lava rock, minerals and shells. Upstairs, learn about Native Hawaiians, with exhibits on ancient sports, religion and the kapu (taboo) system.

Hilo

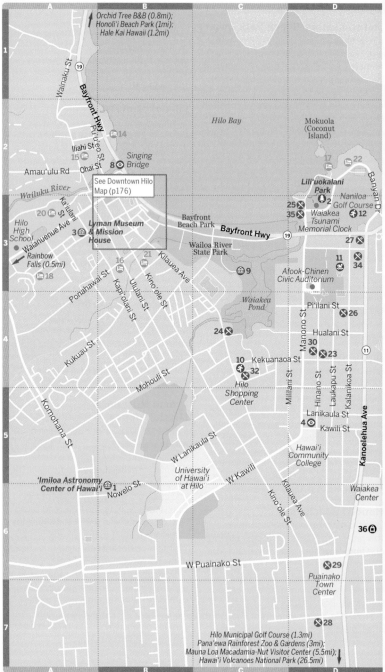

Orchid Tree B&B (0.8mi);
Honoli'i Beach Park (1mi);
Hale Kai Hawaii (1.2mi)

Wainaku St

Bayfront Hwy

19

Hilo Bay

Mokuola
(Coconut
Island)

Iliahi St

Pu'ueo St

14

15

Ohai St

8 Singing
Bridge

Amau'ulu Rd

17

22

Wailuku River

Lili'uokalani
Park

2

Naniloa
Golf Course

25

35

Waiakea
Tsunami
Memorial Clock

12

20

Ka'iulani Ave

Hilo
High
School

Waianuenue Ave

3 Lyman Museum
& Mission
House

See Downtown Hilo
Map (p176)

Bayfront
Beach Park

Bayfront Hwy

19

27

Rainbow
Falls (0.5mi)

16

21

18

Kīlauea Ave

Wailoa River
State Park

9

Afook-Chinen
Civic Auditorium

11

34

Ponahawai St

Kapiolani St

Ulu'ole St

Kino'ole St

Waiakea
Pond

Pi'ilani St

26

Kukuau St

Manono St

Hualani St

30

23

Mohouli St

24

10

32

Kekuanaoa St

Milani St

Hinano St

Laukapu St

Kalanikoa St

Hilo
Shopping
Center

Lanikaula St

4

Kawili St

Komohana St

W Lanikaula St

W Kawili

Hawai'i
Community
College

Kanoelehua Ave

'Imiloa Astronomy
Center of Hawai'i

1

Nowelo St

University
of Hawai'i
at Hilo

Kīlauea Ave

Kino'ole St

Waiakea
Center

36

W Puainako St

29

Puainako
Town
Center

28

Hilo Municipal Golf Course (1.3mi)
Pana'ewa Rainforest Zoo & Gardens (3mi);
Mauna Loa Macadamia-Nut Visitor Center (5.5mi);
Hawai'i Volcanoes National Park (26.5mi)

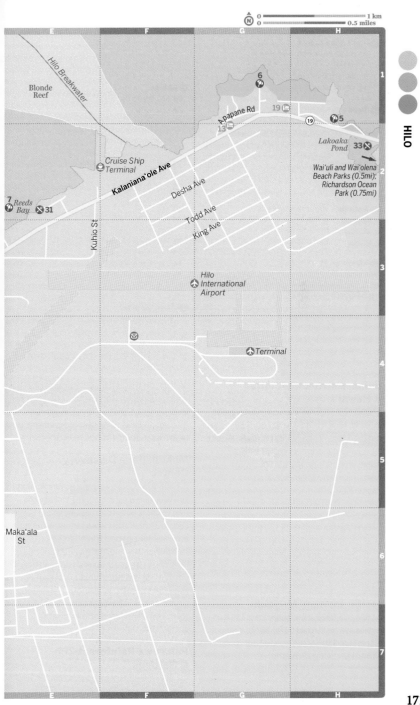

0   ===================== 1 km
0   ===================== 0.5 miles

Blonde
Reef

Hilo Breakwater

Cruise Ship
Terminal

Kalaniana'ole Ave

Kuhio St

Desha Ave

Todd Ave

King Ave

Apapane Rd

13

19

19

6

5

Lakoaka
Pond

33

Wai'uli and Wai'olena
Beach Parks (0.5mi);
Richardson Ocean
Park (0.75mi)

7 Reeds
Bay   31

Hilo
International
Airport

Terminal

Maka'ala
St

Hilo

'Imiloa Astronomy Center of Hawai'i
Museum

(☎ 808-969-9700; www.imiloahawaii.org; 600 'Imiloa Pl; adult/child 6-17yr $17.50/9.50; ☺ 9am-5pm Tue-Sun) 'Imiloa, which means 'exploring new knowledge,' is a $28 million museum and planetarium complex with a twist: it juxtaposes modern astronomy on Mauna Kea with ancient Polynesian ocean voyaging. Who would've thought that the mythical kumulipo (Hawaiian creation story) and the scientific big bang theory have parallels? It's a worthwhile family attraction and the natural complement to a summit tour. One planetarium show is included with admission.

Pacific Tsunami Museum
Museum

(☎ 808-935-0926; www.tsunami.org; 130 Kamehameha Ave; adult/child 6-17yr $8/4; ☺ 9am-4:15pm Mon-Sat) You cannot understand Hilo without knowing its history as a two-time tsunami survivor in 1946 and 1960. This seemingly modest museum is chock-full of riveting information, including a new

section on the Japanese tsunami of 2011, which damaged Kona. Allow enough time to experience the multimedia exhibits, including chilling computer simulations and heart-wrenching first-person accounts.

Mokupapapa Discovery Center
Museum

(☎ 808-935-8358; www.papahanaumokuakea. gov/education/center.html; 76 Kamehameha Ave; ☺ check website for opening hours) FREE
Did you know the Hawaiian archipelago extends far beyond the eight main islands to the Northwestern Hawaiian Islands, a long chain of uninhabited islets and atolls containing the healthiest coral reefs in the USA? Learn more about the islands' pristine ecosystems at this compelling museum, renovated and relocated in early 2014.

Pana'ewa Rainforest Zoo & Gardens
Zoo

(☎ 808-959-9233; www.hilozoo.com; ☺ 9am-4pm, petting zoo 1:30-2:30pm Sat) FREE

HILO SIGHTS

Four miles south of town, Hilo's sprawling 12-acre zoo is a fantastic freebie. Amid well-kept tropical gardens, see a global collection of monkeys, reptiles, sloths, parrots and more. The star is a white Bengal tiger named Namaste. Two play structures and a shaded picnic area make this a perfect family outing.

To get here, turn *mauka* (inland) off the Volcano Hwy onto W Mamaki St, just past the Mile 4 marker.

Rainbow Falls   Landmark

A regular stop for tour buses, the lookout for this 'instant gratification' cascade is just steps from the parking lot. Depending on rainfall, the lovely 80ft waterfall can be a torrent or a trickle. Go in the morning and you'll see rainbows if the sun and mist cooperate. Waianuenue ('rainbow seen in water') is the Hawaiian name for these falls.

To get here, drive up Waianuenue Ave (veer right when it splits into Kaumana Dr) about 1.5 miles from downtown Hilo; follow the signage.

Pe'epe'e Falls & Boiling Pots   Waterfall

Two miles past Rainbow Falls, and just as impressive, is another drive-up lookout, Pe'epe'e Falls & Boiling Pots. This unique series of falls cascading into swirling, bubbling pools (or 'boiling pots') might tempt you to hike in, but stay out of the water; currents are treacherous and many drownings have occurred. Restrooms available here.

EHCC Hawai'i Museum of Contemporary Art   Art Gallery

(East Hawai'i Cultural Center; 808-961-5711; www.ehcc.org; 141 Kalakaua St; suggested donation $2; 10am-4pm Mon-Sat) The best venue for local art is this downtown center, which displays the work of both professionals and amateurs. Exhibits change monthly, while workshops and classes (eg painting, drawing, ukulele and hula) are ongoing. Check the website for special evening concerts featuring top artists.

The Best...
Hilo Freebies

1 Pana'ewa Rainforest Zoo & Gardens

2 Mokupapapa Discovery Center

3 Sweet samples at Big Island Candies (p184)

4 EHCC Hawai'i Museum of Contemporary Art

5 Ho'ike show at Merrie Monarch Festival (p177)

Wailoa Center & Wailoa River State Park   Art Gallery

(808-933-0416; 8:30am-4:30pm Mon, Tue, Thu & Fri, noon-4:30pm Wed) This eclectic, state-run gallery hosts a variety of monthly exhibits. You might find quilts, bonsai, Chinese watercolors or historical photos, all done by locals. Surrounding the center is a quiet state park on the Wailoa River.

The main park landmark is a 14ft, Italian-made bronze statue of Kamehameha the Great, erected in 1997 and restored with gold leaf in 2004. There is also a tsunami memorial and a Vietnam War memorial.

Mauna Loa Macadamia-Nut Visitor Center   Factory

(808-966-8618, 888-628-6256; www.maunaloa.com; Macadamia Rd; 8:30am-5pm) FREE Hershey-owned Mauna Loa provides a self-guided tour of its working factory, where you can watch the humble mac nut as it moves along the assembly line from cracking to roasting to chocolate dipping and packaging. The gift shop sells the finished product at decent prices.

To get here, follow signage about 5 miles south of Hilo; along the Mile 3 access road, see acres of macadamia trees.

🏃 Activities

While Hilo's coast is lined with reefs rather than sand, its gentle waters are ideal for stand up paddle (SUP) surfing; launch from Mokuola (Coconut Island), Reeds Bay or Wailoa River State Park. For surfing, head to Honoli'i Beach Park.

While diving is best on the Kona side, there are decent shore-diving spots in or near Hilo; inquire at dive shops.

Sun & Sea Hawaii   Water Sports
(📞808-934-0902; sunandseahawaii@gmail.com; 244 Kamehameha Ave; SUP half/full day $45/65, 1-/2-tank shore dive $99/$129; ⏰9:30am-5pm Mon-Fri, 9am-4pm Sat, 11am-3pm Sun) This friendly one-stop shop for ocean sports rents SUP packages and sells a variety of snorkeling, diving and swimming gear.

Nautilus Dive Center   Diving
(📞808-935-6939; www.nautilusdivehilo.com; 382 Kamehameha Ave; intro charter dive $85; ⏰9am-5pm Tue-Sat) Hilo's go-to dive shop offers guided dives, PADI certification courses and general advice on shore diving. If you're a certified diver, rent here and head to the best East Hawai'i dive site at Pohoiki Bay in Puna.

Orchidland Surfboards   Surfing
(📞808-935-1533; www.orchidlandsurf.com; 262 Kamehameha Ave; ⏰9am-5pm Mon-Sat, 10am-3pm Sun) Board rentals, surf gear, and advice from owner Stan Lawrence, who opened the Big Island's first surf shop in 1972.

Kawamoto Swim Stadium   Swimming
(📞808-961-8698; 260 Kalanikoa St) FREE For lap swimming, this Olympic-sized, open-air pool is generally uncrowded during the day. Call for opening hours.

Hilo Municipal Golf Course   Golf
(📞808-959-7711; 340 Haihai St; greens fee Mon-Fri $34, Sat & Sun $45) Hilo's main 18-hole course (locally known as 'Muni') offers a well-designed layout, friendly staff and good clubhouse restaurant. Morning tee times are favored by the local contingent;

Left: Onekahakaha Beach Park (p168); **Below:** EHCC Hawai'i Museum of Contemporary Art (p173)

(LEFT) GREG ELMS/GETTY IMAGES ©; (BELOW) LONELY PLANET/GETTY IMAGES ©

call ahead to avoid waiting. While reasonably maintained, expect some weeds and mud, thanks to Hilo rain.

Naniloa Golf Course
Golf

(☎808-935-3000; 120 Banyan Dr; greens fee walk/cart $10/15) Despite its scenic location across from Lili'uokalani Park, this nine-hole course is good mainly for practice or for beginners. Grounds maintenance is so-so, but you might have the course to yourself.

Yoga Centered
Yoga

(☎808-934-7233; www.yogacentered.com; 37 Waianuenue Ave; drop-in class $14; ⏰boutique 10am-5pm Mon-Thu, to 4pm Sun) In an attractive space downtown, this studio offers mostly flow classes and a boutique well stocked with quality mats and clothing.

Balancing Monkey Yoga Center
Yoga

(☎633-8555; www.balancingmonkeyyoga.com; 1221 Kilauea Ave; drop-in class $10) Located at Hilo Shopping Center, this friendly studio offers a variety of daily classes.

🎇 Festivals & Events

Downtown Hilo hosts an art event on the **first Friday each month**, with live music, refreshments and extended hours at shops and galleries.

May Day Lei Day Festival
Hula

(☎808-934-7010; www.leiday.net) Beautiful lei displays, demonstrations, live music and hula throughout the month of May.

King Kamehameha Day Celebration
Historic Celebration

(☎808-935-9338; Mokuola/Coconut Island) Celebration of King Kamehameha, with hula, music, food and crafts, on June 11.

Fourth of July
Independence Day

Entertainment and food all day at Lili'uokalani Park; fireworks display from Mokuola (Coconut Island).

175

Downtown Hilo

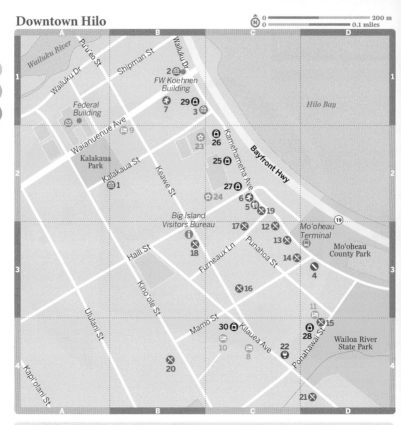

Downtown Hilo

◎ Sights
1 EHCC Hawai'i Museum of Contemporary Art	B2
2 Mokupapapa Discovery Center	B1
3 Pacific Tsunami Museum	B1

✈ Activities, Courses & Tours
4 Nautilus Dive Center	D3
5 Orchidland Surfboards	C2
6 Sun & Sea Hawaii	C2
7 Yoga Centered	B1

🛏 Sleeping
8 D&S Bed & Breakfast	C4
9 Hilo Bay Hostel	B2
10 Lotus Garden of Hilo	C4
11 Pakalana Inn	D3

✕ Eating
12 Abundant Life Natural Foods	C3
13 Cafe Pesto	C3
14 Hilo Farmers Market	C3
15 Koji's Bento Korner	D4
16 KTA Super Store – Downtown	C3
17 Moonstruck Patisserie	C3
18 Ocean Sushi Deli	B3
Paul's Place	(see 11)
19 Puka Puka Kitchen	C2
20 Short N Sweet	B4
21 Two Ladies Kitchen	D4

🍷 Drinking & Nightlife
22 Grapes: A Wine Store	C4

🎭 Entertainment
23 Kress Cinemas	B2
24 Palace Theater	C2

🛍 Shopping
25 Alan's Art & Collectibles	C2
26 Basically Books	C2
Dragon Mama	(see 19)
27 Extreme Exposure Fine Art Gallery	C2
28 Hilo Guitars & Ukuleles	D4
29 Sig Zane Designs	B1
30 Still Life Books	C4

Championship Hula

The **Merrie Monarch Festival** (📞935-9168; www.merriemonarchfestival.org; Afook-Chinen Civic Auditorium; 3-night admission $25-30) swoops into town around Easter (late March or early April) and turns laid-back Hilo into *the* place to be. Forget about booking a last-minute room! This sellout three-day hula competition was established in 1964 to honor King David Kalakaua (1836–91), who almost single-handedly revived Hawaiian culture and arts, which had been forbidden by missionaries for 70 years.

Top hula troupes from all the Islands vie in *kahiko* (ancient) and *'auana* (modern) categories. *Kahiko* performances are strong and serious, accompanied only by chanting. *'Auana* is closer to the mainstream style, with sinuous arm movements, smiling dancers and melodious accompaniment that includes string instruments. The primal chanting, meticulous choreography and traditional costumes are profoundly moving.

The competitions are televised, but to see it live, order tickets by mail on December 26 (no earlier postmarks accepted); see the website for seating and payment info. The 2700 tickets sell out within a month. Book accommodations and car a year in advance.

Big Island Hawaiian Music Festival
Music

(📞808-961-5711; www.ehcc.org; 556 Waianuenue Ave, Hilo High School; adult/child $10/free) A mid-July, two-day concert featuring virtuoso musicians in ukulele, steel guitar, slack key guitar and falsetto singing.

International Festival of the Pacific
Japanese Culture

(📞934-0177; Japanese Chamber of Commerce, 400 Hualani St) FREE August celebration of the Japanese in Hawaii, featuring a lantern parade and Japanese tea ceremony at Lili'uokalani Park.

Hawai'i County Fair
Fair

(799 Pi'ilani St, Afook-Chinen Civic Auditorium; adult/student $3/2) Pure nostalgia comes to town in September, with carnival rides, games and cotton candy.

Black & White Night
Fair

(www.downtownhilo.com; ⏰5-9pm) Downtown Hilo comes alive on the first Friday of November, with shops and galleries open late, artist and author appearances, and lots of live music.

🛏 Sleeping

In true Hilo style, there are few hotels, but the gamut of indie B&Bs, inns, and hostels. Note that many proprietors charge extra for one-night stays.

The Quirky Cottage
Inn $

(📞(770) 530-8788; www.thequirkycottage.net; 577 Kino'ole St; r $40-80) Simple, clean, private and affordable. If these are your priorities, this no-frills inn is perfect. The two suites each include private bath and two separate sleeping areas ($80 for up to four guests); one even has a kitchen. The studio ($40), with fridge and microwave, is a budget traveler's dream. Owners Doug and Sue have run a successful B&B and their experience shows.

Lotus Garden of Hilo
Vacation Rental $

(📞808-936-5212; http://lotusgardenhilo.com; 140 Kilauea Ave; r $79-105, 2br cottage $120, per additional person $15; 📶) To immerse yourself in Hilo's charm, look no further than these brightly painted buildings. Of the two cottages, the Sugar Shack is available by room (shared kitchen and bathroom), while the Lotus is rented as a whole. All accommodations are comfortable, reasonably priced and within walking distance of all you need. Friendly owners live on-site.

Hilo Bay Hostel Hostel $

(☎ 808-933-2771; www.hawaiihostel.net; 101 Waianuenue Ave; dm with shared bath $27, r with/without bath $77/67; 🛜) Perfectly situated downtown, this well-managed hostel occupies an airy, historic building with hardwood floors, remarkably clean restrooms and a kitchen in which you could cook Thanksgiving dinner. The crowd is older and diverse, creating a low-key, relaxed vibe.

Old Hawaiian B&B B&B $

(☎ 808-961-2816; www.thebigislandvacation.com; 1492 Wailuku Dr; r incl breakfast $85-125; 🛜) Perfect for discriminating budget travelers, these three pleasant rooms include private entrances and tidy furnishings. The Hawaiian Room (sleeps four) and Bamboo Room (sleeps three) offer great value. All open to a backyard lanai, with dining table, microwave and refrigerator. Located about a mile above Rainbow Falls.

Holmes' Sweet Home B&B $

(☎ 808-961-9089; www.holmesbandb.com; 107 Koula St; r incl breakfast $90-105; 🛜) Mr and Mrs Holmes's comfy B&B will immediately feel like home. The larger Blue Ginger room, with queen and twin beds, is worth the extra $15. Rooms are wheelchair-accessible and open into a common area with refrigerator and microwave. Located about 2.5 miles west of downtown, up Kaumana Dr, off Ainako Ave.

D&S Bed & Breakfast B&B $

(☎ 808-934-9585; www.dnsbnb.com; 150 Kilauea St; r $100, ste $125; 🛜) Located downtown, this B&B is convivial, casual and family friendly, run by a welcoming young couple. While simple, the rooms include minifridge and dining table and chairs, and they open to a shared patio where breakfast is served.

Uncle Billy's Hilo Bay Hotel Hotel $

(☎ 800-442-5841, 935-0861; www.unclebilly.com; 87 Banyan Dr; r $95-124; ❄ 🛜 🏊) Family-owned and operated by three generations, Uncle Billy's is a bargain. Expect a no-frills hotel in a terrific location. Rooms

Koi Room in the Orchid Tree B&B

PAULA BORCHARDT/GETTY IMAGES ©

overlook a courtyard of palms, red ginger and talkative mynah birds – or beautful Hilo Bay (an ocean view for just over $100 is a steal!).

The hotel runs a convenience store (7am to 9:30pm daily) with a seating area, free wi-fi and powerful air- conditioning.

Arnott's Lodge
Hostel, Campground $

(☎808-969-7097, 808-339-0921; www.arnotts lodge.com; 98 Apapane Rd; dm $28, r with/without bath $75/65; 🛜) Hilo's longest-running hostel remains a solid value, with a variety of lodging options close to beaches. The $75 rooms are especially nice, with private garden views and bathrooms. Fringe benefits, such as free Sunday pizza and beer, add to the free-spirited camaraderie.

Hilo Tropical Gardens Guest House
Hostel, Campground $

(☎808-217-9650; www.hilogardens.com; 1477 Kalaniana'ole Ave; dm $25, d $55-65; 🛜) Dorm and private rooms are tiny, but spick-and-span, amid a wildly lush setting. Pitch a tent (single/double $15/20) and suddenly you're camping in a jungle (warning: mosquitoes are voracious). Located behind Hilo Homemade Ice Cream store, just past Onekahakaha Beach.

Dolphin Bay Hotel
Hotel $$

(☎877-935-1466, 808-935-1466; www.dolphin bayhotel.com; 333 Iliahi St; studio/1br/2br apt from $119/169/189; 🛜) This family-run hotel attracts countless loyal, repeat guests. No surprise. The 18 apartment units, each with full kitchen, are clean and conveniently located within a five-minute walk to downtown Hilo. Enjoy free coffee and locally grown fruit for breakfast amid tropical foliage. For longer stays, ask about the one-bedroom apartments in the **Annex (per day/week/month $119/763/1600)** across the street.

Hilo Bay Hale
B&B $$

(☎808-640-1113, 800-745-5049; www.hilobay hale.com; 301 Ponahawai St; r incl breakfast $139-159; ❄🛜) In a gorgeously restored 1912 plantation home, two main-floor rooms feature private lanai overlooking charming koi ponds, while a ground-floor room

boasts more privacy and space. Guests have access to the kitchen and laundry facilities. With two personable hosts, proximity to town and weekly discounts ($99 to $119 per night), you can't go wrong here.

Orchid Tree B&B
B&B $$

(☎808-961-9678; www.orchidtree.net; 6 Makakai Pl; r incl breakfast $150; ❄🛜) A few miles outside Hilo, this perennial favorite combines B&B friendliness with space and privacy. Couples will appreciate the stylish Koi Room with a gleaming hardwood floor and, yes, koi pond outside. The Hula Room is larger, containing two beds plus lounging area with plump, inviting sofas. Breakfast is served ouside in a communal 'surfer shack' patio.

Around Hilo

Island Insights

According to Hawaiian legend, young prospective chiefs faced a ritual challenge: could they lift the 3.5-ton **Naha Stone**? The man with enough strength to budge the boulder was destined to reign all of the Hawaiian Islands. Along came teenage boy Kamehameha, who reputedly flipped over the stone (and proceeded to conquer and unite the Hawaiian kingdom). Today the Naha Stone, along with the upright **Pinao Stone**, are landmarks fronting the Hilo Public Library (p186).

To get here from Hilo, head north and turn right just past the Mile 4 marker on Nahala St.

Hilo Honu Inn
B&B $$

(✆808-935-4325; www.hilohonu.com; 465 Haili St; r incl breakfast $140-250; 🛜) In a lovely retro home, three custom-designed guest rooms accommodate different budgets. A worthy splurge, the Samurai Suite is utterly memorable, with genuine Japanese detailing, plus tatami floor, *furo* (soaking tub), tea room and sweeping (if distant) views of Hilo Bay.

Pakalana Inn
Inn $$

(✆808-935-0709; www.pakalanainn.com; 123 Punahoa St; r $99-129, with kitchenette $149; ❄🛜) ✦ With hardwood floors and clean-lined furnishings, this six-unit inn is an oasis just a block from the downtown farmers market. Rooms are average sized, but immaculate and airy, occupying the top floor of a building containing two recommended eateries. No on-site host, so you're on your own.

Hilo Hawaiian Hotel
Hotel $$

(✆808-935-9361, 800-367-5004; www.castle resorts.com; 71 Banyan Dr; r $150-200, ste from $250; ❄🛜🏊) Location, location. Hilo's biggest hotel has a prime oceanfront location, adjacent to Lili'uokalani Park. It's an apt choice for a largish hotel feel, air-conditioning, and round-the-clock staff. Rooms were renovated in 2013. If you can't afford an ocean-view room, head to the lobby cafe for morning coffee, free wi-fi and the spectacular view.

Bay House B&B
B&B $$

(✆808-961-6311, 888-235-8195; www.bay househawaii.com; 42 Pukihae St; r incl breakfast $175; 🛜) Just outside Hilo, across the Singing Bridge over the Wailuku River, find three immaculate guest rooms within sight and sound of the bay. Tastefully tropical themed, with classy hardwood and granite floors, each room includes a private lanai for in-room breakfasts. Rates have creeped up over the years, but this remains a solid choice.

Hale Kai Hawaii
B&B $$

(✆808-935-6330; www.halekaihawaii.com; 111 Honoli'i Pl; r incl breakfast $165-179; 🛜🏊) Four rooms below the main house enjoy panoramic ocean views and shared lanai. The Pele Suite is the best value, offering more space and kitchenette. Gourmet breakfasts are served on the upper lanai. Kids 13 and older only.

To get here from Hilo, head north and turn right on Pauka'a Dr, between the Mile 4 and Mile 5 markers.

The Inn at Kulaniapia Falls
Inn $$

(✆808-935-6789, 866-935-6789; www.water fall.net; 1 Kulaniapia Dr; r incl breakfast $189, guesthouse $279; 🛜) ✦ Drive up, up, up 4 miles past acres of macadamia orchards to 850ft above sea level. Your reward? Ten rooms (in two buildings) and a pagoda guesthouse, exquisitely appointed with Asian antiques, in a fantastically verdant setting, complete with waterfall. The unlit road can be tricky at night. All power is hydroelectric.

Shipman House B&B
B&B $$$

(✆808-934-8002; www.hilo-hawaii.com; 131 Ka'iulani St; r incl breakfast $219-249; 🛜) Staying at the Shipman family's grand Victorian mansion is pricey, albeit peerless in historical significance. Queen Lili'uokalani played the grand piano, while

Jack London slept in the guest cottage. Surrounded by museum-quality antiques, three rooms in the main house are sedate and finely (although not luxuriously) furnished. In a separate cottage, two rooms are more casual and private.

🍴 Eating

Hilo Farmers Market   Market $
(www.hilofarmersmarket.com; cnr Mamo St & Kamehameha Ave; ⏰6am-4pm Wed & Sat) Hilo's gathering place is its downtown farmers market, which opened in 1988 with four farmers selling from trucks. Today, the market is bustling and attracts sizable crowds. A single pass through the food tent unearths luscious mangoes and papayas, massive avocados, whole coconuts, and bunches of anthuriums. Unfortunately, the produce sold here is not 100% locally grown. Craft tents entice tourists with 'Hawaiian' woodcarvings and shell jewelry, but most are cheap imports.

If you miss Wednesday or Saturday market days, you'll still find a row of daily vendors selling produce and flowers.

Kino'ole Farmers Market   Market $
(cnr Kino'ole Ave & Kahaopea St; ⏰7am-noon Sat) 🌱 Hilo's 'other' farmers market is low-key and attracts mainly locals, with its 100% locally grown and made products sold by the farmers themselves. The 15 to 20 vendors supply all you need, including fresh produce, baked goods, taro chips, poi (steamed, mashed taro), plants and flowers. Parking is plentiful.

Suisan Fish Market   Fish $
(📞808-935-9349; 93 Lihiwai St; poke per pound $13; ⏰8am-5pm Mon-Fri, to 4pm Sat) For a fantastic variety of *poke* (sold by the pound), you can't beat Suisan, where you know the fish is freshly caught. The *shōyu* (soy sauce) ahi and *limu* (seaweed) ahi are tried and true. The takeout *poke* and rice bowl ($5 to $7) is an incredible deal.

Paul's Place   Cafe $
(📞808-280-8646; 132 Punahoa St; mains $8-12; ⏰7am-3pm Tue-Sat) In a three-table dining room, Paul serves absolutely scrumptious renditions of the classics, including

1 WHAT'S THE BEST SURF BREAK IN OR AROUND HILO?

There's only one: Honoli'i (p169). Thanks to the tradewinds, there's always something to ride here. Of course, it's hard to predict when waves will be extra big or small. It's also ideal because there are no *wana* (pokey sea urchins), unlike at Pohoiki (in Puna), which has sharp lava rock and lots of *wana*.

2 WHAT IS SURFING ETIQUETTE?

Give right of way to the next person in line and don't 'drop in.' Check the waves before entering. If you're in doubt, ask a lifeguard. And keep the beach clean. Don't litter.

3 WHAT MAKES THE BIG ISLAND DIFFERENT FOR SURFING AND OTHER WATER SPORTS?

Hawai'i is a young island, five million years younger than Kaua'i. There are fewer sandy beaches and developed reefs, and often the ocean hits against rocky cliffs. It's a more challenging place to surf.

4 WEREN'T THERE MORE SURF BREAKS BEFORE?

This island has changed a lot due to the lava flows: until 1990 there were 20 great surf breaks in Kalapana. That's why I moved to the Big Island in 1971. Suddenly the lava took Kalapana and [the surf breaks] were all gone. Some of the magic was lost. I still love the Big Island, but I miss the waves of Kalapana very much.

5 CAN DOWNTOWN HILO COMPETE WITH THE INFLUX OF CHAIN STORES?

If people, locals and tourists don't support small businesses, they'll someday be gone. At big chains, you don't get the same service.

Belgian waffles, robust salads and eggs Benedict featuring his special sauce. Everything's healthy, with lots of fresh fruit and veggies. If the place is full, wait or try again. You won't regret it.

Cafe 100   Local $

(☎808-935-8683; 969 Kilauea Ave; loco moco $2-5, plate lunches $5-7; ☺6:45am-8:30pm Mon-Sat) Locals love this drive-in for its generous plate lunches and 20 rib-sticking varieties of *loco moco* (dish of rice, fried egg and hamburger patty topped with gravy or other condiments), including fish and veggie-burger options. With a clean seating area and efficient service, it's local fast food at its finest.

KTA Super Store   Supermarket $

Downtown (☎808-935-3751; 323 Keawe St, Downtown; ☺7am-9pm Mon-Sat, to 6pm Sun); **Puainako Town Center** (☎808-959-9111, pharmacy 808-959-8700; 50 E Puainako St, Puainako Town Center; ☺grocery 5:30am-midnight, pharmacy 8am-7pm Mon-Fri, from 9am Sat) This popular, locally owned chain carries mainstream groceries plus a comprehensive deli with fresh *poke, bento* (Japanese-style box meals) and other ready-to-eat items.

Abundant Life Natural Foods   Market $

(☎808-935-7411; 292 Kamehameha Ave; ☺8:30am-7pm Mon-Tue Thu-Fri, from 7am Wed & Sat, 10am-5pm Sun) Located downtown, this longtime health-food market has a takeout cafe (shuts down 1½ hours before closing time), serving smoothies and other standbys.

Island Naturals   Market $

(☎808-935-5533; 1221 Kilauea Ave, Hilo Shopping Center; smoothies $3-3.75, deli dishes per lb $7; ☺8:30am-8pm Mon-Sat, 10am-7pm Sun) This well-stocked health-food store has a gourmet deli.

Grapes: A Wine Store   Wine

(☎808-933-1471; www.grapeshawaii.com; 207 Kilauea Ave; ☺noon-6pm Tue-Sat) This hidden treasure is owned by a true aficionado and packed to the rafters with global stock. Free wine tastings every other Thursday!

Koji's Bento Korner   Local $

(☎808-935-1417; 52 Ponahawai St; loco moco $3.25-7.50; ☺7am-2pm Mon-Fri, from 9am Sat) The Koji *loco moco* – with two homemade hamburger patties, teriyaki sauce and gravy, one egg, two Portuguese sausages, macaroni salad and kimchee – is the stuff of local cravings.

Ken's House of Pancakes   Diner $

(1730 Kamehameha Ave; meals $6-12; ☺24hr) There's something comforting about a 24-hour diner with a mile-long menu. Choose from macadamia-nut pancakes, Spam omelettes,

Fresh produce at the Hilo Farmers Market (p181)
LUCI YAMAMOTO

EW KIEW
NGON
ET & SMALL SEEDS
$4⁰⁰/lb.
2 lb for 7⁰⁰

B 5⁰⁰
Kaimana
Lychee
Sweet & small seed !

slow-cooked *kalua* pig plates and steaming bowls of saimin.

Miyo's
Japanese $$

(☎808-935-2273; 681 Manono St; dinner $11-15; ⏰11am-2pm & 5:30-8:30pm Mon-Sat) A long-time local favorite, Miyo's is known for homestyle Japanese meals and crowds. Relocated in 2013, it's now larger, louder, and lacks it's former ambience, but the food is worth it. Try classics such as grilled ahi or *saba* (mackerel), tempura or *tonkatsu* (breaded and fried pork cutlets). Reservations are a must.

Restaurant Miwa
Japanese $$

(☎808-961-4454; 1261 Kilauea Ave, Hilo Shopping Center; sushi $5-8, meals $14-25; ⏰11am-2pm & 5-9pm Mon-Sat, 5-9pm Sun) Tucked away in a mall, Miwa is a low-key local favorite for traditional Japanese cuisine, includilng sushi. No surprises here, just satisfying dishes, such as grilled *saba*, teriyaki chicken and *tonkatsu*.

Puka Puka Kitchen
Japanese, Mediterranean $$

(☎808-933-2121; 270 Kamehameha Ave; $10-12; ⏰11am-2:30pm) This hole-in-the-wall serves Japanese-style plates, such as sautéed ahi and chicken katsu, but also various pita pockets, including a veg falafel option. Takeout bento boxes sell out well before lunch.

Sombat's Fresh Thai Cuisine
Thai $$

(☎808-936-8849; 88 Kanoelehua Ave; dishes $8-16; ⏰10:30am-2pm Mon-Fri & 5-9pm Mon-Sat; ⏰) Go here for healthy Thai classics made with local produce, fresh chef-grown herbs and lots of veg options. The restaurant interior is pleasant enough, but located in a deserted commercial building. Ideal for takeout.

Kuhio Grille
Diner $$

(☎808-959-2336; www.kuhiogrille.com; 111 E Puainako St, Suite A106, Prince Kuhio Plaza; breakfast $5-10, lunch & dinner $9-20; ⏰6am-10pm Sat-Thu, to midnight Fri) Large appetites will find satisfaction at this no-frills diner specializing in local favorites: taro corned-beef hash, oxtail soup, fried-rice

The Best...
Hilo for Kids

1 Picnic at Lili'uokalani Park (p169)

2 Cross a footbridge to Mokuola (Coconut Island; p169)

3 Splash around at Onekahakaha Beach Park (p168)

4 Stroll the Pana'ewa Rainforest Zoo & Gardens (p172)

5 Learn about voyaging at 'Imiloa Astronomy Center of Hawai'i (p172)

6 See a $2 movie at Kress Cinemas (p185)

loco moco and *laulau* (meat or chicken wrapped in taro leaves and steamed, Hawaiian style). Best suited for meat eaters.

Ocean Sushi Deli
Sushi $$

(☎961-6625; 239 Keawe St; 6-piece rolls $3-6, meals $12-14; ⏰10am-2pm & 5:30-9pm Mon-Sat) There's zero decor and hit-or-miss service. But rolls are cheap and creative – for example, combining fresh fish with macadamia nuts or tropical fruit. Not outstanding, but good value.

Hilo Bay Cafe
American, Sushi $$$

(☎808-935-4939; www.hilobaycafe.com; 123 Lihiwai St; mains $15-30; ⏰11am-9pm Mon-Thu, to 9:30pm Fri & Sat, 5-9pm Sun) Since 2003, this casually sophisticated eatery has wowed critics and put Hilo on the foodie map. The only drawback was its mall location. Now literally overlooking Hilo Bay, it's got the whole package, including full sushi bar. The eclectic menu features gourmet versions of comfort food, such as Hamakua mushroom pot pie and a local beef burger with garlic-salted fries.

Sweet Stuff

Hilo boasts a superlative lineup of sweets, which Neighbor Islands (and visitors in the know) crave until their next trip.

Big Island Candies (☎808-935-8890, 800-935-5510; www.bigislandcandies.com; 585 Hinano St; ⏰8:30am-5pm) This immaculate candy factory welcomes visitors with generous samples, fantastic displays and beautifully packaged confections. It's a mecca for locals and Japanese tourists – and for anyone with a sweet tooth.

Moonstruck Patisserie (☎808-933-6868; www.moonstruckpatisserie.com; 16 Furneaux Ln; pastries & cake slices $4-5; ⏰8:30am-4pm Wed-Sat) One discriminating foodie described Moonstruck's croissants as the best she's *ever* tasted. Judging from the accolades and local buzz, she might be right. Pastry chef Jackie Tan-DeWitt specializes in classic European pastries and unique cakes, cheesecakes and fruit tarts.

Hilo Homemade Ice Cream (☎808-217-9650; 1477 Kalaniana'ole Ave; scoops $3.50; ⏰11am-6pm) To or from the beach, stop here for locally made flavors that ring true. Try rich macadamia-nut ice cream with zingy *liliko'i* (passion fruit) sorbet.

Itsu's Fishing Supplies (☎808-935-8082; 810 Pi'ilani St; ice shave $1.50; ⏰8:30am-5pm Mon-Fri) For generations, this family-run shop has delighted kids of all ages with soft-as-snow ice shave (served between 2pm and 5pm). The red, yellow and blue 'rainbow' is a classic.

Two Ladies Kitchen (☎808-961-4766; 274 Kilauea Ave; 8-piece boxes $6; ⏰10am-5pm Wed-Sat) Founded by two Hilo ladies, this hole-in-the-wall makes addictive island-style Japanese *mochi* (sticky rice dessert).

Short N Sweet (☎808-935-4446; www.shortnsweet.biz; 374 Kino'ole St; pastries $1.50-5, sandwiches $9; ⏰7am-4:30pm Mon-Fri, 8am-3pm Sat & Sun) Whether you're seeking locally inspired pastries, gourmet focaccia panini, or a wedding cake made to order, this bakery-cafe is sure to please. We dare you to resist the 'homemade Oreo' or anything with tart-sweet *liliko'i*.

Takenoko Sushi　　　Sushi **$$$**
(☎808-933-3939; 578 Hinano St; chef's choice $38, nigiri $2.50; ⏰11:30am-11pm) Drop everything and make a reservation at this superb eight-seat sushi bar. Expect top-quality fish (mostly flown fresh from Japan), a spotlessly clean setting, expert sushi chef and gracious service. Each bite is a memorable experience. Three dinner seating times: 5pm, 7pm and 9pm.

Cafe Pesto　　　International **$$$**
(☎808-969-6640; www.cafepesto.com; 308 Kamehameha Ave, S Hata Bldg; pizzas $10-20, dinner $18-30; ⏰11am-9pm Sun-Thu, to 10pm Fri & Sat) Cafe Pesto is a safe choice, whether for business lunches or dinner with your mother-in-law. Set downtown in a lovely historic building, the versatile kitchen covers all bases with creative salads, risottos, stir-fries, pastas, seafood and chicken. Don't bother with the pizzas.

Ponds　　　American **$$$**
(☎808-934-7663; www.pondshilohi.com; 135 Kalaniana'ole Ave; mains $20-25; ⏰11am-9:30pm Sun-Thu, to midnight Fri & Sat) This steak/seafood/pasta restaurant will suit those hankering for familiar American food with an island twist. A big plus is the airy dining room overlooking 'Ice Pond.' Live music Thursday to Monday.

Queen's Court

American, Local $$$

(☎ 808-935-9361, 800-367-5004; www.castle resorts.com; 71 Banyan Dr, Hilo Hawaiian Hotel; breakfast adult/child $17/10, dinner buffet $40; ⏰ 6:30am-9:30am & 5:30-8pm daily, to 9pm Fri-Sun) This longtime hotel restaurant is known for its all-you-can-eat weekend buffet dinners (seafood on Fridays and Sundays, Hawaiian on Saturdays). The airy dining room offers a spectacular view of Hilo Bay.

Seaside Restaurant

Seafood $$$

(☎ 808-935-8825; www.seasiderestaurant. com; 1790 Kalaniana'ole Ave; meals $25-30; ⏰ 4:30-8:30pm Tue-Thu, to 9pm Fri & Sat) 🍃 This old-school seafood restaurant specializes in fresh fish, from locally caught mahimahi to pan-sized *aholehole* (flagtail fish) raised in on-site Hawaiian-style fishponds. It's a sit-down restaurant, but the vibe is homey and retro. Portions are generous.

⭐ Entertainment

Palace Theater

Theater

(☎ 808-934-7010, box office 808-934-7777; www.hilopalace.com; 38 Haili St) This historic theater is Hilo's cultural crown jewel. Its eclectic programming includes art-house and silent films (accompanied by the house organ), music and dance concerts, Broadway musicals and cultural festivals. On Wednesday morning (from 11am to noon) it hosts 'Hawai'iana Live' (adult/child $5/free), a touching, small-town intro to Hawaiian culture through storytelling, film, music, *oli* (chant) and hula.

Kress Cinemas

Cinema

(☎ 808-935-6777; 174 Kamehameha Ave; tickets $2) When was the last time you saw a $2 movie? Enter on Kalakaua St.

Stadium Cinemas

Cinema

(☎ 808-959-4595; 111 E Puainako St, Prince Kuhio Plaza; tickets adult/child 3-11yr/matinee $9.50/6.25/7.50) Typical shopping mall cinema with the usual Hollywood showings.

The Best...
Hilo Souvenirs

1 Aloha wear by Sig Zane (p186)

2 Antique-style map of Hawaii from Basically Books

3 Nature photography from Extreme Exposure Fine Art Gallery

4 Big Island chocolate at Hilo Farmers Market (p181)

5 Handmade ukulele from Hilo Guitars & Ukuleles

🔒 Shopping

While locals flock to the chain-heavy **Prince Kuhio Plaza** (☎ 808-959-3555; 111 E Puainako St; ⏰ 10am-8pm Mon-Thu, 10am-9pm Fri & Sat, 10am-6pm Sun) south of the airport, downtown is far better for unique shops.

Basically Books

Books

(160 Kamehameha Ave; ⏰ 9am-5pm Mon-Sat, 11am-3:30pm Sun) A browser's paradise, this shop specializes in maps, travel guides and books about Hawaii. Good selection for kids, too.

Still Life Books

Books

(☎ 808-756-2919; http://stillifebooks.blogspot. com; 134 Kilauea Ave; ⏰ 11am-3pm Tue-Sat) Come for quality used books – primarily literary works – and to browse and talk ideas with the owner, a keen bibliophile.

Extreme Exposure Fine Art Gallery

Photography

(www.extremeexposure.com; 224 Kamehameha Ave; ⏰ 10am-8pm Mon-Sat, 11am-5pm Sun) This informal gallery offers excellent nature photography, notably Kilauea's spectacular lava displays, and caters to all budgets, from framed prints to greeting cards.

Hilo Guitars & Ukuleles Music
(www.hiloguitars.com; 56 Ponahawai St; 10am-5pm Mon-Fri, to 4pm Sat) Find a wide selection of quality ukulele, from koa or mahogany collectibles to fine entry-level instruments.

Sig Zane Designs Clothing
(www.sigzane.com; 122 Kamehameha Ave; 9:30am-5pm Mon-Fri, 9am-4pm Sat) Legendary in the hula community, Sig Zane creates iconic custom fabrics, marked by rich colors and graphic prints of Hawaiian flora. You can spot a 'Sig' a mile away.

Alan's Art & Collectibles Antiques
(808-969-1554; 202 Kamehameha Ave; 10am-4pm Mon & Wed-Fri, 1-4pm Tue, 10am-3pm Sat) Glimpse old Hawai'i in this chock-full secondhand shop: vintage glassware, household doodads, aloha shirts, vinyl LPs and some collectible treasures.

Dragon Mama Homewares
(www.dragonmama.com; 266 Kamehameha Ave; 9am-5pm Mon-Fri, to 4pm Sat) Go home with exquisite beddings custom-made from imported Japanese fabric.

Information

Dangers & Annoyances

While relatively safe, be careful in downtown Hilo and avoid Kalakaua Park at night. Throughout Hilo, expect to hear coqui frogs, an invasive species, after dark. If you are bothered by noise at night, when they are most vocal, bring earplugs.

Internet Access

There's free wi-fi at Starbucks in **downtown Hilo** (933-3094; 438 Kilauea Ave; 4:30am-9pm, to 10pm Fri & Sat), **Prince Kuhio Plaza** (959-2492; 111 E Puainako St; 4:30am-10pm, to 11pm Fri & Sat), and their locations inside Target and Safeway, both near Prince Kuhio Plaza.

Bytes and Pieces of Hilo (808-935-3520; www.bytesandpiecesofhilo.com; 264 Keawe St; computer rental per 15/30/60min $3/5/8, wi-fi per day $5; 9am-6pm Mon-Fri, to 4pm Sat;) Four computers for rent, plus wi-fi, printing, faxing and scanning. The shop also sells vintage collectibles. Call to confirm hours.

Hilo Public Library (808-933-8888; www.librarieshawaii.org; 300 Waianuenue Ave; 11am-7pm Tue & Wed, 9am-5pm Thu & Sat, 10am-5pm Fri) If you buy a three-month nonresident library card ($10), you can use internet terminals for free and check out books.

Aloha wear

ANN CECIL/GETTY IMAGES ©

Medical Services

Hilo Medical Center (☎808-974-4700, ER 808-974-6800; 1190 Waianuenue Ave; ⏰24hr emergency) Near Rainbow Falls.

Longs Drugs Kilauea Ave (☎808-935-3357, pharmacy 808-935-9075; 555 Kilauea Ave; ⏰pharmacy 7am-7pm Mon-Fri, to 6pm Sat, 8am-5pm Sun); Prince Kuhio Plaza (☎808-959-5881, pharmacy 808-959-4508; 111 E Puainako St, Prince Kuhio Plaza; ⏰pharmacy 8am-8pm Mon-Fri, to 7pm Sat, to 5pm Sun) General store and pharmacy; store hours run longer than pharmacy hours.

KTA Super Store (☎pharmacy 808-959-8700; 50 E Puainako St, Puainako Town Center; ⏰pharmacy 8am-7pm Mon-Fri, from 9am Sat) Supermarket with pharmacy. Store hours run longer than pharmacy hours.

Money

Bank of Hawaii Kawili St (☎808-961-0681; 417 E Kawili St); Pauahi St (☎808-935-9701; 120 Pauahi St)

First Hawaiian Bank (☎808-969-2222; 120 Waianuenue Ave)

Police

Police (☎808-935-3311; 349 Kapi'olani St) For nonemergencies.

Post

Downtown Post Office (☎808-933-3014; 154 Waianuenue Ave; ⏰9am-4pm Mon-Fri, 12:30-2pm Sat) Located in the Federal Building.

Main Post Office (☎933-3019; 1299 Kekuanaoa St; ⏰8am-4:30pm Mon-Fri, 9am-12:30pm Sat) Located near Hilo airport.

Tourist Information

Big Island Visitors Bureau (☎808-961-5797, 800-648-2441; www.gohawaii.com/big-island; 250 Keawe St) Basic info and brochures only.

ⓘ Getting There & Away

Air

Hilo International Airport (ITO; ☎808-934-5838; http://hawaii.gov/ito; 2450 Kekuanaoa St, Hilo) Almost all flights to Hilo are interisland, mostly from Honolulu.

Bus

Hele-On Bus (☎808-961-8744; www.heleonbus.org; adult/senior or student $2/1) All buses originate at Mo'oheau terminal (329 Kamehameha Ave) in downtown Hilo. From here, buses go around the island, but service is infrequent, sometimes only very early in the morning (for work commuters) or only a few times daily. If you're going to a major destination (such as Kailua-Kona or a South Kohala resort) and staying within the area, the bus is a feasible option. Check the website for current routes and schedules.

Car

The drive from Hilo to Kailua-Kona (via Waimea) is 95 miles and averages 2½ hours. Driving on Saddle Rd can cut travel time by about 15 minutes. For rental information see p291.

For a retro adventure, see **Happy Campers Hawaii** (☎808-896-8777; www.happycampershawaii.com) which rents VW Westfalia pop-top campers/Vanagons that sleep up to four. From $120 per day, they're a steal – in great condition, with kitchenettes, sink with running water, cookware, bedding and more. Pick up and drop off in Hilo.

ⓘ Getting Around

Bicycle

Cycling is more recreation than transportation in Hilo. **Mid-Pacific Wheels** (☎808-935-6211; www.midpacificwheelsllc.com; 1133c Manono St; ⏰9am-6pm Mon-Sat, 11am-5pm Sun) rents mountain and road bikes for $25 to $45 per day.

Bus

The Hele-On Bus (p187) covers much of Hilo, although service can be infrequent. Check the website for current routes and schedules.

Car

Free parking is generally available. Downtown street parking is free for two hours; finding a spot is easy except during Saturday and Wednesday farmers markets.

Taxi

The approximate cab fare from the airport to downtown Hilo is $15.

AA Marshall's Taxi (☎808-936-2654)

Percy's Taxi (☎808-969-7060)

Puna

Even among locals, Puna is its own world, not far away but _far out._ The driving force is change. Here, the low-key plantation community has been inundated by an eclectic mix of mainland retirees, nouveau hippies, off-the-grid minimalists, funky artists, Hawaiian sovereignty activists, organic farmers, _pakalolo_ (marijuana) growers and entry-level homeowners. While diverse, even divergent, all Punatics relish the laid-back, wristwatch-free lifestyle. They share a deep affinity for the volatile land, which Kilauea Volcano has repeatedly slathered with lava and blessed with black-sand beaches. If day-tripping here, avoid morning and evening rush hour: Puna, the fastest-growing district statewide, has become a sprawling suburb of Hilo.

Ukuleles at the Maku'u Craft & Farmers Market (p193)
189

Puna Itineraries

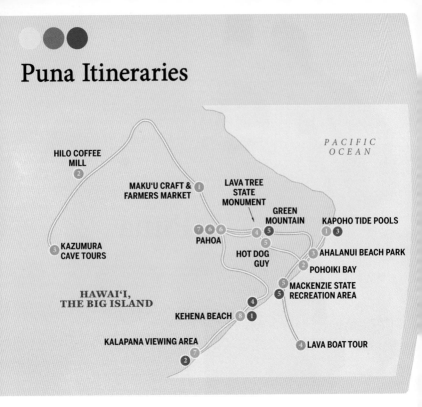

HILO COFFEE MILL ②

MAKU'U CRAFT & FARMERS MARKET ①

LAVA TREE STATE MONUMENT

GREEN MOUNTAIN

KAPOHO TIDE POOLS ① ③

PACIFIC OCEAN

⑦ ⑥ ⑥
PAHOA

④ ⑤

③ KAZUMURA CAVE TOURS

HOT DOG GUY ⑤

③ AHALANUI BEACH PARK

② POHOIKI BAY

⑤ MACKENZIE STATE RECREATION AREA ⑤

HAWAI'I, THE BIG ISLAND

④

KEHENA BEACH ⑧ ①

④ LAVA BOAT TOUR

KALAPANA VIEWING AREA

② ⑦

One Day

① **Kapoho Tide Pools** (p197) Early morning is the best time to enjoy the serenity of these lava pools containing fish and an occasional sea turtle.

② **Pohoiki Bay** (p198) Ace surfers and bodyboarders can opt to hit the formidable breaks here instead.

③ **Ahalanui Beach Park** (p198) Follow up at this easy-access hot pond; never empty, but soothing nevertheless.

④ **Lava Tree State Monument** (p196) Stroll through thick tropical forest, keeping your eyes peeled for hollow 'lava trees,' fascinating oddities of nature.

⑤ **Hot Dog Guy** (p197) If you're hungry, grab a bison, reindeer or beef hotdog grilled to order.

⑥ **Pahoa Fresh Fish** (p195) If a hotdog won't do, push on to Pahoa and fill up on fantastic fish and chips.

⑦ **Kalapana Viewing Area** (p201) If you're lucky and the flow is accessible, book a hiking tour to see red-hot lava. Hiking distances vary, but could be 3 or 4 miles one way over difficult terrain – expect a strenuous half-day to full-day adventure.

⑧ **Kehena Beach** (p199) If lava isn't viewable, take it easy at this freewheeling, clothing-optional black-sand beach.

◉ THIS LEG: 25 MILES

Two Days

1 Maku'u Craft & Farmers Market
(p193) If you're here on a Sunday, start day
two by visiting this market – it distills the
essence of funky, DIY Puna.

2 Hilo Coffee Mill (p193) On other
days, wake up to fresh coffee and breakfast
fixings at this friendly cafe. Coffee fans, the
informative farm and mill tour is not to be
missed.

3 Kazumura Cave Tours (p192) Head
underground to explore the world's longest
lava tube, mesmerizing in its size, darkness
and silence.

4 Lava boat tour (p203) If lava is flowing
into the ocean, it's a rare chance to get
up close with Lava Ocean Adventures. Be
prepared for choppy waters and unavoidable
splashes.

5 MacKenzie State Recreation Area If
the flow is inland or underground (or if you'd
prefer peace and quiet), cobble together a
picnic lunch and laze away the afternoon on
a bed of ironwood pine needles.

6 Paradissimo Tropical Spa (p193)
End your day with a pampering facial or
massage – aah.

7 Kaleo's Bar & Grill (p195) Make a
reservation at Pahoa's standby for well-
made Hawaii Regional Cuisine. Another
winner is Paolo's for Italian dishes in a cozy
dining room.

⟶ THIS LEG: 70 MILES

Puna
Highlights

1 Best Beach: Kehena Beach (p199) Let
it all hang out at this bohemian black-sand
beach, home to Punatics of all persuasions.

2 Best View: Molten lava close-up (p202)
Hoof it over miles of rocky terrain and muddy
jungle to get up close to red-hot lava.

3 Best Activity: Kapoho Tide Pools (p197)
Snorkeling the shallow lava-rock tide pools
awash in fish are fantastic for all ages and levels.

**4 Best Day Pass: Kalani Oceanside
Retreat** (p200) Devote a day to your
health, with yoga, massage, swimming and
nourishing food at this longtime retreat.

**5 Best Scenic Drive: Hwy 132 to Hwy
137** (p196) Puna's highways and byways
are all scenic, but these two are especially
mesmerizing and cover all of Puna's must-
see sights.

Lava flowing from Kilauea Volcano near Kalapana (p201)
STUART WESTMORLAND/GETTY IMAGES ©

Discover Puna

Keaʻau & Around

POP KEAʻAU 2253

Between Hilo and Volcano, you'll whisk past former sugar plantations and mini villages. The main town, Keaʻau, is just a cluster of gas stations and stores, including a supermarket, off Volcano Hwy (Hwy 11). Past Keaʻau toward Pahoa, however, burgeoning residential subdivisions have transformed Puna into sprawling suburbs. If you want to explore Hawaii Volcanoes National Park from a balmier home base than Volcano, consider the lodgings tucked away here.

◎ Sights & Activities

Hiʻiaka's Healing Hawaiian Herb Garden   Gardens
(☎808-966-5956; www.hiiakas.com; 15-1667 2nd St, Hawaiian Paradise Park; adult/senior & child $5/3, with guided tour $15/10; ⊗by appointment) 🍃 Learn about medicinal plants at this lovingly tended acre of native, Polynesian-introduced and international herbs. The founding gardener and herbalist sells *noni* (Indian mulberry) and kava concoctions.

Fuku-Bonsai Cultural Center   Gardens
(☎808-982-9880; www.fukubonsai.com; 17-856 Olaʻa Rd; ⊗8am-4pm Mon-Sat) FREE Although well-intentioned, this bonsai nursery is mostly a salesroom for its commercial specialty: dwarf schefflera that can be grown indoors. Displays of mature bonsai are interesting, but grounds are poorly maintained.

To get here from Keaʻau, drive south on Hwy 11 and turn left on Olaʻa Rd between the Mile 9 and Mile 10 markers.

Kazumura Cave Tours   Caving
(☎808-967-7208; http://kazumura cave.com; off Volcano Hwy, past Mile 22; tours from $30; ⊗by appointment Mon-Sat) Since discovering that his property lies atop Kazumura Cave – the world's longest lava tube – Harry Schick has become an expert on lava caves and gives small tours (six people maximum) at reasonable cost. Be prepared to climb ladders and walk over rocky terrain, even on the shortest, easiest tour. Minimum age is 11; English proficiency

Hikers on Kilauea Volcano
SAMI SARKIS/GETTY IMAGES ©

s required. Make reservations at least a week ahead.

Kilauea Caverns of Fire
Caving

(☎ 217-2363; www.kilaueacavernsoffire.com; off Volcano Hwy, before Mile 11; tours $29-79; ☺by appointment) These tours through Kazumura Cave can run a bit large, up to 20 for the one-hour walk and up to eight for the three-hour adventure. But the shorter tour is a decent option for families, as the minimum age is five.

🛏 Sleeping & Eating

For groceries, stock up at **Foodland** (☎ 808-966-9316; 16-586 Old Volcano Rd; ☺6am-10pm) or **Kea'au Natural Foods** (☎ 808-966-8877; 16-586 Old Volcano Rd; ☺8:30am-8pm Mon-Fri, to 7pm Sat, 9:30am-5pm Sun), both at Kea'au Shopping Center, at the junction of Volcano Hwy and Kea'au–Pahoa Rd.

Butterfly Inn
Inn $

(☎ 808-966-7936, 800-546-2442; www.thebutterflyinn.com; Kurtistown; s/d with shared bath $55/65) Geared for women travelers, this longstanding inn is a safe, supportive place in a comfortable home in Kurtistown. Two tidy rooms with private entrances share an ample kitchen, living room, dining deck, bathroom and outdoor hot tub.

Hilo Coffee Mill
Cafe

(www.hilocoffeemill.com; 17-995 Hwy 11; ☺8am-5pm Mon, Tue, Thu & Fri, 7am-4pm Sat; 🛜) This tidy cafe makes for a pleasant stop, with ample seating, light meals, friendly staff, coffee (brewed and beans) and adjacent roasting room. Owners give personal, informative, 90-minute farm tours (with/without meal $20/15). Located roadside between the Mile 12 and Mile 13 markers.

🔒 Shopping

Dan De Luz's Woods
Arts & Crafts

(☎ 808-968-6607; Hwy 11, past Mile 12; 🛜) Master woodworker Dan passed away in 2012, but the grandson whom he trained is carrying on the family craft. The shop still carries numerous calabashes by this much-loved local talent.

Pahoa

This former plantation town is the region's scruffy hub, attracting a variety of eccentrics and transplants. Rampant development hasn't toned down the fringe element here!

The main thoroughfare is signposted as Pahoa Village Rd. As you enter town, there are two shopping malls on either side of the highway: one with a supermarket and a hardware store, the other with Longs Drugs. In town, you'll find banks, gas stations, a post office and **Big Island BookBuyers** (15-2901 Pahoa Village Rd; ☺10am-6pm Mon-Sat, 11am-5pm Sun), a well-run used bookstore.

◎ Sights & Activities

Maku'u Craft & Farmers Market
Market

(Hwy 130; ☺8am-2pm Sun) Crowds converge here for wide-ranging offerings, including psychic readings, massage, surfboard repairs, orchids, jewelry and, yes, fruits and vegetables. Freshly cooked food includes Hawaiian, Mexican and Thai cuisine. Morning **cultural workshops** (☺9am) give way to **live music** through the afternoon.

You can't miss it on the *makai* (seaward) side of Hwy 130 between the Mile 7 and Mile 8 markers.

Jeff Hunt Surfboards
Surfing

(☎ 808-965-2322; http://jeffhuntsurfboards.com; 15-2883 Pahoa Village Rd; rental per day $25; ☺10am-5pm Mon-Sat, 11am-3pm Sun) Jeff Hunt is one of the island's best board shapers, and at his little hut you can buy one, talk surfing and rent soft-top boards.

Paradissimo Tropical Spa
Spa

(☎ 808-965-8883; www.spaparadissimo.com; 15-2958 Pahoa Village Rd; facials from $25; ☺11am-5pm Tue & Thu-Sat) Owner Olivia is a tender soul with talented hands, and the organic spa products she uses feel like alchemy for the skin. Sauna and massage are also available.

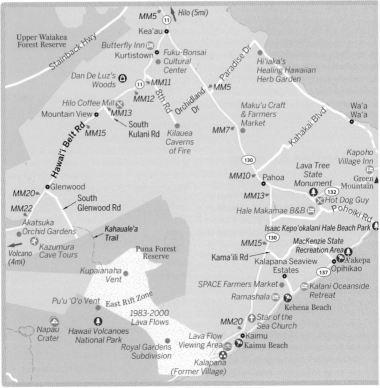

Map labels:
MM5 · Hilo (5mi) · Kea'au · Upper Waiakea Forest Reserve · Stainback Hwy · Butterfly Inn · Kurtistown · Fuku-Bonsai Cultural Center · Paradise Dr · Hi'iaka's Healing Hawaiian Herb Garden · Dan De Luz's Woods · MM11 · 8th Rd · Orchidland Dr · MM5 · Hilo Coffee Mill · MM12 · Maku'u Craft & Farmers Market · Wa'a Wa'a · Mountain View · MM13 · South Kulani Rd · Kilauea Caverns of Fire · MM7 · Kahakai Blvd · Hawai'i Belt Rd · MM15 · Kapoho Village Inn · Lava Tree State Monument · MM10 · Pahoa · Green Mountain · MM20 · Glenwood · MM22 · South Glenwood Rd · MM13 · Hot Dog Guy · Hale Makamae B&B · Pohoiki Rd · Akatsuka Orchid Gardens · Kahauale'a Trail · Isaac Kepo'okalani Hale Beach Park · Kazumura Cave Tours · Volcano (4mi) · Puna Forest Reserve · MM15 · MacKenzie State Recreation Area · Kama'ili Rd · Kalapana Seaview Estates · A'akepa · Opihikao · Kupaianaha Vent · SPACE Farmers Market · Kalani Oceanside Retreat · Pu'u 'O'o Vent · East Rift Zone · Ramashala · Kehena Beach · Napau Crater · Hawaii Volcanoes National Park · 1983-2000 Lava Flows · MM20 · Star of the Sea Church · Royal Gardens Subdivision · Lava Flow Viewing Area · Kaimu · Kaimu Beach · Kalapana (Former Village)

Pahoa Community Aquatic Center
Swimming

(☎808-965-2700; 15-2910 Puna Rd; ⏰9am-5:30pm Mon-Fri, 9am-4:30pm Sat & Sun) For lap swimming, try this fantastic outdoor Olympic-sized pool behind the Pahoa Neighborhood Facility.

🛏 Sleeping

Hedonisia
Hostel, Vacation Rental $

(☎808-430-2545, 808-430-9903; http://hedonisiahawaii.com; 13-657 Hinalo St; dm from $27, r with shared bath $55-70; 📶) 🖉 A former junkyard converted into an organic farm/ramshackle hostel compound, with technicolor murals, Gilligan's Island huts, wild pigs and a school bus. Like-minded free spirits are invited to volunteer in the hostel for discounted stays. Located about 4 miles east of Pahoa.

Hawaiian Sanctuary
Vacation Rental $

(☎800-309-8010; http://sustainable-hawaii.org; Mile 12, Hwy 130; r with shared bath $75-95) 🖉 This permaculture farm offers internships for those interested in sustainable agriculture and going back to nature. Nightly stays are also offered, so visitors can eat vegan food and soak up the vibe. Located about 1.5 miles from central Pahoa.

Jungle Farmhouse
Vacation Rental $$

(☎800-745-5049, 808-640-1113; http://pahoa.info; 15-3001 Mako Way; per night/week $139/700) Kick back at this beautifully maintained house, full of handpicked vintage furnishings, with three bedrooms, 1.5 baths, laundry facilities and an airy screened patio. Outside, enjoy fruit trees, chickens (fresh eggs!) and ducks. A

fantastic value, there's no extra charge for extra guests (maximum four total), and the weekly rate is a steal.

Hale Moana B&B
B&B $$

(☑808-965-7015; www.bnb-aloha.com; 13-3315 Makamae St; studio $110, 1-/2-br ste $145/165; @☎) In a clean-cut subdivision, this B&B (formerly known as Hale Makamae) is immaculate, family-friendly and a bargain. The suites are especially comfy, with well-equipped kitchenettes and enough space to spread out. The owner landscapes her 2-acre grounds superbly and is German fluent.

Eating

For such a small town, Pahoa has a decent bunch of eateries.

Pahoa Fresh Fish
Fish & Chips $

(☑808-965-8248; 15-2670 Pahoa Village Rd; mains $5-7; ☺8am-7pm) Utterly unassuming in an ugly strip mall, this place makes fantastic fish and chips. Who knows what the friendly lady behind the counter is doing? Who cares? We'll come back for her perfectly battered and fried *ono* (wahoo) and mahimahi anytime.

Sirius Coffee Connection
Cafe $

(15-2874 Pahoa Village Rd; ☺7am-6pm Mon-Sat, to 3pm Sun; ☎) Yes, real espresso does exist in Pahoa! This simple space offers good coffee, internet and computer access, friendly service and baked goodies.

Island Naturals
Market $

(15-1403 Pahoa Village Rd; sandwiches $6-10; ☺7:30am-7:30pm Mon-Sat, 8am-7pm Sun; ☑⚕) Here you'll find organic produce, healthy sandwiches, hot mains and the local nouveau hippie crowd.

Malama Market
Supermarket $

(Pahoa Village Rd, Pahoa Marketplace; ☺7am-9pm) Pahoa's biggest grocer is best for basics.

Kaleo's Bar & Grill
Hawaii Regional Cuisine $$

(☑808-965-5600; 15-2969 Pahoa Village Rd; lunch mains $9-16, dinner mains $14-30; ☺11am-9pm; ☎) Pahoa's top sit-down restaurant serves island-fusion fare – such as a tempura ahi roll, orzo pasta salad, and coconut chicken curry – in a relaxed, family-friendly atmosphere. There's live music most nights. Definitely make a reservation on weekends.

Paolo's Bistro
Italian $$

(Pahoa Village Rd; mains $13-26; ☺5:30-9pm Tue-Sun) ☑ This cozy, eight-table eatery executes Northern Italian dishes wonderfully. Bring your own *vino*.

Ning's Thai Cuisine
Thai $$

(15-2955 Pahoa Village Rd; mains $10-14; ☺noon-9pm Mon-Sat, from 5pm Sun; ☑) Come for reliable Thai curries, lively salads and an emphasis on local, organic ingredients.

Luquin's Mexican Restaurant Mexican **$$**
(**808-965-9990; 15-2942 Pahoa Village Rd; mains $10-19; 7am-9pm)** If you're craving Mexican fare, go to Luquin's for a fix, but it's nothing to write home about. The *liliko'i* (passion fruit) margaritas are memorable, however.

Entertainment

Akebono Theater Live Music
(**808-965-9990; Pahoa Village Rd; tickets $10-20)** This historical theater hosts all kinds of music, from Big Island Elvis to visiting jam bands. It's located behind Luquin's Mexican Restaurant.

Getting There & Away

Traffic between Hilo and Puna is a nightmare during commuting hours. By all means, avoid driving toward Hilo in the early morning and toward Kea'au and Pahoa in the late afternoon.

Hele-On Bus (**808-961-8745; www.heleonbus.org; adult/senior or student $2/1)** goes from Hilo to Kea'au and Pahoa several times daily.

Island Insights

Puna is home to the island's biggest concentration of nonconformists, New Agers, nouveau hippies and organic farmers – and it's also the island's gay capital. Here you'll find cruising and rainbow flags, gay-friendly places to stay, workshops and gatherings.

Highway 132

A good way to explore Puna is to navigate the triangle formed by three highways: Hwy 132, Red Road (Hwy 137) and the Kalapana Hwy (Hwy 130). It's even better on a bike!

LAVA TREE STATE MONUMENT

Entering this **park** (**daylight hours**) FREE beneath a thick canopy of (invasive) albizia trees is an otherworldly experience. A short, paved loop trail passes through a tropical vision of Middle Earth, full of wild ferns, orchids, bamboo and strange 'lava trees.' These were formed in 1790 when Kilauea Volcano engulfed the rainforest with a flood of lava up to 10ft deep, enveloping moisture-laden ohia trees before receding. The lava hardened around the trees, which burned away, creating the hollow trunks left today.

To get here, follow Hwy 132 about 2.5 miles east of Hwy 130. Restrooms are remarkably tidy.

'Lava tree'
JOHN ELK/GETTY IMAGES ©

Red Road (Highway 137)

Nicknamed Red Road because its northern portion was originally paved with red cinder, Hwy 137 was repaved with black asphalt in 2013. It's still a mystical drive that meanders through tunnel-like canopies of milo and *hala* (pandanus) trees.

If exploring Puna on a day trip, drive east from Pahoa on Hwy 132; it's otherworldly as the jungly overgrowth thickens. Then head south on Red Road, which navigates from tropical jungle to vast ocean vistas. Return to Pahoa on Hwy 130, less scenic but avoiding backtracking.

Between this 'triangle' of highways, two back roads make intriguing detours or shortcuts: **Pohoiki Rd** connects Hwy 137 with Hwy 132, winding through storybook forest. Look for the roadside **Hot Dog Guy** (cnr Hwy 132 & Pohoiki Rd; hotdog $5-7; ⊙daily 'when it's not pouring'), selling bison, reindeer and beef hotdogs grilled to order.

Further south, **Kama'ili Rd** connects with Hwy 130 and, although less striking, is a pleasant country ramble.

KAPOHO TIDE POOLS

The best **snorkeling** in East Hawaii is this sprawling network of **tide pools** (suggested donation $3; ⊙7am-7pm), officially named Wai Opae Tide Pools Marine Life Conservation District. Here, Kapoho's lava-rock coast is a mosaic of protected, shallow, interconnected pools containing a rich variety of marine life, including saddle wrasses, Moorish idols, butterfly fish and sea cucumbers. Go deeper, heading straight out from the blue house, to see beautiful coral gardens (do not touch); sea turtles like the warm pocket a bit further south (keep 50yd distance).

Wear reef shoes to avoid cutting your soles on the lava rock. From Hwy 137, a mile south of the lighthouse, turn onto Kapoho Kai Dr, which ends at Wai Opae; turn left and park in the lot established by residents ($3 donation). This is not a public park, so there are no restrooms. If residents offer a portable toilet (for obvious reasons), they will request a

1 YOU TAUGHT HAWAIIAN STUDIES AT KALANI. WHAT ARE SOME GOOD HAWAIIAN PHRASES FOR TRAVELERS?
Everyone should learn the words used everyday like aloha and *mahalo* (thanks). In response, you might try 'no problem' *(A'ole pilikia)* or 'It's my pleasure' *(Na'u ka han'oli)*. It's a little more formal and a little more difficult!

2 PUNA IS CAPTIVATING. WHAT ARE SOME OF YOUR FAVORITE PLACES?
I surf, so the Pohoiki breaks are always calling. I like the first bay break called Elevators because it just rocks you up. Another place I really like is the lava tube at MacKenzie State Recreation Area. It's right behind the cliff 'where the spirits jump off.' Kehena Beach is a favorite of course – go before 10am for the best sun and water, and to see the dolphins.

3 DO YOU HAVE ANY TIPS FOR LAVA VIEWING?
The first place I always tell people to go is the new black-sand beach at Kaimu. The lava flow is changing all the time, which is important to remember. Also, there's no safe or right way to go to see the lava. It's a volcano – there's always an element of risk.

4 WHAT'S A GOOD KALANI ACTIVITY FOR PEOPLE WHO WANT A TASTE OF WHAT IT'S ABOUT?
Without a doubt, Ecstatic Sun-Dance. When we started this in 2000, six people and a dog showed up. Now we get about 300 people every Sunday and there's day care (but no dogs allowed). Everyone comes out – it's a highlight of this community.

Detour:
Cape Kumukahi Lighthouse

Hwy 132 goes east until it meets Red Road at **Four Corners** near Kapoho. Once a small farming village, Kapoho became the victim of Pele (Hawaiian goddess of fire and volcanoes) in January 1960 when a volcanic fissure let loose a half-mile-long curtain of fiery lava in a nearby sugarcane field. The main flow of *pahoehoe* (smooth, flowing lava) ran toward the ocean, but an offshoot of *'a'a* (rough, crumbly lava) crept toward the town, burying orchid farms in its path. Two weeks later Kapoho's nearly 100 homes and businesses were buried.

When the lava approached **Cape Kumukahi**, however, it parted around the lighthouse, which survived. Old-timers say that the lighthouse keeper offered a meal to Pele, who appeared disguised as an old woman on the eve of the disaster, and so she spared the structure. Today, the lighthouse is just a tall piece of white-painted metal scaffolding, at the end of an unpaved 1.5-mile road from Four Corners. This is the easternmost point in the state, where you can breathe among the freshest air in the world.

From the lighthouse, trek 10 minutes over *'a'a* toward the sea to a rugged beach, too rough for swimming, but starkly memorable.

---

small donation to offset its maintenance; bring dollar bills.

KAPOHO BEACH LOTS

Slightly further north, there's top-notch snorkeling beyond the locked gates of this seaside community. Vacation rentals, such as **Pualani** (📱805-225-1552; www.big islandhawaiivacationhomes.com; Kapoho Beach Lots; 2-br house $150; @), an airy house with hot tub and wraparound lanai, are plentiful. Check vrbo.com and airbnb.com for listings.

If you stay here, you'll have access to **Champagne Pond**, a tranquil pool with sandy shores frequented by green turtles. It drew controversy when increased use by those driving here (on a rough 4WD-only road from Kumukahi Lighthouse) caused sanitation and other problems. Tread lightly.

AHALANUI BEACH PARK

The 'hot pond' is a spring-fed **thermal pool** (🕐7am-7pm) deep enough for swimming, easily accessible and often crowded. Water temperatures average 90°F (32°C) and the pool is very calm. During high tide, waves crash over the adjacent

seawall, circulating the water, but there's still risk of bacterial infection. Early and late soaking is the best crowd-beating strategy. There are picnic tables, portable toilets and a daily lifeguard. Don't leave valuables unguarded.

ISAAC KEPO'OKALANI HALE BEACH PARK

This beach park, which goes by **Isaac Hale** (house; pronounced *ha*-lay) is a rocky locals' beach along **Pohoiki Bay.** Waters are too rough for swimming, but addictive to experienced bodyboarders and surfers who regard Pohoiki as the island's top break, despite the omnipresence of sharp *wana* (sea urchins). It's a scenic spot to witness pounding waves and local talent.

Some might find the local crowd and vibe intimidating; smile, ask questions and you'll be fine. There are picnic tables, outdoor showers and good **camping** facilities on a pristine lawn, with 22 sites and bathrooms with flush toilets and drinking water. A security guard checks permits (sketchy characters used to squat here).

MACKENZIE STATE RECREATION AREA

With a forest of ironwood trees edging sheer 40ft cliffs overlooking the ocean, this is a dramatic, gorgeous spot. During the day, it makes for quiet, uncrowded picnics. The trees provide plenty of shade, and their fallen needles blanket the ground like a carpet. **Camping** is allowed, but recommended only for large groups due to the park's isolation. Locals tend to go elsewhere because the park has a reputation for being haunted and was the scene of a few violent crimes decades ago.

KEHENA BEACH & AROUND

🏃 Beaches

Kehena Beach   Beach
If any place captures the uninhibited vibe of Puna, it's this beautiful black-sand beach where all stripes – hippies, Hawaiians, gays, families, seniors, tourists – do their own thing. If nudity or *pakalolo* (marijuana) bother you, find another beach. On Sunday a drum circle invites dancing and even more communing. Think twice about swimming; the surf is treacherous.

To get here, turn into a small parking lot immediately south of the Mile 19 marker. A steep path leads down to the beach. Don't leave valuables in your car.

◎ Sights

SPACE Farmers Market   Market
(www.hawaiispace.com; 12-247 West Pohakupele Loop, Seaview Performing Arts Center for Education; ⏰8-11:30am Sat) Kalapana Seaview Estates, near the Mile 18, is home to the SPACE (Seaview Performing Arts Center for Education) Farmers

Market, small but varied and lively. Keep an open mind as you browse tarot readers and tie-dyes, green smoothies and gluten-free breads. To get here, turn into

⭐ The Best... Puna Views

1 Underground in Kazumura Cave (p192), the world's longest lava tube

2 Marine life in Kapoho Tide Pools (p197)

3 Molten lava by land or by sea (p203)

4 People-watching at Kehena Beach (p199)

5 Towering foliage in and around Lava Tree State Monument (p196)

Kapoho Tide Pools (p197)
LONELY PLANET/GETTY IMAGES ©

the subdivision, turn right on Mapuana St and left on Kehauopuna St.

🎊 Festivals & Events

Puna Culinary Festival　　Food
(Kalani Oceanside Retreat & various farms; classes & tours $25, dinners $24) In early September, feast on Puna's farm-to-fork bounty at gourmet dinners, tours, markets and cooking classes.

🛏 Sleeping & Eating

**Kalani Oceanside
Retreat**　　　　　　Resort $$
(📞808-965-7828, 800-800-6886; www.kalani.com; r shared bath $95, r $140-245; ⏰day passes 7:30am-8pm, Ecstatic Sun-Dance 10:30am-12:30pm Sun; @ 🛜 🏊) Immerse yourself in the Puna mindset at this rustic 120-acre compound that hums with communal energy. Daily programs include yoga, meditation, dance and alternative healing. Note that workshops/retreats by visiting

Hidden Dangers in the Water

Frolicking in tide pools and hot ponds has a potential downside – bacteria, including staphylococcal. To minimize risk, go early in the morning when fewer people have entered the pools; go during high tide; and avoid Mondays and post-holidays. Most important, do not enter pools with open cuts and shower immediately after swimming.

teachers are separate from ongoing programs. Nonguests can enjoy facilities on a **day pass** ($20). Weekly **Ecstatic Sun-Dance** (admission $15) gatherings attract the dreadlocked and tattooed.

An outdoor dining **lanai** (breakfast/lunch/dinner $13/15/24), open to nonguests, serves healthy buffet-style meals. Rooms are simple, with plywood floors covered in lauhala mats, and the **camping area** (tents s/d $40/55) is peaceful. To get here, turn inland from Hwy 137 between the Mile 17 and Mile 18 markers.

Ramashala   Vacation Rental $$
(☏ 808-965-0068; www.ramashala.com; 12-7208 Hwy 137; r $50-200; 🛜) Almost directly across from Kehena Beach, this architecturally delightful retreat offers six rooms in three sizes: the smallest come with a twin bed and shared bath, while the largest are mini apartments with full kitchens. High ceilings, hardwood floors, numerous windows, tropical grounds and

two yoga studios make for an elegant private retreat.

Absolute Paradise B&B   B&B $$
(☏ 888-285-1540, 965-1828; http://absolutepara dise.tv; Kipuka St; r $99-135, ste $164; 🛜) Be treated as family at this gay-oriented, clothing-optional B&B a five-minute walk from Kehena Beach. The house and rooms, which vary in size and price, aren't extravagant, but are very comfy and clean.

KALAPANA (FORMER VILLAGE)

For generations, Kalapana was a close-knit fishing village near **Kaimu Beach**, the island's most famous black-sand beach. When Kilauea began erupting in 1983, the lava flowed downslope west of Kalapana. But in 1990 the flow inched toward Kalapana's 100 buildings. When **Star of the Sea Church** was threatened, the community moved it to safety in the nick of time.

Within the year, however, the village and beach were destroyed. Hawaiian residents were remarkably accepting of losing their homes to Pele, commenting that 'Pele's taking back the land' or 'She gave it to us and now she's reclaiming it.'

Today Hwy 137 ends abruptly at the eastern edge of the former village. At the dead-end, a makeshift **tourist stop** includes photos of the eruption and an outpost of the Hawaiian sovereignty movement. From here, you can take a short, but hot and rocky walk across lava desert to **New Kaimu Beach** (aka Coconut Beach), where hundreds of baby coconut palms surround a black arc of sand. The water is too rough for swimming, but it's a contemplative spot.

🍴 Eating & Drinking

Kalapana Village Cafe　　Local **$**
(12-5037 Pahoa Kalapana Rd, Hwy 137; mains $8-11; ⏰8am-9pm) At the edge of civilization (or so it seems), this drive-in-style eatery serves decent burgers and plate lunches, plus ice-cold drinks. Restrooms open only to customers.

Uncle Robert's Awa Bar　　Bar
(⏰3-10pm) In the afternoon, sidle up to Uncle's Awa Bar, where you can try kava (native intoxicant), listen to live music and rub elbows with local characters.

Highway 130

From Kalapana, Hwy 130 makes its way north to Pahoa and on to Kea'au.

👁 Sights

Lava-Viewing Area　　Lookout
(☎hotline 808-961-8093; ⏰3-9pm, car entry by 8pm) At the end of Hwy 130, there's a parking lot staffed by informative personnel, plus souvenir vendors and a few portable toilets. From the lot, you can walk over rocky terrain to a public lava-viewing area, but you might see only a plume of hot steam or absolutely nothing. Call the hotline for current info. The flow is unpredictable, so keep your expectations in check.

Star of the Sea Church　　Church
(⏰9am-4pm) The historic Star of the Sea Church (also known as 'Painted Church') is noted for its trompe l'oeil murals that create an illusion of depth and expansiveness. Built in 1929, this tiny Catholic church's first priest was Father Damien, legendary for his work on Moloka'i with people suffering from leprosy. Originally in Kalapana, it's now off Hwy 130 at the Mile 20 marker.

Noisy Neighbors – Coqui Frogs

Hawaii's most wanted alien is the Puerto Rican coqui frog, only an inch long, but relentlessly loud. At sunset, coquis begin their nightly chirping (a two-tone 'ko-kee' call), which can register between 90 and 100 decibels from 2ft away. Even at a distance, their chorus maintains 70 decibels, equivalent to a vacuum cleaner.

Coquis accidentally reached the Hawaiian Islands around 1988, and they've proliferated wildly on the Big Island. Around Lava Tree State Monument, densities are the highest in the state and twice that of Puerto Rico. Besides causing a nightly racket, coquis are disrupting the ecosystem by eating the bugs that feed native birds. Light sleepers: bring ear plugs.

🏃 Activities

At the end of Hwy 130, there's nothing but vast fields of lava rock. Here, the main activity is lava viewing. Whether you see glowing, red lava depends on luck and timing. If lava is flowing into the ocean, a lava-watching boat tour is possible. If the flow is remote, the only option is a strenuous hike, covering miles of rugged terrain, in pitch darkness on the way back.

Bear in mind, the entire lava flow covers private land, and trespassing is illegal (although no one is cracking down on those crossing their property). If you walk across the flow – guided or unguided – you do so at your own risk. Dangers include unstable lava, sharp rocks, fires, gaseous explosion and simply getting lost in the dark. If you are injured, you could be stranded until other hikers discover you. Therefore, it's prudent to join a guided tour if you decide to hike to see the flow.

Lava Ocean Adventures   Sailing
(☎808-966-4200; www.sealava.com; tours adult/child from $150/125) If (and this is a big 'if') lava is pouring into the Pacific, don't miss a once-in-a-lifetime boat ride it see it. Expect a turbulent ride; fit individuals only.

Ahiu Hawaii   Hiking
(☎769-9453; www.ahiuhawaii.com; tour per person $155; ☯departures 8am & 4pm) When the flow is too remote for most tours, these intrepid guides slog through muddy jungle and sharp lava rock to find it. For very strong hikers only.

Volcano Discovery Hawai'i   Hiking
(http://hawaii.volcanodiscovery.com; 4-14hr tours per person $150-400) Run by a geologist, these customizable tours are informative, personalized and professionally run. Group size is limited for safety.

The Best...
Places with the Puna Vibe

1 Anything goes at Kehena Beach (p199)

2 Back-to-nature lodging at Hedonisia (p194) and Hawaiian Sanctuary (p194)

3 Ecstatic Sun-Dance at Kalani Oceanside Retreat (p200)

4 Far-out finds at Maku'u Craft & Farmers Market (p193) and SPACE Farmers Market (p199)

Native Guide Hawaii   Hiking
(☎808-982-7575; www.nativeguidehawaii.com; tour incl lunch per person $150; ☯by appointment) 🏅 For the personal touch, Native Hawaiian and cultural practitioner Warren Costa offers customized all-day tours that reveal gems you wouldn't find on your own.

Poke a Stick Lava Tours   Hiking
(☎808-987-3456; http://lavarefuge.com; tour $100; ☯7:30am-4:30pm) When the flow is accessible from their Kalapana property, this versatile couple takes groups out. They also offer vacation rentals.

Kalapana Cultural Tours   Hiking
(☎808-936-0456; www.kalapanaculturaltours.com; tour approximately $100) Run by a local family, this is a solid choice for evening hikes when the flow cooperates.

Hawai'i Volcanoes National Park

It's safe to say there is no place on earth like Hawai'i Volcanoes National Park. Sulfurous smoke belches from the ground so voluminously it tastes like you're in hell. Ribbons of red lava flow from Kilauea – the most active volcano on the planet, ruled over by the Hawaiian goddess Pele – toward the sea, boiling it upon contact. Waving palm trees fringe white-sand beaches backed by jet-black lava fields, and above it all looms a snowy mountain, Mauna Loa. An entire day could easily be spent exploring sights along the park's scenic drives, but give yourself at least two – and don't miss seeing the lava lake glowing at night. After the sun goes down, soak in a hot tub secreted in the rainforest or put your feet up in front of the fireplace at cozy, romantic lodgings in artistic Volcano village.

Kilauea Volcano (p208)

Hawai'i Volcanoes National Park Itineraries

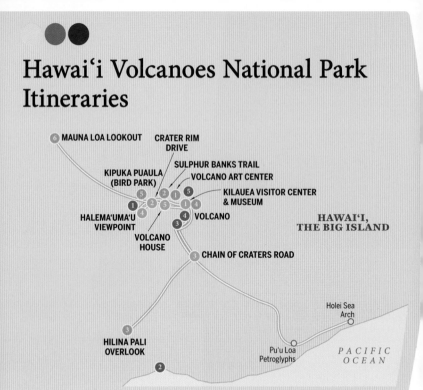

One Day

1 Kilauea Visitor Center & Museum (p208) Start day one early here, near the park entrance, to learn about the volcano and the park's natural history. Check daily schedules of ranger programs, eruption updates, sulfur-dioxide levels and road and trail closures.

2 Crater Rim Drive (p208) If Pele is up to her usual shenanigans, parts of this 11-mile paved loop road will be closed, but you should still be able to visit the Jaggar Museum, walk through Thurston Lava Tube and hike the Kilauea Iki Trail.

3 Chain of Craters Road (p212) Even if it's raining at the visitor center, drive down this scenic road to the coast, where you might still spot sunshine. Along the way, stop to hike to the Pu'u Loa Petroglyphs and snap photos of gravity-defying Holei Sea Arch.

4 Halema'uma'u Viewpoint (p211) After sunset, backtrack along Crater Rim Dr to check out the ethereal glow of the lava lake deep within Halema'uma'u Crater from the patio outside the Jaggar Museum.

5 Volcano House (p222) Even if you're not sleeping here, stop by this historic hotel perched on the rim of Kilauea Volcano. Its fireplace lobby, lounge and restaurant all enjoy crater-view windows.

 THIS LEG: 55 MILES

Two Days

1 **Volcano Art Center** (p209) By the Kilauea Visitor Center, immerse yourself in this high-quality gallery of traditional and contemporary island arts and Hawaiian crafts. If you're lucky, there'll be a hula dance performance or cultural arts demonstration happening.

2 **Sulphur Banks Trail** (p209) Because this is day two, you may be ready for a more serious, all-day hike into the park's volcanic backcountry. If not, opt for this easy, but uniquely scenic trail just a short drive from the visitor center. It connects with the crater-rim walk past the hellish Steaming Bluff.

3 **Hilina Pali Overlook** (p213) Bring a picnic along to this sea-view lookout, reached via a narrow, but paved scenic drive off Chain of Craters Road.

4 **Volcano** (p223) Next it's time for lunch and art-gallery hopping in town, starting at the Volcano Art Center's Rainforest Gallery. Make reservations in advance to take a sustainable farm-and-forest walking tour with Tea Hawaii & Company.

5 **Kipuka Puaulu (Bird Park)** (p219) A short drive west of Volcano lies this rainforest *kipuka* (oasis) spared by dramatic lava flows. An easy mile-long loop trail offers spectacular bird-watching for adults and kids alike – bring binoculars.

6 **Mauna Loa Lookout** (p214) You've come this far already, so why not keep going? Narrow, pockmarked Mauna Loa Rd winds for over 11 miles up 'Long Mountain' to an unforgettable viewpoint over the volcanic caldera down to the coast.

➲ THIS LEG: 50 MILES

Hawai'i Volcanoes National Park Highlights

1 **Best View: Halema'uma'u Viewpoint** (p211) You may have to wait your turn to get a glimpse, but it's worth it.

2 **Best Beach: Halape** (p218) A grueling hot hike with dizzying coastal views leads to this wild beach.

3 **Best Hike: Kilauea Iki Trail** (p216) Trek across a lunar landscape of lava flows inside a living volcanic crater.

4 **Best Activity for Kids: Thurston Lava Tube** (p212) Eerie walk through an underground tunnel carved by lava flows.

5 **Best Entertainment: Volcano Art Center** (p209) Hula dancing, Hawaiian culture and craft workshops, concerts and more.

Volcano Art Center (p209)
ANN CECIL/GETTY IMAGES ©

Discover Hawai'i Volcanoes National Park

Nothing on the Big Island equals the elemental grandeur and raw power of the two active volcanoes encompassed by **Hawai'i Volcanoes National Park** (HAVO; ☎808-985-6000; www.nps.gov/havo; 7-day entry per car $10), established in 1916. With geological history dating back almost half a million years, this awe-inspiring park became Hawaii's first Unesco World Heritage Site in 1987.

The current eruption along Kilauea's East Rift Zone of Kilauea, the park's most active volcano, started on January 3, 1983, making it the longest in recorded history. Nearly 30 years of continuous volcanic action adds up to a lot of lava – some 2.5 billion cubic yards a day (that's 50,000 gallons a minute!), and 500 acres of new land. All of this boil, toil and trouble comes from the Pu'u 'O'o Vent, a smoldering cinder cone along the East Rift Zone.

Kilauea is a shield volcano, which means lava usually oozes and creeps along, with occasional earthquakes, lava fountains and lakes of fire. But it doesn't have the explosive gases of the more dramatic and deadly strato volcanoes found along the Pacific Ocean's Ring of Fire (eg Mt St Helens in Washington), which throw ash and flaming rocks into the air. Though languid, Big Island lava can still be deadly stuff, make no mistake: it consumes trees, houses, roads and anything else in its path.

◉ Sights

CRATER RIM DRIVE

This incredible 11-mile paved loop road starts at Kilauea Visitor Center and skirts the rim of Kilauea Caldera, passing steam vents and rifts, hiking trailheads and amazing views of the smoking crater. At the time of research, the road beyond the Jaggar Museum and Halema'uma'u Overlook to the Chain of Craters Road intersection was closed indefinitely due to eruption activity.

Kilauea Visitor Center & Museum   Museum

(☎808-985-6000; www.nps.gov/havo; Crater Rim Dr; ⏰7:45am-5pm, film screenings hourly 9am-4pm; 👫) Make your first stop the park's visitor center. On-duty rangers and volunteers can advise you about volcanic activity, air quality, road closures and hiking trail conditions.

Jaggar Museum
LONELY PLANET/GETTY IMAGES ©

Interactive museum exhibits are small but family-friendly, and will teach even science-savvy adults a lot about the park's delicate ecosystem and Hawaiian heritage. Pick up fun **junior ranger program** activity books for your kids before leaving.

Geology talks are given twice daily by the outdoor signboards, where ranger-led hikes and other activities are posted. A well-stocked nonprofit bookstore inside the visitor center sells souvenirs, rain ponchos, walking sticks and flashlights. Wheelchairs are free to borrow upon request. There are restrooms and a payphone outside.

Volcano Art Center Arts Center
(📞866-967-7565, 808-967-7565; www.vol canoartcenter.org; Crater Rim Dr; ⊗9am-5pm) 🖋 Near the visitor center, this innovative local art gallery spotlights museum-quality pottery, paintings, woodwork, sculpture, jewelry, Hawaiian quilts and more. The nonprofit shop, housed in the historic 1877 Volcano House hotel, is worth a visit just to admire its solid artisanship. Ask about upcoming art classes and cultural workshops here.

Sulphur Banks Landmark
(off Crater Rim Dr) Wooden boardwalks weave through to steaming Sulphur Banks, where rocky vents and holes are stained chartreuse, yellow, orange and other weird colors by tons of sulfur-infused steam rising from deep within the earth. That rotten-egg stench is from noxious hydrogen sulfide wafting out of the vents. The easy 0.7-mile one-way trail connects to Crater Rim Dr near the parking lot for Steaming Bluff. The latter half of the trail is wheelchair-accessible.

Steam Vents & Steaming Bluff Lookout
(Crater Rim Dr) Pumping impressive plumes of steam in the cool early morning, these vents make a convenient drive-up photo op. Steam is created when rainwater percolates into the earth, is heated by the hot rocks below and then released upward. For an even more evocative experience, take the short walk to the crater rim at Steam-ing Bluff, where the view looks like an inferno with steam pouring over the cliffs.

Kilauea Overlook Lookout
(Crater Rim Dr) The Kilauea Overlook parking lot and picnic area provides a pause-worthy panorama, including views of Halema'uma'u Crater and the Southwest Rift. The latter's rocky fissure is bigger and longer than it looks: it slices from the caldera summit all the way to the coast.

Jaggar Museum Museum
(📞808-985-6051; Crater Rim Dr; ⊗8:30am-7:30pm; ♿) Big draws at this small one-room museum are the views and the real-time seismographs and tiltmeters recording earthquakes inside the park. Other exhibits introduce Hawaiian gods and goddesses and give a short history of the neighboring Hawai'i Volcano Observatory, founded by famed geologist Dr Thomas A Jaggar. Park rangers frequently give geology talks inside the museum. Wheelchairs are free to borrow.

The Best...
Hawai'i Volcanoes National Park at Night

1 Lava lake viewing from Jaggar Museum (p209)

2 'After Dark in the Park' evening programs (p221)

3 Na Leo Manu music concerts (p221)

4 Walking to Thurston Lava Tube (p212) by flashlight

5 Toasting your tootsies by the Volcano House (p222) fireplace

6 Live music and drinks at Uncle George's Lounge (p222)

Hawai'i Volcanoes National Park

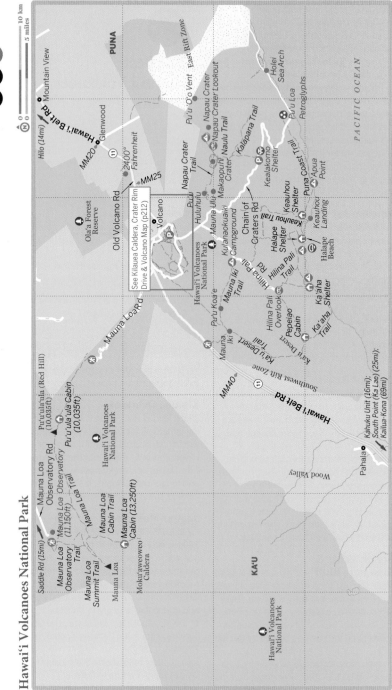

Halemaʻumaʻu Viewpoint Lookout

(Crater Rim Dr) The original Halemaʻumaʻu Overlook off Crater Rim Dr has been closed since 2008 due to ongoing volcanic activity. The next best vantage point is the patio outside the Jaggar Museum. Don't worry, the new viewpoint is still extraordinary: there's absolutely nothing like witnessing a huge smoking volcanic crater or roiling lava lake, especially after dark when the flickering hellfire glow is mesmerizing.

Halemaʻumaʻu is really a crater within the crater of Kilauea Caldera. About 3000ft across and almost 300ft deep, it spews out a rising column of volcanic ash and gases, such as sulfor dioxide, that emerges from the great hole and billows into the sky, partly creating the vog (volcanic fog) that increasingly carpets the island (Kilauea's Puʻu ʻOʻo vent adds the rest).

How active Kilauea Volcano will be when you visit is subject to the whims of Pele, the Hawaiian [...] volcanoes who m[...] so don't count on[...] It's most advant[...] clear nights afte[...] views of the cra[...] near Kilauea Vis[...]

Kilauea Iki C[...]

(Crater Rim Dr) V[...] Kilauea) burst o[...] November 1959, it turned the crat[...] a roiling lake of molten lava and sent 1900ft-high fountains of lava into the night sky. At its peak, the eruption gushed 2 million tons of lava an hour as the landscape glowed an eerie orange for miles.

From the overlook, you can view the steaming mile-wide crater below, which was used for filming the 2001 remake of *Planet of the Apes*.

Look for tiny hikers making their way across the crater floor to appreciate its massive proportions.

Halemaʻumaʻu Crater: A Lake of Fire

On March 19, 2008, Halemaʻumaʻu Crater shattered a quarter-century of silence with a huge steam-driven explosion that scattered rocks and Pele's hair (strands of volcanic glass) over 75 acres. A series of explosions followed, widening a 300ft vent in the crater floor, which as of early 2014 continued to spew a muscular column of gas and ash. The vent bubbles (but doesn't spurt) molten lava.

In 1823, missionary William Ellis first described the boiling goblet of Halemaʻumaʻu, and this prodigious sight attracted travelers from all over the world. Looking in, some saw the fires of hell, others primeval creation, but none left the crater unmoved. Mark Twain wrote that he witnessed: '[C]ircles and serpents and streaks of lightning all twined and wreathed and tied together...I have seen Vesuvius since, but it was a mere toy, a child's volcano, a soup kettle, compared to this.'

Then, in 1924, the crater floor subsided rapidly, touching off a series of explosive eruptions. Boulders and mud rained down for days. When it was over, the crater had doubled in size – to about 300ft deep and 3000ft wide. Lava activity ceased and the crust cooled.

Since then, Halemaʻumaʻu has erupted 18 times; it's the most active area on the volcano's summit. All of Hawaiʻi is the territory of Pele, goddess of fire and volcanoes, but Halemaʻumaʻu is her home, making it a sacred site for Hawaiians.

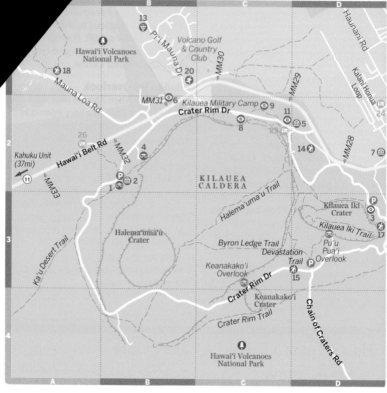

Thurston Lava Tube
Cave

(off Crater Rim Dr; 🚻) On Kilauea's eastern side, Crater Rim Dr passes through rainforest *kipuka* (oases) thick with tree ferns and ohia trees. An often overflowing parking lot is the access point for the ever-popular Thurston Lava Tube. All the tour buses stop here and it's a favorite with kids, so plan to come early or late in the day. A 0.3-mile loop walk starts in ohia forest filled with birdsong before diving underground through a gigantic lava tube that's artificially lit.

Lava tubes are formed when the outer crust of a lava river starts to harden but the liquid lava beneath the surface continues to flow through. After the flow drains out, the hard shell remains. Dating back perhaps 500 years, Thurston Lava Tube is a grand example – it's tunnel-like and almost big enough to run a train through.

CHAIN OF CRATERS ROAD
Turning south off Crater Rim Dr, paved Chain of Craters Road winds almost 20 miles and 3700ft down the southern slopes of Kilauea, ending abruptly at the volcano's East Rift Zone on the coast. Allow at least 90 minutes for the round-trip drive excluding stops. Drive slowly, especially in foggy or rainy conditions, and watch out for endangered nene (Hawaiian goose) along the way.

From the paved road you'll have striking vistas of the coastline far below, but for miles and miles the predominant view is of hardened lava. You can sometimes find thin filaments of volcanic glass, known as Pele's hair, in

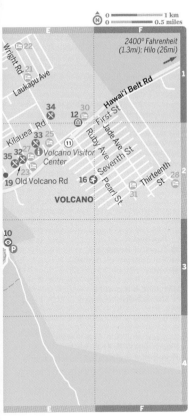

backcountry trek in extreme weather conditions.

Mauna Ulu   Landmark
(off Chain of Craters Rd) In 1969, eruptions from Kilauea's East Rift Zone began building a new lava shield, Mauna Ulu (Growing Mountain). By the time the flow stopped in 1974, it had covered 10,000 acres of parkland and added 200 acres of new coastal land. It also buried a 6-mile section of the original Chain of Craters Road in lava up to 300ft deep. Today the signed turnoff for Mauna Ulu is 3.5 miles down Chain of Craters Road.

The Pu'u Huluhulu Trail (p217) and more demanding Napau Crater Trail (p217) begin here (backcountry permit required for the latter).

Kealakomo   Lookout
(Chain of Craters Rd) About halfway along Chain of Craters Rd, this coastal lookout (elevation 2000ft) has picnic tables and commanding views. Below Kealakomo, the road descends long, sweeping switchbacks, some cut deeply through lava flows.

Pu'u Loa
Petroglyphs   Archaeological Site
(off Chain of Craters Rd) The gentle, 1.5-mile round-trip **Pu'u Loa Trail** leads to one of Hawai'i's largest concentration of ancient petroglyphs. Here Hawaiians chiseled more than 23,000 drawings into *pahoehoe* (smooth-flowing lava) with adze tools quarried from Keanakako'i. At the site, stay on the boardwalk at all times – not all petroglyphs are obvious, and you are likely to trample (and damage) some if you walk over the rocks. The trailhead parking area is signed between the Mile 16 and the Mile 17 markers.

There are abstract designs, animal and human figures, as well as thousands of dimpled depressions (or cupules) that were receptacles for *piko* (umbilical cords). Placing a baby's *piko* inside a cupule and covering it with stones was intended to bestow health and longevity on the child. Rangers occasionally lead hikes exploring petroglyphs beyond the boardwalk – inquire at Kilauea Visitor Center.

the cracks and crevices. The best time to photograph this unique landscape is in the early morning and late afternoon, when sunlight slants off the lava.

Hilina Pali Overlook   Lookout
(Hilina Pali Rd) After a couple of miles of pit craters along Chain of Craters Road, you'll come to the turnoff for Hilina Pali Rd. Drive carefully on this narrow, one-lane paved road – especially because your eyes will be popping at the endless volcanic wastelands and spectacular northward views of Mauna Loa. After 5 miles, you'll pass Kulanaokuaiki Campground. The road ends roughly 4 miles later at the serenely beautiful Hila Pali Overlook.

From the road's end, you may be tempted to hit the **Hilina Pali Trail**, but the shoreline isn't as close as it looks. Hikers must be prepared for a rugged

⊙ **Sights**
1 Halema'uma'u Viewpoint B2
2 Jaggar Museum B2
3 Kilauea Iki Overlook D3
4 Kilauea Overlook B2
5 Kilauea Visitor Center & Museum D2
6 Lava Tree Molds B2
7 Rainforest Gallery D2
8 Steam Vents & Steaming Bluff C2
9 Sulphur Banks C2
10 Thurston Lava Tube E3
11 Volcano Art Center C2
12 Volcano Garden Arts E1
13 Volcano Winery B1

⊙ **Activities, Courses & Tours**
14 Backcountry Office.................................D2
15 Devastation Trail....................................D3
16 Hale Ho'ōla...E2
17 Kilauea Iki Trail D3
18 Kipuka Puaulu (Bird Park) A1
19 Niaulani Rain Forest Tour......................E2
20 Volcano Golf & Country Club B1

⊙ **Sleeping**
Artist Cottage ....(see 12)
21 Chalet Kilauea Collection.......................E1

22 Enchanted Rainforest Cottages.............E1
23 Hale Ohia Log Cabin...............................E2
24 Holo Holo In...D2
25 Kilauea Lodge E2
26 Namakanipaio Cabins &
    Campground A2
27 Volcano Country Cottages.....................E2
28 Volcano Guest House F2
    Volcano Hideaways.......................(see 23)
29 Volcano House...C2
30 Volcano Inn...E1
31 Volcano Rainforest Retreat...................F2

⊗ **Eating**
32 Café Ohi'a E2
    Café Ono ....(see 12)
    Kilauea General Store ....(see 33)
    Kilauea Lodge Restaurant..........(see 25)
    Lava Rock Café ....(see 33)
    Rim Restaurant.............................(see 29)
33 Thai Thai Restaurant E2
34 Volcano Farmers Market........................E1
35 Volcano Store E2

⊙ **Drinking & Nightlife**
    Uncle George's Lounge ....(see 29)

Holei Sea Arch — Landmark

Constantly brutalized by unrelenting surf, the coastal section of Chain of Craters Road has sharply eroded lava-rock *pali* (cliffs). Visible from near the road's end, this high rock arch is a dramatic landmark, carved out of a cliff by crashing waves.

End of the Road — Landmark

(Chain of Craters Rd) Quite. The road ends where the lava says it ends, having swamped this coastal section of Chain of Craters Road repeatedly between 1969 and 1996. The 'Road Closed' sign, almost entirely buried in lava, is a classic photo op. There's a simple info board and portable toilets here, plus a ranger outpost – but don't count on it being staffed unless lava starts flowing again nearby within hiking distance.

MAUNA LOA ROAD

If you really want to escape the crowds, drive 11.5-mile Mauna Loa Rd past hiking trailheads, majestic views and *kipuka* (oases) spared by massive lava flows. The road begins off Hwy 11 near the Mile 31 marker, just over 2 miles west of the park's main entrance. After a mile or so, before reaching Kipuka Puaulu, roadside picnic tables and pit toilets are the only facilities.

Lava Tree Molds — Landmark

(off Mauna Loa Rd) Near the start of Mauna Loa Rd, there's a turnoff to some neglected lava tree molds, deep tube-like apertures formed when lava flows engulfed the rainforest and hardened around the waterlogged trees instead of burning them upon contact. As the trees disintegrated, they left deep holes where the trunks once stood.

Mauna Loa Lookout — Lookout

(Mauna Loa Rd) It's a narrow, winding and potholed drive to the very top of lonely Mauna Loa Rd, passing heavily forested *kipuka* as you come ever closer to the world's most massive active volcano. Mauna Loa has erupted more than 18 times in the past century – the last eruption, in March 1984, lasted three weeks. At the end of the road lies epic Mauna Loa Lookout (6600ft) and the start of the exceptionally challenging, multiday

Mauna Loa Trail (p219; backcountry permit required).

For the best views, wander a short way down the trail for vistas that encompass smoking Kilauea far below.

KAHUKU UNIT

In 2003, NPS and the Nature Conservancy jointly purchased Kahuku Ranch, part of Hawai'i's largest traditional *ahupua'a* (land division). The biggest conservation land purchase in the state's history, this deal added a whopping 116,000 acres to the national park, increasing its size by over 50%.

Today, the park's **Kahuku Unit** remains largely wild and undeveloped. This is a real get-away-from-it-all destination, with no amenities besides outhouses. Four hiking trails – Pu'u o Lokuana (p220), Palm (p220), Glover (p220) and Kona (p220) – lead through green pastures and around volcanic cinder cones, lava tree molds, rainforest and lava flows. The 12-mile round-trip **scenic drive** is unpaved, but usually passable just over halfway in a standard car. Beyond the Palm Trail's upper trailhead, a high-clearance, 4WD vehicle is advised.

At the time of research, the Kahuku Unit (free entry) was open to the public from 9am to 3pm on Saturdays and Sundays, but double-check this at Kilauea Visitor Center before making the trip. The entrance is about 4 miles west of Wai'ohinu (p238), between the Mile 70 and the Mile 71 markers on Hwy 11. Ranger-guided hikes are offered some weekends (advance reservations not usually required.)

🏃 Activities

HIKING

Dust off your hiking boots: rainforest oases, lava deserts, secluded beaches, crater walks and the world's most active volcano all await on the park's 150-mile trail network, rising from sea level to the summit of Mauna Loa (13,679ft).

Be prepared for highly changeable weather: a hot sunny stroll can turn cold and wet in an instant. No drinking water is available, except possibly at primitive campgrounds (where it must be treated before drinking); plan to pack at least 3L of water per person per day. Campfires are prohibited. A compass and binoculars are handy, because misty or 'voggy'

Thurston Lava Tube (p212)

PHILIP ROSENBERG/GETTY IMAGES ©

Detour:
Viewing the Lava Flow Up Close

Lucky travelers can view live lava making the 64-mile journey from the Pu'u O'o Vent to the ocean. Where the lava will be flowing when you visit and whether or not you can reach it are impossible to predict. Sometimes it's an arduous 13-mile round-trip hike from the end of Chain of Craters Road inside the park. Ask at the Kilauea Visitor Center, call the park or check the NPS website for updates.

It's usually a much easier hike to the flow from the free, county-run lava viewing area (p202) outside park boundaries at the end of Hwy 130 in Puna. If the show is really on, there will be surface flows, lava 'skylights' and flaming trees. When the flow mellows or changes course, you'll be able to see a steam plume during the day, and an unearthly red glow after dark. Bring a flashlight and water, and plan to stick around after sunset. You might be able to get even closer to the lava flow on a guided hiking tour or lava boat cruise leaving from Puna (p189).

Of course, all of this information is highly changeable – staying informed about the flow helps manage expectations (especially kids'). Lava entering the ocean is wondrous, but extremely dangerous. The explosive clash between seawater and 2100°F (1150°C) lava can spray scalding water hundreds of feet into the air and throw flaming lava chunks well inland. Unstable ledges of lava crust (called 'lava benches') sometimes collapse without warning. Several observers have been injured, some fatally, over the past decade. Always stay at least 500yd inland from the lava flow and heed all official warnings.

conditions and intense sunlight reflecting off lava can impede navigation.

All overnight hikes require a free permit, available in person up to one day ahead from the **Backcountry Office** (☎808-985-6178; Crater Rim Dr, Visitor Emergency Operations Center (VEOC); ⏰8am-4pm). Ask at Kilauea Visitor Center for directions, or check the park website, which has a downloadable backcountry trip planner covering potential hazards with safety tips and advice for protecting wildlife and archaeological sites.

If you prefer to join a group, the nonprofit **Friends of Hawai'i Volcanoes National Park** (☎808-985-7373; www.fhvnp. org; annual membership adult/student/family $30/15/45) leads weekend hikes and field trips, and organizes volunteer activities such as native forest restoration.

Kilauea Iki Trail Hiking

If you can only do one day hike, make it this one. Beginning at the Kilauea Iki Overlook (p211) parking lot off Crater Rim Dr, this 4-mile, clockwise loop takes you through a jaw-dropping microcosm of the park. It quickly descends 400ft through fairytale ohia forest, then cuts across mile-wide Kilauea Iki crater. Scattered vents lace the crater's surface with ethereal steam plumes, while the wrinkly, often iridescent lava surface is peppered with ohelo shrubs, ohia trees and ferns.

Hitting the trail before 8am is a good way to beat the day-tripping crowds. The faint footpath across the crater floor is marked by ahu (stone cairns) to aid navigation. Don't wander off-trail to explore any steaming vents, lava tubes or caves without an experienced guide.

Geology-oriented trail brochures ($2) are sold at Kilauea Visitor Center.

Halema'uma'u Trail   Hiking

Halema'uma'u Crater was indefinitely closed to hikers at the time of research due to ongoing volcanic activity, though short trail sections through ohia forest along the crater rim were open. When fully open, this 7-mile loop is one of the park's best day hikes, prized for its variety of ecosystems and colorful lava flows.

Devastation Trail   Hiking

Although only 0.5 miles long, the paved, wheelchair-accessible Devastation Trail offers fantastic views of Mauna Loa looming over the sulfur-encrusted caldera. The 1959 eruption of Kilauea Iki toasted this rainforest, leaving dead trees, stripped bare and sun-bleached white, and tree molds. Now ohia trees, 'ohelo shrubs and ferns are colonizing the area anew.

The prominent cinder cone you'll see along the way is **Pu'u Pua'i** (Gushing Hill), formed during the eruption. You can start the trail from either end at the Pu'u Puai Overlook parking lot or the Devastation Trail parking area further west, where Crater Rim Dr turns south.

Crater Rim Trail   Hiking

Almost all of this trail was closed at the time of research, which is a pity since this 11.5-mile loop hike showcases just how dramatically the volcano has altered the landscape over time. Ask at Kilauea Visitor Center about which trail sections are currently open, usually short strolls of under a mile through ohia forest along the rim of **Keanakako'i Crater**, off Crater Rim Dr and Chain of Craters Road.

Pu'u Huluhulu Trail   Hiking

This easy 2.5-mile round-trip hike begins at Mauna Ulu (p213) parking area off Chain of Craters Road. The trail ends atop a 150ft-high cinder cone, **Pu'u Huluhulu**, which is like a crow's nest on a clear day. Summit vistas net Mauna Ulu, Mauna Loa, Mauna Kea, Pu'u 'O'o Vent, Kilauea Volcano, the East Rift Zone and the ocean beyond.

A self-guiding trail brochure ($2), which includes perilous eyewitness accounts of the 1969–74 eruption, is sold at Kilauea Visitor Center.

Napau Crater Trail   Hiking

An incredibly varied and satisfying all-day hike, the Napau Crater Trail passes lava fields, immense craters and thick native forest, ending with distant views of Pu'u 'O'o, the source of Kilauea's ongoing eruption. It's a 14-mile round-trip backcountry hike over rugged terrain, starting from the Mauna Ulu (p213) parking area off Crater Rim Dr. Backcountry permits are required for both day and overnight hikes.

Pu'u 'O'o Vent and its lava-flow path
STEPHAN HOEROLD/GETTY IMAGES ©

Self-registration is available at the trailhead, but it's smarter to pick up your free permit from the Backcountry Office (p216), where you can ask about trail conditions and closures in this geologically unstable area. The trail's first 5 miles follow what was formerly Chain of Craters Road, before lava swamped it; reticulite and Pele's hair (strands of volcanic glass) are strewn over the flows.

You'll pass lava trees and **Pu'u Huluhulu** cinder cone before veering left (east). On clear days the view is magnificent, with Mauna Loa to the northwest, Mauna Kea to the north and the volatile Pu'u 'O'o vent to the east. After descending across *pahoehoe* flows, you'll reach the south rim of jaw-dropping, mile-long **Makaopuhi Crater**.

Exiting a cool fern forest, you come to the rock walls of an old depository for *pulu,* the golden, silky 'hair' found at the base of *hapu'u* (tree fern) fiddlehead stems, with which ancient Hawaiians embalmed the dead. Tour helicopters whir overhead as fantastic views of the partially collapsed Pu'u 'O'o cone appear. Beyond the **Napau Crater lookout**

junction is primitive Napau Campground (pit toilets, no water).

You can shave off about 4 miles round-trip if you start on the Naulu Trail from Kealakomo (p213) down Chain of Craters Road. However, you'll miss some of the grandest views and the huffing vents and cracks peppering the active rift.

Puna Coast Trails
Hiking

You'll experience secluded snorkeling, white-sand beaches, soaring cliffs and savagely beautiful landscapes on these rugged backcountry trails. The main approaches – the Hilina Pali, Keauhou and Puna Coast Trails – are all hot, steep and strenuous, so bring lots of extra water. With an interconnecting trail network, you can design your own overnight trek.

Pick up your free overnight hiking permit (required) at the Backcountry Office (p216), where rangers have information on current trail closures and conditions, and just as importantly, water-catchment levels at primitive backcountry shelters and campgrounds.

With swimming and snorkeling, white sand and coconut trees, **Halape** is the most popular overnight destination,

Hiking, Devastation Trail (p217)

followed by **Keauhou**. Endangered hawksbill sea turtles nest all along the coast here, so travel responsibly.

The easiest route down to the coast is the gently sloping **Keauhou Trail** (6.8 miles one way); the trailhead is past the Mile 6 marker on Chain of Craters Road. The shortest route to Ka'aha is the **Hilina Pali Trail** (3.6 miles one way), which continues to Halape (8 miles), but it begins with a brutal cliff descent; the trail starts at Hilina Pali Overlook (p213).

Kipuka Puaulu (Bird Park) — Hiking

(🚶) If you're looking for a shady, 1.2-mile loop hike easy enough for young kids, this is it. This 100-acre sanctuary is a prime specimen of a rainforest *kipuka* (oasis), spared about 400 years ago by a major lava flow from Mauna Loa. Today native flora and fauna thrive here. The trailhead is just over a mile up Mauna Loa Rd, off Hwy 11.

This hike is best done in the early morning or at dusk, when you'll be enveloped by birdsong. You'll see honeycreepers – the *'amakihi*, *'apapane* and *'i'iwi* – plus the inquisitive *'elepaio* (Hawaiian monarch flycatcher). The trees soar, so bring your binoculars and park yourself on a forest bench. You'll also pass a lava tube inhabited by a unique species of big-eyed hunting spider and lava-tree crickets.

Flora-and-fauna trail guides ($2) are sold at Kilauea Visitor Center.

Mauna Loa Trail — Hiking

(off Mauna Loa Rd) The Mauna Loa Trail begins at the end of Mauna Loa Rd, off Hwy 11. All in, it's an extremely challenging (though nontechnical) 19.6-mile hike that ascends 7000ft and takes at least three days, although four is better for acclimatization and exploring the summit area. Rain, fog, snow and whiteouts can make the trail's *ahu* (cairns) hard to follow.

Two simple bunk-bed cabins are available on a first-come, first-served basis at Pu'u'ula'ula (Red Hill) and closer to the summit. Potable water might be available, but must be treated; inquire at the Backcountry Office (p216) when

The Best...
Hawai'i Volcanoes National Park Day Hikes

1 Kilauea Iki Trail (p216)

2 Kipuka Puaulu (Bird Park)

3 Pu'u Loa Petroglyphs (p213)

4 Glover & Kona Trails (p220)

5 Napau Crater Trail (p217)

picking up your free permit (required). Be prepared for severe winter conditions year-round, as well as wildfires and volcanic eruptions (very unlikely).

The trail begins rising through an ohia forest and above the tree line. After 7.5 miles you'll reach **Pu'u'ula'ula (Red Hill)** at 10,035ft, offering views of Mauna Kea to the north and Maui's Haleakalā to the northwest. The next day, the 11.6-mile hike to the summit cabin (13,250ft) crosses a stark, stirring landscape of multicolored cinder fields, spatter cones and gaping lava fissures. Two miles before arriving at the cabin, turn left at the **Moku'aweoweo Caldera** trail junction for the summit cabin. The other fork leads to the 2.6-mile **Summit Trail**, for tackling the summit (13,679ft) on day three.

To summit the mountain in just one day, there's the Mauna Loa Observatory Trail (p142) off Saddle Rd.

Mauna Iki Trail — Hiking

For solitude in a mesmerizing lava landscape, follow this trail into Ka'u Desert. Starting off Hwy 11 along what's commonly called the **Footprints Trail**, your initial commitment is low and variations allow for great route extensions. However, the entire trail section from the Jaggar Museum to Hwy 11 was closed at the

Hiking & Backpacking Safety Tips

In Hawai'i Volcanoes National Park, both lava desert and coastal trails can be extremely hot and dehydrating. Heat exhaustion is a real danger. Sunscreen, sunglasses and a wide-brimmed hat are essential. When weather conditions turn windy and wet, hypothermia is possible even if temperatures stay above freezing. Always pack extra insulating, waterproof layers too.

Only fit and experienced high-altitude hikers should attempt Mauna Loa. It's critically important to acclimatize first. For 'altitude sickness' (acute mountain sickness, or AMS), descent is the only remedy. The mountain's high elevation causes extreme environmental conditions, making hypothermia a hazard. Winter-rated, waterproof clothing and gear are essential year-round.

time of research due to ongoing volcanic activity.

Look for the Ka'u Desert Trailhead parking area between the Mile 37 and the Mile 38 markers on Hwy 11. Start early, as midday can be brutally hot and dry. Initially, the trail is very clear, level and partly paved, threading through sand-covered *pahoehoe* flows to reach a structure protecting ancient Hawaiian footprints preserved in hardened ash.

Beyond here the trail is marked by easy-to-follow cairns. As you gradually ascend, views expand, with Mauna Loa behind and the immense Ka'u Desert in front. Less than 2 miles from the trailhead, you'll crest **Mauna Iki** and stand likely alone in the middle of a vast lava field.

Pu'u o Lokuana Trail   Hiking

Near the entrance to the park's remote Kahuku Unit, this easy 2-mile loop follows historic ranch roads through pasture lands. After passing lava tree molds, the route wanders around spatter ramparts from Mauna Loa's 1868 eruption. Follow an abandoned airstrip back to the road and climb the cinder cone that gives this trail its name for spectacular views.

Palm Trail   Hiking

A lonely semiloop inside the park's detached Kahuku Unit, this 2.6-mile ramble traverses pasture land with panoramic views. Highlights include ranching-era

relics, remnants of native forest and striking volcanic features along a fissure from Mauna Loa's 1868 eruption. Start at the lower trailhead, an 0.8-mile walk downhill from the upper trailhead.

Glover & Kona Trails   Hiking

Deep inside the park's wilderness Kahuku Unit await the Glover and Kona Trails. The highlight of the 3-mile **Glover Trail** semiloop is standing at the edge of a huge forested pit crater, a deep bowl full of trees looking like the entrance to the underworld. Another semiloop hike nearby, the 3.8-mile **Kona Trail** passes through ranchlands and borders an 1887 lava flow.

The Lower Glover trailhead is on the right about 3 miles uphill beyond the Upper Palm trailhead (high-clearance 4WD recommended). The Glover Trail loops back to the upper trailhead near the end of Kahuku Rd, from where it's a 0.9-mile walk back downhill on the road to the lower trailhead. Alternatively, extend your hike by cutting west to the Upper Kona trailhead and ending at the Lower Kona trailhead, a short walk from the Lower Glover trailhead.

CYCLING

Volcano Bike Tours   Cycling

(🖊888-934-9199, 808-934-9199; http://bikevolcano.com; tours $105-129) If you're into pedal power, Volcano Bike Tours offers guided cycling tours of the park on hybrid comfort bikes. Tours, which take off rain or shine and last three to five hours, follow Crater Rim Dr and Chain of Craters Road.

🌋 Festivals & Events

Check the park website or ask at Kilauea Visitor Center about free (or low-cost) special events, including **After Dark in the Park** natural history lectures, **'Ike Hana No'eau** cultural demonstrations and craft workshops, **Na Leo Manu** evening concerts and **Stewardship at the Summit** daytime volunteer activities.

Volcano Art Center   Music, Dance
(📞808-967-7565; www.volcanoartcenter.org) Free Hawaiian craft demonstrations are given one Friday each month. The center also hosts arts, music and cultural events year-round, including popular concert, dance and theater performances here and at its Niaulani Campus in Volcano.

Hula Arts at Kilauea   Arts, Culture
(www.volcanoartcenter.org; 🚻) 🏖 A free series of outdoor *kahiko* (ancient) hula performances happens near the Volcano Art Center on one Saturday morning each month.

Kilauea Cultural Festival   Culture, Arts
(www.nps.gov/havo/planyourvisit/events.htm; 🚻) 🏖 For over 30 years, this annual cultural festival in July has celebrated traditional Hawaiian arts, crafts, music and hula. Free entrance to the park during the festival.

🛏 Sleeping & Eating

The park's two drive-up campgrounds are relatively uncrowded outside summer. Nights can be crisp and cool, however; you should bring rainproof gear. Campsites are first-come, first-served (seven-night limit).

Namakanipaio Cabins & Campground   Cabin, Campground $
(📞info 808-756-9625, reservations 866-536-7972; www.hawaiivolcanohouse.com; tent site $15, cabin q $80) The park's busiest campground is off Hwy 11, about 3 miles west of the visitor center. Tent camping is in a small, unshaded meadow with little privacy. Facilities include restrooms, drinking water, picnic tables and BBQ grills. Book ahead for simple, A-frame wooden cabins with shared communal bathrooms and hot showers; check-in is at Volcano House.

Pu'u Loa Petroglyphs (p213)

SCOTT DARSNEY/GETTY IMAGES ©

Kulanaokuaiki Campground
Campground $

(www.nps.gov/havo; Hilina Pali Rd) FREE About 5 miles down Hilina Pali Rd, this minimally developed campground has eight tent sites, pit toilets and picnic tables, but no water. Campfires are prohibited.

Volcano House
Lodge $$$

(☎866-536-7972, 808-756-9625; www.hawai ivolcanohouse.com; Crater Rim Dr; r $185-385; 🛜 🍴) With an unforgettable location perched on the rim of Kilauea Caldera, the newly reborn Volcano House has long enjoyed its unique status as the park's only hotel. Ecoconscious renovations have brought long overdue upgrades to the restaurant, bar, fireplace lobby areas, gift shops and 33 spacious, if quite plain and thin-walled, guest rooms. Reserve well in advance.

Both the refurbished **Rim Restaurant** (www.hawaiivolcanohouse.com/dining/; Crater Rim Dr, Volcano House; breakfast buffet adult/child $18/9, lunch prix-fixe menu adult/child $19/11, dinner mains $19-39; ⊙7am-10am, 11am-2pm & 5-9pm), serving better-than-average Hawaii Regional Cuisine (modern island fusion) crafted from local ingredients, and **Uncle George's Lounge** (Crater Rim Dr, Volcano House; ⊙11am-9pm), a pint-sized bar with live music and food, have enormous windows that afford absolutely staggering volcano views (as do certain guest rooms). If you can't spring for the room, just sip a beer. Slowly.

ℹ️ Information

The park (☎808-985-6000; www.nps.gov/havo) is open 24 hours a day, except when eruption activity and volcanic gases necessitate temporary closures. For current lava flows and trail, road and campground status, check the website or call ahead.

The park's main entrance sits at almost 4000ft, with varying elevation and climates inside park boundaries. Chilly rain, wind, fog and vog (volcanic fog) typify the fickle weather here, which can go from hot and dry to a soaking downpour in a flash. Near Kilauea Caldera, temperatures average 15°F (8.3°C) cooler than in Kona, so bring a rain jacket and pants, just in case.

Dangers & Annoyances

Although few people have died due to violently explosive eruptions at Kilauea (the last was in 1924), other volcanic activity hasn't been so beneficent. You'll hear about tourists who ventured onto unstable 'benches' of new land that collapsed, for example.

Heed rangers' and park warnings. Stick to marked trails and don't venture off on your own – getting lost on lava is easier than you think. Watch your step, especially on glass-sharp 'a'a; the bloody abrasions aren't pretty. Wear hiking shoes with good traction and ankle support, and carry at least 2L of water per person (more if you're hiking).

High concentrations of sulfur dioxide permeate the air, especially around Halema'uma'u Crater, sometimes closing Crater Rim Dr altogether. Anyone with respiratory or heart conditions, pregnant women and those with infants or

Bicycling, Hawai'i Volcanoes National Park
PETER FRENCH/GETTY IMAGES ©

young children should be especially careful. When driving through especially voggy areas, keep the car windows rolled up and the air-conditioning running on recycled air. Drivers should also stay alert to avoid hitting an endangered nene (Hawaiian goose).

Websites

Hawaii Department of Health (www.hiso2index. info) Air-quality updates and current sulfur dioxide levels islandwide. For park-specific information, visit www.hawaiiso2network.com.

Hawaiian Lava Daily (http://hawaiianlavadaily. blogspot.com) Stunning photos and videos of Kilauea volcano's red-hot lava action.

USGS Hawaiian Volcano Observatory (http:// hvo.wr.usgs.gov) Kilauea Volcano eruption updates, current earthquake and atmospheric conditions, and hypnotizing web cams.

🅐 Getting There & Around

The park is 30 miles (45 minutes) from Hilo and 95 miles (2¼ hours) from Kailua-Kona via Hwy 11. The turnoffs for Volcano village are a couple miles east of the main park entrance. Hwy 11 is prone to flooding, washouts and closures during rainstorms. Periods of drought may close Mauna Loa Rd and Hilina Pali Rd due to wildfire hazards.

The public **Hele-On Bus** (📞808-961-8744; www.heleonbus.org; adult 1-way fare $2) departs fives times daily (except Sunday) from Hilo, arriving at the park visitor center about 1¼ hours later, with one bus continuing to Ka'u.

In the park, cyclists are permitted only on paved Crater Rim Dr, Chain of Craters Road, Hilina Pali Rd and Mauna Loa Rd.

Volcano

Slow down: this is Volcano. Enveloped by cool mists and a mystical hush, this tiny town is hedged by ohia forest and emerald tree ferns. Many artists and writers find inspiration in this small, soulful place. Pull out your wet-weather gear, however: it can be cold and rainy.

Local

NAME: EN
OCCUPATI
INTERPRET
RESIDENCE:
VOLCANOES

1 WHAT'S
PARK?
BACK TO?
The Kilauea Iki .... can pick it up pretty much outside my door. I hike at least part of it every day. I've done it in a little over an hour – but that's with power walking across the crater. It usually takes two hours minimum.

2 IF YOU HAD ONLY THREE OR FOUR HOURS IN THE PARK, WHAT WOULD YOU DO?
There are shorter trails like Mauna Ulu where you'll see more of the park and fewer people. I'd also go to the Jaggar Museum and the overlook – this is the closest view of Halema'uma'u Crater since the road closures. The walk from the steam vents to the Sulphur Banks is cool too.

3 ASIDE FROM HIKING, WHAT DO YOU LIKE TO DO HERE?
My degree is in anthropology and so I often work at the Pu'u Loa petroglyphs, which are really interesting. Try and go in the early morning or late afternoon when the shadows are most dramatic. We're working to generate more interest in the ranger-led hikes there that take visitors beyond the boardwalk.

4 WOULD YOU RECOMMEND VOLUNTEERING IN THE PARK TO OTHERS?
Volunteering here has been one of the most exciting experiences of my life. Before I came here I knew nothing, but after two weeks of training I felt prepared – I knew about Hawaiian plants and animals, and traditional culture.

The Best...
Hawaiian Cultural Experiences

1 Hula Arts at Kilauea (p221)

2 Kilauea Cultural Festival (p221)

3 Pu'u Loa Petroglyphs (p213)

4 Volcano Art Center (p209)

5 Hale Ho'ola (p224)

⊙ Sights

Rainforest Gallery   Gallery

(📞808-967-8211; www.volcanoartcenter.
org; 19-4074 Old Volcano Rd; ⊙9am-4pm) A
satellite of the Volcano Art Center (p209)
in Hawai'i Volcanoes National Park, this
gallery showcases local artists working in
many different media; the adjacent shop
offers remarkably handcrafted works for
sale. Art workshops and performing arts
events are sometimes held here too.

Volcano Garden Arts   Gallery

(www.volcanogardenarts.com; 19-3834 Old Volcano Rd; ⊙10am-4pm Tue-Sun) Get inspired at
charming artist-owner Ira Ono's working
studio in the fern forest. You'll also discover an art gallery representing dozens of
island craftspeople and fine artists, rotat-
ing art installations, gardens and Café Ono
(p229). Check the online calendar for art
workshops and special events.

2400° Fahrenheit   Gallery

(📞808-985-8667; www.2400f.com; 11-3200 Old
Volcano Rd; ⊙10am-4pm Thu-Mon) Drop by to
watch Michael and Misato Mortara blow
hot glass into mind-boggling bowls and
vases. A tiny gallery displays their finished
masterpieces – don't ask how much. It's
off Hwy 11 at the village's eastern end.

Akatsuka Orchid Gardens   Gardens

(📞808-967-8234; www.akatsukaorchid.com;
11-3051 Volcano Rd; ⊙9am-5pm) Famous for
its unique hybrid orchids, this touristy
showroom bursts with 200,000 bloom-
ing plants, shippable all over the world.
Drop in for an olfactory awakening. It's
off Hwy 11 between the Mile 22 and the
Mile 23 markers.

Volcano Winery   Winery

(📞808-967-7772; http://volcanowinery.com;
35 Pi'i Mauna Dr; tasting flight $5; ⊙10am-
5:30pm) With grapes grown in Mauna Loa's
volcanic soil, this winery inland from Hwy
11 pours bottles with some *very* unusual
(read: supersweet) flavor infusions: tea,
macadamia nuts, honey and guava.

🏃 Activities

Hale Ho'ola   Spa

(📞808-756-2421; www.halehoola.net; 11-3913
7th St; ⊙by appointment only) After a hard
day hiking, relax at this day spa inside a
private home with *lomilomi* (traditional
Hawaiian massage) augmented by hula
music, hot lava-rock stones or steaming
bundles of medicinal herbs. Or maybe a
volcanic mud facial or tropical body treat-
ment – coconut-lemongrass sugar scrub,
anyone? No walk-ins.

Volcano Golf & Country Club   Golf

(📞808-967-7331; www.volcanogolfshop.com; 99-
1621 Pi'i Mauna Dr; greens fees $56, club rental
$20) With a lush setting beneath Mauna
Loa and Mauna Kea, this straightforward
18-hole, par-72 course is a local favorite.

👉 Tours

Niaulani Rain Forest Tour   Walking Tour

(📞808-967-8211/8222; www.volcanoartcenter.
org; 19-4074 Old Volcano Rd, Volcano Art Center's
Niaulani Campus; ⊙9:30am Mon & 11am Sat;
👫) 🌿 FREE Join an hour-long, half-mile
guided nature walk through Volcano's
rainforest. Guides cover the ecological
importance and protection of old-growth
koa and ohia forests, traditional Hawaiian
uses of plants, and the role of birds in the

forest. Call to ask about forest restoration volunteer workdays.

Tea Hawaii & Company
Walking Tour

(📞808-967-7637; http://teahawaii.com; 1hr tour $25) 🌿 Get an insider's look at Hawai'i's specialty tea cultivation on this sustainable farm and forest sanctuary, where you'll tour the tea gardens before tasting hand-picked black, white and oolong brews. Reservations required.

Hawaii Photo Retreat
Walking Tour

(📞985-7487; www.hawaiiphotoretreat.com; 1-/2-/3-day tour $345/690/1035; 🕐by reservation only) Seriously aspiring photographers experience unbridled natural beauty on customized tours with professional shooters Ken and Mary Goodrich, who live in Volcano. Meals and transportation not included.

⭐ Festivals & Events

Volcano Rain Forest Runs
Sports

(http://volcanorainforestruns.com) In August, this half-marathon, 10km run or 5km run/walk passes through Volcano village and nearby ranch lands.

Volcano Village Artists Hui
Arts

(www.volcanovillageartistshui.com) FREE Tour pottery, fiber work, wood scupture, ceramics, woodblock prints, glass blowing and photography studios over a three-day weekend in late November.

🛏 Sleeping

Tranquil B&Bs and vacation-rental cottages grow around Volcano like mushrooms. Most require a two-night minimum stay, or else add a one-night surcharge or cleaning fee. For more listings, check **Vacation Rentals by Owner** (VRBO; www.vrbo.com), **HomeAway** (www.homeaway.com), **Air B&B** (www.airbnb.com) and local rental agent **Volcano Gallery** (📞808-987-0920; www.volcanogallery.com).

Holo Holo In
Hostel $

(📞808-967-8025, 808-967-7950; www.volcano hostel.com; 19-4036 Kalani Honua Rd; dm $24, r with/without bath $75/60; @ 🛜) Don't be put off by this hostel's exterior. Inside, the two six-bed dorms and four private rooms are sizable and cabinlike. The hostel, which has a well-equipped kitchen, is locked from 11am to 4:30pm daily, when guests

Wine tasting, Volcano Winery

must vacate. No credit cards or shoes indoors. Book ahead. The Hele-On Bus stops two blocks away.

Enchanted Rainforest Cottages
Vacation Rental **$$**
(☎808-443-4930; http://erc-volcano.com; 19-4176 Kekoa Nui Blvd; d $85-140; 🛜) Private, well-designed and impeccably kept, these cottages are harbored in a fern forest landscaped with footpaths and koi ponds. Both the light-filled Apapane Guesthouse – with a skylit bathroom, gas stove and full kitchen – and the smaller Hikers' Retreat studio attached to the main house have private lanai, immersing you in a leafy world of bird calls.

Volcano Country Cottages
Vacation Rental **$$**
(☎808-967-7960; www.volcanocottages.com; 19-3990 Old Volcano Rd; d incl breakfast $105-155; 🛜) Nestled in the rainforest, each of these cozy, centrally located cottages has a full kitchen with modern appliances (except for the studio, which has no kitchen).

Privacy is assured, and there's outdoor space too, including a candel-lit hot tub hidden among ohia trees and ferns. Rates include self-catering breakfast fixin's.

Volcano Hideaways
Vacation Rental **$$**
(☎808-985-8959, 808-936-3382; www.vol canovillage.net; 6 Hale Ohia Rd; cottage $140-160; 🛜) On a quiet lane in Volcano town, all three of these historic cottages are spotless and expertly outfitted by energetic hosts, who provide everything from robes and a DVD library to freshly roasted coffee from the owner's farm. Depending upon which cottage you choose, perks include rain showers, whirlpool tubs, gas fireplaces, laundry rooms and kitchens.

Artist Cottage
Vacation Rental **$$**
(☎808-967-7261; www.volcanoartistcottage. com; 19-3834 Old Volcano Rd; cottage incl breakfast $129-149; 🛜) To all the artists and writers reading this: make your creative retreat here. On the grounds of Volcano Garden Arts (p224), this refurbished

Left: Making glass art, 2400° Fahrenheit (p224) **Below:** Market in Volcano
(LEFT & BELOW) LONELY PLANET/GETTY IMAGES ©

redwood cottage full of original art has a sky-lit bedroom and bathroom with a giant walk-in shower. There's a full kitchen and a private outdoor hot tub. It's small – best for one or an intimate pair.

Chalet Kilauea Collection
Lodge $$

(✆800-937-7786, 808-967-7786; www.volcano-hawaii.com; 19-4178 Wright Rd; r $110-200, with shared bath $60-75; 🛜) 🍃 Three properties target three very different kinds of travelers. **Volcano Hale** is for hikers, with shared baths, a kitchen and a wood-burning fireplace lounge. A bit motel-ish, **Lokahi Lodge** is functional for families and has a garden hot tub. Romantic **Chalet Kilauea** evinces a cozy country-cottage atmosphere, with unique rooms and a treehouse suite. Breakfast buffet served (surcharge applies).

Volcano Inn
Inn $$

(✆800-628-3876, 808-967-7773; www.volcanoinnhawaii.com; 19-3820 Old Volcano Rd; r $99-149; 🛜) 🍃 Apart from aesthetic blunders (glaring signage, photos tacked to walls), this inn offers outstanding value. The main building contains immaculate rooms (corner rooms enjoy fern-forest views) and a positive community atmosphere. Family cottages come with kitchenettes and hot tubs. Rates drop for multiple-night stays. Takeout breakfasts and lunches available a la carte.

Hale Ohia Log Cabin
Cabin $$

(✆808-735-9191; www.homeaway.com/vacation-rental/p206956; Hale Ohia Rd; q $150; 🛜) 🍃 Step back in time to 'Old Hawaii' with a couple of nights at this sweet log cabin built in 1906. Century-old *sugi* pine trees grow in the yard, and notice the Hilo's Boy School carving on the cabin wall (the first headmaster built this cabin). There's a king and double bed in an upstairs loft, a modern kitchen and a wood-burning stove.

Volcano Guest House
B&B $$

(📞866-886-5226, 808-967-7775; www.volcanoguesthouse.com; 11-3733 Ala Ohia St; r & ste $95-145, cottage $140-220, incl breakfast; 📶) 🌿 At this ecoconscious, family-run property, heart-warming rooms, suites and cottages with kitchettes sit among rainforest gardens, with a hot tub and laundry for guests' use. It's a value-conscious pick for families.

Kilauea Lodge
B&B $$$

(📞808-967-7366; www.kilauealodge.com; 19-3948 Old Volcano Rd; r & cottage incl breakfast $190-205, house $220-295; 📶) A tastefully renovated 1930s YMCA camp, this 12-room lodge is like a small hotel. Rooms embody upscale country chic with romantic accents like gas fireplaces, Hawaiian quilts and stained-glass windows. The honeymoon room has a wood-burning fireplace and private balcony, but even newlyweds have to share the garden hot tub. For more privacy, rent an off-property house.

Volcano Rainforest Retreat
Vacation Rental $$$

(📞800-550-8696, 808-985-8696; www.volcanoretreat.com; 11-3832 12th St; cottage incl breakfast $145-295; @ 📶) Serenity abounds at these four individually designed cedar cottages, each artfully positioned with huge windows to take advantage of fern-forest views. Each has an outdoor hot tub or Japanese-style soaking tub. For added romance, in-room massage can be arranged in advance. Breakfast supplies provided.

Lotus Garden Cottages
B&B $$$

(📞808-345-3062; www.volcanogetaway.com; r incl breakfast $185-210; 📶) Choose among three sweet cottage rooms with rainforest views. The Aloha Moon and Hula Moon suites have cedar-plank walls, gas fireplaces, rattan furnishings and tall ceilings, while the unique Lotus Suite is outfitted with Asian antiques. Directions will be provided upon booking; no walk-in guests accepted.

🍴 Eating

Despite all the tourist traffic, Volcano has only limited eating options, and most are overpriced.

Café Ohi'a
Cafe $

(19-4005 Haunani Rd; items $3-9; ⏰usually 7am-5pm; 🚶) This humble cafe's daily fresh soups in bread bowls, giant sandwiches and baked goods (try the chocolate-pecan tart) are all perfect for devouring on a hike or at picnic tables right outside. Breakfast croissants and cinnamon rolls kick off the day right.

Volcano Farmers Market
Market $

(http://thecoopercenter.org; 1000 Wright Rd, Cooper Community Center; ⏰7-10am Sun;

Volcano Rainforest Retreat
LONELY PLANET/GETTY IMAGES ©

(👥) 🍴 The whole community comes out to this weekly market to buy farm-fresh produce, takeout meals, flowers, local crafts and more.

Volcano Store　　　Self-Catering $
(19-4005 Haunani Rd, cnr Old Volcano Rd; 🕙5:30am-6:45pm) Basic groceries, camping supplies and a few grab-and-go items. Friendly staff and two gas pumps.

**Kilauea General
Store**　　　Self Catering $
(19-3972 Old Volcano Rd; 🕙7am-7pm) Slim pickings for groceries and premade snacks and meals. ATM and gas available.

Thai Thai Restaurant　　Thai $$
(📞808-967-7969; 19-4084 Old Volcano Rd; dinner mains $15-26; 🕙noon-9pm Thu-Tue, from 4pm Wed; 🍴) Locals claim it's the best Thai on the island. Classic *larb* (minced meat salads) and curries are all authentically flavored and well portioned, but don't let the servers intimidate you into ordering yours too mild. The dining-hall atmopshere can get crowded and stressed (dinner reservations recommended). Avoid tables in the kitschy gift shop or better yet, call ahead for takeout.

Lava Rock Café　　　Diner $$
(📞808-967-8526; www.volcanoslavarockcafe.com; 19-3972 Old Volcano Rd; mains breakfast & lunch $7-11, dinner $11-24; 🕙7:30am-9pm Tue-Sat, to 4pm Sun, to 5pm Mon; 📶👥) This roadhouse joint is nearly always jumping, although the stick-to-your-ribs menu of huge burgers, seafood and pasta won't wow you, whenever it finally arrives at your table. For breakfast (served until 3pm), try the sweet French toast with house-made *liliko'i* (passion fruit) butter. Local musicians often play on Wednesday and Saturday nights.

Café Ono　　　Cafe $$
(http://volcanogardenarts.com/cafeono.html; 19-3834 Old Volcano Rd, Volcano Garden Arts; mains $12-18; 🕙11am-3pm Tue-Sun; 🍴) 🍴 At an art gallery with a lovely garden for dining, you can lunch on organic vegetarian and vegan salads, sandwiches, soups, pastas and cakes. For what you get, it's slightly overpriced. Expect slowed-down service.

**Kilauea Lodge
Restaurant**　　European, Local $$$
(📞808-967-7366; www.kilaualodge.com; 19-3948 Old Volcano Rd; mains breakfast & lunch $8-14, dinner $24-39; 🕙7:30am-2pm & 5-9:30pm) Volcano's only high-end kitchen puts out a daily-changing dinner menu that oddly (and sometimes unsuccessfully) mixes European continental classics like duck *l'orange* and *hasenpfeffer* (braised rabbit) with fresh local seafood. Hardwood floors and a huge stone fireplace make the dinner atmosphere date-worthy. Service is outstanding; too bad the food is mostly mediocre. Make reservations.

ℹ Information

Most services are along Old Volcano Rd, including gas and a post office. Some businesses are cash only.

Volcano Visitor Center (19-4084 Old Volcano Rd; 🕙usually 7am-7pm) Unstaffed tourist information kiosk has brochures aplenty. Next door is a coin-op laundromat, ATM and hardware store selling some camping gear.

Ka'u

Ka'u is a wild and windy place where Big Island myths and ancient mysteries abound.

That makes sense, since Hawaiian history probably all began at Ka Lae (South Point), believed to be the site where wayfaring Polynesians first landed their canoes on Hawai'i. You could spend a day at Green Sands Beach or on the Road to the Sea and come away thinking there isn't much to this arid lava expanse other than a couple of hard-to-reach swaths of sand. But linger a while longer in the USA's southernmost region and you'll see why locals are so rabid to protect it. Ka'u residents have quashed coastal resorts, successfully lobbied for protected nature reserves and become pioneers of off-the-grid living. Even so, pristine areas like Pohue Bay have been slated for development. Are Ka'u's days as Hawai'i's outback numbered? Hedge your bets and head down here right now.

Ka Lae (South Point)
BRIGITTE MERZ/GETTY IMAGES ©

Ka'u Itineraries

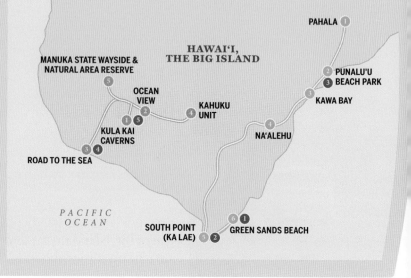

HAWAI'I, THE BIG ISLAND

PAHALA ①

MANUKA STATE WAYSIDE & NATURAL AREA RESERVE ⑤

② PUNALU'U
③ BEACH PARK

OCEAN VIEW

KAHUKU UNIT ④

KAWA BAY

① ⑤ ②

KULA KAI CAVERNS

④ NA'ALEHU

ROAD TO THE SEA ③ ④

PACIFIC OCEAN

SOUTH POINT (KA LAE) ⑤ ②

⑥ ① GREEN SANDS BEACH

One Day

① **Pahala** (p234) Start the day off right at Ka'u Coffee Mill, then drive through the sleepy old sugar-plantation town out to meditative Wood Valley Temple, a Tibetan Buddhist retreat center.

② **Punalu'u Beach Park** (p235) When the wind and the waves are calm enough, wade into the ocean for a morning snorkel with *honu* (green sea turtles) at this phenomenal black-sand beach.

③ **Kawa Bay** (p236) Surfers with the guts and the gear will want to check out the sets at nearby Kawa Bay (aka Windmills), a hidden locals' beach accessed via an unmarked dirt road off Hwy 11.

④ **Na'alehu** (p236) Have you worked up an appetite yet? Keep heading south to sweet little Na'alehu for a hearty plate lunch at Hana Hou Restaurant, a folksy, neighborhood diner with toothsome take-

out picnic fixings, or some soft Portuguese sweet bread from Punalu'u Bake Shop.

⑤ **South Point (Ka Lae)** (p239) Ramble down to the country's southernmost point, where locals go cliff jumping. Just wandering around you'll feel the mana (spiritual essence) of these ancient Hawaiian sites, including a fishing shrine.

⑥ **Green Sands Beach** (p239) This famous olive-green scoop of volcanic sand is about an hour's hike (or a faster 4WD 'taxi' ride) off South Point Rd. Don't count on swimming at this rough-and-tumble spot, known for high surf and howling winds.

➡ THIS LEG: 40 MILES

Two Days

1 **Kula Kai Caverns** (p242) Plunge into one of the Big Island's best underground caving adventures. Soda-straw stalactites, moonmilk puffballs, pillars and columns: a lava tube's exoticism comes alive on guided tours. Children as young as six years old are allowed inside. Reservations are required.

2 **Ocean View** (p241) Fuel up your car's gas tank and stock up on snacks, drinks and to-go deli lunches from supermarkets in southern Ka'u's only commercial center.

3 **Road to the Sea** (p243) Ready for real adventure? You'll need a high-clearance 4WD vehicle to make it to the secluded beaches here, but it'll be worth it when you finally strip off your clothes in a mad dash toward the water. Set off early, say before noon.

4 **Kahuku Unit** (p238) high-clearance 4WD vehicle comes in handy, but isn't absolutely required for exploring this newest addition to Hawai'i Volcanoes National Park. Set on historic ranch lands in the shadow of Mauna Loa's massive lava flows, here hiking trails wind across green pastures, through lush rain forest and around colorful cinder cones and lava tree molds. Keep in mind this wilderness area may only be open on weekends.

5 **Manuka State Wayside & Natural Area Reserve** (p242) If you don't have a 4WD vehicle, or you're already itching to drive back around to the Kona Coast, make a quick pit stop at this little roadside oasis. A family-friendly nature hike strolls through shady native forest where unique endemic plants thrive.

 THIS LEG: 52 MILES

Ka'u Highlights

1 **Best Beach: Green Sands Beach** (p239) Unusual olive sands put this on the Big Island bucket list.

2 **Best View: Ka Lae (South Point)** (p240) Watch crashing surf and dream of paddling to Tahiti.

3 **Best Wildlife Watching: Punalu'u Beach Park** (p235) Where *honu* (green sea turtles) bask in the sun.

4 **Best Activity: Road to the Sea** (p243) Get your kicks on a rugged 4WD adventure.

5 **Best Rainy Day Activity: Kula Kai Caverns** (p242) Take an underground tour of 'living museums.'

Green Sands Beach, South Point (p239)
ALVIS UPITIS/GETTY IMAGES ©

Discover Ka'u

Pahala

POP 1356

A former sugar plantation town now making a living growing coffee and macadamia nuts, Pahala dozes just inland from Hwy 11, south of the Mile 51 marker. Its quiet streets are lined with unrestored early-20th-century plantation houses – just squint to imagine the past. The unhurried town center, with a gas station, bank and post office, is at the corner of Kamani and Pikake Sts.

Wood Valley Temple
PHOTO RESOURCE HAWAII/ALAMY ©

◉ Sights

Ka'u Coffee Mill   Farm

(☎808-928-0550; www.kaucoffeemill.com; 96-2694 Wood Valley Rd; ⊙8:30am-4:30pm) ◢ This down-to-earth coffee farm roasts its own award-winning beans. Taste a variety of brews, which some connoisseurs rate as highly as Kona coffee, at the gift shop stocked with bags of beans to take home.

From Hwy 11, follow Kamani St inland, turn right onto Pikake St, then continue on Wood Valley Rd for about 1.5 miles.

Wood Valley Temple   Temple

(Nechung Dorje Drayang Ling; ☎808-928-8539; www.nechung.org; Wood Valley Rd; requested donation $5; ⊙usually 10am-5pm) Just outside Pahala, this century-old, colorful Tibetan Buddhist temple is wonderfully juxtaposed against a lush 25-acre retreat center where peacocks roam free. The temple's official name, which translates to 'Immutable Island of Melodious Sound,' perfectly captures the valley's wind and birdsong.

Visitors are welcome to join daily chanting and meditation sessions (8am and 6pm), or to just visit the temple and gift shop. A meditative **guesthouse** (s $65-75, d $85; ☎) lets you stay for a few nights.

Turn off Hwy 11 onto Kamani St, then turn right into Pikake St, which becomes Wood Valley Rd; the retreat is about 5 miles inland. It's a meandering drive up valley with farms, forest and one-lane bridges crossing babbling creeks.

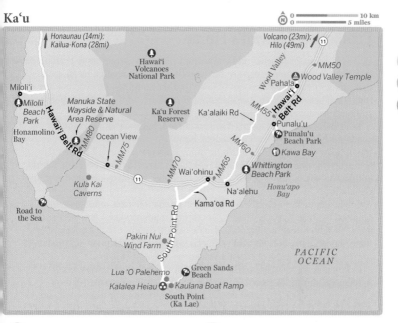

Festivals & Events

Ka'u Coffee Festival — Coffee

(www.kaucoffeefest.com) In mid-May, Pahala wakes up with music, coffee, hula, coffee-farm and mill tours, farm-to-fork food, more coffee and even stargazing. No decaf allowed.

Getting There & Away

Hele-On Bus (☎808-961-8744; www.heleonbus. org; adult 1-way fare $2) One or two daily buses run between Pahala, Na'alehu and Ocean View, continuing up the Kona Coast to South Kohala's resorts. There's also one bus daily except Sunday between Hilo and Ka'u, stopping in Volcano.

Punalu'u

Once a major Hawaiian settlement during ancient times, today Punalu'u harbors a popular black-sand beach, known for sea-turtle spotting, and the Sea Mountain condo development, the only one of its kind on this coast – and perhaps the last.

Beaches

Punalu'u Beach Park — Beach

On a pretty little bay is a black-sand beach where green sea turtles bask and feed. It's also one of the few beaches where rare hawksbill turtles lay their eggs, so be careful not to disturb their sandy nests. Most days the rough, cold waters are not good for swimming as there are forceful undertows – a lifeguard is posted – but when calm, snorkeling is a treat. The park has picnic pavilions, restrooms, outdoor showers, drinking water and a concession stand.

The northern part of the beach is backed by a duck pond and the remains of an old resort, rotting away in testimony to local economics and the anti-development movement. The ruins of the Pahala Sugar Company's old warehouse and pier lie slightly north. Follow a trail up the hill past the cement pier to find the ruins of **Kane'ele'ele Heiau**, an ancient temple where human sacrifices took place, in a vast field. The trail continues all the way to Kawa Bay via secluded coves, now protected as public land.

Protecting Hawaii's Honu

Hawai'i's gorgeous beaches and warm tropical waters attract more than tourists, they also attract *honu* (green sea turtles). Traditionally revered by Hawaiians, these magnificent creatures can be seen feeding, sunning and even nesting on Big Island beaches. Often considered an *'aumakua* (family deity or guardian spirit), *honu* appear in ancient petroglyphs too.

Sea turtles were once a prized source of food, but their capture and consumption was governed by ancient Hawai'i's strict religious laws. In modern times, governance has once again become necessary to prevent further damage to the beaches turtles depend on to reproduce. Development, tourism, hunting and harvesting of their shells have all contributed to a dangerously dwindling population.

Green sea turtles now abound in Hawai'i (look for them munching on seaweed in shallow, rocky areas). Less common are hawksbill sea turtles, called *honu 'ea*. The rarest turtles in the Pacific Ocean, they're easily recognized by their plated shells, beaked noses and clawed flippers. Spot them at Punalu'u or in remote coastal areas of Hawai'i Volcanoes National Park.

Before you get too close to the turtles, consider that only a very small percentage survive to return to reproduce. All Hawaiian sea turtles are endangered species protected by law and you must not approach them any closer than 50yd in the water and 20ft on land (this means kids, too!) – don't imitate tourists who crowd closely around, hassling these gentle reptiles.

To learn more about sea turtles and efforts to preserve critical habitat in Hawaii, visit **Save Punalu'u** (www.savepunaluu.org) and Maui-based **World Turtle Trust** (www.world-turtle-trust.org) online.

Come in the early morning, since the beach park quickly fills with picnickers and tour buses. Camping is allowed with an advance county permit. There are two signed turnoffs for Punalu'u between the Mile 56 and Mile 57 on Hwy 11.

Kawa Bay Beach
Surf's up at Kawa Bay, reached via a dirt road (stay straight, rather than taking any lefts) between the Mile 58 and Mile 59 markers off Hwy 11. Nicknamed Windmills, this is Ka'u's best surf break – paddle out from the beach's northernmost end. Locals also come here to picnic and fish; always respect their space.

Na'alehu

POP 866

Tiny Na'alehu is the southernmost town in the USA – a title it milks for all it's worth.

Alongside giant banyan trees and pastel-colored plantation houses, Na'alehu has a lost-in-time rural feel that's underscored by the beautiful, but boarded-up Na'alehu Theatre, a 1940s movie house along the main road. Na'alehu is northern Ka'u's commercial center, with a supermarket, hardware store, laundromat, library, playground, post office, gas station and ATM. One or two daily Hele-On Bus (p235) services run between Pahala, Na'alehu and Ocean View.

Beaches

Whittington Beach Park Beach
North of Na'alehu, this small beach park has tidepools to explore, a fishpond frequented by birds, and the ruins of an old pier. Despite its name, there's no beach and the ocean is usually too rough for swimming, but hawksbill sea turtles

can often be spotted. Facilities include restrooms, outdoor showers and picnic pavilions (no drinking water). Camping on the grass requires an advance county permit, but proximity to the highway means little privacy.

The turnoff to the park is between the Mile 60 and Mile 61 markers on Hwy 11.

🛏 Sleeping & Eating

Ka'u Coffee House & Guesthouse   Hostel $
(📞808-747-4142, 808-896-9272; 95-5587 Hwy 11; s/d $35/50; ⏰cafe 11am-6pm Mon-Fri; @🛜) On Hwy 11, this family-operated hostel does practically everything right. An upstairs hostel offers clean and tidy rooms and a relaxing community space, while the downstairs cafe serves a cooked breakfast (from $5 for guests), Ka'u coffee and veggie burgers and sandwiches at lunch. The Hele-On Bus stops out front.

Punalu'u Bake Shop   Bakery $
(📞808-929-7343; www.bakeshophawaii.com; 95-5642 Hwy 11; items $3-8; ⏰9am-5pm) Famous island-wide, this landmark bakery packs in locals and busloads of tourists, who come for sandwiches and a variety of flavored, doughy Portuguese sweet bread (purple taro!). Free samples aid in decision-making. Bonus: clean restrooms and a picnic area outside.

Ka'u Farmers Market   Market $
(⏰7am-noon Wed & Sat) A small but quality farmers market sets up in front of Ace Hardware.

Island Market   Supermarket $
(95-5657 Hwy 11, Na'alehu Shopping Center; ⏰8am-7pm Mon-Sat, 9am-6pm Sun) This well-stocked grocery store is the best between Hilo and Captain Cook.

Hana Hou Restaurant   Diner $$
(📞808-929-9717; naaleherestaurant.com; 95-1148 Na'alehu Spur Rd; mains $8-16; ⏰8am-7pm Sun-Thu, to 8pm Fri & Sat; 🛜🚺) Here's your chance to eat 'the southernmost plate lunch in the USA' at a 1940s plantation-era family restaurant. Portions may not be as generous as the prices suggest, though. Stuffed sandwiches and wraps are great for picnicking, but the real draw is home-baked pies, like banana cream and macadamia nut. There's usually live music on Friday and Saturday nights.

Hana Hou Restaurant

Island Insights

For killer coastal views, pull off at the **scenic lookout** above Honu'apo Bay just northeast of Na'alehu. From the lookout you can see the cement pilings of the old Whittington Pier, which was used for shipping sugar and hemp until the 1930s. At the turn of the 21st century, the pier had a more scientific purpose for a few years, when a fiber-optic cable measuring the rising Lo'ihi Seamount, Hawai'i's active underwater volcano, was temporarily attached to the pier's pylons.

Shaka Restaurant   American $$
(☏808-929-7404; 95-5673 Hwy 11; mains breakfast & lunch $8-14, dinner $12-22; ☺7am-9pm)
This sports bar dishes up sloppy plates of grilled burgers, pizza and pub grub (the deep fryer works overtime). Cleanliness is questionable. Live music on most Fridays.

Wai'ohinu & Around

POP 230

Blink and you'll miss sleepy little Wai'ohinu ('sparkling water') between the Mile 65 and Mile 66 markers on Hwy 11. The village's claim to fame is its **Mark Twain monkeypod tree**, planted by the peripatetic author in 1866. The original tree fell during a hurricane in 1957, but hardy shoots sprang up and it's once again full-grown. There's a gas station and general store along the road through town.

◎ Sights & Activities

Four miles west of Wai'ohinu, between the Mile 70 and Mile 71 markers on Hwy 11, lies the entrance to Hawai'i Volcanoes National Park's **Kahuku Unit** (admission free), which offers hikers the chance to explore historic ranch lands and lava flows (for more details, see p215). At the time of research, the Kahuku Unit was only open to the public between 9am and 3pm on Saturdays and Sundays. Check the park **website** (www.nps.gov/havo) for current opening hours and also schedules of ranger-guided hikes (reservations not usually required).

🛏 Sleeping

South Point Banyan Tree House   Vacation Rental $$
(☏808-929-8515, 808-217-2504; www.south pointbth.com; cnr Pinao St & Hwy 11; d $100; 🛜) Fabulous studio apartment digs, equipped with a full kitchen and a hot-tub deck, seem to float in the branches of a giant banyan tree. Flooded with light, the octagonal two-story house is a private escape in a jungle of mango, lychee and 'ulu (breadfruit) trees.

Hobbit House   B&B $$
(☏808-929-9755; www.hi-hobbit.com; d incl breakfast & taxes $170-225) ✿ Powered by the sun and wind, this unique property is a fantastical hideaway. Perched atop a bluff with sweeping ocean views, the honeymoon suite with a full kitchen is a whimsically romantic escape. It's tucked half a mile up, up and up from Hwy 11.

Margo's Corner   Campground, Cottage $$
(☏808-929-9614; www.margoscorner.com; Wakea St, off Kama'oa Rd; tent sites per person $30, cottages $90-130, all incl breakfast; @🛜) Flying the rainbow flag high, this LGBT-friendly guesthouse is an artistic, alternative-minded stopover. Of the two cottages, the Adobe Suite is superior, with its wall of windows, double beds in Star Trek–like berths and private sauna. The garden setting is peaceful and even campers are offered breakfast and hot showers. No smoking on the property.

South Point (Ka Lae)

Ka Lae (literally 'the point') is the southernmost spot in the USA, but more importantly it's also a National Historic Landmark District where most historians believe that Polynesian voyagers first landed in Hawai'i. Turbulent and windy, this sacred place must have looked positively heavenly to ancient seafarers who traveled thousands of miles across open ocean using only waves, winds, sun, moon and stars to navigate.

Ka Lae was one of the earliest Hawaiian settlements, with rich fishing grounds offshore and freshwater available from nearby Punalu'u. These waters still sustain life and local families perch on the cliffs and fish the weekend away. The turnoff for narrow, mostly one-lane South Point Rd is between the Mile 69 and Mile 70 markers on Hwy 11. About 10 miles later, South Point Rd forks: veer right for Ka Lae or left for Green Sands Beach.

For a picturesque alternative, take Kama'oa Rd from Wai'ohinu to South Point Rd, a rolling country drive that deposits you just north of the **Pakini Nui Wind Farm**, where rows of high-tech windmills stand in cow pastures. Heading a few miles further downhill toward the sea, you'll pass the abandoned remains of a US government space-tracking facility that operated here during the mid-1960s.

Beaches

Green Sands Beach   Beach

Also known as Papakolea Beach, this legendary green-sand beach on Mahana Bay isn't really *that* green, but it is a secluded, sandy strand. Its rare color comes from the semiprecious olivine

The Best...

Off-the-Beaten-Track Spots in Ka'u

1 Road to the Sea (p243)

2 Ka Lae (South Point; p240)

3 Kula Kai Caverns (p242)

4 Kahuku Unit, Hawai'i Volcanoes National Park

5 Wood Valley Temple (p234)

KA'U SOUTH POINT (KA LAE)

crystals (a type of volcanic basalt) eroded from a cinder cone above, worn smooth by the relentless surf and then mixed with black sand until it sparkles in the sun. Swimming isn't advisable here (even

Ka Lae cape
MIXA CO. LTD./GETTY IMAGES ©

on calm days) due to strong waves, with frequent high surf and howling winds.

To get here take South Point Rd, turning left after 10 miles. Follow this road until it dead ends at a grassy parking area (don't leave any valuables in your car). At this point you can hike – it's a dusty, hot and long 2.5-mile trek each way, so bring plenty of water – or pay around $10 to $15 for a ride in one of the local 4WD 'taxis' waiting to transport tourists.

If you choose to hike, start by walking toward the water, past the Kaulana boat ramp, and follow the rutted dirt road left through the metal gate. Then just keep going, enjoying the gorgeous undulating coastline and aiming for the uplifted, striated cliff-face in the distance.

Whether you arrive on foot or by 4WD, you'll have to scramble down the cliff to the beach, which has becoming a major tourist attraction despite the difficulty of reaching it. Go early, late or when it's overcast to beat the crowds.

◎ Sights

Ka Lae
Historic Site

(South Point Rd) Hawai'i's southernmost tip, Ka Lae feels like the utter end of the earth. Even with rushing wind filling your ears, an odd stillness steals over this sacred spot pulsing with potent mana (spiritual essence). But don't expect to be alone on the path, which is well-worn by visitors, heading south from the dirt parking area toward the light beacon. Standing near the actual point, you can imagine what it must have been like for ancient Polynesians to land here, fighting violent surf after months at sea.

The confluence of ocean currents just offshore makes this one of Hawai'i's most bountiful fishing grounds. Wooden platforms built onto the cliffs have hoists and ladders for the small boats anchored below, while local fishers brace themselves on lava-rock ledges partway down.

Daredevil locals like to cliff-jump into the surging waters here, but you might want to just peek over the edge, as you're many miles from help and hospitals. Behind the platforms, inside a large *puka* (hole), spy on the ocean raging upward and receding with the waves.

There are no facilities here except portable toilets.

Kalalea Heiau
Temple

Near the dirt parking area for Ka Lae is this ancient temple and fishing shrine where Hawaiians left offerings in hopes of currying favor for a bountiful catch. A standing rock below the heiau is pocked with canoe mooring holes. Enterprising ancient Hawaiians would tether their canoes here with ropes, then let strong currents pull them out into deeper waters to fish.

Kalalea Heiau
THINKSTOCK/GETTY IMAGES ©

Lua 'O Palehemo Historic Site

A short distance inland from the Kalalea Heiau is Lua 'O Palehemo, marked with a tree bent nearly horizontal by battering winds. From this brackish watering hole (*lua* means hole or pit in Hawaiian), views take in the massive flanks of Mauna Loa and the entire coast from South Kona to Puna.

Sleeping

Kalaekilohana B&B $$$

(808-939-8052; www.kau-hawaii.com; 94-2152 South Point Rd; d incl breakfast $269;) It's a rare place that's so welcoming you feel at once like a special guest and part of the family. But the *ho'okipa* (hospitality) here does just that. Upstairs, four airy rooms feature gleaming hardwood floors, luxurious beds, rainfall showers and private lanai. Downstairs, the gracious library and music room, a wide porch and complimentary drinks and snacks invite lingering. Directions will be given upon booking.

Ocean View & Around

Straggling alongside Hwy 11, Ocean View is divvied up between lusher Hawaiian Ocean View Estates (HOVE) *mauka* (inland) and arid Hawaiian Ranchos *makai* (seaward). Together they make up the largest subdivision in the USA. A persistent lack of jobs, blankets of vog and a reputation for illegal drugs keeps residential lots from being fully settled. This is Hawai'i's frontier, where people come to find themselves or get lost, scratching a pioneering existence out of desolate black lava.

Across Hwy 11 from each other near the Mile 76 marker, two shopping centers – Pohue Plaza and Ocean View Town Center – make up southern Ka'u's commercial center, with gas stations, supermarkets, fast food, ATMs and a laundromat. One or two daily Hele-On Bus (p235) services run between Pahala, Na'alehu and Ocean View.

Local Knowledge

NAME: JOHN REPLOGLE

OCCUPATION: CONSERVATION PRACTITIONER, NATURE CONSERVANCY

RESIDENCE: OCEAN VIEW

1 WHY IS KA'U SUCH A SPECIAL PLACE?

Geographically, it's the largest region in Hawai'i. It also has Ka'u Forest Reserve, the largest intact native forest in the state. Most importantly, it's home to Ka Lae (p240) and Kapalaoa – Hawaii's oldest archaeological site (currently closed to the public). Ka'u was once the seat of the Hawaiian Kingdom.

2 WHAT ARE SOME OF YOUR FAVORITE SPOTS IN KA'U?

I like to go to South Point to fish and hang out. The road down is an excellent cycling route. Lua 'O Palehemo (p241) is a place I like to share with people, especially in the early morning when you can see all the way down the coast. I take my grandchildren there a lot.

3 HOW ABOUT GREEN SANDS BEACH?

This is a beautiful, windblown piece of coastline (p239) worth visiting. But it's also fragile – do you see how many people drive there? It's eating away the land and accelerating erosion – it's better to hike anyway to get the full experience.

4 VISITING PUNALU'U AND SEEING THE TURTLES IS A PERENNIAL FAVORITE. DO YOU HAVE ANY TIPS FOR VISITORS?

There's the black-sand beach and the *honu* (green sea turtles), but the Kane'ele'ele Heiau is also there. Punalu'u (p235) was a prominent place in ancient Hawai'i. As for visitors, they should be very careful when swimming – there are major undertows at Punalu'u. While encountering *honu* is a unique experience, the turtles should never be hassled. Stand back and enjoy.

◎ Sights & Activities

Kula Kai Caverns — Caving

(☎ 808-929-9725; www.kulakaicaverns.com; 92-8864 Lauhala Dr; tours adult/child 6-12yr from $20/10) Top-notch underground tours are led by local experts who emphasize respectful stewardship of these 'living museums.' The geologically astounding caves belong to the world's longest lava tube system, reaching back into the bowels of Mauna Loa volcano. On the basic 30-minute tour, you'll enter a short, lighted cave section, where guides present Hawai'i's cultural and ecological history. Reservations are required.

There's also a longer 'crawling' tour ($60) and a two-hour extended twilight tour ($95). Group sizes are kept small, usually with a two- or four-person minimum. Children (minimum age six or eight years) are allowed on most tours.

Manuka State Wayside & Natural Area Reserve — Park

(www.hawaiistateparks.org; Hwy 11) **FREE** This 13-acre reserve offers a very well-done nature trail. Proceeding through native forest on a lava rock path, and assisted by an interpretive trail guide, you'll identify 30 species of plants, and see a pit crater and lava flows. The entrance to the park and picnic area is off Hwy 11, just north of the Mile 81 marker.

Uninviting camping in an open shelter with concrete floors is allowed with an advance state park permit, but it's isolated, not always safe and there's no drinking water.

🛏 Sleeping

Lova Lava Land — Vacation Rental $

(www.lovalavaland.com; Hawaiian Ranchos; yurt/VW bus $60/40; 🛜) 🍃 This off-the-grid 'ecoresort' epitomizes Ocean View ingenuity. Guests sleep in VW buses in the middle of a lava flow and share a central compound with a fully equipped kitchen, herb garden, wi-fi and lava-rock shower. There's also a single yurt with a double bed, hardwood floors and moon roof. It's DIY living, with no on-site staff. A cleaning fee ($30 to $45) may be refundable. Directions will be given upon booking.

Leilani Bed & Breakfast — B&B $$

(☎ 808-929-7101; www.leilanibedandbreakfast.com; 92-8822 Leilani Pkwy, Hawaiian Ocean View Estates; r incl breakfast $99-124; 🛜) On a tropical lot in the Hawaiian Ocean View Estates subdivision, the three plain-jane guest rooms here are a bit tight, but the well-tended grounds, complete with a covered BBQ area, and lanai (which doubles as an art gallery) compensate.

🍴 Eating

Ocean View Pizzaria — Pizza $

(☎ 808-929-9677; Hwy 11, Ocean View Town Center; pizza slice/pie from $3/13, sandwiches $7-12; ⏰ 11am-7pm, to

Lei of Lehua flowers
GREG ELMS/GETTY IMAGES ©

Detour:
Road to the Sea

This high-clearance 4WD road crosses enough loose 'a'a (rough, jagged lava) to shake your fillings loose. Once only for adventurers, these remote black-and green-sand beaches with looming cliffs are not the human-free pockets they used to be. You may find, after all the trouble of getting there, that the sea is too rough to swim and the beach too windy to enjoy. Even so, it's worth the trip for the scenery alone.

To find the **Road to the Sea**, turn *makai* (seaward) off Hwy 11 at the row of mailboxes between the Mile 79 and Mile 80 markers (look for the 'Taki Mana/ Ka Ulu Malu Shady Grove Farm' sign). From there you'll drive 6 miles over rudimentary, seemingly never-ending lava. To reach the first and smaller of the two beaches at the road's end takes 45 minutes or so, depending on how rough you like your ride.

To reach the second beach, drive a half-mile back inland. Skip the first left fork (it's a dead end) and take the second left fork instead. Look for arrows painted on lava rock. The road jogs inland before heading toward the shore again, and the route isn't always readily apparent. There are many places you can lose traction or get lost. Almost a mile from the fork, you'll reach a red *pu'u* (hill). Park there and walk down to the ocean. If you decide to hike the whole distance to the second beach from the split in the road, it's about 1.5 miles each way. Bring as much water as you can carry, because it's a mercilessly hot and shadeless walk.

8pm Fri & Sat) The submarine sandwiches are filling, the pizza just OK. It's a place to eat, not linger. Better for takeout.

Malama Market　Supermarket $
(92-8701 Hwy 11, Pohue Plaza; ⏰6:30am-8pm) Standard groceries, hot *hulihuli* (rotisserie-cooked) chicken, teriyaki-glazed Spam *musubi* (rice ball) and a lot more.

Ocean View Market　Supermarket $
(Hwy 11, Ocean View Town Center) By the post office and an auto-parts store, this community grocery store sells hot food and sandwiches (get here early before they run out).

Hawaiʻi,
the Big Island

In Focus

Hula at sunset
ALVIS UPITIS/GETTY IMAGES ©

The Big Island Today

Drying coffee beans, Honaunau (p74), South Kona

The trick now is to expand sustainable agriculture...and to convince everyone to 'eat local'.

ethnicity
(% of population)

32 — Caucasian
30 — Hawaiian/ part-Hawaiian
19 — Mixed
12 — Japanese
6 — Filipino
1 — Chinese

if the Big Island were 100 people

32 would be 0-24 years old
27 would be 25-44 years old
27 would be 45-64 years old
14 would be 65+ years old

population per sq mile

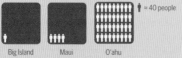

♦ = 40 people

Big Island   Maui   O'ahu

Economic Recovery

Since the 1960s, Hawai'i's economy has rested primarily on tourism, along with agriculture and real estate. But the 2008 national recession squeezed the influx of visitors (just over 1.3 million people in 2013, down 25% from its peak), and hotel occupancy has barely broken 60% since then, although room rates continue to rise. Japan Airlines inflicted another blow by ending its route to Kona International Airport (which Governor Neil Ambercrombie wants to expand) in 2010, and the loss of nonstop flights between San Francisco and Hilo also hurt.

During the recession, the island's overall unemployment rate hovered around 10% and home prices dropped, especially in Puna. The downturn affected the whole state, evidenced by furloughs for government workers (the island's biggest employment sector) and even public schoolchildren. But by early 2014, unemployment had shrunk below the national average of 7%, and real estate prices were rising. Visitors still face some economic fallout, as some state parks have started charging entry fees and have raised camping rates for nonresidents.

ANN CECIL/GETTY IMAGES ©

Sustainable Agriculture

Sugar plantations, which long dominated the state's agricultural landscape, are old news: the last commercial harvest on the Big Island was in 1995. Since then Hawai'i's agriculture has somewhat successfully diversified into signature coffee, papayas, macadamia nuts and orchids – as well as aquaculture and boutique crops from mushrooms, to vanilla to tea. The Big Island is still home to the state's largest cattle operation, Parker Ranch, and the state's last two remaining dairy cattle farms.

The trick now is to expand sustainable agriculture: to employ more island residents, to produce more food and to convince everyone to 'eat local.' The Hawaiian Islands import 85% to 90% of the food eaten here, and it will take many more farms to achieve food security (or, as some activists call it, 'food sovereignty') through greater self-sufficiency.

In 2013, after a long and bitter political fight, Hawai'i County Bill 113 was signed into law by Mayor Billy Kenoi. The law stops biotech companies from operating on the Big Island and prohibits farmers from growing any new GMO (genetically modified organism) crops, with an exemption granted for papayas. Farmers who opposed the bill argue GMOs are necessary to prevent crop-killing viruses that would decimate the industry.

The coffee berry borer (a small beetle native to Africa) was first discovered in Kona in 2010. With almost $30 million in annual revenue at stake, farmers feared economic disaster. Fortunately, a natural fungus that can be sprayed on coffee plants attacks the beetle, somewhat controlling the pest, which can never be eradicated. Quarantines will hopefully prevent the beetle from spreading to other coffee-growing islands.

Nature's Power

On the Big Island, nature is always in the news. Over the past few years, parts of the island have received the unwanted distinction of having the nation's worst drought, notably South Kohala and Ka'u. Meanwhile on the rainy windward side of the island, the longest lava flow in history continues, with spectacular displays inside Hawai'i Volcanoes National Park. New energy development projects are seeking to harness alternative energy sources – including wind, solar, sea and biomass – to sustainably power island homes, transportation and agriculture.

History

Ki'i, Pu'uhonua O Hōnaunau National Historical Park (p77)

LONELY PLANET/GETTY IMA

Hawaii's discovery is one of humanity's great epic tales, starting with ancient Polynesians who first found their way to these tiny islands. Almost a millennium passed before Western explorers, whalers and missionaries arrived. In the tumultuous 19th century, a global melting pot of immigrants came to work on Hawaii's plantations before the kingdom founded by Kamehameha the Great was overthrown, making way for US annexation.

Ancient Hawai'i

Although the discovery of Hawaii may have been accidental, subsequent migrations were not. Polynesians were highly skilled seafarers, navigating over thousands of miles of open ocean in doubled-hulled canoes without maps, and with only the sun, stars, wind and waves to guide them. Beginning around AD 300, they imported to these remote islands

AD 300–600

The first wave of Polynesians voyages thousands of miles by canoe to the Hawaiian Islands.

their religious beliefs, social structures and over two dozen food plants and domestic animals.

When, for unknown reasons, these trans-Pacific canoe voyages stopped around AD 1300, ancient Hawaiian culture evolved in isolation, but retained a family resemblance to cultures throughout Polynesia. Hawaiian society was highly stratified, ruled by a chiefly class called *ali'i* whose power derived from their ancestry: they were believed to be descended from the gods. Ranking just below *ali'i*, kahuna (experts or masters) included priests, healers and skilled craftspeople like canoe makers.

In ancient Hawai'i, clan loyalty trumped individuality, elaborate traditions of gifting and feasting conferred prestige, and a pantheon of shape-shifting gods animated the natural world. Strict religious laws, known as the kapu (taboo) system, governed what people ate, whom they married and dined with, and when they fished or harvested crops – essentially all human behavior. The penalty for breaking kapu was death.

The largest class was the *maka'ainana* (commoners), who could live wherever they pleased, but who were obligated to support the *ali'i* through taxes paid in kind with food, goods and physical labor. The lowest *kaua* (outcast or untouchable) class was shunned and did not mix with the other classes, except as slaves or human sacrificial victims (the latter were exclusively male).

The Best... Ancient Hawaiian Sites

1 Pu'uhonua O Hōnaunau National Historical Park (p77)

2 Puako Petroglyph Preserve (p104)

3 Pu'ukohola Heiau National Historic Site (p110)

4 Halema'uma'u Crater (p211)

5 South Point (Ka Lae; p239)

6 Keanakako'i & Lake Wai'au, Mauna Kea (p135)

First Western Contact: Captain Cook

In 1778, everything changed. On January 18, British naval explorer Captain James Cook, who was in search of the fabled Northwest Passage, accidentally sailed into the main Hawaiian Island chain. Ending 500 years of cultural isolation, his arrival irrevocably altered the course of Hawaiian history. Cook dropped anchor offshore to barter for fresh water and food, as he had elsewhere in the Pacific.

While Cook was already familiar with Polynesian culture from his previous voyages, Hawaiians knew nothing yet of Europeans, nor of the metal, guns and diseases

1778
Captain James Cook becomes the first Western explorer to 'discover' the Hawaiian Islands.

1810
Kamehameha I unites the major Hawaiian Islands into one sovereign kingdom.

1820
First American missionaries arrive at Kailua Bay, praying to convert Hawaiians to Christianity.

their ships carried. When Cook returned to Hawai'i in February 1779, he anchored at Kealakekua Bay to repair his ships and refresh supplies. When Cook tried to take a Hawaiian chief hostage in retaliation for a stolen boat, a battle ensued during which Cook, four of his sailors and uncounted Hawaiians died.

Once 'discovered,' the Hawaiian Islands became a prime Pacific waystation for traders, who would buy furs in the Pacific Northwest and stop here for supplies and fragrant *'iliahi* (sandalwood), then a valuable commodity in China. By the 1840s, the islands also became the whaling capital of the Pacific, with over 700 whaling ships stopping at Hawaiian ports annually. Some locals even jumped aboard to travel the world, since expert Hawaiian sailors were favored recruits by sea captains.

Kamehameha the Great

Kamehameha (meaning, 'Lonely One') was born in the Big Island's North Kohala district around 1753. Belonging to the *ali'i* class, he became a strong warrior under the guidance of his powerful uncle, Chief Kalaniopu'u. As a young man, Kamehameha was present with his uncle at Kealakekua Bay when Captain Cook was killed in 1779.

At the time, the major islands of Hawai'i, Kaua'i, Maui and O'ahu were independently ruled. Kamehameha fought for eight years to become the ruling chief of Hawai'i. Once he succeeded in 1791, he began a monumental campaign to conquer the other major islands. In 1810, after two decades of warfare, Kamehameha succeeded and became the first *mo'i* (king) of the Kingdom of Hawai'i, named after his birthplace.

During his nine-year reign, King Kamehameha I brought relative peace and stability to a society previously in flux with constant power struggles among *ali'i*. When he died in 1819 at his home in Kailua-Kona, two loyal chiefs buried him in a secret place to prevent rivals from stealing his bones, which were believed to hold great mana (supernatural power).

After Kamehameha I's death, his son Liholiho (Kamehameha II) became *mo'i* and his favorite wife, Queen Ka'ahumanu, became *kuhina nui* (regent). In a shocking snub to tradition, those two soon broke the kapu against men and women eating together and ordered many heiau (temples) and *ki'i* (deity images) destroyed. Hawaiian society plunged into chaos.

Christian Missionaries & Hawaiian Converts

Hawai'i's first Protestant missionaries chanced upon a fortuitous time and place to arrive. American Congregationalists from Boston landed at Kailua Bay on April 19, 1820, less than a year after Kamehameha I died. As Hawai'i's ancient religion had just been abolished, the missionaries found a receptive audience. However, new converts often quickly abandoned the church's teachings, reverting to traditional lifestyles.

1828
First coffee trees are planted in Kona by missionary Samuel Ruggles. Coffee beans

1863
Kohala Sugar Company, the island's first sugar plantation, is established.

KAREN MASSIER/GETTY IMAGES ©

The missionaries found one thing that attracted avid, widespread interest: literacy. Ancient Hawaiians had no written language; they preserved their mythology instead through lengthy oral epics, recited word for word by trained kahuna. The missionaries established a Hawaiian alphabet using Roman letters and zealously taught Hawaiians to read and write. This fostered a high literacy rate and the publication of several Hawaiian-language newspapers.

Eventually, however, missionaries banned the Hawaiian language in schools in order to distance Hawaiians from their 'hedonistic' cultural roots. They also prohibited hula dancing because of its lewd and suggestive movements, denounced traditional Hawaiian chants and songs that honored 'heathen' gods, taught women to sew Western-style clothing and abolished polygamy, which was accepted and necessary in this isolated island group.

King Sugar in the Plantation Era

Ko (sugarcane) was a 'canoe plant,' introduced by the first Polynesians. When foreigners realized Hawai'i was ideal for growing sugarcane, they quickly established small plantations using Hawaiian labor. Many missionaries became influential advisors to the Hawaiian monarchy and received large tracts of arable land in return, prompting them to leave the church altogether.

By that time, the Native Hawaiian population had alarmingly declined, due to such introduced diseases as typhoid, influenza, smallpox and syphilis. To fill the labor shortage, plantation workers were imported from overseas. First, beginning in the 1850s, came Chinese laborers and soon after came Japanese and Portuguese immigrants. After the US annexed Hawaii in 1898, Puerto Ricans, Koreans and Filipinos arrived.

The rise of the sugar industry had a major impact on Hawai'i's social structure. Haole (Caucasian) plantation owners and sugar agents became the elite economic and political class, while Hawaiians and foreign laborers without land of their own filled lower-class ranks. Meanwhile, those diverse immigrant groups, along with the shared pidgin language they created, transformed Hawai'i into the multiethnic, multicultural society it is today.

During California's Gold Rush and later the US Civil War, Hawai'i's sugar exports to the mainland soared. As late as 1960, 'King Sugar' remained the state's largest industry. Due to cheaper labor and production costs abroad, however, Hawaii's sugar plantations began shuttering in the 1980s. Today there is only one working plantation left statewide, on Maui.

The Best... History Museums

1 Lyman Museum & Mission House (p169)

2 Hulihe'e Palace (p35)

3 Pacific Tsunami Museum (p172)

4 'Imiloa Astronomy Center of Hawai'i (p172)

5 Laupahoehoe Train Museum (p159)

1882

Macadamia trees are planted on Hawai'i as an ornamental; the nuts aren't eaten till the 1920s.

1893

The Hawaiian monarchy, under Queen Lili'uokalani, is overthrown in Honolulu, ending 83 years of rule.

1912

Duke Kahanamoku wins Olympic swimming medals; he later becomes a global ambassador of aloha and surfing.

Hawaiian Kingdom Overthrown

Under the Hawaiian monarchy, foreigners had no way to own property because the king controlled the lands. With foreigners pushing to secure long-term property rights, in 1848 the kingdom's government enacted the Great Mahele, a revolutionary land reform act. Two years later the government further acquiesced by allowing foreign residents to buy land. Haole sugar growers and land speculators bought huge parcels for minimal sums from chiefs lured by quick money and from commoners ignorant of deeds, taxes and other legal requirements for ownership.

King David Kalakaua, who reigned from 1874 to 1891, fought to restore Hawaiian culture, arts and indigenous pride. He also had a fondness for drinking, gambling and partying, earning him the nickname 'Merrie Monarch.' In 1887 the Hawaiian League, a secret antimonarchy organization run by sugar interests, wrote a new constitution and forced Kalakaua to sign. This 'Bayonet Constitution' stripped the monarchy's powers, making the king a figurehead. It also limited voting rights, effectively allowing only wealthy businessmen and landowners to vote.

When Kalakaua died, his sister Lili'uokalani ascended the throne and tried to restore the monarchy. On January 17, 1893, a 'Committee of Safety,' composed mostly of haole

Koa bowls, Hulihe'e Palace (p35), Kailua-Kona
JOHN ELK/GETTY IMAGES ©

1946
Hawaii's most destructive tsunami, generated by an Alaskan earthquake, kills 122 people on the Big Island.

1959
Hawaii becomes the 50th US state; Daniel Inouye is elected first Japanese American in Congress.

1960
A tsunami generated off South America destroys over 100 buildings and kills 61 people in Hilo.

American residents and supported by US Minister John Stevens and a contingent of US marines and sailors, forcibly arrested her and took over Honolulu's 'Iolani Palace in a tense but bloodless coup d'état.

Becoming the 50th State

After the short-lived Republic of Hawai'i was annexed as a US territory in 1898, the road to statehood was long and bumpy. The islands presented some novel issues for the US federal government, including its distance from the mainland, strong labor unions and a huge nonwhite population. Likewise, statehood was a tough sell to the US Congress, but a series of significant historical events paved the way.

In 1936 Pan American Airways began regular commercial flights from the US mainland to Hawaii, launching the transpacific air age and the beginning of mass tourism. Wireless telegraph service, followed by telephone service, between Hawaii and the mainland alleviated doubts about long-distance communication. And, most importantly, WWII proved both the strategic military role of O'ahu's Pearl Harbor and the Hawaiian Islands generally.

While Southern conservatives, both Democrat and Republic, remained wary of the islands' multicultural melting pot, Hawaii became the 50th US state in 1959. After statehood, tourism exploded, thanks to the advent of jet airplanes and to the commercializing of Hawaii (think tiki craze, Blue Hawaii, aloha shirts and Waikiki). Hotel construction boomed and by 1970 tourism had added $1 billion to state coffers, surpassing both agriculture and US military spending.

Promised Land

In 1921 the US Congress passed the Hawaiian Homes Commission Act, setting aside almost 200,000 acres of government land for Native Hawaiians to lease for $1 per year. Unfortunately many of these lands are remote and lack basic infrastructure (eg roads, water, electricity) and applicants end up waiting for years, even decades. There are over 25,000 residential applicants on the wait list across the state, but fewer than 10,000 leases have ever been granted. Some applicants are elderly or even pass away by the time they receive a lease.

1971

Hilo's Merrie Monarch Festival holds its first hula competition, celebrating a cultural renaissance.

1978

The Office of Hawaiian Affairs (OHA) is established and holds Hawaiian Home Lands in trust for the benefit of Native Hawaiians.

1983

Kilauea begins the volcanic eruption that is currently the longest in recorded history.

Native Hawaiian Renaissance

In 1976, after the homegrown Polynesian Voyaging Society built and sailed the *Hokule'a* – a replica of a traditional Polynesian double-hulled canoe – succesfully round-trip to Tahiti, traditional Hawaiian knowledge was suddenly in demand again. The same year, a small grassroots group, Protect Kaho'olawe 'Ohana (PKO), began illegally occupying Kaho'olawe, an island taken by the US government during WWII and used as a practice bombing site.

After the state held its landmark Constitutional Convention in 1978, public schools started teaching Hawaiian language and Hawaiian-immersion charter schools proliferated. Small but vocal contingents of political activists began pushing for some measure of Hawaiian sovereignty, from complete secession from the USA to a nation-within-a-nation model. Today the US federal government still has not acknowledged Native Hawaiians as an indigenous people, however.

1993
Federal 'Apology Bill' acknowledges the USA's role in the kingdom's illegal takeover a century ago.

2002
Following Democratic Party corruption scandals, mainland-born Linda Lingle is elected Hawaii's first Republican governor in 40 years.

2008
O'ahu-born Barack Obama becomes the first African American US President; he is reelected in 2012.

People of the Big Island

Kahiko (ancient) hula performance with an *ipu* (gourd) drum

ALVIS UPITIS/GETTY IMAGES ©

Mention Hawai'i and you might start fantasizing about sandy beaches, swaying palms and blazing sunsets. But the heart of the Big Island is found elsewhere: in its diverse people. Whether residents are Native Hawaiian, kama'aina (born and raised in Hawaii) or transplanted from afar, they're united by small-town values, respect for multicultural traditions, interrracial tolerance and their enthusiastic pursuit of 'the good life.'

Big Island Identity

The Big Island is far from homogeneous, but overall the mellow vibe tends to smooth sharp differences between and among people. Most residents are easygoing and low-key, with a preference for unpretentious small-town life. Politically, the majority are moderate Democrats, often voting along party, racial, ethnic, seniority and local/nonlocal lines.

Locals embrace their longstanding connections, often maintaining friendships with high-school classmates and invariably bumping into familiar faces whenever they step out. As a rule, loud assertiveness is considered unseemly. It's better to avoid embarrassing confrontations and 'save face' by keeping quiet.

The most vocal, liberal and passionate speakers at community meetings are often brash mainland transplants pushing for environmental conservation, sustainability, slow growth and non-GMO food. 'Loudmouth haole,' locals might think. But other transplants quickly find their feet here: befriending *kama'aina* neighbors, growing backyard gardens, studying hula and simply slowing down and respecting local ways.

Locals generally support progressive trends, in keeping with the Hawaiian concept of *aloha 'aina* (love of the land). While Costco and Walmart might be anathema to politically left-leaning mainlanders, budget-minded locals just trying to get by welcome the discounts and variety. And despite guzzling expensive gas, a monster-sized pickup truck remains *the* status-symbol vehicle for many locals.

Hilo vs Kona

While Honolulu folk view Hilo, the capital town, as 'country' or even *da boonies* (the boondocks), everything's relative. On the Big Island, Hilo is 'town,' where people wear wrinkle-free aloha shirts and wristwatches to work in government offices. With the highest statewide percentage of Japanese Americans (33%), Hilo's plantation roots are clear.

In contrast, Kailua-Kona has become the island's economic powerhouse and a tourist hub. It's busy and 'haole-fied,' with a 48% white population due to an influx of new transplants. As a result, traffic along the Queen Ka'ahumanu Hwy is a nightmare and residents often gripe about the county's shortsightedness in improving Kona's jammed roads, compared with Hilo's well-planned system.

Lifestyle

The typical Hawai'i lifestyle is changing with the influence of newcomers and less-traditional younger generations, but Big Islanders generally center their lives around family. The workday starts and ends early; even workaholics tend to be backyard

Who's Who?

Haole White person, Caucasian (except local Portuguese). Often further defined as 'mainland haole' or 'local haole.' Can be insulting or playful, depending on context.

Hapa Person of mixed ancestry; most commonly referring to *hapa* haole who are part white and part Asian, Hawaiian etc.

Hawaiian Person of Native Hawaiian ancestry. It's a faux pas to call any Hawai'i resident 'Hawaiian,' thus ignoring the islands' indigenous people.

Kama'aina Person who is native to a particular place; literally 'child of the land.' In a retail context, '*kama'aina* discounts' apply to anyone with a Hawaii driver's license.

Local A person who grew up here. Locals who move away from Hawai'i somewhat retain their local 'cred.'

'Ohana Family. Extends beyond bloodlines to include close friends, co-workers, classmates and teammates.

Transplant Person who moves to the islands as an adult. Never becomes a 'local,' even after they've lived in Hawaii for many years.

gardeners, surfers or golfers. Not surprisingly, Hawaii residents have the longest life expectancy in the USA: 81.3 years.

The influx of mainlanders is obvious. Mainland transplants generally arrive with more money and different dreams – say, looking forward to a relaxed retirement, starting a B&B or a coffee estate, or just for youthful experimentation. On the Big Island, many mainlanders feel free to be more unconventional.

O'ahu and Maui expats constitute a newer wave of transplants. 'Hilo still feels like old Hawaii,' they say. Indeed, Big Island real estate remains the most affordable statewide, while urban problems from traffic to crime remain tolerable. 'High density' is still a foreign concept on the Big Island, where commutes can cover a lot of highway.

Regional differences can be stark. For example, Pahoa is teeming with off-the-grid types who grow their own food and live off bare essentials, eschewing creature comforts like hot showers. In Hilo and Kona, such a lifestyle is practically unheard of. There, locals tend toward more conventional 'American dream' lives, meaning marriage, kids, a comfortable home and stable employment.

Multiculturalism

Big Island immigrants are today overwhelmingly white, so the island's diversity stems from historical plantation-era ethnic groups: Native Hawaiians, Japanese, Filipino, Portuguese and Chinese. It's a unique mix that's remarkably different from mainland diversity, as it lacks significant African American and Latino populations.

During plantation days, haole were the wealthy plantation owners, and their legendary surnames remain household names (eg Parker Ranch, Lyman Museum). Their ingrained privilege is one reason why some resentment toward haole still lingers. However, prominent haole families were often close allies of high-ranking Native Hawaiians – or even related by marriage.

Hilo Farmers Market (p181)

Dos & Don'ts for Island Visitors

○ Do be courteous and 'no make waves' (don't make a scene).

○ Do try to use basic Hawaiian words, but don't speak pidgin.

○ Do dress casually like locals do. Remove your shoes before entering homes and B&Bs.

○ Do treat ancient Hawaiian sites and artifacts with respect. Don't collect or move stones.

○ Do ask permission before picking flowers or fruit on private property.

○ Do drive slowly and don't honk your horn except in an emergency.

○ Do give a *shaka* (Hawaii's hand-greeting sign) if another driver lets you merge.

○ Do tread lightly at 'locals only' beaches.

As time passes and the plantation era fades away, the traditional stereotypes, hierarchies and alliances are softening too. Besides, no ethnic group has ever kept exclusive for long anyway on Hawai'i. Instead different groups have freely adopted and shared cultural customs, from food to festivals. Today, folks of all ethnic backgrounds dance the hula, play the ukulele and study the Hawaiian language.

Today there is no ethnic majority in the Hawaiian Islands. Due to intermarriage, you cannot always assume a person's race or ethnicity by surname – many Native Hawaiians have Caucasian or Asian surnames. Generally, locals feel most bonded with other locals. While tourists and transplants are usually welcomed with aloha, they must earn locals' trust by being *pono* (respectful).

Religion

Although Hawaiians abandoned their ancient religion for Christianity soon after King Kamehameha I died, religious traditions survived underground. Today you'll glimpse them in public ceremonies, such as when a kahuna (priest) blesses the land during a groundbreaking. Many ancient historical sites – *pu'uhonua* (places of refuge), heiau (temples) and petroglyph fields – are also religious sites, chosen for the mana (spiritual essence) of the land. Certain natural features, such as Halema'uma'u Crater and Mauna Kea, are still considered sacred.

Many residents do not claim adherence to a particular faith, and the religious milieu is tolerant rather than dogmatic. The largest religious group is Roman Catholic, due to a significant Filipino population, followed by Mormonism, which has attracted many South Pacific converts. Mainstream Protestant Christianity is struggling with declining membership, while evangelical churches are burgeoning. Buddhism is prevalent among Japanese residents, and their temples are often important community centers.

Big Island Cuisine

Tempura ahi roll

BILL ADAMS/GETTY IMAGES ©

Forget pineapple-topped pizza; Hawaii's cuisine is no cliché. It's a multicultural flavor explosion, influenced by the Pacific Rim and rooted in the islands' natural bounty. The first Polynesians brought nourishing staples such as kalo *(taro),* niu *(coconut), chickens and pigs. Later plantation-era immigrants imported rice,* shōyu *(soy sauce), chilies and more. Over time, all these wildly different flavors became 'local.'*

Local Food

Cheap, tasty and filling, local 'grinds' (food) is the stuff of cravings and comfort. There's no better example than that of the classic plate lunch, a fixed-plate meal of 'two scoop' rice, macaroni or potato salad and a hot protein dish, such as fried mahimahi, teriyaki chicken or *kalbi* short ribs. Often eaten with disposable chopsticks on disposable plates, these meals pack a flavor (and caloric) punch: fried, salty and meaty. Nowadays healthier plates come with brown rice and salad greens.

Sticky white rice is more than a side dish in Hawaii. It's a culinary building block, an integral partner in everyday meals. Without rice, Spam *musubi* (rice ball) would just be a slice of canned meat. The *loco moco* would be nothing more than an egg-and-gravy-covered hamburger patty. Just so you know,

Spam-tastic!

Hawaii may be the only US state where you can eat Hormel's iconic canned meat with pride. Here in the nation's Spam capital, locals consume almost seven million cans per year.

Of course, Spam looks and tastes different in Hawaii. It's always eaten cooked, typically fried to a light crispiness in sugar-sweetened *shōyu* (soy sauce), not straight from the can. It's often served for breakfast with eggs and rice, or sliced and rolled into *musubi* (rice balls or blocks wrapped with nori), sold everywhere, even at mainstream chains like 7-Eleven.

During the plantation era, canned meat was cheap and easy to prepare for *bentō* (Japanese-style boxed lunches) taken to the fields. But Spam itself wasn't introduced to the islands until WWII, when fresh meat was replaced by standard US military rations. By the time the war ended, residents had developed an affinity for the fatty pork-based meat product.

If you acquire a taste for it too, pick up *Hawai'i Cooks with SPAM: Local Recipes Featuring Our Favorite Canned Meat* by Muriel Miura.

sticky white rice means exactly that. Not fluffy rice. Not wild rice. And definitely not instant.

One must-try local *pupu* (snack or appetizer) is *poke* (pronounced 'poh-keh'), a savory dish of bite-sized raw fish (typically ahi), seasoned with *shōyu,* sesame oil, green onion, chili-pepper flakes, sea salt, *ogo* (crunchy seaweed) and *'inamona* (a condiment made of roasted, ground *kukui* – candlenut tree – nuts).

Another favorite local food is saimin, a soup of chewy Chinese egg noodles swimming in Japanese broth, garnished with green onion, dried nori (Japanese dried seaweed), *kamaboko* (steamed fish cake) and *char siu* (Chinese barbecued pork).

The traditional local sweet treat is Chinese crack seed. It's preserved fruit (typically plum, cherry, mango or lemon) that, like Coca-Cola or curry, is impossible to describe – it can be sweet, sour, salty or spicy. Sold prepackaged at supermarkets and Longs Drugs stores or scooped by the pound at specialty shops, crack seed is truly addictive.

Native Hawaiian Food

With its earthy flavors and Polynesian ingredients, Hawaiian cooking is like no other. But it's not necessarily easy for visitors to find – look for it at roadside markets, plate-lunch kitchens, old-school delis and island diners.

Kalua pig is traditionally roasted whole underground in an *imu,* a pit of red-hot stones layered with banana and *ti* (a native plant) leaves. Cooked this way, the pork is smoky, salty and succulent. Nowadays *kalua* pork is typically oven-roasted and seasoned with salt and liquid smoke. At a commercial luau, a pig placed in an *imu* is usually only for show (it couldn't feed 300-plus guests anyway).

Poi – a purplish paste made of pounded taro root, often steamed and fermented – was sacred to ancient Hawaiians. Taro is highly nutritious, low in calories, easily digestible and versatile to prepare. Tasting bland to mildly tart or even sour, poi is usually not eaten by itself, but as a starchy counterpoint to strongly flavored dishes such as *lomilomi* salmon (minced, salted salmon with diced tomato and green onion). Fried or baked taro chips are sold at grocery stores, gas stations etc.

A popular main dish is *laulau,* a bundle of pork or chicken and salted butterfish wrapped in taro or *ti* leaves and steamed until it has a soft spinachlike texture. Other traditional Hawaiian fare includes baked *'ulu* (breadfruit), with a mouthfeel similar to potato; *'opihi* (limpet), tiny mollusks picked off reefs at low tide; and *haupia,* a coconut-cream custard thickened with arrowroot or cornstarch.

Hawaii Regional Cuisine

Hawaii was considered a culinary backwater until the early 1990s, when a handful of island chefs – including Alan Wong, Roy Yamaguchi, Sam Choy and Peter Merriman, all of whom still have restaurants on the Big Island – created a new cuisine, borrowing liberally from Hawaii's multiethnic heritage.

These chefs partnered with island farmers, ranchers and fishers to highlight fresh, local ingredients and in doing so, transformed childhood favorites into gourmet Pacific Rim masterpieces. Suddenly macadamia-nut-crusted mahimahi, miso-glazed butterfish and *liliko'i* (passion fruit) anything were all the rage.

This culinary movement was dubbed 'Hawaii Regional Cuisine' and its 12 pioneering chefs became celebrities. At first, Hawaii Regional Cuisine was rather exclusive, found only at high-end dining rooms. Its hallmarks included Eurasian-fusion flavors and gastronomic techniques with elaborate plating.

Upscale restaurants are still the mainstay for Hawaii's star chefs, but now you'll find neighborhood bistros and even plate-lunch food trucks serving dishes inspired by Hawaii Regional Cuisine, with island farms lauded like designer brands on menus.

The Best... Food & Drink Festivals

1 Kona Coffee Cultural Festival (p43)

2 Kona Brewers Festival (p43)

3 A Taste of the Hawaiian Range (p99)

4 Puna Culinary Festival (p200)

5 Ka'u Coffee Festival (p235)

Who Invented Loco Moco?

Among Hilo's claims to fame is the *loco moco* (a hamburger patty, fried egg and gravy over rice). In 1949, the Lincoln Wreckers, a teen sports club, hung out at the now long-gone Lincoln Grill. Amid pinball machines and a jukebox, they'd fill up on cheap hot meals. One guy nicknamed Loco ('crazy' in Hawaiian pidgin) requested a new dish, so the owners offered him a big bowl of rice smothered with a hamburger steak and brown gravy for 25¢. This mishmash made the permanent menu and was named *loco moco* in honor of Crazy. Eventually eggs were added, and the rest is Big Island culinary history.

The Best...
Sustainable Food Websites

1 Hawai'i Seafood (www.hawaii-seafood.org)

....

2 Hawai'i Agritourism Association (www.hiagtourism.org)

....

3 Edible Hawaiian Islands (www.ediblehawaiianislands.com)

....

4 Slow Food Hawai'i (www.slowfoodhawaii.org)

....

5 Hawaii Farm Bureau Federation (www.hfbf.org)

....

Hawaii's Locavore Movement

Many Big Islanders are backyard farmers, growing more apple bananas, star fruit and avocados than they can consume themselves. Still, a whopping 85% to 90% of Hawaii's food is imported, and food security (aka 'food sovereignty') is a hot topic. Small-scale family farmers are trying to shift the agriculture industry away from corporate-scale monocropping (eg sugar, pineapple) enabled by chemical fertilizers, pesticides, herbicides and genetically modified organisms (GMOs).

Diversified agriculture and agrotourism are booming on the Big Island. It's not just about Hawai'i's signature macadamia nuts and Kona coffee anymore, but a delicious range of locally grown edibles: Hamakua Coast mushrooms, vanilla, tomatoes and salad greens; Big Island abalone, lobsters and *kampachi* (yellowtail) from the Kona coast; grass-fed beef and lamb from Waimea; Kona chocolate; organic tea from Volcano and the Hamakua Coast; Ka'u oranges and coffee; yellow-flesh Kapho Solo papayas from Puna; and local honey. While the Big Island's egg and poultry farms are long gone, the state's two biggest cattle dairies still operate here.

Despite the popularity of Hawai'i's farmers markets, supermarkets still typically stock blemish-free Sunkist oranges and California grapes. An exception is the Big Island's KTA Superstores, a minichain that carries 200 products, including milk, beef, produce and coffee, from dozens of local vendors under its Mountain Apple Brand.

Coffee, Tea & Traditional Drinks

Hawaii was the first US state to grow coffee. World-famous Kona coffee wins raves for its mellow flavor with no bitter aftertaste. The upland slopes of Mauna Loa and Hualalai volcanoes in the Kona district offer an ideal climate (sunny mornings and afternoon clouds with light seasonal showers) for coffee cultivation.

While 100% Kona coffee has the most cachet, commanding upwards of $20 to $40 or more per pound, in recent years crops from the island's southernmost district of Ka'u have won accolades and impressed aficionados. Small coffee farms have also fruited in Puna and Honoka'a on the island's windward side.

Ancient Hawaiians never got buzzed on coffee beans, which were first imported in the early 19th century. Hawaii's original intoxicants were plant-based Polynesian elixirs: 'awa, a mild, mouth-numbing sedative made from the kava plant's roots, and noni (Indian mulberry), which some consider a cure-all. Both of these drinks are pungent in smell and taste, so they're often mixed with other juices.

Tea-growing was introduced to Hawaii in the late 19th century, but never took hold as a commercial crop due to high labor and production costs. In 1999 University of Hawai'i researchers discovered that a particular cultivar of tea would thrive in volcanic soil and tropical climates, especially at higher elevations. Small, often organic, tea farms are now spreading around Volcano and along the Hamakua Coast.

Fruit trees also thrive here. Alas, most supermarket cartons contain imported purees or sugary 'juice drinks' like POG (passion fruit, orange and guava). Look for real, freshly squeezed and blended juices at health food stores, farmers markets and roadside fruit stands. Don't assume that the fruit is local, though.

Beer, Wine & Cocktails

Once a novelty, a handful of microbreweries are now firmly established on the Big Island. Brewmasters claim that the mineral content and purity of Hawai'i's water makes for excellent-tasting beer. Another hallmark of local craft beers is the addition of a hint of tropical flavors, such as Kona coffee, honey or *liliko'i*.

Lively brewpubs and tasting rooms where you can sample popular pours include ecoconscious Kona Brewing Company (p42) in Kailua-Kona, the Big Island Brewhaus (p127) in Waimea and **Hawai'i Nui Brewing** (Map p170; ☏808-934-8211; http://hawaiinuibrewing.com; 275 E Kawili; ⊙10am-6pm Mon-Fri) FREE (which also owns the Mehana Brewing Company label) in Hilo. The island's sole winery, Volcano Winery, is untraditional in its guava-grape and macadamia-honey concoctions – they're not to everyone's taste.

Every beachfront and hotel bar mixes tropical cocktails topped with fruit garnish and a toothpick umbrella. Hawaii's legendary mai tai is a mix of dark and light rum, orange curaçao, orgeat and simple syrup with orange, lemon, lime and/or pineapple juices.

Luau

In ancient Hawaii, a luau commemorated auspicious occasions, such as births, war victories or successful harvests. Modern luau to celebrate weddings or a baby's first birthday are often large banquet-hall or outdoor gatherings with the *'ohana* (extended family and friends). Although the menu might be daring – including Hawaiian delicacies such as raw *'a'ama* (black crab) and *'opihi* – the entertainment is low-key.

Hawaii's commercial luau started in the 1970s. Today these shows offer the elaborate pseudo-Hawaiian feast and Polynesian dancing and fire eaters that many visitors expect. But the all-you-can-eat buffet of luau standards is usually toned down for the mainland palate, with steamed mahimahi and teriyaki chicken. Most commercial luau are overpriced and overly touristy, although kids may enjoy them.

Coffee plantation, Kona
DENNIS MACDONALD/GETTY IMAGES ©

Hawaiian Arts & Crafts

WILLIAM WATERFALL/GETTY IMA

Contemporary Hawai'i is a tropical garden of diverse cultural traditions, underneath which beats a Hawaiian heart. Since the 1970s, a revival of indigenous language, crafts, music and hula means visitors will find themselves surrounded by art, both ancient and new. E komo mai (welcome) to this Polynesian island, where storytelling and slack key guitar are among the familiar sounds of everyday life.

Hula

In ancient Hawai'i, hula sometimes was a solemn ritual, in which *mele* (songs, chants) were an offering to the gods or celebrated the accomplishments of *ali'i* (chiefs). At other times hula was lighthearted entertainment, in which chief and *maka'ainana* (commoner) danced together, including at annual festivals. Most importantly, hula embodied the community – telling stories of and celebrating itself.

Dancers trained rigorously in *halau* (schools) under a *kumu* (teacher), so their hand gestures, facial expressions and synchronized movements were exact. In a culture without written language, chants were important, giving meaning to the movements and preserving Hawai'i's oral history – anything from creation stories about gods and goddesses to royal genealogies. Songs often contained *kaona* (hidden meanings), which could be spiritual, but also amorous or sexual.

Today hula competitions take place across the islands, with hula troupes vying in *kahiko* (ancient) and *'auana* (modern) categories. *Kahiko* performances are raw and elemental, accompanied only by chanting and thunderous gourd drums. Costumes are traditional, with *ti*-leaf lei, *kapa* (pounded bark-cloth) skirts, primary colors and sometimes lots of skin showing. Western influences – English-language lyrics, stringed instruments, flowing dresses and pants, sinuous arm movements and smiling faces – may appear in *'auana* dances. Some *halau* even flirt with postmodern dance styles.

Hawaii's own Olympics of hula is Hilo's **Merrie Monarch Festival** (☎935-9168; www.merriemonarchfestival.org; Afook-Chinen Civic Auditorium; 3-night admission $25-30), held around Easter. A newer competition, **Moku O Keawe** (www.mokif.com; Waikoloa Resort Area; admission per night $15-25), takes place at Waikoloa in early November. Don't miss the year-round outdoor **hula performances** (www.volcanoartcenter.org; 👤) ☎ at Hawai'i Volcanoes National Park.

Island Music

It would take a textbook to cover every genre of Hawaiian music, from traditional *mele* to contemporary vocalists, like the late Israel 'Iz' Kamakawiwo'ole, who marry Hawaiian and English lyrics. Away from the islands, however, most people aren't aware of the lasting contributions that Hawaiian musicians have made to modern music: the steel guitar, the ukulele and the slack key guitar.

Spanish and Mexican cowboys first introduced the guitar to Hawaiians in the 1830s. Fifty years later, teenager Joseph Kekuku started experimenting with playing a guitar flat on his lap while sliding a pocket knife or comb across the strings. He invented the Hawaiian steel guitar *(kika kila)*, which lifts the strings off the fretboard using a movable steel slide, creating a signature smooth sound.

Hawaiian Music Online

Hearing Hawaiian music is a great way to get pumped before, during and after your trip. The following websites let you dive right in:

○ **Hawaiian Music Island** (www.mele.com) Online music and video retailer with links to award-winning Hawaiian artists and internet radio stations, with mainland and island concert listings.

○ **Cord International** (www.cordinternational.com) Vintage music purveyor for everything from retro Japanese Hawaiian sounds to Les Paul's luau album.

○ **Mountain Apple Company** (www.mountainapplecompany.com) Music label with the biggest library of contemporary and traditional Hawaiian music, plus free online clips and streaming radio.

○ **Hawaiian Rainbow** (www.hawaiianrainbow.com) Live streaming of mostly traditional Hawaiian music; also available on a free mobile app.

○ **Huapala** (www.huapala.org) Hawaiian music and hula archives include chants and songs searchable by island.

○ **Dancing Cat Records** (www.dancingcat.com) Music label dedicated to Hawaiian slack key guitarists, offering free online album previews.

The Best...
Big Island Albums

1 *'Ohai 'Ula* (2010), Kainani Kahaunaele

2 *Aloha Pumehana* (2009), Darlene Ahuna

3 *Hawai'i Island... Is My Home* (2008), John Keawe

4 *Songs from Hawai'i Island* (2007)

5 *Honey-Boy* (2002), Kekuhi Kanahele

6 *O Ke Aumoe* (1996), George Kuo

Heard all across the islands is the ukulele, derived from the *braguinha,* a Portuguese stringed instrument introduced to Hawaii in 1879. Ukulele means 'jumping flea' in Hawaiian, referring to the way players' deft fingers swiftly 'jump' around the strings. Both the ukulele and the Hawaiian steel guitar contributed to the lighthearted *hapa haole* (Hawaiian music with predominantly English lyrics) popularized in Hawaii and abroad after the 1930s. Today the ukulele is making a comeback as a young generation of virtuosos emerges, led by genre-bending, Billboard chart-topping rocker Jake Shimabukuro.

Since the mid-20th century, the Hawaiian steel guitar has usually been played with slack key guitar (*ki ho'alu,* literally 'loosen the key') tunings, in which the thumb plays the bass and rhythm chords, while the fingers play the melody and improvisations, in a picked style. Legendary musician Gabby Pahinui launched the modern slack key guitar era with his first recording of 'Hi'ilawe' in 1946. In the 1970s, Gabby and his band the Sons of Hawai'i embraced the traditional Hawaiian sound, spurring its rebirth. The list of contemporary slack key masters is long and ever growing, including Big Island–born Keola Beamer.

Hawaiian vocalists are known for a distinctive falsetto singing technique (called *leo ke'ike'i*) that stresses the break *(ha'i)* between lower and upper registers. The unquestioned leader of this style among women remains the late Genoa Keawe, whose impossibly long-held notes in the song 'Alika' set the standard (and set it high). Other notables include jazzy songbird Amy Hanaiali'i Gilliom and younger chanteuse Raiatea Helm, both Grammy nominees.

Traditional Crafts

The lei – a handcrafted garland worn around one's neck or head – is Hawaii's most sensuous and transitory art form. Traditional lei makers may use feathers, nuts, shells, seeds, seaweed, vines, leaves and fruit, as well as fragrant fresh flowers. In choosing their materials, lei makers tell a story – since flowers and plants may embody Hawaiian places and myths – and express emotions such as love, honor and respect.

In the islands' Polynesian past, lei were part of sacred hula dances and given as special gifts to loved ones, as healing medicine to the sick and as offerings to the gods. Today locals often don lei for special events, such as weddings, birthdays, anniversaries, graduations and other public ceremonies. A typical Hawaiian lei costs anywhere from $10 for a single strand of plumeria sold at the airport to thousands of dollars for a 100% genuine Ni'ihau shell lei necklace.

Other bewitchingly beautiful Hawaiian crafts include *lauhala* weaving, *kapa* (pounded-bark cloth) making and intricate featherwork seen in *kahili* (royal standards), capes and lei. When it comes to *lauhala,* weaving the *lau* (leaves) of the hala (pandanus) tree is the easier part, while preparing the leaves, which have razor-sharp spines, is messy work. Making *kapa* (called tapa elsewhere in Polynesia) is no less laborious: large sheets of hand-felted cloth are colorfully dyed with plant

materials and stamped or painted with bold geometric patterns, then scented with flowers or oils.

Ancient Hawaiians were also expert at woodworking, carving canoes out of logs and hand-turning lustrous bowls from a variety of beautifully grained tropical hardwoods, such as koa, kou and milo. *Ipu* (gourds) were dried and used as containers and as drums for hula performances and chanting. Contemporary woodworkers use native woods to craft traditional bowls, exquisite furniture, jewelry and free-form sculptures. Hawaiian bowls are not typically decorated or ornate, but are shaped to bring out the natural beauty of the wood.

All of these traditional Hawaiian crafts have become so popular with tourists that cheap imitation imports from factories across the Pacific and Asia have flooded island stores. Shop carefully, buy local and expect to pay more for high-quality handmade pieces, for example, at the **Volcano Art Center** (☏866-967-7565, 808-967-7565; www. volcanoartcenter.org; Crater Rim Dr; ⊗9am-5pm) 🖉, and Holualoa's **Kimura Lauhala Shop** (☏808-324-0053; www.holualoahawaii.com/member_sites/kimura.html; cnr Hualalai Rd & Hwy 180; ⊗9am-5pm Mon-Fri, to 4pm Sat) 🖉 and **Ipu Hale Gallery** (☏808-322-9069; www.holualoahawaii. com/member_sites/ipu_hale.html; 76-5893 Mamalahoa Hwy; ⊗10am-4pm Tue-Sat) 🖉.

Literature

Hawai'i's oldest storytelling was of ancient myths and legends, originally disseminated by oral tradition. In modern times, Hawaii's written literature was long dominated by Western writers who observed Hawaii's exotic-looking world from the outside, such as James Michener's best-selling historical saga *Hawaii*, Mark Twain's *Roughing It* and Isabella Bird's *Six Months in the Sandwich Islands*.

Since the 1970s birthed an ongoing renaissance of Hawaiian culture and language, locally born writers have created an authentic contemporary literature of Hawaii that evokes island life from an insider's perspective. Leading this movement has

Tobacco leaves, Pu'uhonua O Hōnaunau National Historical Park (p77)

Hawaiiana Classes

Explore Hawaiian language, art, music and dance at a variety of cultural classes, workshops and lessons held all over the island, including at beach resorts and hotels. Check calendar listings in the **Big Island Weekly** (www.bigislandweekly.com) and with the following places:

- **Volcano Art Center** (p267)
- **Society for Kona's Education and Art** (SKEA; ☏808-328-9392; www.skea.org; 84-5191 Mamalahoa Hwy) ✎
- **Donkey Mill Art Center** (☏808-322-3362; www.donkeymillartcenter.org; 78-6670 Mamalahoa Hwy; ⏱10am-4pm Tue-Sat Aug-May, 9am-3pm Mon-Fri Jun & Jul; ⛎) FREE
- **Keauhou Shopping Center** (www.keauhouvillageshops.com; 78-6831 Ali'i Dr) FREE
- **East Hawai'i Cultural Center** (East Hawai'i Cultural Center; ☏808-961-5711; www.ehcc. org; 141 Kalakaua St; suggested donation $2; ⏱10am-4pm Mon-Sat)

Get a head start before your trip with online music lessons by slack key guitarist **Keola Beamer** (www.kbeamer.com).

been **Bamboo Ridge Press** (www.bambooridge.com), which for more than 35 years has published contemporary local fiction and poetry in an annual journal and has launched the careers of many well-known Hawaii writers.

In 1975, *All I Asking for Is My Body,* by Milton Murayama, vividly captured plantation life for Japanese *nisei* (second-generation immigrants) around WWII. Murayama's use of pidgin opened the door to an explosion of vernacular literature. Raised on the Big Island, Lois-Ann Yamanaka has won widespread acclaim for her poetry and stories (*Wild Meat and the Bully Burgers,* 1996), in which pidgin embodies her characters like a second skin.

Indeed, redeeming pidgin – long dismissed by academics and disparaged by the upper class – has been a cultural and political cause for some. The hilarious stories (*Da Word,* 2001) and essays (*Living Pidgin,* 2002) of Lee Tonouchi, a prolific writer and playwright, argue that pidgin is not only essential to understanding local culture, but also a legitimate language.

Family Travel

Stargazing, Mauna Kea (p135)

JOHN HOOK/GETTY IMAGES ©

With its phenomenal natural beauty, Hawai'i is perfect for a family vacation. Nā keiki (kids) can play on sandy beaches galore, snorkel amid tropical fish, zipline in forest canopies and even watch lava flow. Then get them out of the sun (or rain) for a spell at family-friendly museums. Because long drive times can make kids antsy, you may not want to base yourself in just one place on the Big Island.

Planning Your Trip

Mixing up natural and cultural sites and activities, as well as managing expectations, helps maximize children's fun. The latter is especially important when it comes to lava: kids may be sorely disappointed, expecting the fiery fountains dramatically seen on the Discovery Channel. Check current lava flows with the **Hawaiian Volcano Observatory** (http://hvo.wr.usgs.gov/activity/kilaueastatus.php) before booking an expensive helicopter or boat tour.

Choose accommodations based on your family's sightseeing and activity priorities. Resorts offer spectacular swimming pools, along with kids' activity day camps and on-call babysitting services. But some parents prefer the convenience and cost savings of having a full kitchen and washer/dryer, which many condominiums and vacation rentals offer.

Children often stay free when sharing a hotel or resort room with their parents, but only if they use existing bedding. Otherwise, rollaway beds may be available – sometimes free, but usually for a surcharge of up to $40 per night. At condos, kids above a certain age might count as extra guests and entail an additional nightly surcharge. Kids and even babies are welcome at some island B&Bs and inns, but not all.

Because Hawaii is a family-oriented and unfussy place, most restaurants welcome children, except for some high-end resort dining rooms. If restaurant dining is inconvenient, no problem. Eating outdoors at a beach park is among the simplest and best island pleasures. Pack finger foods for a picnic, pick up fruit from farmers markets, stop for smoothies at roadside stands and order plate lunches at drive-ins.

Commercial luau might seem like cheesy Vegas dinner shows to adults, but many kids love the flashy dances and fire tricks. Children typically get discounted tickets (and sometimes free admission when accompanied by a paying adult).

When deciding when and where to visit, know that most families choose the sunny leeward side of the island, staying around Kailua-Kona or on the South Kohala coast. The windward side of the Big Island gets more rain year-round and higher waves in winter, which can nix swimming. Year-round, vog (volcanic smog) can be a factor island-wide. Sometimes the air pollution is negligible, but at other times its health effects can be hazardous, especially for young children and pregnant women.

Resources

Travel with Children (published by Lonely Planet) Loaded with valuable tips and amusing tales, especially for first-time parents.

Lonely Planet (www.lonelyplanet.com) Ask questions and get advice from other travelers on the Thorn Tree's online 'Kids to Go' forum.

Go Hawaii (www.gohawaii.com) The state's official tourism site lists family-friendly activities, special events and more – just search the site using terms like 'kids' or 'family'.

Need to Know

- **Baby food and formula** Sold at supermarkets and pharmacies.
- **Babysitting** Ask your hotel concierge; some resorts offer day-care programs and kids' activity clubs.
- **Breastfeeding** Done discreetly (cover up) or in private.
- **Car seats** Reserve in advance through car-rental companies or Baby's Away.
- **Changing facilities** Ubiquitous in public restrooms except at beaches.
- **Cribs** Book ahead for rentals from Baby's Away.
- **Diapers (nappies)** Sold everywhere (eg supermarkets, pharmacies, convenience stores).
- **Health** Keep hydrated and wear sunscreen. Be careful when hiking over sharp *a'a* lava. Follow ocean safety rules and talk to lifeguards before getting in the water.
- **Highchairs & kids' menus** Available at most sit-down restaurants, except top-end dining rooms.
- **Strollers** Bring from home or reserve rentals with Baby's Away.

What to Pack

Hawai'i's small-town vibe means that almost no place – apart from star chef's restaurants and five-star resorts – is formal, whether in attitude or attire. You can let your kids wear T-shirts, shorts and rubbah slippah (flip-flops) just about anywhere. When visiting Hawai'i Volcanoes National Park and the island's windward side, rain gear and a sweater or fleece jacket will come in handy – those areas experience some wacky weather.

At tourist convenience shops, such as the ABC Store, you can buy inexpensive water-sports equipment (eg floaties, snorkel sets, bodyboards). In Kailua-Kona, Snorkel Bob's (p39) rents and sells all kinds of watersports gear for kids, from reef shoes to snorkel masks. If you do forget some critical item from home, **Baby's Away** (www.babysaway.com) rents cribs, strollers, car seats, backpacks, beach toys and more.

Is My Child Old Enough?

Although parents will find plenty of outdoor family fun for all ages on Hawai'i, some activities require that children be of a certain age, height or weight to participate. Always ask about restrictions when making reservations to avoid disappointment – and tears.

○ **To learn to surf** Kids who can swim comfortably in the ocean are candidates for lessons. Teens can usually join group lessons; younger kids may be required to take private lessons.

○ **To take a boat tour** Depending on the outfit and type of watercraft, tours sometimes set minimum ages, usually from four to eight years. Larger boats might allow tots as young as two to ride along.

○ **To summit Mauna Kea** Not advised for children under age 16 due to high-altitude health hazards.

○ **To ride in a helicopter** Most tour companies set minimum ages (eg two to 12 years) and sometimes also minimum body weights (eg 35lb). Toddlers must be strapped into their own seat and pay full fare.

○ **To go ziplining** Minimum age requirements range from five to 12 years, depending on the company. Participants must also meet weight minimums (usually 50lb to 80lb).

○ **To ride a horse** For trail rides the minimum age ranges from seven to 10 years, depending on the outfitter and if your child has riding experience. Short pony rides may be offered for younger kids.

The Best...
Children's Highlights

1 Three Ring Ranch Exotic Animal Sanctuary (p39)

2 Ocean Rider Seahorse Farm (p85)

3 'Imiloa Astronomy Center of Hawai'i (p172)

4 Pana'ewa Rainforest Zoo & Gardens (p172)

5 Hawai'i Volcanoes National Park Junior Ranger Program (p208)

6 Astronaut Ellison S Onizuka Space Center (p85)

The Natural World

Scuba diving, Kaiwi Point (p81)

DOUG PERRINE/GETTY IMA

Calling this island big is no misnomer: Hawai'i claims twice as much land as the other Hawaiian Islands combined. Its landscape is so diverse that its alpine and lava deserts, wet tropical and dry forests, montane bogs and other ecosystems support the highest concentration of life-zone types on earth. Stewardship of these natural resources is a traditional Hawaiian value, reflected in aloha 'aina — love and respect for the land.

The Land

Myth and science dramatically mix on the Big Island, where plate tectonics and Pele, goddess of fire and volcanoes, conspire to create a powerfully majestic landscape.

Hawaiian volcanoes are created by a rising column of molten rock — a 'hot spot' — under the Pacific Plate. As the plate moves northwest a few inches each year, magma pierces upward through the plate's crust buried deep on the ocean floor, creating volcanoes. Straddling the hot spot today, the Big Island's Kilauea is the world's most active volcano.

Hawaiian volcanoes are shield volcanoes that erupt with effusive lava to create gently sloped, dome-shaped mountains. But they can also have a more explosive side, as Kilauea dramatically reminded onlookers and scientists in 2008. Since its current eruption began in 1983, Kilauea has added more than 500 acres of new land to the Big Island.

In Hawai'i Volcanoes National Park and elsewhere, you can observe hardened lava flows pierced by vents belching malodorous sulfur and walk through spectacular tubes, where past rivers of lava have cooled unevenly. If Pele is feeling frisky, you might witness lava flow, billowing clouds of steam during the day and glowing like hellfire at night.

Wildlife

Born of barren lava flows, the Hawaiian Islands were originally populated only by plants and animals that could traverse the Pacific – for example, seeds clinging to a bird's feather or fern spores that drifted thousands of miles through the air. This evolutionary process accounts for the fact that over 90% of Hawaii's flora and fauna species are endemic (that is, unique to the islands), and also explains why they fare so poorly against invasive species and human-caused environmental changes. Unfortunately, Hawaii holds the ignominious title of being the 'endangered species capital of the world.'

Animals

Scientists estimate that successful species were established on the Hawaiian Islands maybe once every 70,000 years – and these included no amphibians, no mosquitoes and only two mammals, both now endangered: the Hawaiian hoary bat and the Hawaiian monk seal. The former are rarely seen, but the latter are increasingly hauling out onto Hawai'i's beaches (it's illegal to get closer than 50yd).

Up to 10,000 migrating North Pacific humpback whales come to Hawaiian waters for calving each winter. The world's fifth-largest whale, the endangered humpback can reach lengths of 45ft and weigh up to 50 tons. Other whales (such as blue and fin whales) also pass through. By federal law, you may not approach a whale in Hawaiian waters nearer than 100yd.

Show-stealing spinner dolphins are named for their acrobatic leaps from the water. These nocturnal feeders come into sheltered bays during the day to rest, especially along the Kona Coast. Because they are extremely sensitive to human disturbance, federal guidelines recommend that swimmers do not approach any wild dolphins closer than 50yd.

Hawai'i's coral reefs teem with over 500 tropical fish species, including bright yellow tangs; striped butterflyfish and Moorish Idols; silver needlefish and neon-colored wrasse, which change sex (and color) as they mature. Endangered *honu* (green sea turtles), hawksbill and leatherback turtles also swim in Hawai'i's waters and bask on sunny beaches (keep back at least 20ft on land, 50yd in the water).

Hawaii's endemic birds are often spectacular examples of adaptive radiation, but two-thirds are already extinct due to predatory feral animals (like mongooses and pigs) and diseases introduced by non-native birds. In Hawai'i Volcanoes National Park, you can catch sight of brightly colored Hawaiian honeycreepers, the royal 'io (Hawaiian hawk) and the endangered nene (Hawaiian goose), Hawaii's official state bird.

The Best...
Big Island
Nature
Escapes

Plants

Extravagantly diverse flora occupies every island niche. Of course, what you'll see today is not what the first Polynesians or ancient Hawaiians saw. Over half of native forests have already disappeared, mainly due to logging, agriculture and invasive plants. Most 'Hawaiian' agricultural products were originally exotic imports – including papayas, pineapples, mangoes, macadamia nuts and coffee.

In densely populated areas such as Kailua-Kona, you'll notice many of the non-native flowering plants grown in other tropical places around the world (bird of paradise, blood-red anthurium, orchids etc). But head inland to native forests and you'll see mighty koa and silver-tinged *kukui* (candlenut) trees forming a canopy over a mix of endemic flora. Out on lava flows, look for low-lying shrubs bursting with *ohelo* berries, emerald-green *hapu'u* (tree ferns) and blossoming ohia plants.

On the slopes of Mauna Kea, distinctive flora includes the yellow-flowered *mamane* tree and tiny-leafed *pukiawe* shrub with its red, pink and white berries. Back down by the beach, native coastal plants to look for include *'ilima,* its delicate orange-yellow flowers often strung into lei; pink-flowering *pohuehue* (beach morning-glory) with its dark green, glossy leaves; and *naupaka* shrubs, whose pinkish-white flowers look as if they've been torn in half (by a broken-hearted lover, according to Hawaiian legend).

Outdoor Adventures

Kayaking, Kealakekua Bay (p73)

DANITA DELIMONT/GETTY IMAGES ©

Everyone finds their own thrilling way to play outdoors on Hawai'i, whether it's exploring a lava tube or ziplining through the rainforest. How about nighttime scuba diving with manta rays or stargazing atop a volcano? Paddling a kayak, snorkeling with tropical fish and surfing are other diversions at sea, or visit sacred valleys on foot or horseback to get in touch with Hawai'i's true nature.

At Sea

With Hawai'i's long and strong tradition of communing with the ocean, you're sure to get wet on your Big Island vacation. Even if you've never snorkeled or surfed, this is a great place to start, with experienced outfitters on both sides of the island. Not much advance planning is required, save checking the weather – just get up and *go*.

Beaches & Swimming

On Hawai'i, coastal strands come in a rainbow of hues and infinite textures – with sand sparkling white, tawny, black, charcoal or green, and scattered with sea-glass, pebbles and boulders or cratered with lava-rock tide pools.

By law, all beaches in Hawaii are open to the public below the high-tide line. Private landowners can prevent access to their shoreline over land, but not by watercraft. Resort hotels often provide public beach access with limited parking spots, occasionally charging a small fee.

West Hawai'i is most inviting for swimming, including crescent-shaped Mauna Kea Beach and white-sand Manini'owali Beach with its brilliant turquoise waters, or try a short lap in Kiholo Bay's lava tube. East Hawai'i is generally rougher and mostly only for strong swimmers, although local families can be found at Hilo's beaches.

Bodyboarding

Bodyboarding (aka boogie boarding) rivals surfing and stand up paddling as the most popular way to ride Hawai'i's waves. Winter brings the best action to West Hawai'i at Hapuna Beach State Park, White (Magic) Sands Beach Park, Honoli'i Beach Park and Kekaha Kai (Kona Coast) State Park beaches, particularly Manini'owali (Kua Bay). If you really know what you're doing, venture to Puna's Isaac Hale Kepo'okalani Beach Park or Hilo's Honoli'i Beach Park, both in East Hawai'i.

Diving

Hawai'i's underwater scenery is every bit the equal of what's on land. Ocean temperatures are perfect for scuba diving, averaging 72°F to 80°F at the surface year-round. Even better is the visibility, especially in the calm waters along the Kona Coast, ideally during September and October.

About 700 fish species call these waters home, as do spinner dolphins, sea turtles and moray eels, so you won't want for variety – even during on-shore dives. If you've dreamed of diving, this is a perfect spot to learn, with a smorgasbord of dive operators offering open-water certification courses and beginners' dive experiences.

Among the most popular dive spots on the island is Ka'awaloa Cove in Kealakekua Bay. Other good West Hawai'i sites include Turtle Pinnacle, Harlequin, Aquarium and Suck 'Em Up along the Kona Coast, and Puako further north in Kohala. The manta ray night dive is a must, so book early. River runoff on the Hilo side usually means cloudy visibility, but Pohoiki in Puna – East Hawai'i's best site – teems with marine life.

For more tips, check out Lonely Planet's *Diving & Snorkeling Hawaii*.

Fishing

The Kona Coast is a deep-sea fishing fantasy: at least one 'grander' (1000lb or more) marlin is reeled in every year. With over 100 boat and kayak fishing charter companies leaving from Honokohau Harbor, the next one could be yours. These waters are also

Dive Safely & Responsibly

The popularity of diving puts immense pressure on many of Hawai'i's dive sites. Here's how you can help:

○ Conserve Hawai'i's reef and marine ecosystems by using minimal-impact diving techniques.

○ Respect Native Hawaiian sacred places, including fishing grounds.

○ Do not feed any wildlife or disturb marine animals. It's illegal to come within 50yd of sea turtles, dolphins or Hawaiian monk seals, or within 100yd of whales. Don't ride on the backs of sea turtles, as this causes them great anxiety.

Warning! Don't go for a helicopter or plane ride or ascend to high altitudes (eg Mauna Kea, Mauna Loa) for at least 24 hours before or after scuba diving.

rich with ahi (yellowfin tuna) and *aku* (bonito or skipjack tuna), swordfish and mahimahi (dolphinfish). If you get to keep your catch, harborside Bite Me Fish Market Bar & Grill will cook it for you.

Kayaking

The warm, calm seas hugging the Kona Coast, combined with hidden coves and turquoise, fish-filled waters, make Hawai'i prime sea-kayaking turf. (Forget rivers – there are none.) Variants on the sport – fishing, surfing and sailing – are all possibilities, with guides and outfitters along the Kona and Kohala Coasts offering rentals and tours.

Kealakekua Bay, with its smooth waters and abundance of fish and spinner dolphins, is one of the state's most popular kayaking spots. Up north, the pristine coastline around Kiholo Bay offers solitude, while the reefs around Puako beckon paddlers to don their masks.

Snorkeling

On the Big Island, you can step from the sand into crystal tropical waters teeming with vibrant coral and reef fish. Popular West Hawai'i snorkeling spots – like Kealakekua Bay and Kahalu'u Beach Park – are also teeming with tourists. To escape the crowds, go in the early morning (when conditions are best anyway), drive further up or down the coast (like to Beach 69 or Puako), or hike or kayak to more remote spots. In East Hawai'i, snorkelers can drive right up to Hilo's Richardson Ocean Park or detour down to Kapoho in Puna.

Always follow coral-reef etiquette: don't touch any coral, which are living organisms; watch your fins to avoid stirring up sand and breaking off pieces of coral; and finally, don't feed the fish. Snorkel gear rental costs around $10/25 per day/week, depending on quality. Most places rent prescription masks, which are essential for the myopic. Reef shoes are recommended for lava-lined shores.

Catamaran and Zodiac raft tours will transport you to prime spots and provide gear and food. On the Kona Coast, tours leaving from Keauhou Bay (instead of in-town Kailua Pier, or Honokohau Harbor north nearer the airprot) have shorter rides to Kealakekua Bay, meaning more snorkel time for you. Book in advance, especially during high season and for nighttime snorkeling with manta rays.

Surfing & Stand Up Paddling (SUP)

Ancient Hawaiians invented surfing (calling it *he'e nalu,* 'wave sliding'). On Hawai'i today, surfing is its own intense subculture as well as a part of everyday island life. Generally, winter northern swells are bigger and leeward breaks are cleaner. Check local tides, weather and swells online with *Hawaii Surf News* (www.hawaiisurfnews.com).

Along the Kona Coast, surf at Kahalu'u Beach Park, Banyans and Lymans, all south of Kailua-Kona, and Pine Trees near Wawaloli (OTEC) Beach. Down south in Ka'u, Kawa Bay has a left break that locals love. Consistent east-side spots are Honoli'i Cove in Hilo and Waipi'o Bay. Puna's Pohoiki Bay is much hairier, but experienced surfers will dig the reef breaks at Isaac Kepo'okalani Hale Beach Park.

The Best...
Big Island Adventure Tours

1 Lava boat tour in Puna (p203)

2 Ziplining in Kohala (p117)

3 Diving and snorkeling with manta rays along the Kona Coast (p42)

4 Mauna Kea stargazing (p138)

5 Sea kayaking during winter whale-watching season (p81)

Locals are usually willing to share surf spots that have become popular tourist destinations but they reserve the right to protect other 'secret' surf grounds. As a newbie in the lineup, don't expect to get every wave that comes your way. There's a definite pecking order and tourists are at the bottom.

The latest trend in surfing is stand up paddling (SUP) – which, as the name implies, means standing on the surfboard and using a paddle to propel yourself along flat water or waves. It takes coordination to learn, but it's easier than regular surfing.

Both surfboard and SUP rentals and lessons are widely available on the Kona and Kohala Coasts, and from a few outfitters in Hilo.

Whale-Watching

During their annual 6000-mile round-trip between Alaska and Hawaii – one of the longest migration journeys of any mammal – humpback whales breed, calve and nurse in the Big Island's nearshore waters between December and April.

Over 60% of the North Pacific humpback population winters in the Hawaiian Islands, so you'll have a good chance of seeing their acrobatics on a cruise, while kayaking or even from shore – don't forget binoculars. Tours run year-round from Kailua-Kona to view sperm, melon-headed, pilot and pygmy killer whales and, of course, dolphins.

On Land

Hawai'i has 11 of the world's 13 ecosystems, filled with exotic flora and fauna waiting to be seen. The island's unique geology offers all sorts of land-based adventures and it's a premier hiking destination. Travelers should pack a good LED flashlight for cave explorations, a rainproof jacket and binoculars for lava viewing and wildlife-watching.

Caving

Being the youngest Hawaiian Island and still volcanically active, Hawai'i is a caving hotspot, claiming six of the world's 10 longest lava tubes. No visit to the island is complete without exploring their dark, mysterious depths. In Puna you can tour parts of the Kazumura Cave, the world's longest and deepest lava tube. In Ka'u, the Kula Kai Caverns are geological wonders.

Cycling & Mountain Biking

Road cycling is tricky here, with narrow, winding roads light on shoulders. The Ironman route on Hwy 19 north of Kailua-Kona is an exception, and bike rentals are most readily available in Kailua-Kona. The **Hawai'i Cycling Club** (www.hawaiicyclingclub.com) offers information on island-wide cycling routes and events. Kona-based outfitter **Orchid Isle Bicyling** (☏808-327-0087; www.orchidislebicycling.com) organizes daily cycling tours and multiday vacations.

Golf

While playing on a championship course at a Kona or Kohala beach resort in the 'Golf Capital of Hawaii' can cost over $200 a round, Hawai'i's much more affordable municipal courses still boast scenery you probably can't get back home. Afternoon 'twilight' tee times are usually heavily discounted. Club rentals are sometimes available.

Visit www.teetimeshawaii.com for course descriptions and book-ahead tee times.

Helicopter & Air Tours

Flying over the world's most active volcano and gushing waterfalls provides unforgettable vantages you simply can't get any other way. That said, 'flightseeing' tours negatively impact Hawai'i's natural environment, both in noise generated and fuel burned.

Expensive helicopter tours are all the hype, but fixed-wing planes offer a smoother, quieter ride. Questions you should ask before booking either include: Do all passengers have a 360-degree view? Are noise-cancelling headsets provided? For the best views, sit up front.

Helicopter tours fly if it's cloudy, but not if it's raining – wait for a clear day, which is more likely during summer. Most tour companies offer online discounts (book in advance).

Recommended flightseeing outfitters include the following:

Blue Hawaiian Helicopters (☏800-745-2583; www.bluehawaiian.com) Reliable, dependable and high-volume company; departures from Waikoloa and Hilo.

Iolani Air (☏808-329-0018; www.iolaniair.com) Flightseeing tours in small prop planes take off from Kona and Hilo.

Paradise Helicopters (☏866-876-7422, 969-7392; http://paradisecopters.com) More personalized helicopter tours leave from Kona and Hilo.

Safari Helicopters (☏800-326-3356, 969-1259; www.safarihelicopters.com) Tours of East Hawai'i's volcanoes and coastline depart from Hilo.

Hiking

From an afternoon stroll through a lava tube to a multiday summit trek, the Big Island has wild walks. Hawai'i Volcanoes National Park boasts the most varied trails, but you can also hike to secluded Kona Coast beaches or easily explore petroglyph fields without leaving West Hawai'i.

Diving through an underwater cavern
BRANDON SAWAYA/GETTY IMAGES ©

Hike Safely & Responsibly

You don't have to worry about snakes, wild animals or poison ivy on Hawai'i. What you *do* have to worry about is lava – from ankle-twisting *'a'a* (slow-flowing rough and jagged lava) and toxic fumes to collapsing lava benches and hellishly hot conditions. Heed all posted warnings and hike with a buddy. Observe *kapu* (no trespassing) signs (residents of Waipi'o Valley are particularly territorial).

If you plan to hike anywhere here, sturdy, ankle-high footwear with good traction is a must. Flash floods are a real danger in many of the steep, narrow valleys that require stream crossings (yes, including Waipi'o Valley). You'll need to come prepared for winter mountaineering conditions if hiking to the summit of Mauna Loa or Mauna Kea is in your sights.

Camping permits are required for all overnight hikes, including in Hawai'i Volcanoes National Park and Waimanu Valley. It's best to bring your own backpacking gear from home. For anything else you need (or forgot to pack), try the Hawaii Forest & Trail (p81) headquarters in Kailua-Kona.

Both Hawaii Forest & Trail and Hawaiian Walkways (p156) offer recommendable guided hiking tours. Helpful resources for independent hikers include the following:

Na Ala Hele (www.hawaiitrails.org) Online maps and directions for public-access trails, including the long-distance Ala Kahakai National Historic Trail.

Sierra Club – Moku Loa Group (www.hi.sierraclub.org/Hawaii/outings.html; donation per hike for nonmembers $3) Island-wide group day hikes and volunteer opportunities doing trail maintenance and ecological restoration.

Horseback Riding

In Hawai'i's hilly green pastures, *paniolo* (cowboys) wrangle cattle and ride the range. Up in North Kohala and Waimea especially, as well as around Waipi'o Valley, you can arrange trail and pony rides and customized horseback tours. Book ahead.

Stargazing

From atop Mauna Kea, where international superpowered telescopes are trained on the heavens, scientists explore our universe. You can too – on Mauna Kea itself, with the eye-opening nightly stargazing program at the visitor information station. Kids under 16 can participate, but it's recommended they don't go to the summit.

Ziplining

If you're keen to zoom along suspended cables while the landscape whizzes by far below, several zipline outfitters now dot the island. Tours offer a totally different perspective on the island's forests, waterfalls and coastline. Plan on spending half a day on an adrenaline-pumping tour (minimum age and weight requirements apply).

Survival
Guide

Beach in Kona
GLOWIMAGES/GETTY IMAGES ©

A-Z
Directory

●●●

Accommodations

Rates

The following price ranges are for a double room with private bathroom in high season. Unless otherwise stated, taxes of 13.41% aren't included.

○ **$** under $100

○ **$$** $100 to $200

○ **$$$** over $200

Reservations

Availability is scarcer during high season (mid-December through March or April, and June through August), around major holidays and special events. Book months in advance for peak periods, when room rates rise.

Amenities

○ Accommodations offering online computer terminals for guests are designated with the internet icon (**@**). An hourly fee may apply (eg at hotel business centers).

○ The wi-fi icon (**⧉**) indicates wireless internet access; a daily fee may apply. Look for free wi-fi in common areas (eg hotel lobby, poolside).

○ A surprising number of hotels offer only wired in-room access; getting online may cost $12 or more per 24 hours.

○ Air-conditioning (**❄**) is a standard amenity at most resorts. At some hotels, condos, hostels, B&Bs and vacation rentals, only fans may be provided.

Hotels & Resorts

○ Ranging from no-frills motels to mega beach resorts, hotels typically offer full-time staff, daily housekeeping and amenities such as swimming pools (**⛱**), bars and restaurants.

○ 'Rack rates' refer to the the highest published rates. Hotels often hugely undercut rack rates to book as close to capacity as possible. Reserve ahead online for discounts.

○ At some hotels, rates depend mainly on the view. Even partial ocean views cost 50% to 100% more than garden or mountain (or parking lot) views.

○ Many hotel properties are entirely nonsmoking by law, with high penalty fees for noncompliance. If you need a smoking room, you must specifically request one (they're rarely available).

Condominiums

○ Condos typically include separate bedroom(s), a full kitchen and a washer/dryer. Most condos are located around Kailua-Kona and bookable online. Units are privately owned and inconsistent in quality.

○ Most condos require multiple-night minimum stays and offer weekly discounts. Condos are best for weekly or monthly stays; otherwise, the mandatory cleaning fee (averaging $75 to $150) negates any savings.

B&Bs, Inns & Guesthouses

○ Hawai'i's B&Bs either serve breakfast or provide groceries for guests to prepare their own. Inns and guesthouses typically do not offer breakfast. Apartment-style amenities might include a kitchenette.

○ Most B&Bs, inns and guesthouses require multiple-night stays. Always book ahead. Drop-in guests are discouraged and same-day reservations are hard to get.

○ Rates typically cover two guests, with extra-person surcharges of $15 to $35. Children may not be allowed.

○ Besides **Vacation Rentals by Owner** (www.vrbo.com), **HomeAway** (www.homeaway.

Book Your Stay Online

For more accommodations reviews by Lonely Planet authors, check out http://hotels.lonely planet.com. You'll find independent reviews, as well as recommendations on the best places to stay. Best of all, you can book online.

com) and **Air B&B** (www. airbnb.com), check online listings with the following:

Affordable Paradise (📞 808-261-1693; www. affordable-paradise.com)

Hawaii's Best B&Bs (📞 808-885-4550; www. bestbnb.com)

Hawaii Island B&B Association (www.stayhawaii. com)

Camping & Cabins

The island's best camping and cabins are inside Hawai'i Volcanoes National Park. State and county parks run the gamut; in general, easy-access roadside spots, especially at county beach parks, can be hangouts for drunkards and druggies.

Hawaii State Parks (📞 808-961-9540; https:// camping.ehawaii.gov/camping/ welcome.html; 75 Aupuni St, Room 204, Hilo; ⊘8am-3:30pm Mon-Fri) Advance state-park camping permits are required. Nonresident fees are $18 per campsite for up to six people ($3 for each additional person), $50 per A-frame shelter and $80 to $90 per cabin.

County of Hawai'i Department of Parks & Recreation (📞 808-961-8311; https://hawaiicounty. ehawaii.gov/camping/welcome. html; 101 Pauahi St, Suite 6, Hilo; ⊘7:45am-4:30pm Mon-Fri) Advance county-park camping permits are required. Nonresident campsite fee is $20 per person per night.

Happy Campers Hawaii (📞 808-896-8777; www. happycampershawaii.com; rental per day from $120) Rents VW campervans with kitchenettes that can sleep up to four people, but you'll need separate campsite reservations. Pick-ups and drop-offs in Hilo (free airport shuttle service).

Climate

Location
The leeward (western) side of the island is usually hot and dry, while the windward (northeastern) side receives abundant rainfall year-round.

Elevation
The mountainous upcountry is noticeably cooler and wetter. This elevation difference is most marked on Mauna Kea and Mauna Loa, where overnight temperatures dip below freezing.

Seasons
When you're most likely to see major storms and flooding, the winter wet season (December to March) is rainier than the summer dry season.

Climate

Hilo
°C/°F **Temp**

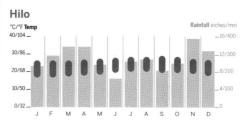

Kailua-Kona
°C/°F **Temp**

Mauna Key
°C/°F **Temp**

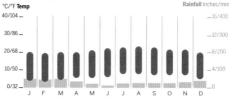

Customs Regulations

Non-US citizens and permanent residents may import the following duty-free:

- 1L of liquor (if you're over 21 years old)

- 200 cigarettes (1 carton) or 100 non-Cuban cigars (if you're over 18)

- $100 worth of gifts

Hawaii has stringent restrictions against importing any fresh fruits and plants. Because Hawaii is a rabies-free state, the pet quarantine laws are draconian.

Before leaving Hawaii, make sure that any fresh flowers or produce has been commercially packaged and approved for travel (or else you'll be forced to surrender those pineapples at the airport).

Discount Cards

Children, students, seniors, state residents and active and retired military personnel usually receive discounts at museums and attractions. All but children need to present valid ID proving their status.

Electricity

120V/60Hz

120V/60Hz

Food

Meals are early and start on the dot in Hawaii: typically 6am breakfast, noon lunch and 6pm dinner. Dress codes are relaxed (called 'island casual'), with no jackets or ties normally required. Men can get away with an aloha shirt and neat khaki or golf shorts at most resort restaurants.

The following price ranges refer to an average main course at dinner in a restaurant (lunch is usually much cheaper) or a set meal at a casual takeout eatery. Unless otherwise stated, taxes and tip are not included.

- **$** under $10

- **$$** $10 to $20

- **$$$** over $20

Gay & Lesbian Travelers

The state of Hawaii has strong minority protections and a constitutional guarantee of privacy that extends to sexual behavior between consenting adults. Locals tend to be private about their personal lives, so you will not see much public hand-holding or open displays of affection. Everyday LGBTQ life is low-key, and there's no 'scene' to speak of – it's more about picnics and potlucks, not nightclubs.

Connect with the following community resources:

Gay Hawaii (www.gayhawaii. com) Free website.

Odyssey Magazine Hawaii (www.odysseyhawaii.com) Free statewide monthly publication, archived free online.

Out in Hawaii (www.outinhawaii.com) Free website.

Out Traveler (www.out-traveler.com) Gay-oriented Hawaii travel articles free online.

Purple Roofs (http://purpleroofs.com) Directory of gay-owned and gay-friendly B&Bs, vacation rentals, guesthouses and hotels.

Pacific Ocean Holidays (☏ 808-923-2400; www.gayhawaiivacations.com) Personalized vacation packages for gay and lesbian travelers.

Internet Access

In this guide, the wi-fi icon (☏) indicates that wi-fi is available. The internet icon (@) indicates that there's an online computer for guests or customers. Either could be free or fee-based.

● Wi-fi is now available at many accommodations; it's usually free at B&Bs, condos and vacation rentals.

● Bigger towns have at least one coffee shop offering free wi-fi or a pay-as-you-go internet cafe charging around $6 to $12 per hour.

Language

Hawaii has two official languages: English and Hawaiian. There's also an unofficial vernacular, called pidgin, a creole language whose colorful vocabulary permeates everyday local speech. While Hawaiian's multisyllabic, vowel-heavy words may look daunting, the pronunciation is actually quite straightforward.

Legal Matters

If you are arrested, you have the right to an attorney; if you can't afford one, a public defender will be provided free. The **Hawaii State Bar Association** (☏808-930-0872; www.hawaiilawyerreferral.com) makes attorney referrals.

In addition to Hawaii's road rules (see p292), be mindful of the following laws:

● Bars, clubs and liquor stores may require photo ID to prove you're of legal age (21 years) to buy alcohol. You must be 18 years old to buy tobacco.

● Drinking alcohol anywhere other than at a private residence, hotel room or licensed premises (eg bar, restaurant) is illegal, which puts beach parks off-limits.

● Possessing marijuana or nonprescription narcotics, hitchhiking and public nudity are all illegal in Hawaii.

● Smoking is generally prohibited in all public spaces, including airports, bars, restaurants and businesses.

Maps

Published by **University of Hawai'i Press** (www.uhpress.hawaii.edu), the fold-out, full-color topographic *Map of Hawai'i* ($4.95) details every bay, beach and gulch on the Big Island. **Franko Maps** (www.frankosmaps.com) makes full-color, waterproof and rip-proof laminated island maps showing beaches, snorkeling and diving spots, with a nifty guide to tropical fish. For exploring off the beaten path, Odyssey Publishing's Ready Mapbook series offers comprehensive road and street atlases for East Hawai'i and West Hawai'i ($16.50 each).

Money

ATMs

● ATMs are available 24/7 at most banks, convenience stores, shopping centers and airports.

● Expect a minimum surcharge of $2.25 per transaction, plus any fees charged by your home bank.

● Most ATMs are connected to international networks (eg Plus, Cirrus) and offer decent exchange rates.

Hawai'i vs Hawaii

The *'okina* punctuation mark (') is the Hawaiian language's glottal stop, which determines the pronunciation and meaning of words. In this guide, Hawai'i (with the *'okina*) refers to the island of Hawai'i (the Big Island), to ancient Hawai'i and to the Kingdom of Hawai'i pre-statehood. Hawaii (without the *'okina*) refers to the US state.

285

- Hawaii's two largest banks are **Bank of Hawaii** (www.boh.com) and **First Hawaiian Bank** (www.fhb.com).

Checks

Out-of-state personal checks are generally not accepted, except at some privately owned lodgings (eg B&Bs, condos, vacation rentals).

Credit Cards

Major credit cards are widely accepted. Typically they're required for car rentals, hotel reservations, buying tickets etc. B&Bs, condos and vacation rentals may refuse credit cards or else add a 3% surcharge.

Taxes

A 4.17% state sales tax is tacked onto virtually everything, including meals, groceries and car rentals (which also entail additional state and local taxes). Lodging taxes total 13.41%.

Tipping

Tipping is *not* optional; only withhold tips in cases of outrageously bad service.

Airport skycaps & hotel porters $2 to $3 per bag, minimum per cart $5

Bartenders 15% to 20% per round, minimum $1 per drink

Housekeeping staff $2 to $5 per night, left under card provided; more if you're messy

Parking valets At least $2 when handed your car keys

Restaurant servers & room service 15% to 20%, unless a gratuity is already charged

Taxi drivers 15% of metered fare, rounded up to next dollar

Traveler's Checks

Rather archaic nowadays, traveler's checks in US dollars are still accepted like cash at bigger tourist-oriented businesses in Hawaii, such as resort hotels. Smaller businesses such as grocery stores usually refuse them.

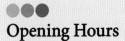

Opening Hours

Banks 8:30am to 4pm Monday to Friday, some to 6pm Friday; 9am to noon or 1pm Saturday

Bars & clubs noon to midnight daily, some to 2am Friday and Saturday

Businesses (general) & government offices 8:30am to 4:30pm Monday to Friday, some post offices also 9am to noon Saturday

Restaurants breakfast 6am to 10am, lunch 11:30am to 2pm, dinner 5pm to 9:30pm

Shops 9am to 5pm Monday to Saturday, some also noon to 5pm Sunday; major shopping areas and malls keep extended hours

Public Holidays

On the following national holidays, banks, schools and government offices (including post offices) close, and transportation, museums and other services operate on a Sunday schedule. Holidays falling on a weekend are usually observed the following Monday.

New Year's Day January 1

Martin Luther King Jr Day Third Monday in January

Presidents' Day Third Monday in February

Prince Kuhio Day March 26

Good Friday Friday before Easter Sunday (in March or April)

Memorial Day Last Monday in May

King Kamehameha Day June 11

Independence Day July 4

Statehood Day Third Friday in August

Labor Day First Monday in September

Columbus Day Second Monday in October

Veterans Day November 11

Thanksgiving Fourth Thursday in November

Christmas Day December 25

Safe Travel

For visitors who have an accident or become victims of crimes, the **Visitor Aloha Society of Hawaii** (VASH; ☎808-926-8274; www.visitoralohasocietyofhawaii.org) offers short-term nonmonetary assistance.

Hazards & Trespassing

Flash floods, rock falls, tsunami, earthquakes, volcanic eruptions, shark attacks, jellyfish stings and yes, even possibly getting brained by a falling coconut — the potential dangers in Hawaii might seem alarming at first. But like the old saying goes, statistically you're more likely to get hurt crossing the street at home.

Of course, that's not to say that you shouldn't be careful. First educate yourself about potential risks to your health and safety. This advice becomes even more important when you're engaged in outdoor activities in a new and unfamiliar natural environment, whether that's a snorkeling spot, a jungle waterfall, a high-altitude mountain or an active (and thus unpredictable) volcanic eruption zone.

Wherever you choose to explore, remember to mind your manners and watch your step. Hawaii has strict laws about trespassing on both private land and government land not intended for public use. Trespassing is always illegal, no matter how many other people you see doing it. Respect all 'Kapu' or 'No Trespassing' signs.

Always seek explicit permission from the land owner or local officials before venturing onto private or government land closed to the public, regardless of whether it is fenced or signposted as such. Doing so not only respects the *kuleana* (rights) of residents and the sacredness of the land, but also helps ensure your own safety.

Practicalities

- **Newspapers** Major dailies: *Hawaii Tribune-Herald* (p51); *West Hawaii Today* (p51); *Honolulu Star-Advertiser* (www.staradvertiser.com)

- **Radio** About 25 FM and five AM radio stations; National Public Radio (NPR) at lower end of FM dial

- **Time** Hawaii-Aleutian Standard Time (HST) is UTC-10. Hawaii doesn't observe Daylight Saving Time (DST). 'Island time' means taking things at a slower pace or being late.

- **TV & DVD** All major US TV networks and cable channels; DVDs coded region 1 (US and Canada only)

- **Weights & measures** Imperial system (except 1 US gallon = 3.79L)

Theft & Violence

The islands are notorious for thefts from parked cars, especially rentals (which are obviously tagged with bar-code stickers). Thieves can pop a trunk or pull out a door-lock assembly within seconds. They strike not only at remote trailheads when you've gone for a hike, but also at crowded beach and hotel parking lots where you'd expect safety in numbers.

As much as possible, do not leave anything valuable in your parked car. If you must, pack all valuables out of sight before arriving at your destination. Some locals leave their car doors unlocked with the windows rolled down to discourage break-ins and avoid costly damages (eg broken windows).

Stay attuned to the vibe on any beaches at night, and in places like roadside county parks, where drunks and drug users sometimes hang out. In rural areas of the island, there may be pockets of resentment against tourists, so be respectful as you explore off the beaten path.

Tsunami

Hawai'i is always at risk of tsunami, which have killed more people statewide than all other natural disasters combined. Hawai'i's tsunami warning sirens are tested on the first working day of each month at 11:45am, using the yellow speakers mounted on telephone poles. If you hear them at any other time, head for higher ground away from the coast. Telephone directories have tsunami evacuation zone maps. Turn on the radio or TV and listen for news.

Telephone

Cell Phones

International travelers need a multiband GSM phone to make calls in the USA. Popping in a US prepaid

ℹ Important Numbers

- Emergency (police, fire, ambulance): ☎ 911
- Local directory assistance: ☎ 411
- Long-distance directory assistance: ☎ 1-(area code)-555-1212
- Toll-free directory assistance: ☎ 1-800-555-1212
- Operator: ☎ 0

rechargeable SIM card is usually cheaper than using your home network. SIM cards are available at telecommunications and electronics stores, which also sell inexpensive prepaid phones, including some airtime.

Among US cell-phone service providers, Verizon has the most extensive network; AT&T and Sprint get decent reception. Coverage is good in bigger towns but spotty or nonexistent in rural areas.

Dialing Codes

- All Hawaii phone numbers consist of a three-digit area code (808) followed by a seven-digit local number.
- To call long-distance from one island to another, dial 1 + 808 + local number.
- Always dial 1 before toll-free numbers (800, 888 etc). Some toll-free numbers only work within Hawaii or from the US mainland and Canada.
- To call Canada from Hawaii, dial 1 + area code + local

number (note international rates still apply).

- For all other international calls from Hawaii, dial 011 + country code + area code + local number.
- To call Hawaii from abroad, the international country code for the USA is 1.

Payphones & Phonecards

- Payphones are a dying breed, usually found at shopping centers, hotels, beaches, parks and other public places.
- Some payphones are coin-operated (local calls usually cost 50¢), while others only accept credit cards or phonecards.
- Private prepaid phonecards are available from convenience stores, supermarkets, pharmacies, etc.

●●● Tourist Information

101 Things To Do (www.101thingstodo.com/big-island) Free publication describing major attractions.

Big Island Visitors Bureau (Map p176; ☎ 808-961-5797, 800-648-2441; www.gohawaii.com/big-island; 250 Keawe St, Hilo) Basic info and brochures only.

This Week (www.thisweek.com) Free tourist publication with handy maps.

●●● Travelers with Disabilities

Accommodations

Major hotels are equipped with elevators, phones with TDD (telecommunications device for the deaf) and wheelchair-accessible rooms (which must be reserved in advance); most B&Bs and small hotels are probably not.

Guide & Service Dogs

Not subject to the general quarantine rules for pets if they meet the Department of Agriculture's minimum requirements (see http://hdoa.hawaii.gov/ai/aqs/guide-service-dogs for details). All animals must enter the state at Honolulu International Airport.

Tourist Information

For Hawaii-specific info on airports, all-terrain beach wheelchairs, transportation, medical and other support services, visit the **Disability & Communication Access Board** (☎ 808-586-8121; www.hawaii.gov/health/dcab/travel; Room 101, 919 Ala Moana Blvd, Honolulu) website. **Access Aloha Travel** (☎ 800-480-1143, 808-545-1143; www.accessalohatravel.com) is a full-service local travel agency.

Transportation

Rent wheelchair-accessible vans from **Wheelchair Getaways** (☎ 650-589-5554, 800-638-1912; www.wheelchairgetaways.com). Car-rental agencies may offer hand-controlled vehicles; reserve them well in advance. If you have a disability parking placard from home, bring it with you. Pu'uhonua O Hōnaunau National Historical Park and Hawai'i Volcanoes National Park lend wheelchairs free of charge.

●●● Visas

Double-check current visa and passport requirements *before* coming to the USA via the Visas section of the US **Department of State** (http://travel.state.gov) website and the Travel section of the **US Customs & Border Protection** (www.cbp.gov) website.

Currently under the US Visa Waiver Program (VWP), visas are not required for citizens of 37 countries for stays up to 90 days (no extensions) if they register online at least 72 hours before arrival with the **Electronic System for Travel Authorization** (ESTA; https://esta.cbp.dhs.gov/esta/), which costs $14. Canadian visitors are generally admitted visa-free for stays up to 182 days.

Upon arrival, the Department of Homeland Security (www.dhs.gov) requires that almost all foreign visitors (currently excluding most Canadian citizens) have their digital photograph taken and electronic (inkless) fingerprints scanned; the process typically takes less than a minute.

Transport

●●● Getting There & Away

Flights can be booked online at www.lonelyplanet.com/flights.

✈ Air

Hawaii is a competitive market for airfares, which vary tremendously by season, day of the week and demand. In general, return fares from the US mainland to Hawai'i cost from $400 (in low season from the West Coast) to $800 or more in high season from the East Coast.

Airports

There are few direct flights to the Big Island from the US mainland or Canada. Most domestic US and international flights arrive at Honolulu International Airport on O'ahu. Travelers must then catch an interisland flight to one of the Big Island's two primary airports, Kona or Hilo.

Interisland airfares vary wildly; expect to pay from $80 to $180 one way. Round-trip fares are typically double that without any discounts.

Usually, the earlier you book, the cheaper the fare.

Hilo International Airport (ITO; Map p170; ☏ 808-934-5838; http://hawaii.gov/ito; 2450 Kekuanaoa St, Hilo) Almost all flights to Hilo are interisland, mostly from Honolulu.

Kona International Airport at Keahole (KOA; Map p82; ☏ 808-327-9520; http://hawaii.gov/koa; 73-7200 Kupipi St) Mostly interisland and some US mainland and Canada flights arrive at Hawai'i's main airport, 7 miles northwest of Kailua-Kona.

Airlines

In addition to Hawaiian Airlines, the following carriers currently fly directly from the US mainland or Canada to the Big Island (usually to Kona): Air Canada, Alaska Airlines, American Airlines, Delta Air Lines, United Airlines, US Airways and WestJet.

The main interisland carrier – reliable Hawaiian Airlines – flies into Kona and Hilo. Commuter-oriented Mokulele Airlines flies into Kona and Kamuela (Waimea) airports with small turboprop planes. Another commuter carrier, Island Air, sometimes flies larger prop planes to Hilo.

Hawaiian Airlines (HA; ☏ 800-367-5320; www.hawaiianair.com)

Island Air (WP; ☏ 800-652-6541; www.islandair.com)

Mokulele Airlines (YV; ☏ 866-260-7070; www.mokuleleairlines.com)

●●●

Getting Around

🚌 Bus

It is possible to reach many places around the island with Hele-On Bus (p96), but services are infrequent, especially on Sundays and holidays. Always check the website or call for current schedules, routes and fares, which are all subject to change. Most routes originate from Mo'oheau Bus Terminal in downtown Hilo.

The one-way adult fare is $2 (including a free two-hour transfer), or buy a 10-ride ticket sheet ($15) or monthly pass ($60). You cannot board with a surfboard or bodyboard; luggage, backpacks, skateboards and bicycles are charged $1 each.

🚲 Bicycle

○ Cycling around the Big Island is only for the adventurous and very fit who can cope with rain, sun, strong headwinds, narrow roads and oblivious drivers.

○ In towns, cycling can be convenient for those comfortable riding in traffic. Dedicated bicycle lanes are scarce, however. The best places to rent, buy or repair bikes are in Kailua-Kona.

○ Bicyclists are generally required to follow the same state laws and road rules as vehicle drivers. Cyclists under age 16 are legally required to wear helmets.

🚗 Car

Automobile Associations

○ For 24-hour emergency roadside assistance, free maps and discounts on car rentals and accommodations, join the **American Automobile Association** (AAA; ☎593-2221, from Neighbor Islands 800-736-2886; www.hawaii.aaa.com; 1130 N Nimitz Hwy, Honolulu; ⊕9am-5pm Mon-Fri, to 2pm Sat).

○ AAA has reciprocal agreements with automobile associations in other countries (eg CAA); bring your membership card from home.

Driver's License

○ US citizens with a driver's license from another state or international visitors with a valid driver's license issued by their home country can legally drive a car in Hawaii if they are at least 18 years old.

○ Car-rental companies will generally accept foreign driver's licenses written in English with an accompanying

Road Distances & Times

To circumnavigate the island on the 225-mile Hawai'i Belt Rd (Hwys 19 and 11), you'll need at least five hours.

FROM HILO

DESTINATION	DISTANCE (MILES)	TIME (HOURS)
Hawai'i Volcanoes National Park	30	¾
Hawi	76	1¾
Honoka'a	41	1
Kailua-Kona	86	2
Na'alehu	66	1½
Pahoa	20	½
Waikoloa	72	1¾
Waimea	55	1¼
Waipi'o Lookout	50	1¼

FROM KAILUA-KONA

DESTINATION	DISTANCE (MILES)	TIME (HOURS)
Hawai'i Volcanoes National Park	98	2¼
Hawi	53	1¼
Hilo	86	2
Honoka'a	53	1¼
Na'alehu	59	1½
Pahoa	102	2¼
Waikoloa	26	¾
Waimea	40	1
Waipi'o Lookout	63	1½

photo. Otherwise, be prepared to present an International Driving Permit (IDP), obtainable in your home country, along with your foreign driver's license.

Fuel & Towing

○ Gasoline (petrol) is readily available in bigger towns. Fuel up before driving remote highways (eg Saddle Road).

○ Gas prices in Hawaii currently average $4.30 per US gallon. Expect to pay 40¢ to $1.10 more per gallon than on the US mainland. Prices are lower in Hilo than Kailua-Kona.

○ Towing is mighty expensive, costing about $65 to start, plus $6.50 per mile towed. Avoid trouble by not driving up Mauna Kea's summit road in anything but a 4WD vehicle, and never driving off-road, especially in sand or mud.

Insurance

○ For damage to your rental car, an optional collision damage waiver (CDW) costs an extra $15 to $20 a day.

○ If you decline CDW, you will be held liable for any damages up to the full value of the car.

○ Even with CDW, you may be required to pay the first $100 to $500 for repairs; some agencies will also charge you for the car-rental cost during the time it takes to be repaired.

○ If you already have vehicle insurance at home, it might cover rental cars; ask your insurance agent in advance.

○ Some credit cards offer reimbursement coverage for collision damages if you rent the car with that card; check this before your trip.

○ Most credit-card coverage isn't valid for rentals over 15 days or for 'exotic' models (eg convertibles, 4WD Jeeps).

Car Rental

The majority of visitors rent a car. Most agencies require drivers to be at least 25 years old; a few may rent to younger drivers for a hefty daily surcharge (check before booking). Having a credit card, not just a debit card, is usually necessary.

The daily rate for renting a small car usually ranges from $35 to $75, while typical weekly rates are $150 to $300; taxes, fees and surcharges can easily add $10 or more per day. 'Green' hybrid cars and 4WD vehicles are more expensive. Rates usually include unlimited mileage.

Book in advance online, then recheck periodically for lower rates. Reserve child-safety seats ($10 per day, or $50 per rental) when booking. Joining the rental agency's rewards program in advance (it's usually free) might entitle you to additional discounts and shorter queues at the airport.

Agencies serving both Kona and Hilo airports (except where otherwise noted) include the following:

Advantage (☎ 800-777-5500, 808-961-9193; www.advantage.com) Hilo airport only.

Alamo (☎ 877-222-9075; www.alamo.com)

Climate Change & Travel

Every form of transport that relies on carbon-based fuel generates CO_2, the main cause of human-induced climate change. Modern travel is dependent on airplanes, which might use less fuel per kilometer per person than most cars but travel much greater distances. The altitude at which aircraft emit gases (including CO_2) and particles also contributes to their climate change impact. Many websites offer 'carbon calculators' that allow people to estimate the carbon emissions generated by their journey and, for those who wish to do so, to offset the impact of the greenhouse gases emitted with contributions to portfolios of climate-friendly initiatives throughout the world. Lonely Planet offsets the carbon footprint of all staff and author travel.

Avis (☎ 800-331-1212; www.avis.com)

Budget (☎ 800-527-0700; www.budget.com)

Dollar (☎ 800-800-4000; www.dollar.com)

Enterprise (☎ 800-325-8007; www.enterprise.com)

Harper Car & Truck Rentals (☎ 800-852-9993, 808-969-1478; www.harpershawaii.com) The only agency with no restrictions on driving 4WD vehicles to Mauna Kea's summit. Damage to a vehicle entails a high deductible; rates are generally steeper than at other major agencies. Free Kona and Hilo airport shuttle service.

Hertz (☏ 800-654-3131; www.hertz.com)

National (☏ 877-222-9058; www.nationalcar.com)

Thrifty (☏ 800-847-4389; www.thrifty.com) Kona airport only.

Road Conditions & Hazards

○ Roads and bridges can flood during rainstorms, especially in Hilo, Puna and Ka'u. Watch out for muddy, rocky landslides by gulches along the Hamakua Coast.

○ Driving off-road or to Mauna Kea's summit is not for standard cars or novice 4WD drivers. In such remote areas, you'll be miles from any help.

○ On narrow, unpaved and/ or potholed roads, locals may hog both lanes and drive over the middle stripe until an oncoming car approaches.

○ In hyphenated addresses, such as 75-2345 Kuakini Hwy, the first part of the number identifies the tax zone and section, while the second part identifies the street address. If numbers suddenly jump unsequentially, you've just entered a new zone, that's all.

Road Rules

Slow, courteous driving is the rule. Generally speaking, locals don't honk (except in an emergency), don't follow close (ie tailgate) and let other drivers pass and merge.

○ Drive on the right-hand side of the road.

○ Talking or texting on handheld devices (eg cell phones) while driving is illegal.

○ Driving with a blood alcohol level of 0.08% or higher or when impaired by drugs (even if legally prescribed) is illegal.

○ It's illegal to carry open containers of alcohol (even if they're empty) inside a vehicle; unless they're full and still sealed, store them in the trunk.

○ Seat belts are required for drivers and front-seat passengers.

○ Children aged three and under must be secured in a child safety seat. Those aged four to seven must use a booster or car seat (unless the child is 4ft 9in tall and can use a lap-only seat belt in the back seat).

○ Speed limits are posted and enforced.

○ Turning right at a red light is permitted unless a sign prohibits it.

○ At four-way stop signs, cars proceed in order of arrival. If two cars arrive simultaneously, the one on the right has the right of way.

○ When emergency vehicles approach from either direction, carefully pull over to the side of the road.

Motorcycle & Moped

○ You can legally drive a moped in Hawaii with a valid driver's license issued by your home state or country. Motorcyclists need to have a valid US state motorcycle license or specially endorsed IDP.

○ The minimum age for renting a moped is 16 years; for a motorcycle it's 21.

○ Rental mopeds cost from $50/250 per day/ week; motorcycle rentals start around $100 per day, depending on the make and model. A sizeable credit-card deposit is usually necessary. Most rental agencies are in Kailua-Kona.

○ Helmets are not legally required for those 18 years or older, but rental agencies often lend them for free – use 'em.

○ State law requires mopeds to be ridden by one person only and prohibits their use on sidewalks and freeways. Mopeds must always be driven single file at speeds not exceeding 30mph.

A-Z

Glossary

aʻa – type of lava that is rough and jagged

aeʻo – Hawaiian black-necked stilt

ahu – stone cairns used to mark a trail; an altar or shrine

ahupuaʻa – traditional land division, usually in a wedge shape that extends from the mountains to the sea

ʻaina – land

aliʻi – chief, royalty

aloha – the traditional greeting meaning love, welcome, good-bye

aloha ʻaina – love and respect for the land

anchialine pool – contains a mixture of seawater and freshwater

ʻapapane – bright red Hawaiian honeycreeper

ʻaumakua – protective deity or guardian spirit, often an animal or ancestor

awa – see *kava*

broke da mout – delicious; literally, 'broke the mouth'

crack seed – Chinese preserved fruit; a salty, sweet and/or sour snack

e komo mai – welcome

grinds – food; to *grind* means to eat

ha – breath

hala – pandanus tree; the leaves *(lau)* are used in weaving mats and baskets

hale – house; hut

haole – Caucasian; literally, 'without breath'

hapa – portion or fragment; person of mixed blood

hapuʻu – tree fern

heʻe nalu – wave sliding, or surfing

heiau – ancient stone temple; a place of worship in Hawaii

holua – sled or sled course

honu – turtle

hoʻokipa – hospitality

hula – Hawaiian dance form, either traditional or modern

hula ʻauana – modern hula, developed after the introduction of Western music

hula halau – hula school or troupe

hula kahiko – traditional hula

ʻiʻiwi – scarlet Hawaiian honeycreeper with a curved, salmon-colored beak

ʻiliahi – Hawaiian sandalwood

ʻio – Hawaiian hawk

ipu – spherical, narrow-necked gourd used as a hula instrument

kahuna – knowledgable person in any field; commonly a priest, healer or sorcerer

kalo – taro

kamaʻaina – person born and raised or a longtime resident in Hawaii; literally, 'child of the land'

kanaka – man, human being, person; also Native Hawaiian

kane/Kane – man; if capitalized, the name of one of four main Hawaiian gods

kapa – see *tapa*

kapu – taboo, part of strict ancient Hawaiian social and religious system

kava – a mildly narcotic drink (*ʻawa* in Hawaiian) made from the roots of *Piper methysticum,* a pepper shrub

keiki – child

ki – see *ti*

kiʻi pokaku – stone carvings; petroglyphs

kiawe – a relative of the mesquite tree introduced to Hawaii in the 1820s, now very common; its branches are covered with sharp thorns

kiʻi – see *tiki*

kipuka – an area of land spared when lava flows around it; a rainforest oasis

ko – sugarcane

koʻa – fishing shrine

kokua – help, cooperation; please

kona – leeward side; a leeward wind

Ku – Polynesian god of many manifestations, including god of war, farming and fishing

kukui – candlenut tree and the official state tree; its oily nuts were once burned in lamps

kuleana – rights

kumu – teacher

kupuna – grandparent, elder

lanai – veranda; balcony

lau – leaf

lauhala – leaves of the *hala* plant, used in weaving

lei – garland, usually of flowers, but also of leaves or shells

limu – seaweed

lomilomi – traditional Hawaiian massage; known as 'loving touch'

Lono – Polynesian god of harvest, agriculture, fertility and peace

luakini – a type of *heiau* dedicated to the war god Ku and used for human sacrifices

luau – traditional Hawaiian feast

mahalo – thank you

maka'ainana – commoners; literally, 'people who tend the land'

makai – toward the sea; seaward

mana – spiritual power

mauka – toward the mountains; inland

mele – song, chant

menehune – 'little people' who, according to legend, built many of Hawaii's fishponds, heiau and other stonework

milo – endemic hardwood tree

mo'i – king

nā keiki – children

naupaka – a native shrub with delicate white flowers

Neighbor Islands – the term used to refer to the main Hawaiian Islands outside of O'ahu

nene – a native goose; Hawaii's state bird

'ohana – family, extended family; close-knit group

oli – chant

'opihi – an edible limpet

pahoehoe – type of lava that is quick and smooth- flowing

pakalolo – marijuana; literally, 'crazy smoke'

pali – cliff

paniolo – cowboy

Pele – goddess of fire and volcanoes; her home is in Kilauea Caldera

pidgin – distinct local language and dialect, created by Hawaii's multiethnic immigrants

pikake – jasmine flowers

piko – navel, umbilical cord

pono – righteous, respectful and proper

poi – staple Hawaiian starch made of steamed, mashed taro

pupu – snack or appetizer; also a type of cowry shell

pu'u – hill, cinder cone

pu'uhonua – place of refuge

rubbah slippah – rubber flip-flops

shaka – hand gesture used in Hawaii as a greeting or sign of local pride

talk story – to strike up a conversation, make small talk

tapa – cloth made by pounding the bark of paper mulberry, used for early Hawaiian clothing (*kapa* in Hawaiian)

ti – common native plant; its long shiny leaves are used for wrapping food and making hula skirts (*ki* in Hawaiian)

tiki – wood- or stone-carved statue, usually depicting a deity (*ki'i* in Hawaiian)

ukulele – a stringed musical instrument derived from the *braguinha*, which was introduced to Hawaii in the 1800s by Portuguese immigrants

'ulu – breadfruit

Behind the Scenes

Our Readers

Many thanks to the travelers who wrote to us with helpful hints, useful advice and interesting anecdotes:
Lee Hundley, Amy MacNaughton

Author Thanks

Sara Benson

Mahalo nui loa to all of the locals who shared insider tips. Big thanks to my coauthor Luci Yamamoto, as well as to Cat Craddock-Carrillo, Kathleen Munnelly, Martine Power, Mark Griffiths and all of the other in-house LP staff who helped create this book. Thanks most of all to Jonathan Hayes for Fridays at the King Kam, Mondays at the Manago and Kona coffee almost every morning.

Luci Yamamoto

Mahalo to the locals who teach me more about Hawai'i every time I return. Thanks to those who helped me at LP, including Cat Craddock-Carrillo, Kathleen Munnelly, Martine Power, Mark Griffiths and Dianne Schallmeiner. Deepest appreciation to my coauthor Sara Benson, a real pro, and to my parents, who still make Hilo home to me.

Acknowledgments

Climate map data adapted from Peel MC, Finlayson BL & McMahon TA (2007) 'Updated World Map of the Köppen-Geiger Climate Classification', Hydrology and Earth System Sciences, 11, 1633–44.

Cover photographs: Front: Kukio Beach, North Kona Coast, Philip Rosenberg/Visual Photos/PacificStock; Back: Pololu Valley, North Kohala, James Flint/Alamy

This Book

This 2nd edition of Lonely Planet's *Discover Hawai'i, the Big Island* guidebook was researched and written by Sara Benson and Luci Yamamoto. The previous edition was written by Luci Yamamoto and Conner Gorry. This guidebook was commissioned in Lonely Planet's Oakland office, and produced by the following:

Commissioning Editor Kathleen Munnelly
Coordinating Editor Fionnuala Twomey
Product Editor Anne Mason
Senior Editors Claire Naylor, Karyn Noble
Book Designer Clara Monitto
Regional Senior Cartographer Mark Griffiths
Cartographer Julie Dodkins
Assisting Editors Penny Cordner, Kate Evans, Kate James
Cover Researcher Naomi Parker
Thanks to Anita Banh, Cat Craddock-Carrillo, Brendan Dempsey, Lauren Egan, Ryan Evans, Larissa Frost, Genesys India, Jouve India, Martine Power, Anna Richardson, Alison Ridgway, Wibowo Rusli, Dianne Schallmeiner, Tony Wheeler, Juan Winata, Wendy Wright

SEND US YOUR FEEDBACK

We love to hear from travelers – your comments keep us on our toes and help make our books better. Our well-traveled team reads every word on what you loved or loathed about this book. Although we cannot reply individually to your submissions, we always guarantee that your feedback goes straight to the appropriate authors, in time for the next edition. Each person who sends us information is thanked in the next edition, the most useful submissions are rewarded with a selection of digital PDF chapters.

Visit **lonelyplanet.com/contact** to submit your updates and suggestions or to ask for help. Our award-winning website also features inspirational travel stories, news and discussions.

Note: We may edit, reproduce and incorporate your comments in Lonely Planet products such as guidebooks, websites and digital products, so let us know if you don't want your comments reproduced or your name acknowledged. For a copy of our privacy policy visit lonelyplanet.com/privacy.

Index

000 Map pages

NOTES

302

How to Use This Book

These symbols give you the vital information for each listing:

☏	Telephone Numbers	🛜	Wi-Fi Access	🚌	Bus
☺	Opening Hours	🏊	Swimming Pool	🚢	Ferry
P	Parking	🍴	Vegetarian Selection	M	Metro
☺	Nonsmoking	🍴	English-Language Menu	S	Subway
✳	Air-Conditioning	👶	Family-Friendly	🚋	Tram
@	Internet Access	🐾	Pet-Friendly		

Look out for these icons:

★	Must-visit recommendation
FREE	No payment required
🌿	A green or sustainable option

Our authors have nominated these places as demonstrating a strong commitment to sustainability – for example by supporting local communities and producers, operating in an environmentally friendly way, or supporting conservation projects.

All reviews are ordered in our authors' preference, starting with their most preferred option. Additionally:

Sights are arranged in the geographic order that we suggest you visit them, and within this order, by author preference.

Eating and Sleeping reviews are ordered by price range (budget, mid-range, top end) and within these ranges, by author preference.

Map Legend

Sights
- 🏖 Beach
- 🛕 Buddhist
- 🏰 Castle
- ✝ Christian
- 🕉 Hindu
- ☪ Islamic
- ✡ Jewish
- 🗽 Monument
- 🏛 Museum/Gallery
- 🏚 Ruin
- 🍷 Winery/Vineyard
- 🦓 Zoo
- ◉ Other Sight

Activities, Courses & Tours
- 🤿 Diving/Snorkelling
- 🛶 Canoeing/Kayaking
- 🎿 Skiing
- 🏄 Surfing
- 🏊 Swimming/Pool
- 🚶 Walking
- 🏄 Windsurfing
- ➕ Other Activity/Course/Tour

Sleeping
- 🛏 Sleeping
- ⛺ Camping

Eating
- 🍴 Eating

Drinking
- 🍷 Drinking
- ☕ Cafe

Entertainment
- 🎭 Entertainment

Shopping
- 🛍 Shopping

Information
- ✉ Post Office
- ℹ Tourist Information

Transport
- ✈ Airport
- ⊗ Border Crossing
- 🚌 Bus
- 🚡 Cable Car/Funicular
- 🚲 Cycling
- ⛴ Ferry
- 🚝 Monorail
- P Parking
- S S-Bahn
- 🚕 Taxi
- 🚉 Train/Railway
- 🚋 Tram
- ⊖ Tube Station
- U U-Bahn
- M Underground Train Station
- • Other Transport

Routes
- Tollway
- Freeway
- Primary
- Secondary
- Tertiary
- Lane
- Unsealed Road
- Plaza/Mall
- Steps
- Tunnel
- Pedestrian Overpass
- Walking Tour
- Walking Tour Detour
- Path

Boundaries
- International
- State/Province
- Disputed
- Regional/Suburb
- Marine Park
- Cliff
- Wall

Population
- 🔴 Capital (National)
- ◉ Capital (State/Province)
- ● City/Large Town
- ● Town/Village

Geographic
- 🏠 Hut/Shelter
- 🗼 Lighthouse
- 👁 Lookout
- ▲ Mountain/Volcano
- 🌴 Oasis
- 🌳 Park
-)(Pass
- 🌲 Picnic Area
- 💧 Waterfall

Hydrography
- River/Creek
- Intermittent River
- Swamp/Mangrove
- Reef
- Canal
- Water
- Dry/Salt/Intermittent Lake
- Glacier

Areas
- Beach/Desert
- Cemetery (Christian)
- Cemetery (Other)
- Park/Forest
- Sportsground
- Sight (Building)
- Top Sight (Building)

Our Story

A beat-up old car, a few dollars in the pocket and a sense of adventure. In 1972 that's all Tony and Maureen Wheeler needed for the trip of a lifetime – across Europe and Asia overland to Australia. It took several months, and at the end – broke but inspired – they sat at their kitchen table writing and stapling together their first travel guide, *Across Asia on the Cheap*. Within a week they'd sold 1500 copies. Lonely Planet was born.

Today, Lonely Planet has offices in Franklin, London, Melbourne, Oakland, Beijing and Delhi, with more than 600 staff and writers. We share Tony's belief that 'a great guidebook should do three things: inform, educate and amuse'.

Our Writers

SARA BENSON

Coordinating author, Kailua-Kona & the Kona Coast, Mauna Kea & Saddle Road, Hawai'i Volcanoes National Park, Ka'u After graduating from college, Sara jumped on a plane to California with just one suitcase and $100 in her pocket. Then she hopped across the Pacific to Japan, living for long stretches on Maui, Hawai'i, the Big Island and O'ahu and tramping all around Kaua'i, Moloka'i and Lana'i. Sara is an avid hiker, backpacker and outdoor enthusiast who has worked as a seasonal ranger for the National Park Service and as a volunteer at Hawai'i Volcanoes National Park. Already the author of more than 55 travel and nonfiction books, Sara also co-wrote Lonely Planet's *Hawaii* and *Discover Honolulu, Waikiki & O'ahu* guides. Follow her latest adventures online at www.indietraveler.blogspot.com, www.indietraveler.net, @indie_traveler on Twitter and indietraveler on Instagram.

Read more about at:
lonelyplanet.com/members/Sara_Benson

LUCI YAMAMOTO

Kohala & Waimea, Hamakua Coast, Hilo, Puna Luci Yamamoto is a fourth-generation native of Hawai'i. Growing up in Hilo, she viewed the cross-island drive from Hilo to Kailua-Kona as a rare, all-day adventure. Then she left for college in Los Angeles and law school in Berkeley – and even the Big Island seemed small indeed. Since covering Hawai'i for Lonely Planet, she's opened her eyes to the true greatness of her home island. Currently living in Vancouver, she feels privileged when *kama'aina* still consider her a 'local girl.' Follow Luci via her blog yogaspy.com and website luciyamamoto.com.

Published by Lonely Planet Publications Pty Ltd
ABN 36 005 607 983
2nd edition – Sep 2014
ISBN 978 1 74220 627 1
© Lonely Planet 2014   Photographs © as indicated 2014
10 9 8 7 6 5 4 3 2
Printed in China